Wink

Wink

THE INCREDIBLE LIFE
AND EPIC JOURNEY OF
JIMMY WINKFIELD

ED HOTALING

McGraw-Hill

Camden, Maine ◆ New York ◆ Chicago ◆ San Francisco ◆ Lisbon ◆ London ◆ Madrid
Mexico City ◆ Milan ◆ New Delhi ◆ San Juan ◆ Seoul ◆ Singapore ◆ Sydney ◆ Toronto

Also by Ed Hotaling

They're Off! Horse Racing at Saratoga

The Great Black Jockeys:
The Lives and Times of the Men Who Dominated
America's First National Sport

The **McGraw·Hill** Companies

1 2 3 4 5 6 7 8 9 10 DOC DOC 0 9 8 7 6 5

Library of Congress Cataloging-in-Publication Data
Hotaling, Edward.
 Wink : the incredible life and epic journey of Jimmy Winkfield / Ed
Hotaling.
  p.   cm.
 Includes bibliographical references and index.
 ISBN 0-07-141862-8 (hardcover : alk. paper)
 1. Winkfield, Jimmy, 1882–1974. 2. African American jockeys—
United States—Biography. 3. Jockeys—United States—Biography. 4.
Horse racing—United States—History. 5. Horse racing—Europe—
History. I. Title.
 SF336.W475H68 2005
 798.4'0092—dc22   2004017321

Photo on page iii of Winkfield in France courtesy Dr. Amie Carey.
Jacket photo of Winkfield on Alan-a-Dale courtesy Kentucky Derby
Museum.

To Greg, Luc, and Marthe

There is nothing I love as much as a good fight.

—Franklin Delano Roosevelt

CONTENTS

Preface   ix

Prologue   1

One: Bluegrass Boy   5

Two: "A Race War Is On"   26

Three: Winnie's Diamond   40

Four: "Winkfield's Dead!"   50

Five: Win the Futurity and . . .   68

Six: "Winkfield, I Don't Like to Be Double-Crossed!"   79

Seven: Invading Russia   91

Eight: Edna or a Life   103

Nine: James and Alexandra   120

Ten: Wink's World War I   142

Eleven: The Odyssey   155

Twelve: An American in Paris   170

Thirteen: Kings, Queens, and Wink   187

Fourteen: Marriage and Divorce   198

Fifteen: Josephine and Friends   218

Sixteen: Winkfield Shot; Winkfield Stabbed   230

Seventeen: Chickens, Rabbits, and Nazis   244

Eighteen: The Nazis versus Wink   252

Nineteen: The Backstretch   263

Twenty: You Can't Come In   290

Notes   300

Selected Bibliography   321

Acknowledgments   325

Index   329

PREFACE

JIMMY WINKFIELD WAS THE QUINTESSENTIAL AMERICAN.
Optimistic. Determined. A fighter who withstood every blow and
kept coming.

When the Spanish-American War was breaking out across
Chicago's front pages, this eighteen-year-old stable boy from a
backwater Kentucky town made headlines of his own through sheer
daredevilry.

Already a two-time Kentucky Derby winner when racism
blocked him from becoming the top athlete in America's biggest
sport, he became the champion jockey in the land of the czars instead. Hundreds of thousands hailed their "black maestro" in an
arena bigger than any in America. The day after a Serbian nationalist assassin fired the first shot of World War I, Jimmy Winkfield
cantered into the sun before Moscow's screaming fans and won a
race with a purse nearly three times that of the Derby back home.

I caught a glimpse of him in Paris in the early 1960s. Somebody
in Haynes's American restaurant on the Right Bank said something
like, "Do you know who that is over there? It's Jimmy Winkfield.
He was once one of the world's best jockeys. Maybe the best."

Looking across the room, I saw an elderly man, handsome and
well dressed. He stood only five feet tall but seemed magnified by
the aura in which he moved—a composed but benevolent dignity.
He was a man at peace, and I was moved to admiration, but no, I
didn't know who he was.

I know now, though.

While researching my first book, a history of racing in Saratoga
Springs, New York, I learned something that has been left out of
our history books: that America's first big sporting events, horse
races, starting from earliest colonial days, were dominated by black
jockeys. More amazing still, most were slaves, yet they led extraor-

dinary lives as professional athletes. After the Civil War, they moved north and began to conquer every racetrack in sight. Their rapid rise was so unstoppable that it led to white protests against black domination of horse racing. But then, in a fog of hard times and Jim Crow backlash, they disappeared.

So I set about writing another history—*The Great Black Jockeys*—and discovered that the last of them, Jimmy Winkfield, hadn't vanished after all; he had escaped overseas to a new life, a life unburdened by racism but repeatedly ransacked by the cataclysms of the twentieth century. Seen through a prism, his life *was* that century.

As I wrote, friends worried about my hermetic withdrawal. They needn't have. One day, shut in my house, I was huddled with Guglielmo Marconi in the worst storm anybody could remember on Coney Island, where Jimmy was riding in the biggest race in the country and getting brutally cussed out by his boss. Some days I journeyed to Odessa, on the Black Sea, and watched the last moments of racing in Czarist Russia before the racetrack went up in flames. Sometimes I was trudging past the Transylvanian Alps as Jimmy helped lead more than two hundred fifty thoroughbreds on a 1,100-mile trek to freedom while hunger and the Bolsheviks dogged his exhausted steps. Or I would take a steamer to Paris, where, in company with Josephine Baker, I celebrated the arrival of Lucky Lindy and his *Spirit of St. Louis,* then bopped out to Jimmy Winkfield's villa to watch him train his thoroughbreds, unaware that in a few years his house and stables would be confiscated by the Nazis.

As I pressed on with the writing, racing down the backstretch to the half, this American jockey's story took off on its own into the homestretch, becoming the book you hold in your hands. The story seemed to write itself. It really is one of those rare and fabulous tales of courage and persistence—a story torn from America's heart.

So get ready for Jimmy Winkfield's spectacular odyssey from small-town Kentucky to the capitals of Europe and the epochal events of a crowded century, battling all comers simply to go on living the life he chose. You may never have heard of Wink—just as I had never heard of him that long-ago night in Paris—but after reading his story, you will never forget him.

PROLOGUE

THE FANS WERE AWED BY THE AMERICAN IN THE 1911 GERMAN
Derby—first by the striking sight of his straw-yellow silks against
his black skin, then by his astonishing talent. The reporters called
him "*Der Neger*"—which in German at the time was closer to "Negro" than to the ugly English epithet.

As he swung his colt around to join the parade to the starting
post the American had to be startled by the thousands in the grandstand. They were laughing. The sight of a black man surprised and
delighted many of them—millions of Germans had never seen a
black man; some even wanted to touch him—but they were actually
laughing about something else.

The name of his horse. Whose hilarious name they immediately transferred to the jockey, and laughed all the more.

The name was Monostatos.

"Monostatos!" cried the Germans as Jimmy Winkfield rode by.

As soon as they saw Jimmy, Wolfgang Amadeus Mozart's last
opera, *Die Zauberflöte* (*The Magic Flute*), must have been spinning
in their heads. In that wildly popular opera, Monostatos is the name
of the black Moor, a lusty servant who forces the world to confront its prejudices as he sings, mockingly:

"I must forgo love because a black man is ugly . . . Dear, good
moon, forgive me: a white skin has seduced me! White is beautiful, I must kiss her."

Not everyone was amused. Circulating through the crowd that
day may well have been a minor horse dealer and bookmaker named
Christian Weber. Within a few years, Weber would be one of only
four intimates of another young thug, the wallpaper hanger and
failed watercolorist Adolf Hitler; they would be the only men with
whom Hitler used the affectionate "du" form of "you." Between
meetings of their tiny new National Socialist Workers (Nazi) Party,
Hitler and Weber would stroll the streets of Munich, carrying dog

whips for their next brawl with the Communists. And a decade after that, with Hitler installed as chancellor of Germany, his favorite horseman would rise like a shooting swastika from mere bookie to society star of the Third Reich, as dashing as a Nazi could be. He would found the Hauptreitschule, or Main Riding School, for Hitler's rapidly expanding personal army, the SS, or Schutzstaffel (safety squadron). And in June 1940, in occupied France, Weber and his fellow horsemen would scheme to commandeer fabulous thoroughbreds and racing stables, including Jimmy Winkfield's own.

But that was still three decades in the future when Jimmy, on Monostatos, charged into the 1911 German Derby. Much more immediately—in the late editions of that evening's newspapers, in fact—news of the Derby would reach Vienna, where Jimmy and Hitler were both living at the time. Already dreaming of an all-white, all-German future, the twenty-two-year-old Hitler would likely learn about this strange hero of the German reporters in the *Berliner Tageblatt*, the liberal, sophisticated newspaper that he most loved to hate, edited as it was by Theodor Wolff, a brilliant Jew. Certainly Hitler would not be amused by the reports on Germany's premier sporting event. The crowd loved the Moor, and worse, they were betting on him.

"*Der Neger gewinnt!*" the fans were screaming near the top of the Derby home stretch in the city of Hamburg. "The Negro is winning!"

Maybe he was, and maybe he wasn't. They would find out in twenty-five seconds.

Had Jimmy had the luxury to pick faces from the screaming crowd, he might have glimpsed other strands of his future that day in Hamburg. Soldiers, functionaries, and relatives of Kaiser Wilhelm II were there; the Kaiser himself had been there a few days before. In their cold eyes Jimmy might have glimpsed the first, senseless world war, in the botched resolution of which were sown the seeds of the second. And there were playboy Russian aristocrats and their consorts in the stands as well. In their extravagance Wink might have sensed the revolution that in a few years would

surge past his Moscow hotel, sweeping him up in its tide and separating him from another family, another fortune.

But Jimmy wasn't looking for faces or signs. Having been torn
from one country, he didn't know and, at the moment, might not
have cared that future cataclysms would tear him from two others.
He had a race to win, and twenty-five seconds to do it in. In whatever corner of his brain was not devoted to the absolute exigencies
of the moment, he might have been asking himself, as he was
known to do on occasion, "What's a little black man from Chilesburg, Kentucky, doing in a spot like this?"

Chapter One

BLUEGRASS BOY

Jimmy Winkfield never forgot the sunlit spot where he was born on an old back road in Kentucky, eight miles east of Lexington. Richard Chiles, a farmer from Virginia, kept a stagecoach tavern there for some forty years before the Civil War, so they called it Chilesburg. When Chiles died in 1853, another white man, Sam Uttinger, bought the property and sold a lot with a farmhouse to a free black couple named George and Victoria Winkfield.

George's father was white, and the Winkfield surname originated with an old family and its field, Winecas Field, in Berkshire County, England. Weirdly enough, considering what would happen to Jimmy, Winecas Field was practically next door to the celebrated horse races at Ascot. But just how those English Winkfields planted themselves in the far-off blue fields of Kentucky, and what they did there, is a story buried long ago in the hurts and loveliness of that conflicted state.

George and Victoria had a boy, Augustus, in 1855, another boy, Samuel, in 1856, a girl, Rachel, in 1857, and the Civil War didn't slow them down. They had a third boy, William, in 1862, and a second girl, Bettie, in 1864, and kept right on going, and after the war a sprinkling of farmhouses sprang up around the Winkfields. The people there would not forget Sam Uttinger. They would revere him for having been brave enough to sell to George and Victoria amid the racial hatreds and violence of those days—eventually they would even change the name of the place from Chilesburg to Uttingertown.

Whatever magical effects resulted from ancient Winecas Field's proximity to Ascot, George and Victoria were not involved in what outsiders took to be Kentucky's raison d'être: race horses. They stuck to what were really the state's two biggest farm industries, raising tobacco and hemp. Of course, they kept chickens, and probably pigs, too, since the family recipes included the jellied pork loaf known as headcheese, and they likely sharecropped on bigger properties nearby. By 1880, give or take, they had presented tiny Chilesburg with seventeen new citizens. The youngest was Jimmy. Some of Jimmy's older sisters, among them Rachel, Bettie, and Margaret, settled elsewhere, in nearby towns like Lexington and Danville. Some of the brothers did not. They just stayed right there in the sun, farming and raising families on either side of Chilesburg Road, a golden lane that was lucky if it was two wagons wide and half a mile long and that ended in the middle of a yellow wheat field. A few—Gus, Sam, William, Moses—settled close by. All told, the Winkfields ended up with a nice little chunk of the Bluegrass, but the youngest had other ideas.

By 1887, when Jimmy was seven, he was riding saddle horses bareback or hopping off them to perch on a plank fence and watch the thoroughbreds dance down a dirt lane. Jimmy was baby-cheeked, bright-eyed, slender, good-looking, inquisitive. He loved to dress up, dress to kill, and from later pictures it was clear that when he did, the first thing he would do was pose, with his unusually large hands on his hips, leaning forward to find out what was happening next. All ears, all eyes, ready for action.

Records of the dates and circumstances are lost, but George and Victoria both died when Jimmy was very young—and he was out of

Chilesburg in a flash. He went to live with one of his sisters in Lexington, which happened to be the hub of America's horse racing universe, the center of its biggest horse-breeding state. Shaped like a wheel, Lexington had fourteen turnpikes shooting out of it like spokes, and once you got spinning around that big wheel, it could fling you anywhere in the world.

The Winchester Pike, the first turnpike Jimmy ever took, came in at three o'clock on the wheel and ran straight into Lexington's heart and soul, at Sixth and Race streets, on the eastern edge of town. This was the Kentucky Association racetrack, oldest in America, founded in 1826. It gave everybody in Lexington, eventually including Jimmy, a powerful sense of tradition. The famous antebellum statesman and perennial presidential candidate Henry Clay had been an officer of the racing association, and John C. Breckinridge had been its president, with a sideline as vice president of the United States.

But to everybody in American racing, the track was still just good old Chittlin' Switch, so called after the railroad switch next door, where the horses were shipped in, and the prized chitterlings—pork tripe—that the track kitchen featured for the trainers, jockeys, and the rest of the help on the "backstretch," the stable and training area. Hard by the track was the black neighborhood whose labor and talent kept it going. This was where Jimmy's sisters lived, and where he got his first job as a shoeshine boy; as relevant a profession as you could exercise in unpaved America, where everybody's shoes and boots were a mess.

All around east Lexington Jimmy found his heroes, America's great black jockeys. Now forgotten, they were once known across the land. They had begun as slaves. They came off the Old South's big horse farms, or from plantations that happened to have racing stables too, and they wound up dominating America's first professional sport from colonial times to the Civil War. Theirs was a strange world even within that strangest of worlds, American slavery. While still slaves, a few of the best competed to the applause of tens of thousands of white and black Americans from

New Orleans to New York and made the sporting news the next morning. These slaves lived adventurous lives of travel, excitement, and public praise that other Americans, white or black, could only dream of. They even achieved what felt like freedom—if only for those minutes on a horse and the only race that mattered was the one around the track and the only colors that counted were the colors on their backs, their stables' racing colors. Several moved up to training horses and a few to managing major stables, hiring and firing the black and white help, running the entire business because the white owners didn't know how, all while still trapped in slavery.

They first appeared on the scene decades before the American Revolution. One of them, Austin Curtis, was America's first great professional athlete and star of the colonies' first premier racing region—along the raging Roanoke River on the Virginia–North Carolina border. Like all the others, he is unknown to historians, and you will not find him in any textbook. A brilliant tactician, Curtis made his owner, a North Carolina founding father named Willie Jones, the richest horseman in America. They got along and as slave and master formed the nation's first brilliant athlete-manager combination. Curtis was freed for services to America during the Revolution, services that included the extremely dangerous job of keeping Jones's valuable thoroughbreds out of the hands of the then-conquering British cavalry.

Dumped in Charleston off a slave ship right after the Revolution, the teenaged hunchback called Simon became the most celebrated rider across the South, from the Atlantic Ocean to the Mississippi. Before 1810 he was brought to Tennessee, where he became the invincible nemesis of General Andrew Jackson. With a mare named Haynie's Maria, Simon beat every horse Jackson could throw at him. The wise-cracking, banjo-strumming Simon had a wicked mouth, and he was so brilliant in the saddle he could get away with turning it on anybody, the bigger the better. One day the six-foot, one-inch General Jackson issued an order to the four-foot, six-inch slave jockey.

"Now, Simon, when my horse comes up and is about to pass you, don't spit your tobacco juice in his eyes, and in the eyes of his rider, as you sometimes do," said the future president of the United States.

"Well, Gineral," said Simon, his famous whine dripping sarcasm. "I've rode a good deal agin' your horses, but"—and here he dropped a "shit" or some other oath—"none were ever near enough to catch my spit."

When Jackson left the White House, after winning his wars against state "nullification" of federal laws, against the Bank of the United States, and against Congress (not to mention the British navy at the Battle of New Orleans), somebody asked Old Hickory if there was ever anything he couldn't beat.

"Nothing that I can remember," Jackson said, in the ultimate compliment to Simon, "except Haynie's Maria."

Jackson actually brought his own slave jockeys to the White House and operated a top-level racing stable on the grounds—the only time the White House was ever a major sports power.

Another slave jockey, Charles Stewart, raced up and down the East Coast before he became an assistant trainer in Virginia and proceeded to buy his future wife and her children. Free African-Americans often bought their loved ones out of slavery, but Stewart was a slave who owned slaves. A few years later, his owner sent him west to breed his stallion, Medley, and the two of them, man and horse, walked six hundred miles through the Cumberland Gap and on to Kentucky. After single-handedly managing a major breeding service there, he went on to Louisiana and became the manager of that state's top racing stable, employing white and black help. Yet he remained a slave until the Civil War freed him.

A jockey named Cornelius rode one of the grandest American horses of all time, a thoroughbred named Boston, who from the records appears to have been superior even to Man o'War or Secretariat. In his best year, 1838, Cornelius and Boston captured eleven victories in eleven starts, which was a lot more than it sounds like today. In those days, horse races were in heats, often 4-mile heats, and a horse would have to win two out of three or three out of five heats. So a single race typically totaled at least 8 or 12 miles each. A race that went to 20 miles—in five heats—was not unheard of. In 1838 and 1839, the slave Cornelius, riding at tracks from Virginia up to Long Island, seeing more of the world than most Americans ever would, lost only once as he piloted Boston for 143 miles before tens of thousands of screaming fans.

Duncan Kenner, Louisiana's favorite son, whose name is honored across that state today, bought Abe Hawkins for $2,350. Abe was expensive, but he was a damn good jockey. When the Yankee troops arrived in 1862 and took over Kenner's fabulous sugar plantation on the Mississippi, Kenner escaped on one of his thoroughbreds while the Union troops lounged around getting drunk on his best wines. Nobody knew where Abe, then the South's best jockey, was until he turned up in St. Louis in the middle of the war, racing and winning. Then he starred at the big track in Paterson, New Jersey, and at the spectacular wartime race meeting at Saratoga. He was the only other man known the country over as just "Abe."

One day right after the war, a New Orleans gentleman approached the then-rich black jockey at Saratoga and asked if he knew that his old master, the famous Duncan Kenner, had been ruined by the war.

"Do you ever see him?" Abe asked.

"Yes, I see him rather often."

Then, said Abe, "Tell him I have ridden a great many races here in the North and have made right smart of money. It is all in the bank and it is his if he wants it, because I am just as much his servant as I ever was."

With the Civil War's destruction of their base—the countless little racecourses all over the Deep South—black jockeys declined in number, but they remained strong in the border state of Kentucky, which had fallen under the control of federal troops by 1862, though it remained a slave state through the war. Even in the midst of lightning Confederate raids on the Bluegrass horse farms—notably by General John Hunt Morgan—thoroughbred racing had never stopped in Kentucky. And after the war, many of the major southern stables took their remaining black jockeys to the hugely popular northern tracks, where they tested the limits of Yankee tolerance.

The most unforgettable black jockey lived right there in Jimmy's Lexington. For years, through the mid-1880s, Ike Murphy had been the highest-paid athlete in America, white or black, making $15,000 to $20,000 a year. He was equally renowned for his integrity in a game dominated by gamblers and full of cheats. They called him Honest Ike.

Just as it had done for Ike, growing up in Lexington offered Jimmy at least a bit of insurance against dishonesty, for the simple reason that the sport was the livelihood of almost everybody in town, so they had to protect it. Not that everybody did. One day, a couple of local horse traders tried to unload a colt on a New York tycoon named Clarence Mackay for $10,000. The colt turned in a wicked fast workout over three-eighths of a mile for the benefit of a Mackay agent, and the sale was about to be signed. But somebody discovered the three-eighths pole had been secretly moved at five-thirty that morning, which accounted for the colt's rare speed. The deal was off. And years later, developers putting up housing on the old track site uncovered a graveyard of jockey's batteries. The Lexington homestretch was uphill, and these handheld batteries gave the tired nags a jolt of encouragement as they charged to the finish line.

Besides integrity, Ike had another lesson for Jimmy if he ever cared to ride professionally: be a "money rider"; go for the big ones, which will make your reputation and set you up for more. Ike won the Kentucky Derby three times, in 1884, 1890, and 1891, not to mention four of the then far more important American Derbies at Chicago, five of the Latonia Derbies in Kentucky, and indeed a sampler of almost every important prize in America's biggest sport. Who cared if you won a hundred nothing races in a year? Ike's approach, saving himself for the big ones, gave him a reputed 44 percent winning rate, a record that would never again be approached in America.

The legends of earlier black jockeys gave a kid like Jimmy not merely confidence but the conviction that he was going to make it. Success was all around him. In 1891, when he was eleven, he may have sold a lot of shoeshines just before the dressy, all-day shower that Ike and his wife, Lucy, threw for Tony Hamilton, one of the leading riders in the East, and his bride. Top jocks like Kentucky Derby winners Billy Walker and Isaac Lewis were in the crowd at Ike's $10,000, seven-acre home on East Third Street. A sumptuous luncheon stretched into a vast champagne buffet served from Ike's dining room, parlor, and library. At eight they danced to a "Jockey Quadrille." In a word, Ike Murphy was class—something else Jimmy Winkfield picked up early, if in fact he hadn't been born with it. But Lexington wasn't running out of future heroes, either.

It was a slip of a thirteen-year-old, the same age as Jimmy, who won four of the five races on opening day at Lexington in 1893. This enfant terrible was James "Soup" Perkins, who would go on to win the Kentucky Derby at age fifteen, tying another black rider, Lonnie Clayton, as the youngest Derby winner ever. Jimmy wasn't blind. He could see this would be good work. Soup, for instance, was having a blast, shooting craps between races, mugging for pictures, showering his family with incredible gifts, all the while inhaling buckets of his favorite food. Not chitlins. Soup. Didn't matter what kind.

Soup captured 192 races in 1895, more than any other jockey, which gave him the title of national champion—national champion in the sport that still drew the biggest crowds, usually far bigger than baseball's.

And the younger ones kept coming, one set of black riders serving as models for the next. Though Jimmy's junior by five years, Marshall Lilly would become a different kind of model for him over the years, bringing out an old-fashioned quality that maybe Jimmy didn't know he had until he recognized it in somebody else: manners. Marshall's father had worked for James Grinstead, one of the wealthy white Lexington breeders and stable owners, and the son had an old-fashioned Kentucky gentleman's courtesy that was as formal as his first name. It was easy to see why Marshall and the unfailingly polite Jimmy became good friends; it was not so easy to see the extraordinary separate path that Marshall would take. Though it looked as though Marshall was not going to be much of a jockey, he was developing a strange rapport with the best colts. The better they were, the better Marshall got along with them. As Jimmy would discover, this would take his young friend very far on American turf, or as they said in Kentucky, "to the top of the tree."

Oddly for America, the Kentucky white kids who wanted to be jockeys found themselves chasing black competition. Luckily, they were used to it—it was just a fact of life in Kentucky, at the Louisiana tracks, and in a rare few other places. It even taught some of those white boys about life and tolerance, as Jimmy would learn firsthand from little Roscoe Goose and the breeder Sandford Lyne's son Lucien. But tolerance was the opposite of what was going on in the rest of America in the 1890s, especially in and around New York City, the epicenter of the sport, with its seven huge tracks— Sheepshead Bay, Gravesend, and Brighton Beach in Brooklyn; Jerome Park, just north of Manhattan; Morris Park in Westchester County; the new Aqueduct on Long Island; and Monmouth Park in nearby New Jersey.

In the years of American industrial growth after the Civil War, racetracks had multiplied and expanded in the cities of the North, the Midwest, and California. The black jockeys who before the war had been concentrated in the South and the border states of Kentucky and Tennessee had begun appearing at the booming new tracks, following the money. This was quite independent of the black population shift of the time, the migration from the farms and small towns of the Old South to the cities of the North and Midwest, but the two movements coincided, and black jockeys shared the migrants' hope for freedom.

As racing boomed, the purses started exploding until, in 1888, they peaked with the Futurity Stakes, worth $40,900. The richest annual event yet in American sports, it was staged at the Coney Island Jockey Club in Brooklyn, a pretty layout along Ocean Avenue, with fine restaurants, shade trees, and lovely lawns, right off breezy Sheepshead Bay. And who won it? One of the great black jockeys of the day, Shelby "Pike" Barnes, from Beaver Dam, Kentucky. Tony Hamilton, another black jockey, was second.

Then came the backlash. Ike Murphy was one of the first victims. In 1890, on the fabulous racer Salvator, he met the great white jockey Edward "Snapper" Garrison and a horse named Tenny in a match race—one against one. It was one of the most ballyhooed events yet in American sports history, a mile and a quarter over the Sheepshead Bay track in Brooklyn. Each man was given credit for inventing the term "grandstand finish," and that's what they gave the crowd. Grabbing the lead at the start, Ike and Salvator broke the mile record, then the record for a mile and an eighth. But Snapper and Tenny bore down on them in front of the stand, Snapper spurring and frantically changing whip hands. A poet of the day called the finish:

> *One more mighty plunge, and with knee, limb, and hand*
> *I lift my horse first by a nose past the stand.*
> *We are at the string now—the great race is done,*
> *And Salvator, Salvator, Salvator won!*

But disaster followed quickly. Murphy entered the Monmouth Handicap at the gorgeous new Monmouth Park in New Jersey, America's most spectacular sports arena yet. Before the race, he dropped by Monmouth's startling iron grandstand to pay a visit to his wife, Lucy, who was accompanied by Ike's valet. They had the waiter bring them a refreshing glass of imported Apollinaris water. Then he was off to battle on the highly regarded mare Firenzi. But Ike handled her badly. Not only did he finish seventh out of seven, but he had trouble dismounting, to put it mildly. When the race was over, the *New York Times* reported, "what strength he had was gone, and he fell out of the saddle in a heap on the track."

Although Murphy was accused of having taken drugs or too many drinks, none of it was proved. The Apollinaris company even issued a formal statement that it was only selling water. The much more likely explanation was that Ike was weak from "flipping," forcing himself to vomit to make the required weight. But that was all it took for the racing establishment and the media to go after Murphy, and he was soon being denied decent mounts as he lost the support of the once idolatrous press and stable owners. He could do nothing right. Embittered, he told a reporter, "When I won it was all right, but when I lost, and when not on the best horse, they would say, 'There, that nigger is drunk again.' I tell you, I am disgusted and soured on the whole business."

They went after Tony Hamilton, too. He won the even richer Futurity ($67,675) of 1890 and was second only to Alfred "Monk" Overton in winning percentage that year—both of them above an astronomical 33 percent—only to have the *Times* note that Tony's trainer knew "more about languages than Prof. Garner ever dreamed of in the wilds of Africa, and so is able to hold successful converse with Hamilton." A few years later, "reporting" on Hamilton's dispute with the authorities, the *Times* said Hamilton's recent erratic riding "had been variously accredited to too free use of opium, to overindulgence in gin, and to downright rascality." For good measure it referred to him as "a muckle-headed negro."

You might wonder how an athlete could perform under such a barrage, but all black Americans had been hearing that all their lives, and Hamilton, for one, still managed to win. In addition to the Futurity, he took the pricey American Derby, New York's three important handicaps, and much else. All this, despite the fact that it was much harder for the top black jockeys to garner publicity and retain the agents who could win them the best mounts. The most crushing blow, though, was the financial Panic of 1893 and the recessions that followed through the nineties. As the economy collapsed and American racing shrank, the fight for the dwindling number of jobs turned more vicious, and blacks were pushed out at an accelerated rate. At the close of 1900, one magazine called Willie Simms "about the last of the long list of famous colored jockeys." But one more would now fight ferociously to get on that list and in the process reach still unmatched heights in American sports.

Through the 1890s, Kentucky remained a haven. For black kids riding there, it was like being enrolled in an all-black school. It gave them comfort, camaraderie, and confidence, and convinced them they were not only as good as anybody else, but better. In fact, black riders so ruled Kentucky racing that they even prompted an unheard-of labor rebellion against black dominance. In 1895, white jockeys at the Latonia racecourse, in northern Kentucky on the Ohio, publicly protested what they called the "colored trust." Black riders were getting all the good mounts, they complained. The *Kentucky Post* quoted them as saying that "favoritism was being displayed by the principal horse owners. . . . The colored boys were getting the best of it . . . and are multiplying so fast that a good white boy has little chance at all." The *Post* said a couple of white jocks had already left Latonia and others were "thinking of forming a union among the white boys." Obviously, there was plenty of fuel for an explosion.

One day at the Newport racecourse—also on the Ohio and practically next door to Latonia—the black rider Coley Thompson was driving down the stretch on the long shot Myosotis and just loving the loneliness of it all. Suddenly, out of nowhere, he felt the white jock Jesse Mathews breathing furiously down his neck on the favorite, Bon Jour, as if to say, "Bonjour!" There was only a sixteenth of a mile to go. Jesse tried to pass Coley on the outside. To stop him, to halt this grand theft of a horse race, the black boy swerved to the right, bumping Bon Jour and almost knocking the white boy out of the saddle. As the badly shaken Jesse straightened up, Coley bumped Bon Jour again. This time Jesse drew his whip and hit the black rider with the butt end. It was like hitting him with an iron rod, because the butt was weighted with lead for better balance and control. Coley's mouth was a torn pocket, his nose an old faucet pouring blood.

Jesse and Bon Jour went on to win, and Myosotis was disqualified, but it wasn't over. Jesse "weighed out"—hit the scales for the required weight check after the race—and strolled into the jockey room. Coley flew at him, and they went at it like gamecocks. Neither was a hundred pounds, but they were all wiry muscle. Soup Perkins got into it, too, but the teenagers were finally separated. Jesse said Soup hit him. Soup said he was trying to break it up. It's impossible to know who started it, but it was a fight the black jockeys could not win. And as Jimmy would find out the hard way, it would get a lot worse.

As the black jockeys continued to star at Lexington, Jimmy Winkfield was still nowhere in sight. "In '96," he'd recall, "I was goin' to school at nights and drivin' a carriage for some white folks during the day." White folks in Lexington needed a lot of carriage rides, because they couldn't do much business within walking distance. They would have to see a man about a horse two miles out on the Georgetown Pike—at the Nursery Stud owned by New York financial titan August Belmont. Or they'd have a horse trade a half mile out on the Richmond spoke, where Henry Clay's granddaughter reigned at Ashland, the family estate. Or they'd have a party at Lucien Lyne's father's place, six miles out on the Nicholasville Pike. And Jimmy was just the man to take them there.

But there was something special about Jimmy: driving rich white folks around had an unexpected effect on him. He wasn't depressed by what they had and he didn't. On the contrary, he was encouraged by what he could get someday, too. He was even more encouraged by what he already had and could take with him: the feast of the Bluegrass. In time, he would fall further under the spell of the *Poa pratensis* that bloomed bluish in late May.

These were Jimmy's blue fields as much as anyone's. They stretched far beyond the thirteen-mile radius of the Lexington wheel, reaching across twelve hundred square miles of north-central Kentucky to form a welcoming plateau surrounded by rolling hills—a natural amphitheater. It was as if the rest of nature could gather in the surrounding foothills and look down, taking delight at the bucking, four-legged blue bloods growing up on the plateau's calcium-rich grass and limestone waters. To hear jealous

surrounding counties tell it, the Bluegrass reached even farther, covering eight to twelve thousand square miles. In fact, American
"bluegrass" first took root just south of the Kentucky border. An
Irish-born surgeon, Dr. Redmond Dillon Barry, transplanted the
delicious Irish blade into Tennessee in the late 1790s, which helped
that state become the country's principal horse racing region in the
early nineteenth century, before Kentucky claimed the title.

Jimmy fell hopelessly under the spell of his Kentucky, just as Ike
Murphy had. Somehow, both saw beyond the horrific racism of
the day. And besides, life was slightly better in the Bluegrass. For
one thing, they had plenty of friendly company. The Bluegrass had
one of the biggest concentrations of black residents in Kentucky,
including a growing black middle class in the segregated towns. For
another, the Ku Klux Klan had been in decline for several years
through most of the South and would not arise again nationally
for another two decades. Indeed, Klan outfits rarely got a toehold in
the area because, as one of Jimmy's descendants would explain, the
"rich white folks" were not about to allow murderers and arsonists
to run around their multimillion-dollar farms with their thoroughbreds and highly talented jockeys and trainers. The reduction of
the Klan threat in the horse country was a major reason for the
survival of black jockeys.

In 1896, Jimmy might have been in on one of Lexington's
biggest carriage jobs. People were streaming to Ike's, but for the last
time: he had died of pneumonia in his mid-thirties. It was a lung
disease common among jockeys, whose crash dieting, intensive exercising, and sweat baths weakened their resistance to infection. Ike,
for one, had crash dieted for years. On that early February day, more
than five hundred mourners rode or walked to East Third to pay
their respects to Lucy. The African-American Masons and Knights
Templar escorted the funeral cortege, a record queue of carriages
that circled African Cemetery No. 2 on snow-buried East Seventh
Street.

Lucy loved flowers, and they were sent by the thousands. Tony
Hamilton and Robert "Tiny" Williams sent a giant blooming

horseshoe. Ed Brown, a former slave jockey who had become a leading trainer, sent lilies of the valley, as did Ed Corrigan, the Irish operator of Chicago racetracks. A wreath arrived from Fred "The Flying Dutchman" Taral, the best white jockey of the decade. They were honoring one of the athletes of the century, soon to be forgotten—but not by sixteen-year-old Jimmy Winkfield.

The carriage rides were not quite over. In the national press, guesses at the worth of Ike's estate ranged wildly, from $30,000 to $125,000. But whatever the total, Lucy could not manage either the money or the house, so she moved in with her mother, several blocks away. For a while she went to the expense of hiring a carriage every day to visit Ike's grave and anoint it with fresh blooms, and it's possible that Jimmy was one of Lucy's drivers on those sad days. Wherever Jimmy was, he was certainly harboring a clear notion of who the next Ike Murphy was going to be.

On Saturdays, Jimmy and his friends would go to the racetrack. He'd play marbles with the stable boys, getting tips on the likely winning horses and making new friends. Most important, he got to watch the jockeys close up, wishing he were up there himself. In the spring of 1897, when he was seventeen, a man offered him a job at the track for $8 a month plus board. "I was rich," he would say later. "I galloped [exercised] an old mare that year that won five races, and each time she win the owner give me $5 and the jockey $5." His friends took to calling him Wink.

"Next spring, Bub May hired me for $10 a month and board. His daddy was mayor of Lexington, and in the summer of '98 they took some horses to Chicago."

One August afternoon, the Spanish-American War was stealing the headlines—AMERICAN AND SPANISH TROOPS IN PORTO RICO SOON TO BE WITHIN FIRING DISTANCE—but Wink had more important things to worry about. He and the other stable boys had their savings on a colt named Jockey Joe in the sixth race at Chicago's Hawthorne track. The colt's odds were as long as fifty to one with some of the bookies. But what Wink and his friends knew, and nobody else did, was that Joe had burned up the track in his morning gallops.

They still balked at playing him to win the whole thing. He had never won a race—he had never been in a race—and he was up against other two-year-olds the experts liked a lot better. The race was full of some of America's best jockeys, too, like the white riders Willie Martin, who liked to win big in front of a screaming grandstand; future international stars Lester and Johnny Reiff; and Irish-American sensation Tommy Burns, on his way to leading the country with 277 wins that year. These stars weren't the least bit worried about Jockey Joe, because he didn't even have a real jockey.

He had Winkfield. Although just a stable boy and exercise rider, Jimmy himself was actually going to be riding Jockey Joe because the Mays couldn't afford anybody better at the moment. That was another reason the stable boys decided to play it safe, and they finally found a bookmaker to give them twelve to one on their savings if Joe just came in second. But Wink had a lot more at stake. He would be riding to win, and after he did, the world would take notice of Jimmy Winkfield, war or no war.

On racing's "western circuit," which meant the Midwest and California, you couldn't get any better than Chicago. It was not the ultimate, not the East, not Saratoga, which symbolized American racing at its best. But with racing in a deep recession across the country, the money at the Saratoga races that day was no better than at Chicago. In fact, this $400 sprint and every other race at rustic Hawthorne had a bigger prize than any at tony Saratoga, where the first race was for a measly three hundred 1898 dollars. It was won by an eight-to-one long shot named Nigger Baby.

A few tracks were already using various versions of a claptrap starting gate, but everybody hated them. They apparently left the horses a nervous wreck, too. One, tried out in 1894 at Maspeth, New York, involved a simple "gate," or metal bar, that was swung across the track. That was all right, but officials also decided the system required the sounding of three loud gongs—one for the horses to line up in front of the gate, a second to alert the jockeys to get ready, and a third gong announcing that the gate would now be swung open. By that point, the high-strung thoroughbreds were ready for long-term psychotherapy.

So, instead, nearly all the big tracks had begun using what they called the "webbed barrier," which was much quieter. A man—the "starter"—would stand on a platform and wait for his assistants to push the horses' rumps this way and that until they were all lined up in front of what looked like a tennis net stretched across the track, but higher and made of rubber. The barrier would be sprung by the starter when he thought the horses were about as lined up as they were going to get. So on this August afternoon in 1898, in the last race on the Hawthorne card at Chicago, a quick sprint of five-eighths of a mile, the webbed barrier flew up.

And they were off in the first real race of his life. Winkfield, the stable boy, was quickly several lengths behind the field, his visions of at least a twelve-to-one payoff fading fast. But by the far turn, he had ranged up into contention, though there were still five horses in front of him. Suddenly, he had another vision: an opening. It wasn't much. A reporter described it as just "large enough for a rabbit to get through." The stable boy shut his eyes, dug in his spurs, and steered for the hole. Willie Martin shouted at him not to try it, but Wink didn't hear or didn't care. The others were going to have to get out of his way.

Jockey Joe crashed into Charmante, who in turn smashed into Numa, who was knocked off stride and thrown into the air, landing on his head and rolling over. His jockey, a white rider named Ellis, sailed over the fence and into the gutter alongside the rail. But Wink got through. And now, at the top of the homestretch, he was ahead by a neck. The other stable hands were in racetrack heaven, whooping it up and screaming encouragement at Wink when Martin pulled alongside him on a colt named Approval. Flying on the grandstand side, Martin got past Wink to win at the wire. Good thing Wink and company had just bet to place.

Ellis was badly shaken up, and many who saw the race pointed the finger squarely at Winkfield. "A stable boy's anxiety to win narrowly escaped causing a tragedy at Hawthorne," a *Times-Herald* story began. The *Chicago Daily News* called him "a stable lad over-anxious to win out at any cost." But Wink's brazen first ride got him his first headlines, the rarest of feats, especially for a black rider. Though he had almost killed Ellis, he had shown he had guts, a fiery drive. The *Times-Herald* proclaimed: JOCKEY WINKFIELD TRIES TO GET THROUGH WITH A LONG SHOT AT HAWTHORNE AND SCATTERS HIS FIELD. Best of all, he was now officially known to the public as "Jockey Winkfield."

The bad news: his debut was also the first time he got into trouble, big trouble. The stewards called him into the grandstand to question him. "Where have you been riding?" they asked.

"I jes' rode," said Jimmy.

"Ain't you never rode before, boy?"

"No, suh," replied Jimmy.

So the stewards looked at one another—and then suspended him for a year. At least in theory. A month later, Bub May called Winkfield out of the stables and snuck him onto Jockey Joe at Newport, Kentucky's little "outlaw track," so called because, like other small operators, it ignored the rules of New York City's aristocratic Jockey Club, which enjoyed the fantasy that it controlled racing. Wink and Jockey Joe came in second again, this time without incident, and the suspended jockey couldn't wait to get back in the game legitimately.

From the start, Bub and his father, W. H., took care of Wink. The trainer son and stable owner daddy were his first surrogate fathers, and it was all for the better. Maybe the Mays were cold and remote, all business and horses, like a lot of small-timers trying to make it, but they let Wink goof off and gamble with the stable hands, and they taught him the rudiments of the business, mostly by example. They proved their faith when they let him ride at Hawthorne and when they threw him back on Jockey Joe at illegal Newport—at some risk to themselves if the Jockey Club ever found out about it. In the summer of 1899, after Winkfield's one-year banishment to the backstretch, they were ready to give him another shot.

People like the Mays would always give Jimmy a shot. Perhaps it was his courage in the saddle or his brash confidence out there on the track. Or something deeper—his good manners, his innate class, his quick mind. He was fun, too, easy to have around. And he liked to work, for a price. Smart as hell, he had never been too good to shine shoes, drive a carriage, or work a man's filly, but it certainly was not what he had in mind. And he had shown in his debut at Chicago that he was not going to waste a shot.

In July, this Bluegrass boy with cheek found himself in America's metropolis, at once Babel and Babylon. Second in the world, in size and almost everything else, only to London, New York City was what racetrackers of the day were already calling "the Big Apple." Apples, of course, were a horse's favorite treat, and one day at the Fairgrounds Race Course down in New Orleans, a black stable hand had been overheard telling another that his stable was off to "the big apple." The one who heard it was a New York turf writer, who later, in the 1920s, would popularize the nickname in his column in the *Morning Telegraph*, "Around the Big Apple with John J. FitzGerald."

Wink was confined to a thin slice of the apple, the outer rim of New York's newest borough, Brooklyn. He was on narrow Coney Island, which along its five-mile stretch accommodated three of the country's most important racetracks: the Gravesend track at the western end of Coney, Sheepshead Bay at the eastern end, and Brighton Beach in the middle.

Ten million Americans trekked to Coney every summer. On a single day, Wink might have seen two hundred thousand people at the beaches and boardwalks and amusement parks, the fireworks and electric-light shows, the racetracks. But he had little time for sightseeing himself. He was lucky if he noticed the Atlantic Ocean right in front of his eyes, busy as he was at the Brighton Beach track. His workouts on a youngster named Avenstoke were really impressing May senior. So his son Bub put the two-year-old in a race, hiring a brilliant little Irish braggart named Winnie O'Connor to ride him, and the colt won "post to post"—leading from start to finish. Avenstoke was so impressive that afternoon that Bub's father was offered $10,000 for him.

The old man reacted like the cantankerous farmer who got an incredible offer for a property and still couldn't part with it.

"If somebody thinks that colt's worth that kind of money, then she must be better than we figured," said W. H.

He was about to take his stable to Chicago, which reminded him of the near disaster from the year before when Jockey Joe and the wild boy exploded through the hole in the stretch. Then he took another look at the boy—a year on the ground behind him but still full of fire, totally unfazed by the Big Apple and everything around him. He was thoroughly impressed by the job Winkfield had done with Avenstoke in the mornings, how he had made the unproven colt look like a Kentucky Derby winner. Best of all, the boy's suspension was up. Hell no, he wasn't going to take $10,000 for Avenstoke. And he didn't need some expensive star like that loud-mouthed Irish brat Winnie O'Connor on him either.

"When we get to Chicago," W. H. growled, "let's give Winkfield a chance on him. I like the looks of that boy!"

So the Mays trained their stable out to the southwest side of Chicago—to the old Harlem track in Cicero, next door to Hawthorne. They put Avenstoke in a race ten days after his win at Brighton Beach, a wicked turnaround for a baby who had just been dragged halfway across the country. Presiding over their little booths and blackboards in front of the grandstand, the bookies preferred an unkindly named two-year-old, Unsightly. He was nine to five. They made Avenstoke their second favorite, at two to one, on the strength of his Brighton win under O'Connor and Winkfield's workouts. Somehow the colt looked fresh as he stepped onto the Harlem track—this time in the large, strong hands of his familiar exercise boy.

The barrier flew up for the six furlongs. Wink came away in the lead and held it. There was no explosion this time; he never even used his whip. As Unsightly drove out of third in the stretch, Wink pulled an extra burst of speed out of Avenstoke. It was as if the neophyte jockey knew what he was doing, and he obviously did, coolly hand-riding his colt all the way to the wire. Up in the stand, the press boys were scribbling fast: "W. H. May's colt . . . had no trouble winning. . . . Avenstoke is undoubtedly a good colt." And the kid? Like Avenstoke, he was officially no longer a "maiden"—he had won a race—yet he seemed like much more than a new jockey with one win. He already looked like a veteran. A phenom. One to watch.

W. H. and Bub were bursting with pride in the winner's' circle as they accepted the $400 winner's purse, and Wink, still sitting on Avenstoke, had just learned that applause felt really good. And it felt good making the bosses happy. Nobody in the grandstand could possibly know the warmth of a winner's circle when it's the first time.

Seven weeks later, Wink looked like the real thing again on Avenstoke, winning on a card that featured champions like Tommy Burns and Carroll Mitchell. Straight through that October, the recent stable hand added eight wins on different mounts at Harlem and Hawthorne. Then W. H. May and Co. shifted a few miles east to the Lakeside track at Roby, Indiana. It was damp, drizzly November—so cold Wink thought his huge hands would freeze on the reins. But it didn't stop him: he piled on five more wins at Roby and wound up his first Chicago season with fifteen wins and fifty-six finishes "in the money"—in first, second, or third place.

After tallying the thousands in profits his protégé was bringing in, Bub signed him to a three-year deal for $25 a month—a paltry wage, but normal for a talented beginner. The following spring, when the Mays took him down to New Orleans, Winkfield lost no time proving he was worth a lot more as he finished third on the list of the Big Easy's top jockeys. If he thought his wage was unfair, he was not stupid enough to say so. If he had, his career might have been over before it started, and he might never have found himself in the race of his dreams, and in the race of his nightmares.

Chapter Two

"A RACE WAR IS ON"

Wink guided his colt along the north side of the grandstand, trotted onto the track, and got a thrill known to only a few hundred humans before him. It was May 3, 1900, and he was riding at Churchill Downs on Derby Day.

He bounced his colt into the centennial midafternoon, joining six other jockeys and horses for the first race of the day, to be followed by the Derby three races later.

It was especially exciting for a Kentucky boy. Heart thumping, he tried to drink in the overflowing grandstand, topped by two five-year-old steeples, Churchill's soon-to-be-famous "twin spires." Cantering around the first turn toward the starting point, he heard the muffled roar of thousands, each mumbling about the entries as they scratched numbers on their programs.

It was the biggest crowd that had ever seen him ride, two or three times the size of the mobs that watched big-city baseball, just as big as the armies of wise guys who jammed the tracks around New York City. In fact, the twenty to thirty thousand men and women who gazed on Wink and his fellow jocks added up to the biggest turnout in the Derby's first quarter century. Some had come

down to Louisville that morning from Chicago, switching from the
train to the Fourth Street tram out to Churchill. Others had ridden over from St. Louis on the Southern Railway or hopped the
Iron Horse from Wink's country—Lexington and the Bluegrass—
where you had your choice of railroads.

Jack Chinn, a Kentucky colonel lounging by the judges' stand,
said there were only seven men in Frankfort, the state capital, who
were not at Churchill. Apparently one was needed "to guard the
six of them that are in jail."

A lot of people used their feet. "They'd walk twenty miles to get
there," Winkfield would remember, "and then couldn't find a place
to sleep."

The rise of Louisville as a racing mecca was a defeat for Winkfield's adopted hometown. Try as it did, Lexington had never been
able to turn its ancient equine tradition into a modern facility on a
par with those of the bigger cities on the sport's western circuit—
Chicago, Nashville, New Orleans, St. Louis, and Louisville. By
the standards of Winkfield's day, Louisville was a veritable metropolis, population 205,000, eight times bigger than Lexington.
The German Karl Baedeker's renowned guidebook went out of its
way to point out that "the 'Kentucky Derby' is held here in May"—
before adding that Louisville also produced nearly $80 million in
manufactured goods (in 1900 dollars), had "the largest leaf tobacco
market in the world," a mule market rivaling that of St. Louis, and
very extensive sales of "Kentucky whiskey."

The opener on Derby Day was a dash of five and a half furlongs—a little less than three-quarters of a mile, a furlong being
an eighth of a mile. It would start on the far side of the one-mile,
oblong course, after the first turn, so that the horses would finish
in front of the screaming grandstand. Even on that far side it was
obvious this was Derby Day, with the infield clogged with carriages and with neighboring housetops sprouting spectators. What
they saw was a terrible start.

Eight minutes dragged by as the starter and his assistants kept
trying to get the horses in a line. And no track announcer shouted

"They're off!" into a microphone. It would be ages, the 1950s, before racetracks would install what turf writer Joe Palmer thoughtfully described as "the damn public address system." Instead, with Wink and the other guys finally at the ready, the starter sprang the net barrier for the opening race and at the same time shouted, "Go!" It was the fans themselves who, squinting to figure out what was happening on the far side of the track, suddenly shouted, "They're off! They're off!"

The name of Wink 's colt summed up both of their brief lives: The Rush. Wink had won on the three-year-old a month earlier at Memphis. This time Rush moved into second halfway through the sprint, and when Wink called on him, he took the lead at the top of the stretch and won as he pleased, by two lengths. It felt good. It was a good warm-up. And it was a huge advantage to get an early feel for both the Derby Day madness and the track surface (which was the fastest Derby Day track anybody could remember). This is one reason why even out-of-town jockeys accept mounts in earlier races on big days. But nothing could fully prepare Wink that afternoon.

If riding on Derby Day was an honor shared by only a couple of hundred Americans until then, the thrill of being in the Derby itself was known to fewer than 120 (and only 500 or so more over the next century). It would last barely more than two minutes, but it was the culmination of years of preparation for stable owners and trainers, months of anticipation for the crowds, and weeks of pent-up excitement for the jockeys—or, in the case of Kentuckians like Winkfield, a lifetime. Reporters tried desperately to catch the tension of a Derby afternoon, which a century later would still be one of the most nerve-racking in sports. The *Courier-Journal*'s man wrote of "the tense, nervous excitement which comes with the anticipation of a great contest at hand." The *Louisville Times:* "It places a greater tension upon the feelings than any other sport. It equals almost the sharp pangs of battle."

Waiting in the paddock behind the grandstand, Wink heard the loud clang of the bell out on the trackside judge's stand, the first tremendous jolt of Derby excitement. It was time to saddle the colts.

And now, in a remarkable reversal of roles, a white stable owner hunched over and gave the black jockey "a leg up" into the saddle. People on tiptoes, trying to see it through the crowd, assumed Wink was placing his left foot in owner-trainer J. C. Cahn's linked hands, then lifting himself and swinging his right leg over the colt's rump. But that's not how it was done. It would be too much work for the jockey, requiring too much energy at this critical moment. Instead, Wink kicked back his left leg and cradled his shin, not his foot, in Cahn's right hand. It really was a leg up. Then Cahn lightly guided him up toward the saddle, and Wink swung his leg easily over Thrive. And it was the black jockey, not a white owner or white trainer, who was now in charge.

Then another jolt. A glorious shriek pierced the grandstand's buzz. It was the clarion call of the bugle, a tradition at American racetracks since the early 1800s. The specific call that Wink heard that afternoon was the U.S. Cavalry's "First Call," which since 1834 had been summoning soldiers to their first daily formations. It had recently been adopted by racetracks up and down the East Coast to call the riders to the "Parade to the Post." American tracks have used it ever since.

And with that the boy from Chilesburg rode into a moment of pure pageantry, the most elegant show in sports, if not in all America. Along the rail on the far side, the people he worked with— exercise boys, grooms, hotwalkers, 80 percent of them black—could barely see the pageant, but once they heard the bugle, they could feel it. Even the crowds on the housetops felt the moment, and the bugle hushed the crowd watching from their carriages on the south side of the grandstand. It all but silenced the grandstand audience, 80 percent of them white. Along the rail in front of the grandstand, a reporter noted "the black mob down the fences."

The show began with a single-file procession of the most beautiful animals in the kingdom—in reddish bay, brown, black, gray, and white, with various markings, from a star or blaze on the face to white stockings, and the jockey's silk jackets and caps making a kaleidoscope of the stable owners' colors. No athletes in America got a better introduction. In fact, black athletes got no introduction at all in other mainstream sports: though still starring in horse racing, they were kept out of the latest national pastimes of basketball and college football. It was true that in 1884, major league baseball had finally welcomed its first black player, Moses Fleetwood Walker, of the Toledo nine, but he would also be the last black player until Jackie Robinson six decades later.

And it was obvious to Winkfield and everybody else that tolerance wasn't going to last in horse racing, America's biggest sport by far. If Jimmy was only the latest black rider to make his Derby debut, he had seen and felt enough of the racism all around him to know that he was also going to be one of the last in the Louisville classic. On this day, though, he found another black rider among the seven. As Winkfield waited his turn to emerge from the paddock, Monk Overton rode onto the track in the pink and black of the Woodford Buckner stable. Overton was aboard a local favorite, Kentucky Farmer, who was warmly applauded.

Oh, Monk could tell Wink a thing or two about the old days, especially about the black domination of the early Derbies, a fact that would soon be deleted from the sport's history books. (The old black jockeys wouldn't be anything racing people would deign to talk about for almost a century.) Wink's fellow black jockeys had captured thirteen or fourteen of the twenty-five Kentucky Derbies so far (the records are still incomplete), including the inaugural Derby, won by Oliver Lewis. But that did not tell the story of how prominent blacks were among the "also-rans." All but two or three of the fifteen jockeys in the first Kentucky Derby, in 1875, were black. In Overton's time, the 1890s, Churchill Downs had fallen into hard times and could attract only three to eight horses to its famous Derby; still, most of the jockeys were black. All but one of the riders were black in the 1891 and 1895 Derbies, all three were black in 1892, and six of the eight were black in the 1896 running.

Wink doubtless knew that Monk himself had ridden against Ike Murphy twice in the Derby, losing to him by only half a length the second time. Monk had never won the Derby, though. This was his eighth try, and you can almost hear Wink and his smart-ass colleague stable boys yelling:

"Hey, Monk, when you gonna win one?"

But they all respected Monk, knowing that long ago he had turned in not only one of the most memorable moments of the century for a black athlete but one of the most spectacular days ever at the races. On July 10, 1891, at Washington Park in Chicago, Monk Overton became the first American jockey ever to win all six of his races on a single day's card, but that doesn't nearly tell the story. After each race, the bookmaking companies, at their booths in front of the stand, kept betting against Monk's chances of winning yet again. The clerks at the blackboards would get out their chalks and scratch longer odds each time on Monk's mounts. At the end of the day, an extraordinary fact emerged: not a single bookmaking firm had made money. Some lost as much as $6,000, a pile in those days. For some, it was a near-death experience. A bookie nicknamed The Ghost decided to stay with Overton in his personal bets and won an astounding $11,000, but he must have looked like his nickname, because Monk had cost his firm, Griff & Co., and the others, combined, a jaw-dropping $120,000.

"The ring will never get its money back," The Ghost said of Monk's tour de force. "I withdraw from Griff & Co."

The fans, on the other hand, were loving it. Sticking with Monk, they cleaned up again and again. When the day was done, Monk was swimming in public praise even as the rigidly racist white baseball leagues were keeping black athletes out. 'MONK' WINS SIX RACES/SKILLFUL COLORED JOCKEY/EXCITING FINISHES AROUSE GREAT ENTHUSIASM, headlined the *Tribune*. "Once he was well on his winning way, the public followed him and raided the [betting] ring on his mounts, winning a ton of money . . . the spirited finishes bringing the crowd of 4,500 to its feet three or four times. Overton was wildly cheered . . . and 'Monk' beamed."

Winkfield had been keeping a close eye on the colt right behind Monk's. He was named after a white hero. Naming race horses after people was a common practice, and in this case the honoree was a Lieutenant Gibson—"one of the gamest fellows and best shots in the hills," said a reporter. He was leading federal troops trying to neutralize "confederate" gangs in the Kentucky boondocks, including the "kuklux." As the equine "Lieut. Gibson" cantered past Wink, everybody in the stands thought of the kuklux and their ilk, who at the moment were concentrating on white people—breaking into their mountain homes, beating them, sometimes killing them, and wrecking the houses—for being irreligious or for political reasons, like union organizing.

The human lieutenant would be in action again soon in the case of two white people, a Mrs. Hall and her son, murdered by the kuklux over in Letcher County, Kentucky, not far from Boone's Fork. Gibson would lead a company of soldiers and deputies against the accused, one May Reynolds and his men. The final battle would take place near Whitesburg, a town famous for its hospitality, including its roomy thirty-by-thirty-foot jail. Gibson would capture some of May's gang, including two of the Bentley boys, Mac Konts, Ikey Potter, Sol and Lige Flemings, the Wright brothers, and the Newton brothers. But May Reynolds would escape, along with John Reynolds, Creed Potter, and some others—a most unfortunate turn of events for Gibson. As a reporter who dared venture into those mountains said of the lieutenant, "The head of the Kentucky river is an awful unhealthy place for him just now, for May Reynolds has sworn against Gibson particularly."

When the fans saw that colt in the parade, they had the same question everybody in the mountains put to that reporter: "Have they ketched the kuklux yet?"

Jimmy Winkfield knew the boy in royal purple who sat on Lieut. Gibson. In fact, he knew Jimmy Boland only too well. The Jimmies had just beaten each other in their April meeting at Memphis. This time Boland's mount was favored by the bettors and probably even by the stars, given the signs: he not only was named after the lieutenant but boasted an illustrious grandsire, Iroquois, who in 1881 had become the first American-bred horse to win the original Derby, at Epsom Downs in England.

A minute later, the Louisville fans were shouting the twin spires off for hometown owner Hiram Scoggan's two entries, their jocks shamelessly aglow in stars and stripes.

Wink brought up the rear of this parade on the seven-to-one shot Thrive, the unfamiliar black jockey's satiny orange and blue silks catching the falling sun. The horses pranced a quarter of a mile up the stretch to the starter's stand. The race route: back down the stretch past the crowd, a mile around the track, and down the stretch again to finish the mile and a quarter in front of the best seats in the house. Wink and the other six jocks looked like ghosts, as if they had drained not only every last drop of water and every last ounce of fat from their bony little bodies but their blood, too. Approaching the barrier, their stable colors flashed in the sun. The colts nervously threw their manes, twisted their necks, bounced forward, backed up, threatened to launch their hind hooves, as Wink and the boys punched and wrenched their necks back.

"Go!" The rubber barrier twanged as it hit the rail.

They got away in a great charge, their massive chests rising and falling, the riders a jumble of colors. Wink's outsized, long-fingered hands held Thrive back until their first move. As they reached the roaring grandstand for the first time, Wink pulled on Thrive, then cut straight over to the rail for the shortest trip. He was sitting fourth. Up front, Lieut. Gibson shot ahead into the first turn. The white jockey Crowhurst, in a good spot aboard one of Hiram Scoggan's flag bearers, Highland Lad, yelled at Clyde Van Dusen, who was on the other Scoggan entry, Florizar:

"Van! How much do you think I will win by?"

But Lieut. Gibson was still towing the field at a fast clip. So Wink jockeyed Thrive to a comfortable spot, where he watched and waited. And waited. When he got to the three-quarters pole, Wink began his drive. And what a drive! The tough black crowd along the backstretch went wild as they saw their friend from Chilesburg acting like he actually belonged in the Kentucky Derby. For a black jockey, this was the hardest-to-please crowd of all and the most important. Wink's young cohort Marshall Lilly would be cowed by these railbirds a few years later when he got one of his shots at becoming a jockey. Marshall raced the bejesus out of his mount as he approached the black stable hands just so he wouldn't have to hear them razzing him to death. As a result, when he got by them, Marshall's horse had nothing left.

Under Winkfield's whip, Thrive was fifth at the mile. Heading into the stretch they collared jockey Crowhurst on the tiring Highland Lad and pounded past them into third. The roaring, rasping crowd strained to see if Thrive had anything left. They got their answer. Wink and his colt put on a wicked stretch run, bearing down on flag-bearing Florizar, whom Van Dusen had eased up when it was clear he couldn't beat Lieut. Gibson. It was clear that Wink couldn't, either. Still he drove furiously for second. It was not to be. "I'd have caught Florizar if the wire hadn't a bobbed up when it did," Wink said after the race. But by grabbing third he was at least "in the money," or among the top three finishers, which still made him part of history. As for Florizar's rider, Clyde Van Dusen would finally get to the winner's circle nearly thirty years later, in 1929, as a trainer, on a horse that shared his name.

TOW-ROPED HIS FIELD ALL THE WAY, was how the *Courier-Journal* headlined Lieut. Gibson's wire-to-wire triumph. It might have made some of the sharper turf fans recall Gibson's grandsire, whose trainer had cabled home the order of finish in the 1881 Epsom Derby in code: IROPERTOW, an anagram for the first three finishers, IROQUOIS, PEREGRINE, TOWN Moor. As for Lieut. Gibson's 2:06 ¼, it would stand as a Churchill Downs record for eleven years. It would take seventy-three years for the next century's speediest Derby laureate, Secretariat, to do it only 6 and $^{17}/_{20}$ seconds faster.

But Winkfield knew what many did not, that there was another race on at that moment. As the lieutenant was draped in his garland of roses, Wink bolted for the jockeys' room, where the riders weighed out. This was to show they hadn't cheated by dropping some of the lead slivers that had been inserted into their saddles so their colts would carry the required weight for the Derby, 122 pounds. Wink had weighed in at under 104, so they had stuffed more than 18 pounds of lead into his seat.

He made damn sure to weigh out first so he could be the first to talk to the press. A year into the game, he had already mastered the press moves: how to become better known to owners and trainers so he could get good horses. Now he landed one of his earliest big clippings, a post–Kentucky Derby interview. Wink was covered in gray dust, and his eyes were still watery from the wind. As the reporters all saw, he had the look of a champion, too—dirty and breathless—and it impressed the hell out of them.

The interview began with that eternal reporter's question "How do you feel?" One of the Louisville papers printed Winkfield's answers in country-boy English—with an imagined black accent as rendered by the white reporter or editor. "How do I feel? I feels fine. I does. Thrive's a good horse. Of course I couldn't ketch dat Gibson. He's too good."

If the white Jimmy Boland had said "ketch," as the mountain people did, as most Americans did, it would have come out "catch" in the paper on this momentous occasion. As a matter of fact, this Michigan country boy's own remarks were printed with perfect diction and grammar. Boland was quoted as saying of Lieut. Gibson: "He can turn the same trick every day in the week and furnish some special performances. I'm proud of having ridden a Kentucky Derby winner." The *Courier-Journal* found Boland not only literate but charming, and modest. "I don't know what to say," he commented, laughing. "What Gibson did speaks for itself. A cook could have won if he didn't fall off."

But it was Winkfield, basking in the first sunshine of his career, who made more of a name for himself than anybody else that day, even if the editors sometimes spelled his name "Winfield." They were so bamboozled by this brazen kid's mouth they put his name in a headline the next morning and even spelled it right: WINKFIELD SAID A COOK COULD HAVE WON ON GIBSON "JUST AS EASY" (never mind that it was winning rider Boland who had actually said that). Wink earned $300 for third place from Cahn, who had hired him out from the Mays. Cahn added a bonus of $25. "Usually I didn't get anything unless I won," Wink would recall, "and then only five or ten dollars." He came in second in another important contest that spring, the battle for most wins at Churchill, when he garnered thirteen, second only to Boland.

But this twenty-year-old was getting too good too fast for some of the white jockeys, and they were about to let him know it. They would stop him if they had to kill him to do it. The competition for jobs was getting deadly as American racing came under increasing financial pressure and many of the richest stable owners began to move abroad for higher purses there, especially to England and the high prestige of winning classic races in the sport's motherland. They took along their jockeys, by then nearly all of them white, including, in the year 1900, Tod and Cassius "Cash" Sloan, Johnny and Lester Reiff, and Danny Maher.

It was the first massive flight abroad by American athletes, and the biggest ever. With their aerodynamic, crouched-over riding positions, as opposed to the straight-backed English, the Americans thrilled their hosts and stole a high percentage of their races. A popular American magazine, *Munsey's*, was agog. Fourteen-year-old, sixty-four-pound Johnny Reiff, it reported, was making the equivalent of $100,000 a year. The black jockey Willie Simms had introduced "the American seat" a few years earlier, but it was the famous white jockey Tod Sloan who got the credit, perhaps in part because he crouched even more. Admiring him from back home, *Munsey's* called Tod "the most brilliant jockey that ever sat on a horse," and England, though at first it ridiculed him for replacing jockeyship with "monkeyship," finally adopted not only this

Yankee Doodle Dandy crouching on a pony but his crouch, too. Sang the winner of a newspaper poetry contest in England:

Of Toddy Sloan now let us sing,
Whose praises through the country ring,
Undoubtedly the jockey king,
Proclaimed by everybody.

Jimmy Winkfield wasn't going anywhere. Luckily for him, he was as good at handling money as he was at riding horses. But there was another, terrible lesson in store for him. He learned it three months after the 1900 Derby, on a fast track near Chicago. He was as hot as that first week in August, taking four races in two days at the Harlem course in Cicero, just outside the city. On Wednesday, he boarded a veteran campaigner named Dr. Walmsley, the bettors' second choice in the six-furlong sprint. As Wink started to move the six-year-old down the backstretch, a white boy named J. O'Connor, probably thinking he was hidden in the herd of a dozen horses, crashed Wink and Dr. Walmsley into the rail. It was a double-decker sandwich crash, combining two thousand pounds of muscular horse flesh with the weight of two unprotected riders, but O'Connor was on the safe side of it and bounced away on the chestnut Alfred C. as another white jock went on to win.

As his mount lay there with two broken ribs, Winkfield was rushed to a hospital with scary-looking leg injuries. He could have been killed. As it was, he would be out a full week. At first, the white boy's horse was blamed and banned from Harlem, the *Chicago Record* saying that O'Connor just couldn't control him. But then track officials concluded that something more sinister was afoot. Under the headline WAR AMONG JOCKEYS: RACE CONFLICT AT LOCAL TRACK/ WHITE AND COLORED RIDERS ADOPT ROUGH-RIDING TACTICS, the *Record* reported, "A race war is on between the jockeys riding at the local tracks. Jealous because of the success of so many colored riders, the white boys accepting mounts at Harlem, it is said, have taken desperate measures to put their rivals out of business."

The story went national. The *Thoroughbred Record*, one of the industry's bibles, picked it up, using the "race war" line, and gave Winkfield a boost in the process: "Last Wednesday Winkfield, one of the most successful of the colored boys riding at Harlem, was crowded against the fence, bruising his leg. . . . Horse and rider escaped luckily at that."

But the black jocks weren't going to take it. On Thursday, the appearance of a crack two-year-old filly named Miss Bennett pushed the Harlem crowd to eight thousand, and the fans got to see something else, too—the black riders fighting back. "The colored boys, becoming convinced they were badly used (the day before), retaliated . . . and took a hand in the rough tactics," said a Chicago reporter. It might seem amazing today that black jockeys, who with their families faced the terrifying horrors of racism, would dare to fight back, but they did. Their successes on the western circuit— from Chicago to Kentucky to New Orleans—gave them confidence, and the farther north they got, the more daring they became.

The Chicago "race war" got wilder on Friday, as the black jockeys got the upper hand in the unholy mess that was the fifth race. First, two white boys were knocked off their mounts, one of them in a bad spill on the far side of the Harlem track. Then, right in front of the grandstand, a jockey bumped a colt named Henry Burt, who in turned banged the white rider of a Hiram Scoggan entry. The fans were horrified as the Scoggan filly was lifted almost off her feet by Henry Burt, then slammed into the rail and hit the ground. As the white boy was sprawled in the dirt in his stars-and-stripes silks, stiff as a corpse, four other horses sailed over him and the filly as if it were a steeplechase. "The entire field of horses seemed to pass over the prostrate horse and jockey, and the latter lay cold and still for a time," but the white boy survived. On Saturday, another rider was fined a hefty $100 for whipping an opponent's horse in the head in a furious drive. Again the papers said it was racially motivated, but they did not say which jockey was white and which was black.

The *Chicago Record* concluded: "The officials, who are aware of the jealousy, are doing all they can to adjust matters and keep peace among the boys, but have not yet succeeded in preventing the accidents."

As for Winkfield, he had won the publicity sweepstakes again. As he lay in the hospital, the Chicago papers speculated on when he would make it back and then wrote about him when he did, a week later. Unfortunately, his lower legs were still bothering him, and he didn't win any races his first day back; in fact, as he nursed his ankles, he managed to win only five in Harlem's last month, although he did keep his owners in the money twenty-four times. It was a relief to go back to Kentucky. That fall he made his debut at the Latonia course up on the Ohio, riding there and at Newport through November.

The softness of Christmastime sent sentimental Jimmy back to his brothers and sisters and friends in Lexington. He married a girl named Edna that year. The records tell us nothing about her up to then, except that she lived in Lexington and was nineteen, about a year younger than Jimmy. He might have known her from their Bluegrass childhood, but he had been away with the May stable for most of the past two years, so it was a whirlwind, holiday love affair. And in only a couple of months, with the arrival of spring, love and marriage would have to make way for his whirlwind career.

Chapter Three

WINNIE'S DIAMOND

Wink and his mount, a three-year-old bay called His Eminence, felt the Kentucky Derby crowd without looking. The surrounding sea of humanity numbered about twenty thousand again this year, versus the mere eleven thousand who had just helped Connie Mack open the 1901 Philadelphia Athletics baseball season.

"At 4:47 o'clock a flash of red appears just to the left of the stand," noted the *Courier-Journal*'s man in the press box. "It is Winkfield on His Eminence, wearing the colors of Frank Van Meter's stable."

Applause rippled through the grandstand. Wink was almost unique now, one of a dwindling number of black athletes in American racing. There were a few in boxing, but none in any other mainstream sport.

It was April 29, 1901, the first time the Derby had not been run in the merry month. Such a state of affairs would happen only once more, in 1945, when it so disturbed Kentuckians' rhythms that they scheduled the Derby on the first Saturday of May forever after. Wink seemed off to a big season. At Memphis, he had taken the

Tennessee Derby, still a rival to Louisville's grand event. Tennessee, after all, had been the center of American racing before Kentucky. Wink had captured the important Congress Sweepstakes at Memphis, too, and had set a record for the mile and fifty yards, 1:42 ½.

More than a bit of déjà vu hung over this Kentucky Derby. Here were the two Jimmies again, Winkfield and Boland, the only riders to appear in both the last Derby of the nineteenth century and the first of the twentieth. Just like last year, Wink had been on the Mays' crack sprinter, The Rush, in the first race of Derby Day. Again Wink and The Rush won going away, and again they set a record for the distance. And just like last year, Wink had been hired out from the Mays by another owner—this time Van Meter—for the Derby itself.

But if Winkfield now commanded respect, he was hardly the star at Churchill that afternoon. The one who sparkled most was tiny Winfield O'Connor, a year younger than Wink and "one of the best jockeys in the world," frothed one of the newspapers. "O'Connor is several pounds the better jockey that has a mount in the Derby." That meant Winnie could weigh several pounds more and still beat the rest of them. Weight was a big deal in the Winnie O'Connor story, because he had once been the lightest American jockey ever. The previous lightest may well have been a pre-teenager who rode in Virginia before the American Revolution, when it was common to throw eleven- and twelve-year-old boys on a half-ton race horse so as not to slow him down too much. As this colonial child sat in the hanging seat-scale, he displaced all of forty-seven pounds, which moved a diarist to observe: "Strange that so little substance in a human Creature can have strength & skill sufficient to manage a Horse in a Match of Importance."

When Winnie O'Connor made his professional debut for Mike Daly's famous Brooklyn stable, he, too, was only twelve and weighed just forty-five pounds. He was called "the lightest jockey who ever rode a race horse."

At this moment in 1901, however, the Irish kid from Brooklyn had added eight years and more than sixty pounds and was on his way to becoming the winningest jockey in the country. A national celebrity, O'Connor stopped only at the best hotels, sporting the best suits from the boys' department, cigars that looked bigger than he was, and diamonds that lit his way. He was constantly giving clog-dancing exhibitions and being gossiped about in the papers, as were other top white jockeys. This in turn gave them a leg up in the workplace, plastering their names in the minds of stable owners looking for riders. The winner of the last Derby, Fred "The Flying Dutchman" Taral, created a cloud of publicity for himself by running around with the boxer John L. Sullivan while the papers called them "Big and Little Casino." In the midst of all the talk, Taral commanded a jaw-dropping $12,000 a year from any stable owner who wanted first call on his services, and eight thousand for second call. O'Connor had a similar glow about him, whereas Wink could tap-dance all night and get nothing for it.

Winnie's spectacular current distinction was a diamond display that might have blinded Wink that afternoon. Diamonds were a man's best friend, especially for an Irishman like Winnie who had come up from the bottom. Or like John Morrissey, who for the second Derby had provided Churchill Downs with a French machine that could replace human bookmakers. It allowed a bettor to make a $5 wager on a horse, then added up the total amount bet on that horse—in French, the *pari mutuel*, or mutual bet—and divided that sum by the number of bettors to determine the horse's odds. No messing with a bookie in a checkered jacket. Anti-gambling forces screamed that these efficient, immoral machines would lure more innocents to the track, that they had brought an epidemic of suicides to the boulevards of Paris, but Morrissey figured they would buy him more diamonds. He had risen from the gangs of New York to become boxing champion of America, the nation's biggest casino operator, and a congressman. But when he had wanted to distinguish himself in the presence of president-elect Lincoln, he had summed it all up with a $5,000 diamond pin blazing from his shirtfront, set off by more diamonds on his cuffs.

It was hard, though, to get closer to your stones than did Diamond Jim Brady, the railroad-car builder, who attended the Derby when Wink was a boy. Brady owned twenty-seven thousand diamonds, it was said, including the ones decorating his underwear.

Yet Winnie O'Connor got even closer to his jewels. As he pulled off his shirt that afternoon and prepared to slip into a white silk jacket with blue sleeves, he revealed, noted one writer, a startling gift from a recent employer, one Prince Poniatowski. It was a pin in the shape of a jockey's head, constructed entirely of diamonds and, for the time being, stitched into Winnie's pale pink chest. The only black chest in the jockeys' room was bare.

The fact that he had to follow Winkfield in the post parade must have been a pinprick of another sort for O'Connor, but now the little northern star and his beautiful brown colt, Sannazarro, had their moment as they brought half of Churchill's grandstand to their feet. The bettors, though, liked a colt with the forgettable name of Alard Scheck. He was the odds-on favorite at seven to ten, meaning he was so good you had to wager $10 to get a mere $17 back, including your own ten, if you won. His owner was a Memphis brewer named Johnny Schorr, and a huge Tennessee contingent had come up to see Alard embarrass the Kentuckians.

Wink and the four white boys rode up to the starting line, where starter Curley Brown used a word that young Americans would later think they invented. "He cautioned them to keep cool," said a reporter. The fatherly Curley lectured, "You can't start running now, boys, so don't try it." Although old man Curley got a lot of sympathy from the jocks for treating them equally, Curley's insistence on a fair start was more about money. "The public must be protected," he said, "and every boy must do his best to get off." Wink remembered a trick to get off even better than his best.

"Come up to the line quietly," said Curley. But Wink's colt made a break to the side, knocking the other four out of line. "Keep that horse still there, Winkfield!" Stunts at the start like that, to mess up the other horses and riders, were the oldest tricks in the book before starting gates locked horses in. Then Winnie broke, too. But the delay wasn't bad: only four minutes went by before

Curley shouted, "Go!"

Before the colts had traveled fifty yards, His Eminence was a half-length in front. Perfectly judging the pace of the race, knowing that his mount had plenty left, Wink kept him relaxed. Passing the cheering grandstand crowd for the first time, the colt was still in the lead, and he held it on the far side, cruising under Wink's hold. Into the final turn, Wink was three lengths in front, headed for a Kentucky boy's thrill of a lifetime. O'Connor and Boland whipped furiously, trying to drive their horses into contention.

This was the point where Alard Scheck, the favorite under the crack Scottish boy J. Woods, was supposed to make his move and come flying down the stretch, but today wasn't his day. Despite the Scot's urging, the horse refused to surge. Up front, Wink shook up His Eminence, who responded courageously with his long legs and clean stride. As he looked over his shoulder going down the stretch, Wink saw the others hopelessly beaten. Winnie and Sannazarro were second; Boland, on Driscoll, third.

Wink halted His Eminence in front of the crowd, which included Kentucky's governor and both of its U.S. senators. As they erupted into thunderous applause and Wink was handed a bouquet, his eyes filled with tears. Never had a black American been honored like this, other than on a racecourse. A blanket of evergreens and red and white roses was draped over the colt's back, a tradition started six years earlier with a collar of white and pink roses for Willie Simms's colt, Ben Brush. It would be another quarter of a century before a journalist would dream up the Derby's nickname, the Run for the Roses.

The black fans were delirious, and not because Wink was black. A "southern tip" had been spread about His Eminence—in other words, a tip that originated with the black help on the backstretch, inside information from the stables—and inspired heavy betting. And now a stable worker, or as the *Courier-Journal* put it, "a proud darky paraded [His Eminence] up and down in front of the stand, while the crowd cheered some more."

Wink's eyes still hadn't dried as he headed for the jockeys' room. There, the other jocks went out of their way to say His Eminence had won fairly. "I got a good start and was not interfered with," said Woods, the Scot. "It was the nicest race I ever rode in." Winnie made it sound like it was the horses versus him—"The best horse beat me"—and put in a little bid to steal Wink's mount for the richer American Derby. "In my opinion," O'Connor proclaimed, "His Eminence has a splendid chance to win the American Derby at Chicago in June."

"I got him away a little early," Wink told the reporters, "and after that I just breezed him around the track." But those two minutes and seven and three-quarters of a second would freeze forever in his mind. Wink would replay this race so often in his head, as he did so many others, that six decades later he would describe it in almost the same words: "I got him away in front and stayed there. Was nothin' to it." Those big hands helped:

> All the way, I kept a good hold of his head and never moved on him. In the stretch, I looked back and saw Sannazarro coming along. I tell you, I shook up His Eminence some then, and he came in easy. I think I could have won in faster time if I had wanted to work him, but he had it all his own way anyhow, so what was the use?

Winkfield seemed a lot calmer than after the previous year's Derby. He was getting used to the excitement; traveling from New York to Chicago to Kentucky to New Orleans to Memphis and back will do that for a farm boy. Getting slammed into the rail and almost killed had also contributed to his quieter outlook. Stable owner Frank Van Meter cashed in $4,850 for the Derby, and although, to the newspapers, he assigned himself all the credit for instructing Wink, he privately betrayed his admiration for his jockey by awarding him a hefty $500 bonus. There is no record of how much Bub May charged Van Meter for Wink's services, but May doubtless had been able to jack up that price lately on the strength of Wink's ever more obvious talents. May rarely had horses that approached the

standards of the Derby or other big races—with Wink, he had more
jockey than horse—so renting out Wink as often as possible provided May with a good extra income. In return, May almost certainly sweetened Wink's $25-per-month contract, which had a year
to go. And in the bargain, the Derby win meant Wink was much
more in demand, with those potential bonuses just in front of him,
like the rabbits at a greyhound track.

Wink, indeed, was launched. One newspaper ran a handsome
headshot of him, with his almond eyes and striped silks. A sidebar
began with the reporters' usual odd obsession with shades of brown,
as opposed to shades of white: "Winkfield, the jockey who rode His
Eminence to victory in Kentucky's classic event, is a little chocolate colored negro whose home is in Lexington." But Jimmy Winkfield was alone on his way to the top. No other black athlete joined
him. Only a few remained on the jockey lists, among them Simms,
Overton, and Tommy Knight, all fading fast.

A newspaper article that appeared on Derby Day—a front-page
account of Reverend Dr. Charles Parkhurst's speech at the Madison
Square Presbyterian Church in New York City—showed how tense
the climate was for black people. Parkhurst was helpfully enlighten-
ing his fellow Christians on his recent trip to the South:

> The Southerner does not like the Negro any better than
> the average Northerner does, and the two carry themselves
> toward the Negro with just about the same amount of
> Christian consideration; only, of the two, the Southern
> white man has perhaps this advantage, that he does not
> make quite so flamboyant a pretense of loving the Negro
> as his Northern confrere does. The Southern white man
> dislikes the Negro, and he owns up to it. The white man in
> the North dislikes the Negro and lies about it.

Of those who read this over their breakfast before heading out
to the Kentucky Derby, how many applauded Winkfield as he rode
up to the stand? But Wink was fearless. It was as if, having figured

out the game, he couldn't be stopped. On that Derby Day alone, he was in the money in five of six races, with three firsts, a second, and a third. He finished that spring meeting by winning ten of his forty races. Already, people were starting to see him as a *money rider*— meaning he was interested only in the best horses and richest races. They had said it about Ike Murphy, too. Usually it was meant as an insult; athletes weren't supposed to be money-grubbing, but who in America wasn't? Getting clobbered by those white jockeys in Chicago made Wink choosier about his mounts, too. There was less rough riding in the richer events, where the judges had to be more alert and at least act fairer.

The money-rider tag fit. Winkfield thought about money all the time. He had gotten the mount on His Eminence for the colt's maiden win as a two-year-old, which helped him get the assignment for the 1901 Kentucky Derby. He was not concentrating on any old race. He got the maiden win of the best horse in the West at the moment, named Garry Hermann. He also took the important Turf Congress Handicap at Churchill two days after the Derby, and then the Clark Handicap, still a racing fixture today. A week later, he added the Latonia Derby up the road, across the Ohio River from Cincinnati, where the official chart book pointed out that winner Hernando was "most judiciously ridden." Wink was aiming for the big ones.

Jimmy Winkfield had become the premier jockey of the West, a position he solidified by changing employers. It is not clear whether he waited until his contract with Bub May was up, in the second half of 1902, or Bub let him out early. But Wink now signed with the more prominent Patrick Dunne, son-in-law of a powerful Chicago stable owner named Ed Corrigan, who could help make things happen for Wink. Dunne had seen what everybody else saw. "May brought him up," as Phil Chinn, an old Kentucky colonel, put it, "but May never had to teach that boy how to ride. He was a natural from the start. He had no particular style; he just sat up there like a piece of gold."

But he was in a dangerous spot, too. An obvious target. No longer just one of a handful of surviving black jockeys, he was far ahead of the others. Jess Conley would have only fifteen wins in 1901; Simms, only six; Overton, four. They couldn't even see Wink way out there in front. After winning two races at Latonia on May 13, he hopped a train to Worth, on the southwestern outskirts of Chicago, to win another on May 14, three more on May 15, one more on May 16, two more on May 17, one more on May 18—who could keep up with him?

This time it really was the jockey who deserved the credit because, with all of his triumphs, he hadn't yet been on a horse that would rate a word in the long history of the turf—until he reached the Windy City. America's lone black sports star spent June through November of 1901 burning up all the tracks in Chicago—Hawthorne, Harlem, the old Washington Park, Worth—and Lakeside, just across the Indiana line, racking up seventy-two wins. Then he got the leg up on a funny-looking two-year-old named McChesney.

This colt had a huge white splash down his nose, which sometimes stuck out of a hood with thick blinkers, so he wouldn't be distracted by all the wonderful things available for a colt to gaze at. McChesney also had tall white stockings, which looked ridiculous on him, like today's athletic socks. Funniest of all was how short he was, not much taller than five-foot Jimmy Winkfield, and with his narrow rear he looked like some abstract leather sculpture. His rear legs would drag as he paraded to the post. But if McChesney was an ungainly animal at a canter, galloping transformed him magically into a beautiful machine, an advanced experiment in pure speed. When you had a horse like McChesney, you wanted a jockey like Winkfield.

One October day at the Harlem oval, riding at his usual 105 pounds, Wink took McChesney over six and a half furlongs— just thirteen-sixteenths of a mile—in a wicked 1:18 $^4/_5$, but the colt wasn't even close to running all out. And while a two-week turnaround between races would be considered tight a century later, Wink and McChesney came out the very next day for another six and a half furlongs. "McChesney put up his usual high-class performance," the *Daily Racing Form* marveled, "and raced everything into the submission by the time the head of the stretch had been reached." His time: exactly the same. This time the *Racing Form* checked the books and found that Wink and McChesney had just set a new American record for the distance.

Five times Winkfield got on the two-year-old in that 1901 season, and five times he won, helping this lightest and brightest of chestnuts advance toward the history books. But the colt would soon deliver a terrible shock to Wink.

After Chicago, Wink dropped down to the Big Easy, where he wrapped up a lovely year on horseback by winning the highlight of the season, the New Orleans Christmas Handicap. Loaded with lead to make 123 pounds aboard the chestnut George Arnold, Wink made it a terrific holiday for the fans, giving them a breathtaking finish as he won by just a head and lowered the track's mile mark to 1:39.

By his own count, Winkfield won more than 161 races in 1901. In only his second full year of riding, he was competing at the summit. Yet America's only great black jockey was mysteriously left out of the rankings by the important *Goodwin's Annual Official Guide to the Turf.* This seemed especially odd since only four of the nation's jockeys had more wins. Winnie O'Connor was number-one with 253. Curiouser still, the guide's publisher, F. B. Goodwin himself, had traveled to Louisville for the 1901 Derby, in which Wink beat Winnie. Goodwin had left Wink off his lists in 1899 and 1900, too, though Wink's stats had been much better than many of those included. The *Guide* did list a few of the vanishing black jockeys who weren't doing so well. Maybe the trouble was that Winkfield was refusing to vanish, which some in the sport and in the newspapers made clear they didn't like. It was not a good sign for America's lonely leading black athlete, or for the immediate future of American sports.

Not that it slowed down Wink.

Chapter Four

"WINKFIELD'S DEAD!"

The crowd pushed and pulled for a closer look at the four heads poking out of the top halves of their doors in the Churchill Downs paddock. Nearby, owners were giving last-minute instructions to their jockeys in the 1902 Kentucky Derby and answering questions from reporters and fans.

The favorite was a colt named Abe Frank. His owner explained how he got his name.

"Why, boys," said George C. Bennett, "this horse is named after Abe Frank, a Jew cotton broker of Memphis, and by the way he's one of the finest fellows that ever lived. He's a prince, and while he's swift, he's not quite as fast as his namesake here."

"Do you think Abe Frank will win?" somebody asked.

"There isn't any doubt about it," said Bennett. "And I want to say that if he does win the Kentucky Derby, I wouldn't trade places with President Roosevelt. Ain't that right, Coburn?"

"We'll win it all right," said Monk Coburn, the white jockey wearing Bennett's green-with-white-diamonds silks.

Major Thomas Clay McDowell patted Alan-a-Dale on the mane and spoke with Wink. The major presided over Ashland, the Lexington estate of his great-grandfather on his mother's side, the famous statesman Henry Clay. Back in the 1820s, Ashland had been called the White House of Kentucky as Clay ran repeatedly for the presidency. Wink already knew how to talk to such men. As a bootblack, carriage driver, and exercise boy, he had observed people like McDowell close up. Now he was learning how to do business with them.

McDowell made it easier. He may have been the grandest man in Lexington, but at just thirty-six years old, he was also one of the boys—a jolly, fat-cheeked, mustached young man under a derby that fit his head like a sausage casing. The whole thing was packed into a round-collared shirt, open tweed coat, and matching vest stretched over a happy stomach. Two important items hung from this gut, a gold chain protruding from a stopwatch pocket and field glasses dangling on a string.

Two of the four Derby colts were flying Ashland's black-and-white silks: Alan-a-Dale and The Rival, under Nash Turner, the latest great white jockey to come down from the North just for the Louisville classic. Tom told Wink to get away fast, take the lead, and keep it as long as possible. He wasn't expecting Wink to win; he didn't think the colt could go a mile and a quarter, and besides, Alan-a-Dale had been much slower than The Rival in workouts. So Tom was running him as a "rabbit," to get off fast and tire the other two horses while letting The Rival save himself. Then The Rival would take over and go on to win.

It wasn't exactly a secret. Like everybody else, T. W. Moore, owner of the fourth horse, Inventor, knew The Rival was the Ashland horse to beat. You didn't bring in one of the North's top jockeys and not stick him on your best horse. Moore himself had hired the black rider Robert "Tiny" Williams, who'd seen his day. And what a day. Williams had won the Travers at Saratoga, Chicago's prestigious American Derby, and the fabled Queen's Plate in Ontario. Now, Moore told Tiny to hold back and keep pace with The

Rival, letting Alan-a-Dale and Abe Frank wear themselves out. The Rival and Nash Turner were his only real threat.

But only four horses? These were indeed the years of extremely thin fields and small purses in the Kentucky Derby as Churchill Downs struggled to survive. In the fifteen Derbies from 1891 through 1905, ten had fields of five or fewer, but the legendary modern trainer "Sunny Jim" Fitzsimmons, who in Winkfield's day was a small-time jockey on outlaw tracks, said those good small fields required smarter jockeys. "With these big fields, they ride their own race, and if everything goes just right, they win," he said. "But it took more skill and judgment to beat a good four- or five-horse field like you had then because you had to study each horse in the race."

The bugle called them to the post. Monk Coburn rode out on Abe Frank, and a stable boy rubbed the jockey's leg with a rabbit's foot, shouting, "Good luck for Abe!"

"Abe's all right," said Monk.

A groom patted Alan-a-Dale, a shimmering chestnut with perfect conformation and a wide blaze down his face, and yelled, "Ride him good, Wink!"

"If there's a race in him, I'll get it out," said Wink, smiling.

They stepped onto the track and turned left toward the starting line a quarter of a mile up. High above the brilliantly colored parade to the post, six poles flew the Stars and Stripes above the thick crowd of fifteen thousand. Bringing up the rear, Alan-a-Dale glistened in the sun, and his jockey seemed to as well: Wink was the only rider in the Derby who'd been singled out in the newspaper accounts. It was obvious why. Only Ike Murphy and Willie Simms had captured two Kentucky Derbies, and only Ike had won two in a row, a decade ago. Could Wink join them with a double?

It seemed that Jimmy Winkfield could do anything. From New Year's Day to May Day 1902, from New Orleans to Memphis to Nashville to Chicago, Wink had picked up another twenty-two wins and fifty-nine finishes in the money for his delighted bosses. In March, he had interrupted his Memphis season for the Crescent City (New Orleans) Derby, which lured one of the biggest crowds ever, added another major jewel to his collection, and earned him a picture in the *Picayune* (JOCKEY WINKFIELD. THE BLACK ARTIST). You could hear his growing confidence when he met the press down there.

"I came all the way from Memphis to ride Lord Quex," the twenty-two-year-old announced. "He ran a splendid, game race. He would have beaten the others a city block, though, if the track had been dry."

How hot was Wink? On the last day of April, he won two races at Nashville, including the important Belle Meade Stakes, took the train five hundred miles north, and the next morning was at the Worth Race Course on the southwest side of Chicago, where Sam Hildreth was having a monster May Day. Hildreth had known hard times. His father was a small-time stable owner who dragged his wife and ten kids all over the West, barely surviving, but young Sam learned something rare along the way: how to make extremely smart horse trades. And today, before Wink rode in, Sam's own black-and-white silks had led the way in four of the first five races.

After each victory, a lengthening conga line trailed Sam to his cottage on the grounds, where his new friends swam in liquor before staggering back to the races. The track's champagne salesmen quickly took over the party, figuring it would be smart advertising to supply free bubbly to the conga line. At the end of the day, it was up to Wink, who had just arrived at the track, to slip into black and white himself and win the sixth race for Hildreth, a mile for all ages. All the way around Worth's first turn and down to the half, Wink was sixth, hopelessly boxed in on a five-year-old named Vulcain and lugging the top weight of 115 pounds—Wink plus about 10 pounds of lead. But by now, this sort of thing didn't bother Wink. At the top of the stretch, he called on Vulcain, who responded and ran down the rest of them to win by a length. With that, the line of drunks staggered all the way to the Hildreth stalls, spraying the horses with their champagne and concluding what Sam would always call Hildreth Day at Worth.

But Winkfield couldn't stay for the party that Thursday. On Saturday he needed to be three hundred miles south-southeast, at Churchill, for the 1902 Kentucky Derby. So Wink was in black and white again—McDowell's this time—as he approached the post. The starter was J. J. (Jake) Holtman, the opposite of fatherly Curley Brown. A hard-nosed, gaunt-faced, ruddy German from Chicago, Jake scared the hell out of jockeys up and down the East Coast, but not jockeys this good.

"Me boys," he told Wink and the others, "it's goin' to be a mile and a quarter. Don't forget it, and don't get restive tryin' to get away a sixteenth of an inch in the lead." The boys grinned.

For centuries, races had been launched by the human voice— "Go!"—often along with flags, drums, or pistols—but now Jake found himself contending with another wild card besides humans and horses. For the first time, he had to use the electric Maxwell starting machine. Before the race, Jake had stood under a big umbrella and let loose with his usual string of invectives as he tested the damn machine. The Maxwell contraption was not a line of gated boxes that held the horses, like the starting gates of the future. It merely stretched a tape across the track, then released it, but it called for insane timing. With nobody holding their bridles, Wink and Alan-a-Dale and the others approached the tape, all in a rough line, then jumped into a gallop, at which exact moment Jake had to act, too. "Holtman's fingers closed in on the button, the circuit was complete, the tape went high in the air, and they were off to a perfect start."

Alan-a-Dale broke so quickly Wink lost his right stirrup. "I fished for it, though, and I got it before we reached the stands," he'd remember. It was a quarter mile down to the stands, then a mile around the track. "Nash Turner led past the stands, but then I moved up on the turn and went into the lead by maybe three, four lengths goin' down the backstretch."

Tiny Williams kept Inventor in check, watching Nash on The Rival and paying no attention to Wink, just waiting for the rabbit to tire. But Wink and Alan-a-Dale showed no signs of slowing as they zipped down the backstretch, covering the first half mile in a taxing forty-eight seconds. At last, though, Alan did seem to be tiring, and the other three jockeys began to move, preparing to inhale the weakening front-runner. The shouts came from the stands: "They'll all catch him!" "He's done now!"

Wink looked back, and then he felt Alan's knees start to go. "I felt him beginnin' to bobble, gettin' weak in the legs. I still had a length." He was heading into the far turn before the homestretch. "I was really holdin' him now, trying to save him. I knew I was goin' to have to do somethin' special to win."

Somehow he kept the lead around the turn, but the other three drove on Alan-a-Dale inch by inch, and as they turned for home, Abe Frank was half a length back while Inventor and The Rival were poised at Abe's throat.

"Abe Frank wins!"

"Come on, Inventor!"

The crowd roared, standing on their toes, craning their necks to see. It did look like Alan-a-Dale was all in, but now Wink was ready with that "somethin' special." He was aware that in the off-season the crews at Churchill blanketed the oval with a protective layer of sand, which was pushed to the outside when the racing season began. So just as Abe Frank caught Alan-a-Dale on the outside, Wink moved out and—though no one could see this from where they sat—forced Abe into the sand, where the favorite practically stopped dead.

But then came Tiny on Inventor and Nash on The Rival. Wink ever so subtly drifted right again, escorting them out onto the edge of the sand, but it didn't stop them. Both were coming furiously as Wink was saved by the wire and won by a nose.

Alan was led to the winner's circle, and after Wink dismounted, the colt was paraded in front of the crowd, then taken back across the infield, where the black stable hands mobbed him: "Alan-a-Dale!" What they didn't notice was the limp that was entering the colt's walk as he cooled out. Fifty or sixty other stable hands crowded around Wink in the paddock and patted him on the back.

"Nice race," the twenty-two-year-old "old pro" observed calmly. Then they all but carried him through the crush to the jockeys' room—and the reporters. But even then Wink wasn't telling them his secret—how his unheralded colt, who could go three-quarters of a mile at most, maybe a mile, had dethroned the kings in that quarter-mile stretch. He simply explained that he began to set the pace at the first turn.

"Gee, but he can run!" Wink said, disarmingly. Then he spoke softly, thoughtfully. "I had sense enough to know that he couldn't stand that clip for the full distance. So I just eased up on Alan-a-Dale a little to save him for the stretch. I just hand rode until I saw Coburn set down on Abe Frank about the eighth pole." What did he think of Inventor's effort?

"Say, let me tell you Inventor is a good colt. He surprised me. He made Abe Frank look like a pewter nickel." Will Alan-a-Dale win the American Derby in Chicago?

"He don't suit me for the American Derby," Wink said, brash again, brimming with confidence; whether the colt would go to Chicago might be McDowell's call, but Wink seemed to be saying he wasn't interested. He'd come a long way from Chilesburg.

"Gee, I'm glad we won this Derby, though," said Wink the businessman. "You know this ain't no little race. People talk about a race like this."

Newspapers called it one of the best Derbies ever. "Very few horses have ever won such a race as Alan-a-Dale," one reporter said, "and won it on his courage and stamina." Little did he know. But Wink was too polite and too smart to let out the real story, so he didn't—until years after the Derby.

It so happened that earlier in the spring, Alan-a-Dale had developed a bad knee and got so gimpy McDowell figured the three-year-old couldn't stand hard training under a jockey's weight. So they had him pull a sulky, a harness horse's light two-wheeled vehicle, over the trotting track down in Memphis. Only occasionally would they toss a boy into the saddle. As it also happened, Wink was that boy at least once. And he also exercised The Rival, so he knew long before the race that Alan was much faster. But how would he get to ride Alan-a-Dale when McDowell's other rider would be the celebrated white boy from the North?

"The Major had contracted Nash Turner to ride one of the horses, and I'd ride the other." Wink recalled. "Nash was a good jockey, pretty famous then, and he was a white boy, so he was goin' to get his pick"—unless Wink could do something about it. "For a month I pulled Alan-a-Dale in workouts. I never let him go better than 2:11 for a mile and a quarter, and all the time I galloped The Rival at about 2:09. So when Nash came down on the mornin' of the race, naturally he pick The Rival."

Like all competitors at his level, Wink never stopped calculating, and like the best jockeys, he knew his opponents—equine and human—and how they ran. Of course, he could have gotten into trouble with McDowell for concealing Alan-a-Dale's speed in workouts or for floating out even his own stable mate during the race. But Wink was never caught doing the former, and he managed to avoid blame for the latter by not singling out The Rival—by pushing Monk and Nash and Tiny and their mounts into that nice big soft sandbox together.

"For a long time, people keep asking me how come the second half of that race so slow," he would one day joke. "Well, I tell you why it was slow. I was ridin' four horses!"

After the race, Nash had a different version, not very convincing. "Switching me to ride The Rival caused Mr. McDowell to win the Derby," Nash said. "I was put on the worst horse so as to confuse the other boys"—as if Nash Turner would have agreed to such self-effacement. But his scenario did agree with Wink's in one respect: it could be taken for granted that Turner would get the better mount.

Jimmy Winkfield had become the second jockey in history, after Isaac Murphy, to win consecutive Kentucky Derbies, an achievement that would not be matched until Ron Turcotte did it seven decades later, in 1972 on Riva Ridge and 1973 on Secretariat, to be followed only by Eddie Delahoussaye in 1982 on Gato Del Sol and 1983 on Sunny's Halo. Four riders in more than a century and a quarter. As for the colt, Alan-a-Dale became the first Derby-winning son of a Derby winner, Halma, who had won in 1895 with Soup Perkins up. That wouldn't happen again for another four decades, when Reigh Count's Count Fleet did it in 1943.

And Tom McDowell? He collected $4,850 and gave Wink a terrific $1,000 bonus. He also gave a grand to the famous Turner, although Nash had earned the stable only $300 for coming in third. Was it that Tom couldn't have a white jockey and a black jockey looking equal, that third-place Nash had to be treated better by getting the same bonus as the winner? Or had he made a deal with the celebrated Nash in order to get him to Louisville?

McDowell did give Wink some slight public credit. "The race was in [Alan-a-Dale] and Winkfield brought it out." But Tom also changed his tune a bit on Alan. Rather than cast him as a mere rabbit, he said he didn't give any instructions at all to Wink and Nash. "Both boys are good race riders, and I told them to go in and win." McDowell suddenly had high hopes for his colt with the pretty highlands name. But Alan was suffering. It was not until the stable hands led him across the infield that you could see he was lame, especially in the left foreleg, and it got worse as he cooled off.

Alan-a-Dale never ran again that year. To his credit, McDowell had not dared to start him before the Derby—but should he have let him run even then, in early May? And what about Wink? He had felt Alan bobbling as they took the far turn. Should he have beaten him down the stretch the way he did? They still ask those questions about some of the three-year-olds entering the Derby today. But Alan-a-Dale would recover and would turn in three more years of racing, including a mile record of 1:37 ³/₅ at four, followed by a good career as a sire.

Wink was now in more than one headline. The *Courier-Journal* profiled him in a sidebar that revealed more about others than about Wink:

Jim [it may have been the first time the papers called him that] Winkfield, who rode Alan-a-Dale to victory, is as black as the ace of spades and a jockey whose last two years' riding has won him money and reputation. Winkfield's success as a jockey is said to be due to his good judgment and cold nerve. He has confidence in himself and usually as much in his mount. Winkfield's mounts made such a good showing at Churchill Downs last year that numerous persons played horses to win just because the colored boy had the mount on them. He has started off with a big feather in his cap this year.

But Wink's head was not likely to be turned by the *Courier-Journal*. After all, the morning of the Derby, it had run a two-column ad for a distillery with a picture of an old black man and the catchline OLD WHISKY! OLD HOSS! OLD NIGGER! Meanwhile, the same newspaper highly approved of the latest speech to Congress by a Kentucky representative, against the notion of "social equality" between blacks and whites. "There is still in Kentucky a wide gulf, which no man and no woman can cross or wants to cross. This gulf separates the white people from the Negroes, and no culture, no ability, or refinement or public service can atone for a taint of color in the blood."

Yet the *Courier-Journal* did not speculate that a taint of color in the blood might help you win the Kentucky Derby. In any case, Winkfield wasn't distracted by the newspaper's foolishness. He now took aim at what was then an even bigger target—the American Derby, set for Chicago a month and a half after the Louisville classic. With a value of $18,875, more than quadruple the Kentucky Derby purse, it was second in prize money and prestige only to New York's Futurity, worth $44,500 in 1902.

Phil Sheridan, the Civil War general, headed the Chicago group that had launched the American Derby in 1884 to inaugurate the Washington Park race course. Derbies—races for three-year-olds—had become not only America's biggest but its most beloved sports events. Nearly a century after the original Derby at Epsom Downs in England, in 1780, came the first American version, the Jersey Derby, founded at Paterson in 1863. The Kentucky Derby was first run in 1875, and then derbies sprouted up all across the states, attracting the most promising colts and fillies. Part of the thrill was the chance to see them compete as they came into their real racing years, though some had hit the tracks for the first time at two.

States and cities saw derbies as wonderful promotions. There were derbies in Tennessee, Ohio, California, Texas, and Illinois, not to mention the St. Louis, Chicago, Crescent City (New Orleans), Brooklyn, Latonia (Kentucky), and Tijuana Derbies. But the American Derby was the biggest of them all. It had been an important stage for Jimmy's fellow Lexingtonian Ike Murphy, who won the first three editions and then the fifth. By 1902, black jockeys had taken half of the fourteen American Derbies. This was the Chicago stage that Winkfield was aiming for as he chased Ike Murphy in the derby record books. He wasn't even close yet. Though Wink had chalked up five derbies to date—the Tennessee, New Orleans, and Latonia, and two of the Kentucky classics—he still had miles to ride to catch Ike's twelve major derbies. But those miles were lined with fans, even in turn-of-the-century America, and back home, the *Lexington Herald* bragged about Wink: "He is one of the leading jockeys in the country and is known as 'the Derby rider.' " Up the road and across the Ohio, the *Cincinnati Enquirer* said Wink was riding better than any jock in the country.

It was onward and upward after his 1902 Kentucky Derby win. Winkfield won twenty-one of eighty-one more starts at Churchill that spring, slightly beating his sizzling 25 percent winning record there the year before; then he headed for the Windy City, as people were already calling Chicago. Without missing a hoofbeat, he swelled his stable owners' coffers by finishing in the money thirty-one more times in the next six weeks, including sixteen firsts. In June, he was given a leg up again on the funny-looking but brilliant McChesney, one of the leading picks to win the American Derby.

The buildup to the 1902 Chicago spectacular was one of those rare moments when jockeys become better known than their mounts. A well-known gambler of the day, "Kid" Weller, had opined that two colts, Heno and McChesney, "outclass everything else in the race, and they will be ridden by two of the best jockeys in the country." One was John Bullman, under contract to August Belmont of New York and aiming to tie Ike's record of three consecutive American Derbies. The other was Jimmy Winkfield, "who has won most of the stakes around Chicago this year."

Trainer-owner Sam Hildreth made two slick moves as he plotted to capture the American Derby. First, he secured the services of Winkfield from Pat Dunne, and second, he bought McChesney, the colt Wink had set a speed record with the year before. Though Sam and Wink were each born to large, rural Kentucky families that struggled for a living, their thoughts about this were exactly the opposite. Wink never complained about whatever hard times his family had. You'd get no deprivation narratives out of him. Hildreth, on the other hand, poor-mouthed his circumstances forever. Even as this clever horse trader was starting to hit it big on the Midwest circuit, he managed to look dirt-poor, too, in his rumpled three-piece suits and the tiny bowler perched above his permanently starved, mustachioed face. And in what was a remarkable state of affairs in 1902, the white owner was actually jealous of the rare successful black jockey. "I wondered what Nash Turner or Birkenruth or Winkfield, or the other jockeys who had the leg up on my horses in these later days would think," Hildreth said later, "if I'd offered them, for a single winning mount, the equivalent of what I'd received for a whole month's hard work. . . . or if they'd been compelled to sleep in the hay, or in a little bunk over the stalls, as I had."

The three-year-old McChesney was now "about the most noted race-horse" in the country, as the turf historian W. S. Vosburgh would recall, but the colt remained a revelation to people seeing him run for the first time. With his shrunken body and white stockings, he did a wonderful job of hiding his talents, like the future Seabiscuit. "McChesney was a great, awkward-looking chestnut," said Vosburgh, "but seen in action he was quite a different horse, his motion being perfect."

In the American Derby run-up, McChesney was weeks from being ready. Winkfield got to work on it right away. The jockey's five-foot, 105-pound frame looked like it would crush poor Mc-Chesney, but on Monday of Derby Week, Wink brought him back almost to form. In a stiff mile and a quarter over the Harlem course, the colt wanted to stop before the final eighth, but Wink hustled him. "The game youngster responded and reeled off the final furlong in :13 flat," wrote one reporter. The jockey was stepping up, too. The next day Billy Caywood was riding the speedy favorite, The Don, owned by celebrated betting man Charles E. Ellison. The Don shot to the lead, and Ellison was already counting his money when Wink came flying on a Pat Dunne colt named Allan to get up at the last second and take the win. As was happening so often now, Wink starred in a *Chicago Daily News* multitiered headline that day. OWNER CHARLES E. ELLISON ATTEMPTED A KILLING ON HIS COLT, it said, BUT WINKFIELD'S STRONG RIDE STOPPED THE KILLING.

Wink never forgot that for many of the owners it was about money, *their* money. This put him in a powerful but perilous position. In about two minutes' time, he had just earned $2,510 for Dunne, but he had cost the influential Ellison. And on a huge week like this one in Chicago, the kid from Chilesburg was being sized up by an even richer crowd as many more were following the Chicago developments from the Big Apple. The most powerful, and probably the wealthiest, trainer of the day, John E. Madden, was shipping two colts from Brighton Beach in Brooklyn to Chicago to run against Wink and McChesney.

Jimmy and Madden knew all about each other. Madden's home and farm, Hamburg Place, shared a Lexington turnpike with Chilesburg. But then Madden's reach extended across America. At the moment, the dangerous ex-boxer was a consultant to the patrician Yankee William C. Whitney, the transit czar and one of the richest men in New York City. Diamond Jim Brady was back there at Brighton Beach, too, betting heavily on Madden's horses and trying to pick the winner of the American Derby. New Yorkers also wanted to know this: when would twenty-two-year-old Jimmy Winkfield become a player in the Big Apple?

The movers and shakers on the ground in Chicago included John Drake, the Iowa governor's playboy son who had already hired Wink's Chilesburg friend Lucien Lyne to ride in the American Derby. Drake was one of the biggest gamblers in the country, but you couldn't get much bigger than Elias J. "Lucky" Baldwin. With his brim hat and brush of a mustache, Baldwin looked like Mark Twain, and his life was like something out of Twain, too. Having struck it rich on Nevada mining stock, Lucky created a racing and breeding empire, unloading a nice pile of his $20 million into sixty thousand acres of Los Angeles County and laying it out with lakes, vineyards, orchards, bridges, and rustic homes. Its principal avenue was bordered by eucalyptus and split down the middle by a three-mile row of pepper trees.

Lucky Baldwin hired trainers as good as the younger Sam Hildreth and jockeys as good as Ike Murphy to teach the youngsters at his Rancho Santa Anita, a mere speck of which would survive, in time, to become Santa Anita Race Course. Lucky did love his women and at Saratoga wouldn't so much as allow another male in his coach. Sometimes he selected only blondes or only brunettes to accompany him, and they'd watch as he dumped $5,000 to $50,000 on a single nose.

Lucky had a colt called Cruzados whom the press had derided as a quitter. Lucky would show them. Cruzados would take on Wink and McChesney and seven others in a warm-up for the American Derby: a mile and an eighth at Washington Park's neighboring track, Harlem, on Wednesday of Derby week. A lot of people were saying Cruzados didn't look fit and questioned not only his heart but his physical ability to go the Derby's mile and a half, which enraged Lucky all the more. In view of all this, it was surprising that the colt was going as second choice in the prep race, but then a lot of the money bet on him had to be coming from Lucky and his agents. McChesney was the fans' pick at seven to ten.

A special treat was in store, too. If Wink and his buddy, the black jockey Tommy Knight, on Belle's Commoner, were close at the finish, they had orders to keep right on going for another three-eighths, to give their owners a good line on what might happen in the mile-and-a-half Derby.

They were off! Cruzados jumped to the lead while Wink hung back, saving McChesney around the first turn but without choking him. Wink's face nearly broke into a grin down the backstretch. Here he was, the Chilesburg kid, giving his champion chestnut a final workout for the American Derby. They were bunched into two groups of three nearing the far turn, with a seventh colt on the far outside.

Lucky was cheering Cruzados home, praying he had enough, but Wink and McChesney were practically running up his rear. Wink was also squeezed between two other horses, with nowhere to move. Yet McChesney was on the bit, absolutely "wild for his head"—desperate to take over as they approached the half-mile post and far turn. Under the clench of his rider's outsized hands, the suddenly gorgeous chestnut gained with every perfect stride. Wink waited for the widening of the turn. There he could slip through on the inside, then make his triumphant entry into the stretch and charge down the screaming grandstand, a conquering hero.

Without warning, Cruzados turned his critics into prophets. He quit—stopped almost dead, "as though hit on the head with a sledgehammer," said a witness. He stopped so suddenly that Wink, trapped, didn't even have time to check.

McChesney never actually touched Cruzados but was thrown off stride. He went down heavily, all 1,100 pounds falling toward the inside rail, then performing an almost complete somersault. The colt landed on Wink, slid along the track, and lay motionless. Under the rail, the black jacket with a white sash was lying motionless, too. There was a long stillness at the far turn. Too long. People in the stands started mumbling the news, then shouted:

"Winkfield's dead!"

Stable boys rushed to the jockey's side. The track ambulance was called, and he was taken first to the paddock. The first medical report: he was not dead. He had a broken thigh, dislocated hip, broken collarbone, and broken shoulder bone. He was rushed first to the nearby Garfield Park sanitarium, where they dressed his wounds, then on to a hospital. He was in excruciating pain. And the prognosis was frightening: "With the best of care . . . and good luck combined, Winkfield will not be able to ride again this season, and the injury to the leg may be so bad that he will never ride again."

When he woke up, groaning, the first question Winkfield asked was: "Is the horse hurt?"

"Not much," somebody answered.

"I am glad of that," Wink said. He closed his eyes and rested.

Tommy Knight, on Belle's Commoner, had pulled away to win. McChesney had struggled to his feet and limped slowly along the track, waiting for somebody to take him to the stable. By the time he got there, the limp was gone, and he submitted to a needle without a whimper. Six stitches closed the nasty cut under McChesney's left eye, extending along the cheek. He had a torn left nostril, a badly scratched nose, and hair scraped off a large area of his rump. He would not race again for months, but otherwise he was miraculously okay.

That night, Sam Hildreth was in denial as he feverishly worked the wires for an eastern jockey to ride McChesney in the American Derby. Chicago racing officials had the same disease, refusing to admit that their grandest moment had lost America's grandest horse, not to mention the grandest rider in the West. Around midnight, they telegraphed the press: "McChesney in good shape this morning and undoubtedly starts Saturday. Reports from Winkfield very favorable."

In fact, the morning hospital reports, while not clear on whether Wink had fractured his thigh, confirmed a dislocated hip and broken clavicle. They said he was in high spirits but was sorry he could not race in the Derby. And again: "Winkfield seemed more interested in the injuries to McChesney than to himself and asked that a telegram be sent to Harlem asking the colt's condition and probability of starting in the Derby."

It wasn't only about loving a horse. It was about being the favorite in a nearly $20,000 event featuring the best riders and horses in the country, with additional piles staked by the owners and gamblers. As few athletes would be, Winkfield was acutely aware of the sums, reputations, and futures at stake, including his own.

Everyone within earshot could hear Lucky blustering the next day. He was furious, and he issued a challenge for the future: "If anybody thinks my horse cannot go a mile and a half, I will right now challenge any of the Derby colts to a mile and a half race for $20,000 a side, winner to take all." Cruzados never quit, Lucky insisted. The colt on the rail bumped him, forcing him to the outside, where another horse struck his leg, cutting it to the bone just above the hock joint. This slowed Cruzados right in front of McChesney, who stumbled and crashed into the rail. Maybe, maybe not. Whatever the case, it cost both Cruzados and McChesney—and Wink—their chances in the American Derby, which Wink's neighbor Lucien Lyne would go on to win aboard a colt named Wyeth.

Back home on East Third Street, Edna could read about the accident in the *Lexington Herald*. Jimmy would be coming home again in a few days, and he would never be happier to see her than after he had nearly been killed. Edna was perfect for Jimmy, a wonderful wife. They lived in a more than comfortable neighborhood in Lexington's black section, which comprised at least half the town, and her girlfriends would tell how she had turned their townhouse into a delightful retreat for Jimmy during his all-too-brief returns.

This time, however, she must have fought back tears. As she waited for his train, she tried to accept the devastating news in the morning *Herald*—that his career, their livelihood, was in jeopardy: "Jimmy was so disabled that he cannot ride any more this year." But Wink would have something to say about that, and so surely would Doc Allen, the most valuable friend to be had by a man practicing the world's most dangerous sport. Dr. James M. Allen, the Winkfield family physician, meant more to Wink than all the doctors in Chicago put together.

As usual, Wink proved the papers wrong. Doubtless with Doc Allen's help, he was back in the saddle within a month of his near-death experience and winning again in Chicago, capturing the Harlem Stakes, then the Twentieth Century Stakes. As the other Lexington paper, the *Leader*, put it, Winkfield, "contrary to the usual rule, retained all of his skill and nerve as a jockey in spite of his terrible fall." Of course, Wink had slowed down a touch as he nursed his wounds, but despite his Chicago encounter with the angels and his weeks in bed, he added at least twenty wins through the rest of the year. *Goodwin's Official Turf Guide* could no longer ignore him. Its researchers found he had eighty-eight wins for the year and a 54 percent in-the-money record for his bosses.

Winkfield spent the winter in the Big Easy, where his last win of 1902 came on Christmas Day, just as it had in 1901. Edna most likely didn't join him in New Orleans, where he had no choice but to live a mostly solitary life, getting up at ungodly hours to work horses, reporting to the tracks in the afternoon, and managing his business affairs by himself. But wintering there also gave him a chance to plug into the latest gossip, including a bulletin on another race war, this one in San Francisco. It seemed like another case of a black jockey letting himself get too good. The jock, a boy with the bayou name of Batiste, had made the mistake of becoming the top rider in his San Francisco stable. Not long after that, the Irish-American talent Tommy Burns, along with Monk Coburn and some other white boys, ganged up on Batiste, who after that fled back home to New Orleans. "They made it so warm for the colored boy," said the *Picayune*, "that his employer thought it best to send him here."

As for Wink, he concentrated on healing while setting his sights on something no jockey had ever done before: winning three Kentucky Derbies in a row.

Chapter Five

WIN THE
FUTURITY AND . . .

I
f he was still hurting, you couldn't tell as Winkfield charged
into the 1903 Kentucky Derby fresh off twenty-two victories—
twenty-one at New Orleans and one in the prestigious Tennessee Oaks at Memphis. Now the papers were calling him a "star
rider" and "one of the great race riders of the world." Winkfield
and everybody else just knew he was about to become the only
jockey besides Ike Murphy to win three Kentucky Derbies—even
better, the only one to win three in a row.

Churchill Downs was on the way up, too. An ambitious
Louisville tailor, Matt Winn, had just convinced a group of local
investors to help him buy the joint, and the front door looked like
the entrance to a happy circus, with vendors and crap games and
gamblers spread out in all directions. Winkfield was the first Derby
jockey to appear in the shiny new paddock, and he was sitting on a
live one, a colt called Early. The heavy favorite.

Last one in was the bigoted Henry Booker, scowling when he
saw the crowd's attentions to Wink and Early. In some ways,

though, Booker was a white match for Wink—a country boy from Decatur, Illinois, and a family of fifteen kids, five of them jockeys. And you could understand his bitterness. The game had taken one of his jockey brothers, killed last summer in the East. Then there was Booker's mediocre mount, named Judge Himes. He was owned by Charlie Ellison, the Chicago plunger whose favorite colt, The Don, Wink had beaten in Chicago. Nobody in the paddock paid much attention to Booker or Judge Himes.

Clean-cut and rangy, Early was all controlled energy and shimmering muscle. Once Wink got a leg up, the colt opened his eyes wide and got up on his toes as he walked out of the paddock toward the track. Flying the Irish emerald green of Pat Dunne, Wink and Early were bathed in applause as they stepped onto the track.

Twenty-five thousand watched from the freshly painted grandstand, with its twenty-seven new iron boxes, and from Matt Winn's new $20,000 clubhouse, with its Victorian palms and ferns and café tables staked out by the gowned grand dames of Louisville. About a thousand black fans were in the grandstand, most with their money on Wink. The assistant starters had pushed the six horses into a pretty good line for the start when Wink pulled one of his old tricks. He turned Early just a hair.

"You little nigger!" starter Jake Holtman shouted. "Who told you that you knew how to ride? You are not down at New Orleans now, so come on and get in line!" More insults were hurled at the jocks until the three-year-olds were aligned once more, and the lead assistant starter yelled, "Let her go!"

Wink broke Early well and moved him up in the pack. He made another strong move at the half, right in front of the stable hands on the far rail, who were backing Early and liked what they were seeing. So did the grandstand. "What a cinch for Early! It's a shame to take the money!" Nobody knew it exactly, but it was a historic moment for black American athletes. Many in the white crowd were cheering for Winkfield because he was on his way to a Derby first—three in a row—although it was mostly about their money.

Wink gunned Early past three others, including Booker aboard Judge Himes. It was all over, no doubt about it. A reporter spotted a man with a bet on Early high in the stands, sailing his hat over the crowd. Just to the left of Matt Winn's shiny new press box, which believe it or not could hold six scribblers, "a girl in a cream-colored gown"—they did wear gowns to the Derby—stood on a chair and "shriek[ed] with excitement." As Wink turned into the stretch, his visions of matching Ike Murphy came into sharper focus than the finish line. Early was a length and a half up on Judge Himes.

As Early started to tire a little at the eighth pole, Booker called on his colt. Wink would say he had thoughts of leaning over and interfering with Booker or the colt—he figured being such a huge betting favorite, the judges would never take him down—but he played it clean. The white boy pulled alongside, and Wink turned, looked at him, and laughed. But Early was gasping for air. Wink shook him up, all hands and feet and whip, begging Early to give him another furlong. But Judge matched strides with Early until ten feet from home, and as they passed under the wire, the cheering stopped: Judge Himes had won the Kentucky Derby by half a length.

Wink got a big headline all right, but not the one he wanted: ILL-TIMED RIDE BY WINKFIELD, THE GREAT JOCKEY, RESPONSIBLE FOR THE RESULT. He had moved Early too early. The article read: "It was the opinion of ninety-nine out of each one hundred spectators that the best colt in the race finished second."

Henry Booker was vicious in victory. Describing the stretch run, he said: "As soon as I got upon equal terms with Early, I took special note of his condition. Winkfield turned around at me and laughed. It was then that I was sure I did not have a chance. That nigger, I was sure, was trying to make a sucker out of me. I thought that he wanted me to come up to him so that he could draw away. I knew that I had all the others beat off, so I just went on. I passed Early. 'I have got that nigger beat,' I said to myself. . . . He did not ride up to his usual form. . . . It was a bad ride and helped me win."

Everybody blamed Winkfield, including Winkfield. Tears came

that day, as they had after he won his first Derby. In the jockeys' room, his voice broke as he admitted, "I made my run too soon. . . . I wanted to win for the boss." Wink knew it was an emotional defeat for Pat Dunne, who had sold Early a week before to a Chicago firm for twelve thousand but delayed the deal to run him in the Derby in his Irish green. Still, some felt Dunne should share the blame because he had not conditioned Early for the grueling mile and a quarter.

Eventually, Wink lightened up on himself:

> Maybe I made my move too early, but then I was eight lengths off the leaders, and there was only a half-mile of running left when I went for the lead. Racing is like that. You win two runnings of the Derby in a row, each time beating an odds-on favorite, then you get beat yourself on the only odds-on favorite choice you ride in the race.

But a lot of milk money had been lost that day, and the scene at Churchill reminded a reporter of a recent murder:

> The tremendous crowd greeted the victor like the sad thousands watching the funeral train of the assassinated President McKinley as it wended its way from the Capitol to Canton. Near the roof of the stand, there were sobs and sighs and tears. Below, on the lawn, the warm blood froze in the veins of men who had bet their thousands on Early.

The tide was starting to turn against Winkfield. Two days after the Derby, the *Louisville Times* ran a racist cartoon of Early's owner towering over a caricatured Wink sweating it out in his overcoat. Another, captioned "A Colored Sport," had a black man holding a betting slip—a reminder of the threat that black attendance supposedly represented for Louisville's whites. Wink started hearing personally from the kuklux or their many friends in Kentucky, foaming at the thought of a black star in America. He received death threats and was told he'd never ride in the Kentucky Derby again.

But he was not run out of racing—not yet. In fact, as the music-hall chanteuse Lillian Russell saw, he stayed very hot indeed. Lil showed up in the Churchill crowd nine days after the Derby. The reigning American beauty queen and comedienne was captivating the nation in her tours with the Weber and Fields vaudeville troupe. To her corn-fed beauty, plunging *avant-scéne*, and gorgeous legs, she added the scandal of dressing in men's clothing and smoking cigarettes in public with an air of disdain.

Offstage, Lil lived at the racetrack, always on the arm of a millionaire around the clubhouse, as long as he lasted. The copper magnate Jesse Lewisohn, who tried to keep up with her at Saratoga, was reportedly ordered by his doctor to choose between Lil and his health. For some odd reason, he chose life. Lil was on Diamond Jim Brady's arm, too, or right behind him on his gold-plated bicycle as they whirled around Central Park. He had the bicycle regilded every two weeks and decorated the handlebar with Lil's monogram in diamonds and emeralds. The rumors that she got past the diamonds on his underwear were far-fetched, according to another fashion plate of the day, E. Berry Wall, who said Brady couldn't have been intimate with her because "he was much too fat for that." But Lil began to out-eat even Diamond Jim, diving into fourteen-course dinners, convinced that an iron corset could reshape her into an ever more extreme hourglass, the shape of American beauty, "as tempting," said a gossip writer, "as a baked apple dumpling."

Lil knew her ponies. It was hardly true, as one of her biographers claimed, that she picked them by impaling her program at random with a hatpin. She really knew them. And that day at Churchill, she squeezed into one of Matt Winn's new box seats and picked half of the six winners, although her program has not survived to show whether the three included Wink's win that afternoon. From the 1903 Derby forward through another Chicago season, Jimmy Winkfield enriched his employers' coffers many times, guiding home seventeen winners along the way. But the anonymous threats kept coming, and one day the pressure drove him to drink.

Moonshine was all over the place. Beyond the Kentucky River, the mountaineers, as they called themselves, sweetened their moonshine with brown sugar to produce "white licker," which in turn produced the most powerful headaches. But this one incident with Wink happened in Chicago when he got to drinking bad whiskey one time with some friends. After waking up with a horrific headache, his eyes swollen and hurting, he went to a doctor, who asked him if he'd been in a fight. No. He'd been playing cards and drinking. Then something was wrong with the liquor, the doctor said, because it had affected the blood vessels in Wink's head and eyes. Wink didn't think much of it, and he would quickly forget it because a major change was in store for him. Pat Dunne was taking him to the most famous race meeting in the country, up north, in the foothills of the Adirondacks. It was Lil's favorite place, and Diamond Jim's and, it seemed, every other star's.

Saratoga was all about horses and money and gambling. As in many a grand resort, it went to your head. It didn't matter who you were, once you got there your mind kept exploding with ideas— how to make money, reach the top, and have a hell of a time doing it. The place was a drug. It gave you a sense of security and power. What did it was the tremendous concentration of wealth, which proved that other people had done it—and not just a few of them. But at Saratoga, the part about having a hell of time seemed just as important, and it had been going on for a century already. When President Lincoln set aside a day of prayer and thanksgiving for the Union victory at Gettysburg, Saratoga's racetrack was mobbed. And when, after the terrible battle at Petersburg in Virginia, Lincoln wondered where his playboy–Harvard grad son, Bob, was—the young man's mother, Mary Todd Lincoln, had made it plain he was much too intelligent to be in the war—Bob was, in fact, at Saratoga, dancing to a twenty-two-piece band at the Union Hotel. Somebody asked him if he was a relative of the president's. "Distant," said Bob, "about 400 miles."

Seven Saratoga hotels accommodated more than a thousand

guests each; two of them, more than four thousand each. Henry James caught the Saratoga spirit of power and play when he surveyed the hotel "piazzas," endless, high-columned front porches lined with big wicker chairs, and declared:

> They come from the uttermost ends of the Union—
> from San Francisco, from New Orleans, from Alaska. As
> they sit with their white hats tilted forward and their chairs
> tilted back, and their feet tilted up, and their cigars and
> toothpicks forming various angles . . . I seem to see in their
> faces a tacit reference to the affairs of a continent.

The hotel crowds made the rounds of the mineral springs, which along with the horses made Saratoga unique. At Newport, somebody said, you go into the water; at Saratoga, the water goes into you. Or they went out to the trout-filled waters of Saratoga Lake, where crew races were launching the curious future traditions of intercollegiate sports—bright college colors and strange college cheers:

"Cornell, yell, yell, ell, Cornell!"
Quickly (Harvard): "Rah-rah-rah!"
Slowly (Brown): "Rah-rah-rah!"
Loudly: C-O-L-U-M-B-I-A.

A chef at Moon's Lake House overdid it frying sliced potatoes, thus inventing potato chips. One day, a grand wedding party collected on Moon's verandah, seven brides with seven platefuls of those flaky fried potatoes. When Wink hit town, they were still a delicacy, known as Saratoga Chips.

Nobody was as moved by the possibilities of watery, horsey Saratoga as the New York mass-transit tycoon and Democratic kingmaker William C. Whitney. Populism had finally captured the Democratic Party, so some of its richest members—the Whitneys, Vanderbilts, Belmonts, and friends—turned away from public and political affairs and to other pastimes instead. In the two years before Wink climbed aboard the train to the Spa, Will Whitney had taken over Saratoga racing, rebuilt the track, and created a series of stakes races that made the Kentucky Derby look like chump change. It reinvigorated the old resort.

SARATOGA ON VERGE OF BOOM, screamed the *New York Daily Tribune.* "America has never had a resort that equaled Saratoga." Victor Herbert, who created operettas like that season's *Babes in Toyland,* played the Grand Union Hotel with his Pittsburgh Symphony. Bombastic John Philip Sousa, who wrote "Stars and Stripes Forever" and "The Washington Post March," oompah-pahed his band into Congress Park across Saratoga's own Broadway. Italy's Enrico Caruso, who that season made the most successful debut ever at the Metropolitan Opera and created a deathless Canio in *I Pagliacci,* also did the little park, while the singer-actor Chauncey Olcott relaxed in his own Saratoga garden and thatched-roof cottage, having scored with the tearjerker *My Wild Irish Rose.*

But the most exciting place in town, Canfield Casino, which the writer Herbert Asbury would call "the greatest gambling asset the United States has ever known," was also a major target of horse racing's most powerful enemies, the various antigambling movements across the land. A few years before, the crusading newspaperwoman Nellie Bly invaded both the casino in the park and the racetrack on the eastern edge of town, her exposé inspiring a stack of headlines in the *New York World*: WILD VORTEX OF GAMBLING AND BETTING BY MEN, WOMEN, AND CHILDREN and SPORTS, TOUTS, CRIMINALS AND RACE TRACK RIFF-RAFF CRAZED BY THE MANIA FOR GOLD.

Nellie Bly found "a bleached-haired actress" and "girls more than ten and less than fifteen" befriending men at the casino, "large poker games conducted by women for women at every hotel," and, at the racecourse, "painted faces and penciled, inviting eyes" and a little girl who asked, "Mama, did that lady get all those rings for Christmas?" But Nellie might have secretly liked the races, because the biggest scandal she uncovered at the track was the fact that in the special betting room reserved for women, they got worse odds than the male bettors in the grandstand.

It was the close connection between the casino and the racecourse, between gambling and the sport, that was going to spell bad news for Wink's livelihood. Just before he got there, the Wall Street investor John "Bet-a-Million" Gates lost $375,000 in a single afternoon at the track. To get it back, he immediately headed down Union Avenue to Canfield's, which was sort of an off-site annex to the track, and started playing faro (a card-picking game) and roulette. By ten that night, Gates was out another $150,000, so he asked Richard Canfield to raise the house limit to $10,000 a bet. Said Canfield, sarcastically, "Are you sure that's enough?" At two in the morning, Gates had won back the $150,000 he'd lost at the Casino and at dawn, when he quit, he had cut the previous day's losses to only $225,000. That season, Canfield's sucked half a million dollars out of Saratoga. It's not known how much the renovated track sucked out, but the antigambling forces were watching.

Through this dreamy land of northern summer rode the young man from Chilesburg, Kentucky. Jimmy Winkfield made his Saratoga debut in one of Will Whitney's creations, the Saratoga Special Stakes, worth $21,500, four times more than the Kentucky Derby. He managed fifth on Boxwood, who "showed improvement," the chart said. With racing's aristocracy in the audience—Whitney, August Belmont II, Joseph E. Widener of Philadelphia, Julius Fleischmann—he rode in two more famous events, the United States Hotel Stakes and the Albany Handicap. Unfortunately, his horses did not share his ambitions.

Competition at this level was too rich for Pat Dunne's blood, and especially for his bloodstock—his horses. But as Bub May had done, Pat was able to make money by hiring out his classy jockey. Wink now got tapped to fly the purple and white of the southerner Green B. Morris, who was born poor, still had more molasses in his mouth than our Bluegrass jockey, and had assembled one of the most successful stables around. Morris rode Wink in the $10,000-plus Grand Union Stakes. Named for Saratoga's best-known hotel, it was the final prep for the biggest sports event in the country, the $36,600 Futurity at the end of August.

Wink's mount, Rapid Water, broke from the ninth post and in one of his patented drives, Wink closed a big gap, moving from

eighth to fifth in the stretch. He finished third, two lengths behind the winner, Highball, under the lightweight white jockey
Grover Cleveland Fuller. The black jockey out of the West had just
beaten colts owned by names like Whitney, Belmont, and Widener,
and most important, he had half a length on John Madden's much-
touted The Minute Man. Madden was no fool. He yanked the fine
Irish-American Frank O'Neill, that season's Travers Stakes winner, off The Minute Man and gave Jimmy Winkfield the biggest
shot of his life—the Futurity, one week away. Wink would wear
the "cherry, white hoops on sleeves" of the country's top trainer-
owner, the "Wizard of the Turf," in the country's biggest race.

It was a chance to win real respect, a chance to be front-page
news in the New York dailies, to become one of the few rich black
men in America. Even if he didn't win, a relationship with the
wildly successful John Madden could change his life. Look at Ed
Brown, the black trainer, who had just started working for Madden
and was doing extremely well for himself. And, after all, maybe it
was meant to be. Didn't you hit the Madden farm, Hamburg Place,
only a mile before little old Chilesburg on the Winchester Pike?

Madden had a hell of a chance to win. In fact, he kept telling
people all around Saratoga that he would definitely win, "and Madden rarely makes an idle boast," said the *New York World*. For starters, the Wizard would have two other colts in the race besides The
Minute Man. So Wink accepted Madden's offer.

But a funny thing happened on the way to the Futurity. Another stable owner wandering among the Spa's cathedral elms also
wanted Wink. This was W. M. Scheftel, who was going to run the
Grand Union winner, Highball, in the Futurity. When Highball's
jock, Grover Cleveland Fuller, jumped ship to ride for the wealthy
Englishman Sydney Paget, Scheftel zeroed in on Wink. And he
had an in with Wink that was more important than the Winchester Turnpike: Scheftel's trainer was none other than Wink's other
old neighbor and ex-boss, Bub May.

After picking up a nice piece of change for winning the Grand
Union, Bub wanted more. He wanted to put some luster in his

reputation by capturing the Futurity with his former protégé, the now-famous "colored boy" from Chilesburg. But he wasn't relying on sentiment to lure Wink—he was offering him cash, the unthinkable sum of $3,000, as much as another jockey might get for winning it.

"I'm ridin' for Madden," Wink said quietly but clearly.

"Well, there's $3,000 here if you change your mind," said Bub.

Of course, to take Bub's money would be jumping contract—the verbal but clear contract he had with Madden—and nobody had yet discovered a dishonest bone in gentlemanly Jimmy Winkfield. Still, Wink did have an inner voice that said: take care of Jimmy. And, having been surrounded by gamblers—from the poorest cheaters who ran the games behind the stables to the wealthy cheaters who ran their own games—he might not have been terribly disappointed to be bribed by the kindly gent who had brought him up. Three thousand dollars! It began to look as good as a future with John Madden. Wink faced the toughest choice of his life.

Chapter Six

"WINKFIELD, I DON'T LIKE TO BE DOUBLE-CROSSED!"

I changed my mind," Wink explained years later. "At the last minute, I told Mr. Madden I'd got mixed up, that I'd already promised Bub May I'd ride for him. 'Course I didn't fool Madden a minute."

Jimmy Winkfield could not truly appreciate John E. Madden's emotional stake in the Futurity. Winning the country's biggest sports prize would preserve his place of eminence among the most prestigious social crowd in America—many of them fellow members of the Coney Island Jockey Club, which staged the race. Madden's standing with people like William K. Vanderbilt, Pierre Lorillard, and the Whitneys, Belmonts, and Wideners was worth more to him than the winner's share of the $36,600 purse. But now Madden had a major problem: nobody to ride his lead horse, and the race just days away.

Everybody was following the Futurity developments, even

Guglielmo Marconi, inventor of the wireless telegraph. Toward the end of August, Marconi arrived in stormy New York City aboard a drenched Cunard liner. "My purpose in coming to America this time," said the publicity-minded genius, "is to consult with Mr. Edison." But Marconi also enjoyed getting wireless news on the way over of "the international yacht races, the tennis championships, and the breaking of the trotting record by the famous mare Lou Dillon." If his ship had been at sea a day later, Marconi would have gotten the news of Wink's Futurity.

The Sheepshead Bay racecourse looked out over Coney Island toward the white-capped ocean, but the crowd at the track couldn't see through the rain. It was the worst weather in memory for what New York City had turned into a Futurity Holiday, and it sliced attendance to twenty thousand, half the number expected. Padding through ankle-deep mud in the paddock, Madden kept up appearances, telling the press, "I think I will win." But the morning papers still didn't list a jockey for The Minute Man, the colt Wink had ditched at the last minute.

Madden couldn't just change his mind again and go with Frank O'Neill, who had ridden The Minute Man at Saratoga. It was too late: he had already closed a deal with O'Neill to ride Adbell. Madden did have another jockey on his third colt, but he needed a better one, like Wink, on The Minute Man. He finally got one, too: August Belmont's rider, John Bullman, whose original mount was a late scratch. Meanwhile, Wink had his own last-minute problem: Highball's long stride and small hooves were not a good match for the prevailing mud.

Gong!

And with that electric sound, the fans started yelling, "They're off! They're off!"

But Highball, The Minute Man, and the sixteen other colts just stood there.

It turned out the man in charge of the gong on the judge's stand was just testing it. Whenever he did press the button that sounded the gong for real, it would be a sign for the starter to spring the rubber barrier. That was how it worked at Sheepshead Bay, and by now the jockeys all knew it. Right now, the starter was still trying to get the horses aligned. As the crowd peered through the rain to see what was going on, the starter spent eight minutes trying to align the two-year-olds.

"I want you to get that horse in line, Bullman! What are you doing there, Burns? Bring that horse in!"

Gong!

They were off in the soaking Futurity! Highball broke poorly and had trouble with the slop, but Wink kept him in a drive almost the whole way. Then he leveled off until the last two furlongs of the six-furlong sprint, when he made a splashy run at the leaders. But through the mist, the crowd made out the orange-and-white colors of Sydney Paget's Hamburg Belle, Grover Cleveland Fuller up, swimming in first in three inches of slop. Whitney's Leonidas was second by a head, and wading in third was The Minute Man. Wink and Highball ended up fifth. Charging into the jockeys' room after the race, Paget yanked Grover out of his bath to congratulate him. Madden was furious. Denied his headline, the Wizard exploded.

"Winkfield, I don't like to be double-crossed. If you're not goin' to ride my horses, you're not goin' to ride for anybody."

Wink had made a big mistake, and he knew it. "I got too smart for my pants," he admitted later. But he wasn't alone in those early days of big money going to the heads of star athletes, and he wasn't alone in taking on Madden. Two years earlier, Winnie O'Connor had infuriated Madden by riding all out and winning at Saratoga on a colt named Yankee when Madden had wanted Winnie to hold the colt back. He was secretly planning to run him in the 1901 Futurity, and a loss at Saratoga would have lengthened his odds in the big one.

Old-timers told O'Connor that Madden would never forgive him, and indeed the Wizard boycotted Winnie, wouldn't say a word to him, until the Futurity came up and he couldn't find a rider for Yankee. In desperation, Madden was forced to talk to Winnie in the paddock, which meant giving him an order.

"Go inside and ride my Yankee."

"Go inside yourself and ride him," said the chesty Winnie. Madden caved in.

"Ride him and I'll give you $10,000, win or lose."

Yankee won the Futurity, but Madden never hired Winnie again. In Wink's case two years later, the punishment did not fit the crime. Anybody who jumped contract could expect to be fired, but as Wink would tell it later, Madden meant to make sure nobody else would hire him either. It couldn't have happened at a worse time. One by one, American racetracks had been collapsing financially for more than a decade. Maryland's Pimlico Race Course had shut down in 1890, not to reopen for nearly twenty years, and New York's Jerome Park, where the Belmont Stakes was first run, was turned into a city reservoir. The gathering antigambling forces were scoring victories, too, including a New Jersey ban on pari-mutuel wagering that closed the gorgeous new Monmouth Park only three years after it opened. And it was both zero financing and antigambling protestors that shut down Saratoga for a season in 1896, before Will Whitney came along in an isolated rescue. Nationally, Wall Street's latest crisis, the Panic of '97, and another series of recessions, made hard times for everyone, which meant worse times for black jockeys. For the few of them still around, fights for jobs at the declining tracks raged out of control. The historian Charles Parmer:

> A black boy would be pocketed, thrust back in a race; or his mount would be bumped out of contention; or a white boy would run alongside, slip a foot under a black boy's stirrup and toss him out of the saddle. Again, while ostensibly whipping their own horses, those white fellows would slash out and cut the nearest Negro rider. . . . They literally ran the black boys off the track.

It wasn't just white jockeys ganging up on the few black jockeys left. Whether intolerant or not, many owners didn't want to risk their investments by riding a black jockey only to squint through their field glasses to see him getting murdered on the backstretch. And when a powerhouse like Madden talked, people listened. Even Bub May deserted Wink: when Highball started the next time, Wink was not in the saddle. Racing around the Big Apple for the next couple of weeks—from Sheepshead Bay up to Morris Park in Westchester and back to Brighton Beach on Coney Island, the "Great Jockey" of the West looked like the Worst of the East. He just couldn't get a decent mount. At one point under the Madden hex, he went for more than a month, into mid-October, with only two mounts, and in nine races after the Futurity, he never got an animal that could do better than fourth.

Of course, he could always tell his grandchildren—if, at this rate, he lived that long—that he rode Man o'War. It was quite a moment. Under Wink, Man o'War had charged ahead of Grover Cleveland Fuller, the winning Futurity rider, and was in a drive. Unfortunately, he and Grover Cleveland were also in fourteenth and fifteenth place, respectively, which was how they finished. Wink's Man o'War was a pathetic four-year-old who had come to the races eighteen years before his legendary namesake.

Jimmy Winkfield's calvary—or cavalry of dogs—finally ended at the new but extremely modest "poor people's track" in Jamaica, Queens. Compared with Saratoga, these were not encouraging surroundings. To get there, you took the Long Island Rail Road, or a local trolley. You could watch from the infield for 75 cents or from the one-thousand-seat grandstand for $2. Then things got confusing. Because of the one-mile course's egg-shaped construction, the Jamaica finish line was on a slant, which made it hard to tell the winner. "Unless a horse won by five lengths or more," said one expert, "the official result invariably was greeted by howls of protest." But Wink never gave them anything to howl about at Jamaica. He couldn't get a single ride.

There was a way out. Get out of the country. Maybe you could find an American stable owner to hire you for his English or Continental operations and cash in on the boom in racing over there. Or, sign with an agent for one of the foreign owners trying to snag the next crouching, aerodynamic Tod Sloan. Had he not sabotaged Madden, Winkfield might already have found an owner to send him abroad. Many of the top white jockeys he had ridden against had escaped the collapsing American scene. It was the only major talent drain ever in American sports. At least a dozen future Hall of Famers, including Tommy Burns, by far the winningest jockey of the past five years, and many other stars had left for Europe or England, or soon would. The weekly *Thoroughbred Record*, the industry bible—or in this case, mouthpiece—made believe it didn't care: "At one time, it was fashionable to bewail this general exodus, and say that the foreigners were securing all of our best riding talent. Experience has shown that they never will be missed."

It was a pathetic defense, and the best jockeys kept on fleeing. Look at Lucien Lyne, Winkfield's Lexington neighbor and the luckiest of them all. In 1902, Lyne had won the American Derby, the second-richest race in the country, then captured the Futurity, too. With that, Wall Street tycoon James R. Keene decided he was going to pluck Lucien off America's dying tracks and send him to England. Well, maybe he would, and maybe he wouldn't, because Lucien, like many other young riders, had a big advantage that Wink didn't have. A father. True, Lucien's father, the Lexington breeder Sandford C. Lyne, was so intense he could be a little frightening. There was the time he had custody of a valuable brood-mare named Ravello, imported from England while in foal with a very high-bred colt. The night of the foaling, Lyne began to panic. He had terrible nightmares featuring the pigs on his Lexington farm.

> I dreamed that the pigs on my place had got loose, and the foal having been born, the pigs had eaten it! I awoke in a cold perspiration. I couldn't realize that it was a dream, but slipped on my clothes and rushed out. It was between four and five in the morning, and the day just breaking. I expected to find the remains of the pigs' slaughter, but there was the mare and the foal, safe and sound. I never forgot it.

Now Sandford Lyne bottled that intensity and got on a train to New York to meet with Keene. He signed for his son, a minor, an amazing contract, paying the seventeen-year-old the highest retainer yet for an American athlete at home—$20,000 a year for two years. In addition, he would be paid for second call on his services and an extra fee for each race, thus clearing about $40,000, whereas fatherless, agentless Wink had to handle his own finances, schedules, and negotiations.

Winnie O'Connor, the top rider of 1901, also had a watchful father, a Wall Street broker, and finally Winnie's day arrived as well, with a deal second only to Lucien's. He would ride for Baron Rothschild in France for $15,000 a year for three years plus other expenses. Jerry Ransch, the top American rider of 1902, went to France, too. For Fred "the Flying Dutchman" Taral, it was Germany, where he won the 1902 Deutsche Derby and was wined and dined by visiting American moneybags like James R. Keene at Carlsbad.

But Jimmy Winkfield was left out. Since Willie Simms, the only prominent black jockey to get a European job had been Tony Hamilton, the much-abused American star of the Gay Nineties. Tony had secured a deal to ride in Vienna, then part of the Austro-Hungarian Empire, before scoring big on the Russian turf in 1901. Other American riders had preceded him to Russia and Poland, including Tod Sloan's brother Cash. While Simms had introduced the extreme American crouch to England, it was Cash who first showed it to Russia. And like the white American Cash Sloan, the black American Tony Hamilton was a sensation. He started his Russian career by winning the Moscow Breeders Stakes and was even bigger in Russian-controlled Warsaw, Poland. A Polish historian would write: "He was very gifted and had many marvelous victories both in Warsaw and at the other major racetracks of Russia."

European racetracks seemed paved with gold, but Jimmy could see no way to penetrate that world. Then a third Lexington stable owner—after Bub May and John Madden—entered his life. This was John Oliver (Jack) Keene, the most flamboyant of the trainers who had fled to Europe. He was no kin to Lucien's new angel, the

Wall Streeter James R. Keene, who also owned a Lexington farm but almost never bothered to visit there. Jack was born on the Bluegrass farm that had been in his family for seven generations, ever since the state of Virginia had awarded the Keenes one of the first land grants in Kentucky, long before it became a state. Now thirty-three, Jack had developed a love of horses early on and particularly loved getting them into shape for the races. But he had also come down with a hopeless case of wanderlust, and it was anybody's guess where he might be at any moment. Once, when he found himself broke in the Northwest, he got a loan, hit on a series of bets, and took off for Japan. Of course, Jack always mixed his travel bug with horses, so he cabled home from Japan to have some stock shipped out, and he operated a brief but successful racing campaign under the rising sun.

But Jack had one big dream. His love of thoroughbreds and the land that nourished them was almost mystical, so his dream didn't need to make sense. There it was, stuck in his head: an indoor racing and training center built entirely of Kentucky limestone. The stone stands, the clubhouse, the stables would all be part of Jack's home, like any other room. And even the one-mile-plus training track would be enclosed in limestone—endless quantities of the same bright Bluegrass rock the richest farmers used to outline their spreads back in the early nineteenth century. Those natural walls had defined the Bluegrass until mile upon mile of limestone became too expensive and had to be replaced with black- or white-painted fences. Many of those pretty old walls were still around, though.

So an architect drew up an actual plan for Jack's folly—a palatial building that would house his residence, a clubhouse (with a library, of course), a stable, and even a track. "Some of the horses," noted one commentator, would be stabled "just across the hall from the vast living room." But the huge edifice was still but a gleam in crazy Jack's eye when he got distracted again. He heard from Carroll (Carl) Mitchell, who had been America's leading jockey in 1900 but was now one of the happy expatriates in Russia. Mitchell wrote Jack that he should come over and make some big money. Jack, reading the magic word, said he was interested, and when word got around Russia, Finance Minister Sergei Witte offered Keene a spectacular 10 percent of the Witte stable's earnings for 1902—plus a salary of $1,000 a month and expenses, including the $500 it would cost to sail to Germany and hop the train to Warsaw. Jack was gone. He eventually trained for the Warsaw banker Henry Bloch as well and immediately became Russia's top trainer, winning 116 races in three and a half months. For Bloch alone, Jack's horses captured seventeen of twenty races and earned 185,000 rubles, or $98,400, far better than most trainers back home were doing for all their employers put together.

To Keene, it was obvious what had been wrong in Russia; nearly all the top imported thoroughbreds were English-trained. "The superiority of the American trainers over the Englishmen has been proven in almost every place where Americans have gone," he declared when he returned to Lexington after his first Russian season. And he intended to milk that cash cow. One of the Americans' secrets was aluminum horseshoes, so he grabbed a big supply in Lexington and shipped them to Russia. He had already signed with Mikhail Lazareff, the leading stable owner over there, for 1903. An Armenian oilman, Lazareff was one of Czar Nicholas II's richest subjects and "a political general" in the army, a mostly honorary rank, similar to the Union army's political generals in the Civil War, although many of the latter saw plenty of action. Having decided to soak up some of Lazareff's excess rubles, Jack Keene hired Carl Mitchell as well as an American foreman and blacksmith to join him in Russia.

It worked. The American team swept almost every big race in Russia, thanks mainly to their stunning three-year-old, Irish Lad. This was a son of Czar Nicholas's fabled sire Galtee More, who won the English Triple Crown (the Derby, the St. Leger, and the 2,000 Guineas), then was purchased from the British government in a series of intense negotiations, more intense than you might think. The Russians agreed to pay 20,000 guineas, a record for a horse in training—in other words, a horse still racing—but the czar's lead negotiator, a General Arapov, nearly blew it.

The talks included dinner at a restaurant, where the Russian general mistook some of the wives for prostitutes and became aroused, or as another report put it, "overexcited." The human stallion's under-the-table manners jeopardized the deal but didn't kill it. In their spectacular 1903 season under the czar, Keene, Mitchell, and Galtee More's lad won the jewel of the racing calendar, the All-Russian Derby, worth 40,000 rubles, or $21,200—more than three and a half times that 1903 Kentucky Derby, which Wink should have won but didn't. In second place behind Mitchell was that other American jockey, Tony Hamilton.

Then Keene got into trouble: a one-year suspension for drugging one of his horses. Guilty or not, he should not have been surprised. Just as the English did, the Russians thought the Yanks had "a shadowy side. They brought a terrible plague—doping." Keene's was the first major case of alleged American doping in Russia, and when Keene got home he denied it, telling American reporters, quite convincingly, that the Russians were punishing him for winning too much. He lost his appeal to the Racing Society but had earned $20,000 in salary and commissions, so he planned to return for the 1904 season. So he said.

Keene also said he would bring a new jockey back to Russia, and who better than Winkfield, who was in New York when he heard of Keene's interest in him? It was probably then, in late October or early November, that Winkfield got out of his contract with Dunne. He headed south to sign with the mysterious Lazareff, but when his train pulled into Lexington, Keene wasn't there—he had slipped down to Memphis to buy some horses. So Winkfield hung around, yakking with local reporters about the deal, until Jack got back three days later. Then came the page one news:

PAPERS SIGNED
Winkfield Agrees to Ride
For Gen. Du Lazaroff
For 13,000 Roubles

Actually, Wink was being lied to about the salary. Almost certainly getting its information from Keene, the paper reported that the 13,000-ruble salary was worth $7,800, whereas, at the exchange rate Keene used to report his glorious Russian prizes, the salary would really be about $1,000 less. It was far below Lucien's $20,000-with-perks or Winnie's $15,000-plus. But those were the American industry's best deals, and Wink's was still far better than anything the vast majority of other athletes, white or black, could pull off at home. And it beat begging for mounts in the hostile Big Apple.

It must have sounded extra sweet to hear Keene extol the future that awaited any American horseman in Russia. "There is a splendid chance for a man who is willing and able to gather in some rubles and kopecks," Jack had already told the *Record*, and he raved on, insisting Russia would become one of the leading racing countries. "Men of all degrees of fortune are buying a horse or two" over there, he said, "and a quarter of a million people saw some part of the Moscow Derby." Even if he only meant some part of the Derby Day card, it was beyond imagining.

But Keene was apparently lying about something else. His personal plans were very murky. Was he really planning on going back to Russia, or was he just going to send Winkfield over there alone and get a commission from Lazareff for the deal? It looked as if he never intended to go back. Before leaving Russia toward the end of the summer, he had wired a huge sum to Lexington to buy land adjacent to his Bluegrass farm. He'd written that he would bring home several Russian mares, loudly opining that Russian thoroughbreds had the strongest constitution and that the mares, mated to an American stallion, would produce the ideal race horse. And now he was buying those horses in Memphis. But didn't the contract oblige Keene to go back with Winkfield? It did not. As with other American jockey contracts, the agreement was not with the trainer but with the stable owner. Keene had merely been acting as Lazareff's representative.

With Keene's intentions still a mystery, and no agent or father for Wink to consult, the *Leader* simply stated, "Winkfield is now

23 years old and being of age can sign his own contract." Wink did sign the Lazareff contract, on November 14, 1903, and a week later Keene announced that he would not return to Russia after all. Jimmy Winkfield would have to confront the unknown land of the czars by himself.

Trying to figure out this amazing young man, an American today might think: this is a twenty-three-year-old country kid, traveling alone, first trip out of the country, leaving Edna in Lexington. How could he do it?

But he was not a country kid. At eighteen, he had traveled to Chicago with the Mays and knocked about the racetracks there; the next year, it was New York City and Chicago and New Orleans, and helping the Mays run the little stable; and the year after that, he was one of the stars in the Kentucky Derby, parading to the post in his shiny orange-and-blue silks before thousands of people, then the winner of two Kentucky Derbies. Next he was negotiating riding fees at Saratoga with some of the wealthiest people in the horse racing industry, including the dangerous John Madden. Not only was he not a kid anymore, but as sometimes happens to major athletes—some, certainly not all—he was far older and more experienced in certain ways than, say, a professor at Harvard University.

And having threaded his way through one train station after another for the past six years, he was not afraid of travel. Besides, as later events would show, Mikhail Lazareff was almost certainly not only booking his passage to Europe, via his agents, but paying for it as well, via Jack Keene. And Jack, who had just spent two years in Russia himself, could certainly tell Wink how to board the steamship from New York to northern Germany, then the train along the Elbe River, and how to meet Lazareff's driver at the station in Warsaw. The vast majority of Americans would have been terrified by such a thing. Twenty-three-year-old Jimmy Winkfield was already good at it.

Chapter Seven

INVADING RUSSIA

W hen Jimmy Winkfield arrived in April 1904 at the farm
outside Warsaw where Jack Keene's string was in training, he discovered that he couldn't talk to anybody.

His new employer, Mikhail Lazareff, had thought so highly of
Keene that he could not find a trainer to replace him, so he used
two, a Pole and a Russian, neither of whom spoke English. The
foreman gave Jimmy a book so he could learn Polish.

Even the Poles were lucky they could speak Polish in Warsaw.
As Winkfield would soon learn, the Russians had controlled the
city for seven decades, after putting down a Polish revolt against
czarist rule, and they treated the Warsaw area like a Russian
province, restricting the use of Polish and introducing Russian in
the schools.

For Jimmy, just seeing Lazareff's horses was a relief. They made
him feel at home. Lazareff lived in St. Petersburg but wintered his
thoroughbreds here, well to the south, so they could be prepped
early enough for the spring races in Warsaw. When Jimmy got
there, Lazareff had about fifty in training, and Winkfield would
later say it was like working for Calumet Farm, whose devil's red-

and-blue silks would dominate American racing. Except that Lazareff's holdings were much bigger than Calumet's would be. Lazareff wouldn't have even noticed it if the combined savings of Bub May, Pat Dunne, and for that matter John Madden and Jack Keene fell through a hole in his pocket. As Jimmy could see, every-thing seemed on a larger scale in Russia, so large that nobody in Lexington would ever believe it, starting with the fact that Russia boasted 38 million horses of different breeds, a third of the world's equine population.

In May, when the races started, Jimmy heard a lot more English in the Warsaw jockey colonies—even American English. In fact, Winkfield already knew most of the boys. Johnny Hoar was at Saratoga with him. Joe Piggott had raced around Cincinnati and the western circuit for years. Billy Caywood, Joe Richards, and black rider James Cannon were there as well. Winkfield tuned in to the clipped accents of the English jockeys, and many of the Poles and Russians spoke English fairly well. As everybody knew, even Czar Nicholas II had to use English in his billets-doux to his German-born empress, Alexandra, who preferred the language of her grandmother Queen Victoria.

As Poland thawed and Winkfield itched to show how brilliant he was, a terrible gloom enveloped all of Russia. The newspapers were full of it—headlines that Winkfield couldn't fully translate yet but whose import he could feel in the worries of the Poles and Russians. It was the Russo-Japanese War. Russia's expansion in eastern Asia had collided with Japan's own desire for a foothold on the mainland. The Russians had leased tiny Port Arthur on the Chinese coast, southeast of Manchuria, and now went ahead with their threatened plan to turn it into an important Russian harbor. On February 8, 1904, before Winkfield's arrival in Warsaw, Japan had responded with a surprise attack on Port Arthur. And a few weeks later, as Winkfield had set about exercising Lazareff's thor-oughbreds, the Japanese backed up that attack by landing troops in Korea en route to confronting the Russians in China.

As Warsaw's racecourse opened, the Japanese forced a passage

across the Yalu River, and both sides prepared for massive land battles. Wink's main concern, naturally, was that this Russo-Japanese
War might interfere with his Warsaw debut, just as the Spanish-
American War had hogged the headlines during his Chicago debut.
But the racing went on, and Wink immediately had to adjust to
an entirely different program. In Russia and Russian-controlled
Warsaw, and everywhere else in Europe, races were on grass, or
"turf"—not dirt, as in America—and many of the tracks were pat-
terned after English courses, with irregular shapes and even with
hills. They were very often beautiful, and a jockey felt as if he were
in a painting. The schedules were different, too. They raced only
three times a week but with fifteen races each day, more than twice
the usual number back home. The main race meetings were at
Warsaw, Moscow, and St. Petersburg, and the big day, with the
featured events, was always Sunday.

Wink wasted no time proving he still had his winning ways. He
won two races on Warsaw's opening day, then the important Breeders Stakes for two-year-olds, the Jubilee Stakes, and finally the
Warsaw Derby itself. He took the Warsaw Oaks, too. (The Poles
and Russians not only imported English-bred horses but used English race names like "Derby" for races by three-year-old colts or
fillies and "Oaks" for three-year-old fillies alone.) News of Wink's
success quickly crossed the Atlantic; he could always manipulate the
newspapers at home, even from this distance, but his Warsaw
Derby called for something special. "According to a cablegram received in Louisville, Jockey Jimmy Winkfield had the winning
mount in the Warsaw Derby, one of the greatest races of the Russian turf." The *Lexington Leader* ran a whole column praising Wink
to the skies: "His fame as a race rider is known all over the world."

By July, he was on his way to becoming a major star again. He
had won twenty-one of forty races in Poland and Russia for an un-
believable 52.5 winning percentage and was unplaced—finished out
of the money—only once. His Armenian boss was raking it in, just
as Wink's American employers had. And it wasn't long before
Wink found Russian fans doing what Americans had done on the

western circuit: betting not on the horse but on the jockey, the high-est compliment in the business. A Russian observer said Wink would be a favorite "even though he'd be riding a goat."

Wink wasn't the only Yank at the top. The New Jersey boy Johnny Hoar was riding for three Polish princes, the brothers Lubomirski, who were among the most powerful figures of Polish and Russian racing. Johnny was at his zenith, riding three or four winners a day in Warsaw. For communication and comfort, it helped that his immediate boss was an American trainer, Frank Frisbie, but success was fragile in Europe. Later in the season, Hoar would be knocked out by inflammation of the lungs, an ancient jockey affliction, and Frisbie would be accused of doping, which cut short his exotic career. Joe Richards, from Detroit, was working for the super-rich Warsaw banker Henry Bloch. Carl Mitchell, who had starred for Keene, was still very popular and riding now for one of the czar's cousins, Count Steinbok-Fermour, reportedly at an astronomical salary of $18,000 for 1904. Joe Piggott, employed by the same royal, was even bigger, taking the Empress Prize at War-saw. He led the money-winning list, just ahead of Wink, until he was thrown out of the saddle and sidelined. That made Wink num-ber one in Poland.

Wink even topped Cash Sloan, Tod's brother, who had set the Polish record two years before with an astounding forty-eight wins in 100 starts, finishing out of the money only nineteen times. Wink beat that, racking up fifty-four wins in 105 starts at Warsaw, a 51 percent record, and finishing unplaced in only fifteen efforts. Wink had a mere thirteen starts in his first year in Russia's big ap-ple—Moscow—but two of them were in very important contests.

Jimmy Winkfield's jaw dropped when he entered the Moscow Central Hippodrome for the first time. Atop the classical Greek entrance, with its twelve towering columns, a team of four sculpted horses, with two single horses on each side, leaped into the sky. The Central Hippodrome was completed in 1834 by Nicholas I, grandson of Catherine the Great, and no American racecourse ap-proached its majesty. In fact, at first glance, it seemed overdone to

any American. To understand it, you had to appreciate the importance of horses in Russia. Jimmy's Kentucky deserved its reputation
as America's horse capital, but now he had to consider a country
that had far more horses—those 38 million.

As with racetracks everywhere, there wasn't much built beyond
the Hippodrome's entrance, only a few offices and refreshment
stands under the long stretches of seats. It was all about the track or,
in this case, tracks, because the vast Moscow Central Hippodrome
had two of them, as well as stables, facilities for recreational riding,
horse shows, and polo. The main track with the towering entrance
was reserved for an equine class that was even more revered there
than thoroughbreds: the trotter. As Wink would learn, the ancient
saga of Russian trotting featured races by the renowned Orlov and
Don breeds and by troikas, which were teams of three Orlov trotters pulling a driver in a light wagon. The stands lining the thoroughbred track were built along clean, modern lines, with only a
few decorative touches on modest towers. Again, the race was the
thing. In this vast horse country par excellence, the Central Hippodrome's tracks drew crowds several times bigger than those back
home, even on Kentucky Derby Day. But the sights and sounds of
the contest were the same—the thundering hooves, the jockey's
shouts among themselves, the screaming crowd—and on this Russian Oaks day, the applause that the new kid from Kentucky heard
was actually for him, as he romped home first.

Wink's brief 1904 season at the Hippodrome brought him two
bigger thrills—and a tragedy. All three came on the day of the
country's premier race, the All-Russian Derby. First, Wink would
get to ride in it, but then his heart leaped higher as he discovered
that one of the other jockeys was his old idol Tony Hamilton, who
had come in second to Carl Mitchell and Jack Keene's Irish Lad in
this derby the year before. It had to have been an emotional pre-
race reunion. Hamilton's mount, Crossing, got away fast, but after
a few strides, he fell, throwing Tony onto the turf. The others rode
right over his body, trampling him so badly he lost one of his eyes.
His career was over. Three years later he died of tuberculosis in

Menton, on the French Riviera—in a private railroad car, said one dubious report, while wrapped in sable and flashing rings on every finger.

After Hamilton's tragedy, Wink must have lost almost all memory of his first All-Russian Derby, but in it he had made a mark on Russian racing with a thrilling fight for second, which ended in an extremely rare dead heat—a tie. Yet even the Derby couldn't get much of a headline that first season in Moscow, as the Russo-Japanese War continued to monopolize the Muscovite press. Czar Nicholas had just declared that Port Arthur must be held at all costs, which meant committing Russia's main army to its defense. The czar's famous trans-Siberian railroad shipped about 30,000 men a month to China's small Liaotung Peninsula, just west of the Korean peninsula, where two enormous piles of human cannon fodder faced each other—180,000 Russians against 130,000 Japanese—for the Battle of Liaotung. Despite the odds, the Japanese prevailed, and the Russians retreated to a town called Mukden.

But Winkfield had to make a living, and a letter to a friend back home showed he had a few complaints. One was the high cost of living, especially the stiff charges for his Russian jockey's license. Did he complain to Edna, too? No letters to her have been found, but she was worried about her Jimmy, and as will be clear later, she was developing some big ideas of her own. Meanwhile, Winkfield also complained about the weight regulations. Under European rules, jockeys could generally ride much heavier, which did allow the Yanks to eat once in a while. But the regulations were often unfair. In Austria, horses ridden by the Americans and the British had to carry seven and a half extra pounds; in Russia, it was ten pounds—simply because, as everybody knew, they were much better riders. This penalty for being an American was especially unfair to Wink, because, unlike many of the Yanks, he could still get down to 105 to 107 pounds. As if that were not enough, American riders were not allowed to ride in more than three races a day because they were considered too good. The idea was to give the Russian boys a chance.

Wink didn't think much of the Russian and Polish jockeys, with one exception—a young Pole named Joseph Klodziak. Joseph worked for Lazareff and was a formal understudy to Winkfield. At home, the idea of a white apprenticed to a black jockey would have shocked a lot of bigots, but it wasn't unheard of. Ike Murphy had taught white boys at a little jockey school run by Lucky Baldwin at his Santa Anita ranch. Like Ike, Wink had the temperament for teaching—quiet, analytical, patient—and he loved to communicate about his sport. Joseph would be only his first formal student.

And what was it that Winkfield and his American colleagues knew about racing horses that Russians didn't? One could start by examining what American trainers knew. Jack Keene said the big thing at home was prepping a horse, which the Russians never did. They had no real workouts for horses; their training consisted entirely of walking and slow galloping, so it was no wonder the horses had a tough time competing. But some Russians had ideas of their own. Lazareff wanted his trainers and jockeys to avoid winning by too much, thus ensuring that their losing opponents exhausted themselves while the better Lazareff horses got a breather at the end. After a few weeks of that, the Armenian figured he'd have the only fresh horses in Moscow. But the general quality of Russian horses was fine; once they were properly trained, both Jack Keene and Wink thought they were as good as or better than any others.

The Yanks could also teach the others the crouch, or "American seat," which both white and black colonial riders had invented in the first place, back in those wild quarter-mile races through the southern pines, when the race would be over in thirty seconds and you had to use everything you had, like the aerodynamic crouch, not only to win but to keep the other rider from knocking you off your horse. At the normal, longer distances in Britain and on the Continent, the proper style was to ride erect. This you would do at an almost gentlemanly rate until the last quarter mile or so, at which point you would try to squeeze everything out of the horse in a final mad dash, but without contorting yourself into a rude, ugly crouch. As for managing their own races, Wink and the others drove harder all the way while at the same time adjusting the pace of their race—Wink's specialty—which made it important to have some knowledge of every horse in the race.

But there was something that Wink did not know and that the czar and his friends in the racing establishment apparently did not care about. It was something that thirty-four-year-old Vladimir Ilyich Lenin, quietly writing away in Geneva, Switzerland, might have called the "oppression of the Russian jockey class." The best of the Russian jockeys was Michael Laks, who in his first thirteen years, from 1903 through 1915, won 535 of 2,466 races, for a 21.6 win percentage. By tradition, when the American Jimmy Winkfield won the Warsaw Derby or the Russian Oaks at Moscow in his first year abroad, Mikhail Lazareff would shake his hand as they shared the honors while grand music wafted across the grandstand. But when Michael Laks won a big event, the owner would hardly notice him. "The owners always shook hands with the foreign jockeys, but never with the Russians," Laks noted bitterly in his memoirs.

It was a hard life for the local boys. As soon as he arrived, Wink had been recognized as a proper jockey—a status the Russian riders found almost impossible to achieve. "All American boys are considered full-fledged jockeys, but a Russian boy remains an apprentice until he has won fifty races," Jack Keene noted at the time. And while the foreign jockeys were accorded instant respect, the Russian jocks had to claw for every penny. "To rise from Russian stable boy to jockey was as difficult as rising from theater usher to cabinet minister," Laks said. "There was an iron rule. Everybody had to go through three colored steps. To be listed as 'Rider,' you had to win twenty-five races, and after that, your name would be written in black in the programs, 'Rider such-and-such. . . .' Fifty wins entitled him to see his name written in navy blue, though the title remained the same. And one-hundred-fifty wins at the Moscow, St. Petersburg, or Warsaw hippodrome brought him the coveted red color and the title of 'Jockey.'" Thus, the reality was even harsher than Keene's portrayal. Throw in the fact that foreign jockeys always rode the best horses, and you can see what Russian riders' chances for success were. Almost none. To the end of their careers, many never officially became jockeys. In contrast, Wink and his fellow foreigners had their names printed in red from the start.

Jimmy Winkfield's proud letters home included pitches for American jobs when he got back, either for the coming winter or in case he wanted to stay home for good. And he had a lot to pitch. By the end of that 1904 season, he stood at the top of the combined Polish-Russian winners' list with fifty-seven wins in 118 starts, for a 48 percent win record. Lazareff earned 300,000 rubles, or $160,000, mostly with Wink in the saddle.

Away from his problems in America, Jimmy Winkfield was a new man. But it was time to go home. The season was over, the contract was over, the Russo-Japanese War was still raging in the East, and the Russian winter was on its way. In early November, Joe Richards, William Doyle, and the ailing Johnny Hoar, three of the white American jocks in Russia, boarded the train to Germany and sailed out of Bremen on the steamship *Kaiser Wilhelm der Grosse*, bound for the States. But Russia's best American athlete, always thinking, always the careful businessman, was not in such a hurry. Like Keene before him, Wink was trying to figure out how to play it both ways. Lazareff had offered him a job for the 1905 season, and he was not going to reject out of hand a salary few Americans could ever dream of. Still, he needed to know what his options at home were. He was not at all sure he wanted to return to Russia.

He missed home, missed his brothers and sisters, missed friends like Doc Allen. He missed the applause of American crowds, even if they weren't close to the size of a Moscow crowd. They were Americans. Most of all, he must have missed Edna. He knew she was making their house on East Third Street a wonderful home for him, a delightful refuge from his travels. As he looked homeward, Wink got in touch with a publicist in Warsaw, one S. P. London, who represented several of the foreign jocks. Mr. London's services for the jocks also benefited the Russian stable owners, keeping the jockeys happy over the winter, in a frame of mind to return. London would send a letter (they were not yet called press releases) to America, along with Wink's picture, to help him get a job for the winter. He did the same for the black American jockey James Cannon and for Wink's understudy, Joseph Klodziak.

Wink hoped a powerful owner would see London's announcement in the *Louisville Courier-Journal* and book him at a winter track like Hot Springs. He thought about getting mounts for the New Orleans, Memphis, and Kentucky Derbies. So Wink, Cannon, and Klodziak marched off to the Novialis Studio to sit for the camera. Unlike many Americans, Jimmy Winkfield had had his picture taken professionally countless times back home, usually after winning races, but he always looked terrible in them, exhausted, gaunt, his cheeks caved in. This portrait of Wink, however, was one of his best ever, perhaps because it was taken after the season, when he could eat a little more. He glowed. His face had filled out, and he wore a tie under a Russian, military-style jacket.

You would have had to study it closely to see a problem with his right eye, a suggestion of wanting to wander to the right. He had noticed it before anybody else, of course, and concluded it was the result of that bad whiskey in Chicago that left him with a powerful headache and swollen, painful eyes. It may have kept him off the stuff amidst the famously heavy drinking at Saratoga and, a stiffer challenge, away from the vodka that was drowning Russia. One writer said sarcastically, "British and American jockeys . . . who could hold their vodka consumption down to a quart or so a day managed to do well." But it was no joke. Alcoholism was, as it remains, an enormous blight on Russia, and Michael Laks wrote that he owed his success to staying in shape, which in turn he owed to a promise to himself: no smoking and no drinking. None. "I did not abandon myself to the dissolute life."

There was something else about Wink's studio portrait: a certain calm contentment in his face. How did he get so relaxed when some of his earlier postrace photos in America showed an athlete who was not only exhausted but looked older and somehow desperate? It might have had something to do with freedom. Almost on arrival in Warsaw, he found that widespread, wide-open, public racism, a way of life for so many back home, didn't exist in most of Europe; officially, at least, he was no longer a second-class citizen. So what the Novialis Studio made was a portrait of the jockey as a free man, yet with a serious, slightly quizzical quality that suggested he wasn't so sure about that.

Jimmy Winkfield headed back to America with James Cannon while, in the end, Joseph Klodziak elected to stay put. On the train west from Warsaw into Germany, Wink took advantage of a brief stopover in Berlin to buy souvenirs, including one for Doc Allen. He hit on something sure to thrill the doc, with his love of elegant precision: a beautiful $50 set of silver-mounted pocket instruments. From Berlin, he rode the train northwest along the Elbe River to Hamburg and its North Sea port of Cuxhaven. On November 26, 1904, he pushed his five-foot frame through the thousands bidding good-bye on the dock and boarded the SS *Belgravia* alone. Cannon would sail out of Cuxhaven a few weeks later. Thus Wink ended what seemed almost a fantasy of performing in the land of the czars.

When the ship's clerk asked him whether he was married or single, Wink for some reason replied, "Single," or so the clerk wrote. His "Calling or Occupation": "jockey." Many of the Europeans were headed for the hopeful, frightening experience of Ellis Island, the immigration center in New York Harbor, dreaming of the kind of success that, though they could not know this and would certainly not have guessed it, Jimmy Winkfield now enjoyed. And Jimmy Winkfield himself proceeded to throw up, if we are to judge from his later memories of seasickness.

As the arriving *Belgravia* steamed past Coney Island, Wink might have dragged himself to the deck, or at least a porthole, to look toward the Sheepshead Bay racetrack, scene of the brutal dressing-down by John Madden that started him on his extraordinary journey. Then the *Belgravia* passed the two other Coney Island tracks, Brighton and Gravesend, entered the Narrows, and sailed by the eighteen-year-old Statue of Liberty. Wink had been away nine months. He was going to let America have another shot at him.

Chapter Eight

EDNA OR A LIFE

Y ANKEE JOCKEYS BACK IN AMERICA, one headline shouted.
MANY STAR RIDERS RETURN TO SPEND THE WINTER HERE.
The stars disembarked at the south Manhattan piers over
several days in late November and early December, but the American boys did not have good news for America. They were all doing
well overseas and planned to go back.

A small crowd welcomed Danny Maher as he walked off the
SS *Cedric* from England, having achieved heights no American
jockey had scaled. He had collected two legs of the English triple
crown, the original derby at Epsom and the St. Leger. He was on
his way to becoming one of England's jockeys of the century—and
an English citizen, too.

"I shall never again ride a season in America," declared another
Irishman standing on a New York pier. It was Winnie O'Connor,
the diamond-chested boy Wink had beaten in the Kentucky Derby.
If Danny was baby-faced, big-talking Winnie was such a wisp of a
twenty-year-old that the ship's clerk had put him down as a girl.

The outright dismissal of America by its star athletes that day
would be almost unheard-of over the next century, but Winkfield

would not join in. He would not reject America, and he had no intention of giving up his American citizenship, though he had certainly suffered more at the hands of American bigots than either Danny or Winnie. Unlike Winkfield, Maher and O'Connor also had the strong support of their parents—O'Connor's even lived with him in Paris and accompanied him over on the boat.

These star athletes benefited from a new development that would one day make fame more important than what one was famous for: the news syndicate, the first step, after the newspapers themselves, in the replication of celebrity. Starting with the Associated Press in 1900, the major papers around the country had begun combining resources to cover national and international news; it was cheaper than sending their own reporters and better than reprinting stories from other papers as soon as they hit the mailroom or the telegraph room. A report from an unnamed syndicate—it carried no credit line, thus giving each newspaper the credit—told the story of the returning jockeys. The report started appearing a week before Winkfield arrived on the *Belgravia*, and it raved about Wink's accomplishments, praising him above all the other jocks who rode in Russia.

The day after the *Belgravia* docked in Manhattan, the *Louisville Courier-Journal* ran the syndicate's report, along with the letter that Wink and S. P. London had whipped up in Warsaw. Certain to be read by many big stable owners around Kentucky, the combination letter and press release looked extremely impressive under a three-column headline, with the Novialis Studio's photographs of Winkfield, Cannon, and Joseph Klodziak, even though Cannon's return was delayed and Klodziak had decided not to come back. Still, as an advertisement of Winkfield's availability in the States, it had one small problem. It said he was so good he already had a contract with Lazareff for the next season. Wink didn't want people thinking he was going back, because it might cost him good mounts while he was here. He contacted the *Thoroughbred Record* in Lexington and made it clear that, because of the Russo-Japanese War, his future in Russia was uncertain. So the Russo-Japanese War was good for something, after all; hopefully, it would be enough to keep American stable owners thinking he couldn't go back.

It was the Christmas season, and doubtless a wonderful one for the returning hero as he visited brothers, sisters, and friends in Lexington and along that sweet half mile of country lane out in Chilesburg. Glowing with pride, Jimmy bestowed the silver-fitted instruments from Germany on a delighted Doc Allen around the corner in Lexington. And most of all, he captured Edna all over again. In their cozy home on East Third Street, she listened wide-eyed as he entertained her with tales of his otherworldly adventures in Poland and Russia—a saga far beyond other Americans' comprehension. How he had won the biggest prize they had in Poland, which those people over there also called the Derby. And the Russian Oaks, just like our Kentucky Oaks, only bigger. Edna couldn't possibly imagine their racetrack, which they called the Hippodrome and which could hold three or four of our racetracks.

And believe it or not, Edna, guess who was riding over there? Old Tony Hamilton. He hurt himself, though, and was finished, but you wouldn't believe how much money he had earned. "Even more than me," Jimmy might have conceded, "so far." Perhaps Edna began to think the impossible: that she would have to go and see for herself.

Winkfield had much more on his mind. What was going on with his old neighbor Lucien Lyne, who had bagged the biggest contract of any of the jockeys, to ride for James R. Keene in England? Swinging around to the Lyne place out on Nicholasville Pike, he would learn that plenty was going on, none of it good. Lucien had failed. His protective father had filed a breach-of-contract suit against Keene, then dropped it as he realized that Keene could get Lucien boycotted on the East Coast, just as Madden had done to Winkfield. So the $40,000-a-year jockey in England was back home and suddenly thrown into the pathetic American job market. He had finished third in the Kentucky Derby that spring, just ahead of one of the few surviving black jockeys, Dale Austin. For that, Lucien got some small percentage of the owner's prize of

$300. It had to make Wink think twice about giving up all that money he was making with Lazareff.

Whatever problems other Americans, black and white, were having with one another, Wink and Lucien could still have a good old time—laughing it up as they compared riding abroad versus riding at home, riding against a king versus riding against a czar, the riches of Europe versus being broke in America. Winkfield had no idea whether he could make a living if he stayed home, so one month after Christmas, he did what he had to do: he rode—at the winter meeting down in Hot Springs. The racing was bigger and better at New Orleans, but a Lexington stable owner had promised him the job in Arkansas. There was plenty of other talent at the Springs, too. Jimmy Boland, who had beaten him in his first Kentucky Derby but lost to him in his second, was riding there, and so was racist Hal Booker, who had beaten Wink in his fourth and last Derby.

For his first American race in more than a year, Wink jumped on a nag named Ladas, a five-to-one shot in an eleven-horse field. At nine, Ladas was the oldest thing in the bunch, giving five years and a whopping seven pounds to the favorite. But Wink burst out of the fifth post position, grabbed the lead, and held it, by a neck, at the finish—a nice "I'm back!" The *Arkansas Gazette* put him back in the papers, too: "Jockey Winkfield, who has been in Russia, rode his first race mount today and won in the last race." But something more important appeared an inch and a half below his name: a photograph of a horse in front of fifteen others in a row. The headline: GUARDS OF THE CZAR, WHO FOUGHT AGAINST THE STRIKERS.

More specifically, said the caption, it was "the Tsar's brother leading a section of the Preobrajensky Regiment of the Guards, which is prominent in the fighting." The Preobrajensky Regiment? That was revealing. Named after a village where Peter the Great had lived near Moscow in the late 1600s, the regiment had been the czars' extremely patriotic and highly feared personal guard ever since. Only a threat to the state could bring it into action.

But what had brought the strikers into action? On Sunday, January 9, 1905—January 22 on the western calendar, three days before Winkfield returned to the saddle in America—nearly 150,000 workers had marched on the czar's Winter Palace in St. Petersburg. Many were singing the national anthem, "God Save the Czar," as they appealed to Nicholas to help them. Their petition said, "We are impoverished, we are oppressed, and burdened with unbearable work." But the czar's troops opened fire, killing some eight hundred and wounding many more. It was Russia's Bloody Sunday—and in many ways, though much larger, its Boston Massacre 135 years later. Obviously, it would not end there. A general strike was called the next day, and the workers' leaders began to organize for further action.

Reading bits and pieces of it in the *Gazette*, Wink must have suddenly found it a lot harder to concentrate on Hot Springs. Putting his own survival first—and now it was a question of survival for him, of surviving as a man—he had to ask himself, as strange as it sounded: How was the workers' insurrection affecting the races in Russia? Did he really want to go back now? Yet there was virtually no work for him at the Springs, either. He got only three mounts. In his final two starts, he finished in the money, but the money was pitiful. The purse for each race's winner: $300, $300, $300—laughable compared to what he could make in Russia.

As Winkfield wrapped up his season in Arkansas, Russia sank further into its twin crises—the would-be Revolution of 1905 and the czar's worst defeat yet in the Russo-Japanese War, with ninety thousand Russians and some fifty thousand Japanese killed in a battle around Mukden on the blood-soaked Liaotung Peninsula. But whatever horrors were unfolding in Russia were not quite enough to make life in America look good for any jockey, with the racing industry still sick. To survive, and more—to be himself, one of the world's leading jockeys—Jimmy would have to say good-bye to Edna, take Lazareff's offer, and return to Russia.

Jimmy Winkfield turned up at the stables in Russian-controlled Warsaw again that spring. He was protected from the country's turmoil by the closed world of horsemen, with its early reveilles, long hours, and single-mindedness. Wink and the other foreign boys couldn't read the Russian and Polish newspapers anyway, nor did the strikes and the war in the East shut down that hermetic world, although the disruptions of training and racing schedules continued. Why hadn't the czar's brutal police shut down the tracks? Because they were one of the few things everybody agreed on. The emperor and the aristocracy on the one hand, including the Lazareffs and the other rich businessmen, and the horse-loving Russian and Polish people on the other—everybody loved the races.

Many thousands of ordinary Poles watched the top jockeys parade to the start of the 1905 Warsaw Derby—worth $11,700, nearly twice the value of the Kentucky Derby. They had to accept the fact that the best of the jocks were from far-off America—especially the new black boy, Winkfield, who had captured this great event in 1904, and the white boys Johnny Hoar and Carl Mitchell. Under the Victorian turret that towered over the Warsaw neighborhood, Wink rode out in a dark cap, loose-fitting jacket, and thigh-high black boots, a baggy outfit that disguised the important fact of that moment. Perched above Galtee Boy's saddle in his short stirrups, he was about to explode.

Head down, rear up, the Yank took off—and won it again, beating out Johnny Hoar, with Joe Klodziak third and Mitchell fourth. And in the next race he did it yet again, winning the coveted Emperor's (Czar's) Prize on four-year-old Karoli, another son of Lazareff's great sire Galtee More, who had made it to Russia despite that horny general. Already acknowledged as another Yankee phenom on the order of Cash Sloan and Tony Hamilton, Wink ran away with four more major stakes in Poland that season. His win percentage of nearly 50 percent and those huge stakes victories were astonishing. In Russia, he repeated in the Oaks and captured both the two-year-old and three-year-old Breeders Stakes.

It was a thrill to win under the four sculpted horses that had been soaring over the Moscow Central Hippodrome since 1834. But those four seemed to be answering a command from a higher power—the soaring equestrian statue of Peter the Great placed in the center of St. Petersburg by Catherine the Great in 1782 and the symbol of the city ever since Alexander Pushkin immortalized it in his poem "The Bronze Horseman" in 1837.

After his Moscow conquests, a twenty-four-hour-plus train ride took Jimmy Winkfield to the czarist capital in the early summer of 1905. If the Bronze Horseman symbolized St. Petersburg, its pure-blooded race horses symbolized the nobility and aristocracy, or so the nobles and aristocrats imagined. And Winkfield could see that thoroughbreds were not hidden away in heavily guarded stables but were often shown off in public. One of novelist Leo Tolstoy's characters rode off to a meeting on a steeplechaser. And in this "shimmering and dizzying" city, historian Solomon Volkov said, the most impressive of the luxurious carriages racing down Nevsky Prospect "were the private carriages pulled by expensive thoroughbreds with a satiny sheen to their coats. The horses, with battery-operated lanterns, were no longer frightened by the recently installed trolleys, nor by the first 'taximotors,' but they still snorted at the exhaust fumes."

This czarist capital of neoclassical buildings, vast squares, and granite embankments along the river Neva was a northern Paris, and Nevsky Prospect its Champs-Elysées. The writer Vladimir Nabokov, six years old at the time, would remember it later as a shopper's paradise of "all sorts of common things: fruitcakes, smelling salts, Pears soap, playing cards, picture puzzles, striped blazers, talcum-white tennis balls, and football jerseys in the colors of Cambridge and Oxford." But the Petersburg that Jimmy Winkfield discovered, and to which he would return several times, was more than a playground of aristocrats and horse-players. With a fast-growing population of well over 1.5 million—about the size of Chicago and counting—Petersburg was far in advance of the relative backwater Moscow, which had been the capital for two and a half centuries before Peter the Great. At once Russia's leading port and its leading industrial city, Petersburg produced ships and submarines, diesel and steam engines, cannon, oil tankers, and steel. It was a city of great factories—and greatly exploited workers. One Petersburger looked down from his window "at the dark factories with such grim fear" that he felt like a panicked guard seeing "the Huns at the city gates."

"Things are in the saddle," as Emerson had written, and "ride mankind." Three months after Bloody Sunday, as Jimmy Winkfield was preparing to win the derby down in Warsaw, the escaped political exile Leon Trotsky slipped into Petersburg. On May Day, from one of his hiding places, Trotsky issued a written challenge to Petersburg's workers:

> Comrades. You are afraid of the czarist soldiers. But you are not afraid to go day in and day out to the factories and mills where the machines drain your blood and cripple your bodies. You are afraid of the czarist soldiers. But you are not afraid to hand over your brothers to the czarist army where they perish in the great unlamented cemetery of Manchuria.

On May 14, south of Manchuria, the Japanese navy delivered a final blow to the czarist fleet, which lost eleven battleships and fifty-eight other ships on that day alone. From his latest hiding place, Trotsky declared, "The Russian fleet is no more. It was not the Japanese who destroyed her, but the czarist government." At the beginning of June, as Winkfield was preparing to win Warsaw's special stakes in honor of the czar, Russian sailors in the Black Sea were refusing to eat the rotten meat they were being served on the battleship *Potemkin*. They mutinied, throwing the ship's officers overboard and steaming to the port of Odessa, where local strikers joined them in firing on czarist soldiers. Trotsky was not going to miss this one, either. Came another Trotskygram: "We should follow the example of the *Potemkin* and throw the whole gang that rules us overboard!"

That strangest of summers in the Petersburg of 1905 saw Leon Trotsky's rise, albeit underground, as the first important revolutionary in the capital; the czar's humiliation in the war with Japan; and the American Jimmy Winkfield's debut out at the Petersburg race-course, the aristocrats' ultimate playground.

It lay to the north across the Neva and beyond Petrowski Park, the resort of the czars, across the Malaya and Srednyaya rivers, bordered by the villas of the rich, on Yelazin Island, where one of the czar's retreats, its palace decorated with English gardens and ancient oaks, commanded a magisterial view of the Gulf of Finland. From there it was but a few miles farther north to the biggest racetrack Wink had ever seen, two miles in length, far bigger than anything in America. It offered races three times a week, from June through mid-August. One of its highlights in that summer of 1905 was Wink's victory in the historic Empress Stakes honoring the czarina.

That summer had another American touch. With U.S. President Theodore Roosevelt as mediator, the Japanese and the soundly defeated Russians signed a peace treaty in early September at Portsmouth, New Hampshire. With that, the Russians saw their hopes squashed in the Far East. They surrendered Port Arthur and the southern half of Sakhalin to Japan, got out of Manchuria, and recognized Korea as a Japanese zone of influence. At the end of October, as a result of both the workers' insurrection and the war, Czar Nicholas was forced to announce that he would share power with a parliament, whose lower house, the Duma, included representatives of the peasants, the workers, and the middle and upper classes. Whether Nicholas really would dilute his power, nobody knew. Certainly nobody believed it in the towns where Nicholas's government now organized hundreds of pogroms, massacres of Jews to divert popular discontent into religious hatred.

In any event, the revolutionaries were not interested in sharing. Trotsky, a gifted orator, rushed from one secret workers' meeting to another and became the leader of the first workers' soviet, or council. That year of their discontent, 1905, proved such an exhilarating political triumph—"the dress rehearsal of the Revolution," as it came to be called—that it was almost a laughable anticlimax when Nicholas's incompetent police finally burst into a December meeting to arrest Trotsky, who turned to the gendarme in charge and said sarcastically, "Please don't interfere with the work of the soviet. If you wish to speak, kindly give your name and I will ask the assembly if they wish to hear you." Then he let the officer read his arrest orders, after which Trotsky turned to him and said, "And now you may leave the meeting of the Soviet Workers' Deputies"—and the confused officer actually left. Of course, the czar's police returned and completed the arrest of Trotsky and nearly two hundred others. But Trotsky had completely upstaged his revolutionary rival Lenin, who had only just arrived in Petersburg from Geneva, far too late to rekindle the revolt. After a year in prison, Trotsky would be exiled to the Siberian village of Obdorskoe, above the Arctic Circle and six hundred miles from the nearest railroad station—for life. Nicholas must have thought, "That should hold him."

Jimmy Winkfield was traveling as well, but in the opposite direction from Siberia. A month before Trotsky's arrest, Wink departed what he must have viewed as history's latest fantastical road show—the wild, prerevolutionary Russia of 1905—and headed home again via Germany. Wink was finding every trip—to Russia, inside Russia, and back home—an eye-opening education in the ways of humanity, an education at least equal and perhaps superior to the educations of most kings and revolutionaries because it discouraged conclusions. Winkfield did not write—or rule, except on horseback. He merely observed, quietly, politely, usually answering inquiries with a smile. And on his way home again, if he thought African- and other hyphenated Americans had identity problems, he had only to look around him on the boat to see how much of the world was in flux. The page of the ship's manifest that included James Winkfield also listed a Slovak family of six, who said they were from Hungary, as did many Slovaks, although Hungary had been subsumed by the Austro-Hungarian Empire; three Bohemians, who couldn't figure out if they were from Bohemia or Austria or Hungary or Croatia or Germany and so named all those places; a twenty-year-old tailor and his wife, who thought they were from either Silesia or Austria; a middle-aged merchant and his wife, who for "Race or People" said "Hebrew" and who knew they were from Austria; and five Germans who knew they were from Germany.

When Jimmy got back to Lexington, he saw once again that there wasn't much reason to stay. With the better treatment and all the chances to make money in Russia, it was an easy choice to return for the 1906 season. But it could not have been such an easy choice for Edna Winkfield. It would take enormous courage for a twenty-five-year-old black girl whose life had been bound by racism and who had hardly ever left Lexington—indeed, it would require great courage for almost any young American woman—to sail for Russia. She did, though, and it was an act of transformation and courage equal to her husband's relocation. Her immediate reward was to see her husband become, at last, a major star not only in Poland but in Russia itself—the horse-crazy land of the czars.

By then, Lazareff was less interested in Warsaw and concentrating on Moscow and St. Petersburg. His best horses would go to Moscow, and his best jockey would go with them. Wink did not capture Russia's biggest single stakes in 1906, but he did extremely well overall. With his Lexington bride to share in his experiences, he won more than a third of his starts (69 of 196) and became the number-one jockey in Russia proper for the first time. Forced out of American racing by racism, the sport's financial crisis, and the Madden boycott, Jimmy Winkfield had simply refused to lose. Instead, he pulled off an amazing, almost unimaginable turnaround: unable to become America's national champion, he became imperial Russia's national champion.

In December, Edna took the train down to Cuxhaven and boarded the steamer *Kaiserin Augusta Victoria* for home, to see their families and to take care of the house on East Third Street. But now she was unstoppable. She returned the next spring, one of the very few Lexington girls who was a world traveler—and suddenly a mother as well. In Moscow, Edna and Jimmy decided to adopt a newborn Russian girl, but the circumstances would remain unclear. Who was the mother? Who was the father? It was the first in a series of mysteries in Wink's life as a husband and father. They named their new baby girl Ida.

By now, the war with Japan was finally over, the attempted revolution was in hiatus, Russian racing was back to a full schedule—and

Wink could look forward to family life, at least between races. Daughter Ida certainly didn't slow him down, as the first-time father headed into one of his best seasons ever. On June 24, 1907, great pillars of dust blinded the drivers as their carriages stretched along the unpaved highway from St. Petersburg down through the Tverskaya District to the gates of Moscow. Trolley cars shuttled the city's tens of thousands of horseplayers to the cavernous, high-columned Hippodrome, the very sight of which had floored Wink when he entered it for the first time three years earlier. By midafter-noon, three of the czar's orchestras were blasting military music across the Members' Pavilion. Many of the czar's most privileged aristocrats had gathered there, led by his generals, owners of stud farms, and sportsmen from across the Empire—not to mention their wives, resplendent in impossibly lavish gowns that set their loges, or private boxes, aglow. What bloody war with Japan? What near revolution?

The Russian multitudes peered down on the black American about to contest the second-biggest feature of the day, the Moscow edition—the most important edition—of the Emperor's Prize. The distance was four versts, or about 2.7 miles, a verst being two-thirds of a mile. In America, the classic early-nineteenth-century distance of four miles had been whittled down to well under two miles, so four versts was a grueling test for any American jockey. But Wink was already used to it. The starter sprang the barrier—the Russians called it "the ribbon"—and the others took off. Wink switched immediately to his strategy for long races. He saved his mount, yet another son of Galtee More, then drove by the others, knocking them off one by one, to win the marathon in just under five minutes. With that, the American champion led the colt in front of the stands, with Lazareff at their side, to great waves of applause roaring through the Hippo-drome. An orchestra played "God Save the Czar" three times—"The people's hymn," a reporter called it, though it would be a full decade before Jimmy Winkfield—and all Russia—would learn that a "peo-ple's hymn" could mean something very different.

An hour brought Winkfield to another moment of a lifetime,

grander than the one before: yet another shot at the Moscow, or All-Russian, Derby, in which he had found himself in a dead heat for second three years earlier. This year's was worth about $21,300. In America it was topped only by the $26,600 Futurity, but in ceremony and prestige, it was in a world of its own. The Russian Derby distance was two versts and 144 *sagenes*—about a mile and a half. With eight others, Wink promenaded the three-year-old Count before the dazzling Members' Pavilion, then to the post. One false start—and they were off. Wink restrained his mount even more than he had in the Emperor's Prize, pulling the three-year-old Count all around the backside. At last, as he entered the long Hippodrome stretch, he began eliminating the others, and—like old Ike Murphy—showed the screaming Russians what a grandstand finish was as he captured Russia's greatest race.

Once again, Czar Nicholas II was not present. In fact, he was not the great horse lover that some of his predecessors had been. Nicholas had a sizable breeding farm but only a small racing stable with about ten horses, few of much quality. He managed to win a lot anyway, because when his horse won he'd keep only 25 percent of the purse and give 75 percent to the second-place finisher. That was a happy solution for a czar who did not need the money and who wanted to keep the horsemen happy, too.

"He never paid his jockeys nothin', though—maybe 4,000 rubles [$2,100 a year]," Wink said later, "so I never rode for him."

To the All-Russian Derby and the Emperor's Prize, Wink added his third Russian Oaks in that breathtaking 1907 with Edna at his side. Even with racing permitted only three days a week in Russia, and with the superior foreign jockeys allowed to ride only three times a day, Wink's record was astounding. His 82 wins from 296 starts earned him a sensational 27.7 percent win record and the number-one ranking once again.

Edna Winkfield left for home early that year, boarding the Hamburg-America Line's *Pretoria* with their five-month-old, Ida, in late August. The ship's clerk looked at her and the baby and for citizenship wrote down, "Claims USA." Wink did not follow his wife home, and Edna did not return come spring. As difficult as the continuing separation must have been for both of them, events would later show that living together had likewise become difficult, a difficulty that may have sharpened during that Russian spring and summer as Edna Winkfield coped with a new baby in a strange land far from home and family, her husband gone much of the time.

Despite an overcast sky and a morning of rain, twenty thousand Russians turned out for the 1908 All-Russian Derby. Ignoring the cool weather, a fashion reporter explained, many of the women wore white to brighten the day. Bouquets, oakwood leaves, and a rainbow of national flags decorated the Members' Pavilion tribunes. Wink cantered a colt named Galop as the seven entries paraded to the tunes of the military bands, while a couple of other vibrations from halfway around the world reminded Wink of home. Aboard Koreshok was the first welcome vibration, the newly arrived American rider Herman Radtke, second-winningest jockey in the United States a few years before and once a rider for Jack Keene's brother, G. Hamilton Keene. The second vibration was another reminder of crazy Jack, right along the rail at the Hippodrome track: an old stone stable, like the ones in Jack's limestone dreams.

It might have been a good thing Czar Nicholas didn't show up for this derby, because one of the stronger colts was daringly named Socialist. A sign of more political trouble to come, maybe, but the fast-moving Socialist was cut short this time, bumped after passing the stone stable. Wink "rated" Galop—adjusted his speed in comparison with the others—perfectly, holding the lead into the far turn, but Radtke applied the whip and drove Koreshok to Galop's tail, Wink still hand-riding. The two Yanks, one white, one black, passed the judge's tower, the Russians screaming, out of their minds. Herman pushed Koreshok to Wink's saddle, but that's all he had. Wink got Galop up to win by a large length.

The tens of thousands of Russians cheered the lone black American who couldn't get a job at home, as he accepted an unforgettable prize, a prize whose value only he would understand on a sad day in the future. It was a gold watch.

That afternoon Wink won the Breeders Stakes for three-year-olds, too—for the second year in a row. And with seventy-four wins in 286 starts in 1908, or a win record a little better than 25 percent, he remained Russia's national champion for the third straight year. Spectacular opportunities surfaced now, and when Wink's latest contract with Lazareff was up, he signed with another power on the turf. This was the Polish prince Stanislaw Lubomirski, one of the three brothers who had earlier hired the Yanks Cash Sloan, Tony Hamilton, and Johnny Hoar.

So 1909 found Winkfield still straddling two countries. In Russia, he won nearly a third of his 156 starts—among them his third Breeders Stakes for three-year-olds at Moscow and his second Empress Stakes at St. Petersburg—and in Warsaw, nearly a fifth of fifty-nine races for a sensational 27 percent overall win record. And with his new prince, Wink was about to discover yet another world, one in which he would wind up battling many of the world's most celebrated jockeys, including his old American rivals, even diamond-chested Winnie.

First, though, in late 1909, he headed home to Kentucky, sailing this time from the French port of LeHavre on the beautiful *Lorraine*. For passenger James Winkfield, under both "Nationality" and "Race or People," the ship's clerk wrote:

"USA Citizen African."

Married or single?

"Married," Wink told him.

Nearest relative or friend? "Nobody."

Home again in Lexington, Winkfield found a few bright spots on the racing scene. His old neighbor, Marshall Lilly, had come up with a horse just as great as his exercise rider. Between Marshall's workouts—at once soothing and inspiring—this marvelous animal, named Colin, won fifteen of fifteen in 1907 and 1908 and a century later would still be considered one of the best ever. A new black jockey had turned up, too, out of Raceland, Louisiana. Jimmy Lee looked even better than Winkfield did at his start. Until 1907, only Monk Overton and the English star Fred Archer had ever won six of six races in one day, but nobody in the world had ever done it when there were only six races on the card. Then, on one June afternoon at Churchill Downs, every race you could have seen, all six of them, were won by Jimmy Lee. Indeed, Jimmy Lee, rather than Jimmy Winkfield, might have become the last of the great black jockeys if he had not disappeared so fast, even as the industry itself was collapsing financially and the other black jockeys were disappearing from the record books. Lee's 1908 Travers win at Saratoga remains the last highest-level American stakes race to be won by a black jockey.

Two final blows had struck the black jockeys just before Wink arrived home for the third time. In 1908, as a little black athlete was again impressing the masses in Moscow, a bigger one, Jack Johnson, clobbered the white Tommy Burns for the world boxing title in Sydney, Australia. You didn't have to be a Wright brother to see that a black man towering over all others in boxing also spelled trouble for the very few black athletes in the one arena where they had once been welcome, the racetrack. As Winkfield would see, though, it would be a couple more years before white America would really respond to Johnson.

The second blow was an attack on Winkfield's entire sport in America, or what was left of it. Thanks to powerful antigambling forces pressuring state and local governments, American racetracks had virtually disappeared by 1908, their number falling from 314 to a mere twenty-five. Then Governor Charles Evans Hughes, who would later become secretary of state and then chief justice of the Supreme Court, backed a draconian bill to halt gambling at the races in New York State. Without betting, of course, there would be no races. The bill passed, making it illegal for anybody to quote odds openly, solicit bets, or record bets in a fixed place. Driving both bookmakers and bettors off the tracks, it brought disaster to the 1908, 1909, and 1910 seasons at the tracks around the Big Apple.

Finally, the New York City tracks shut down completely in 1911 and 1912. These were by far the largest racing operations in the country, the home of the biggest stable owners and the industry's biggest job market. It drove almost all of the remaining top owners, trainers, and jockeys to Europe or England. And, as Winkfield would also witness, when America's top sport did make a comeback in America, it would be missing the athlete who had helped launch it: the soon-to-be-extinct black jockey.

On a February day in 1910 came trouble of a domestic sort. Jimmy and Edna had a monumental fight, and he stormed out of the house on East Third Street. They had not been getting along over the past two months since his return, according to his sister Maggie. Just before the row, he told Maymie Offutt, a close friend of the couple, that he was leaving Edna for good. And it wasn't the first time he'd said it. "When I would be around where he was," Maymie said, "he would speak of going away from her, saying he wasn't coming back anymore." She said he had apparently gotten tired of Edna.

Maria Outen, another close friend, who was at the house just after the blowup, testified that the Winkfields had no children, which left the status of three-year-old Ida a mystery. And Maria hinted at something bigger: "They had a fuss there, and after he left he said he never intended to make this country his home again." Perhaps he put it the way Maria said, and perhaps he didn't: it would have been out of character for this Kentucky lover, this lifelong patriot. But it was not only about Edna now. The other issues—the sport's death agonies, the moribund job market, the racism that had destroyed the black jockeys and that Jack Johnson had brought to the surface again with his victory—were all pieces of a larger picture. In the end, it was simply about whether to stay or to go back—whether to get a job as a mere stable hand in the States and make a life with Edna and three-year-old Ida or to continue a life of achievement and recognition in Russia.

A couple of months after he slammed the door on Edna, Jimmy Winkfield was back in the saddle for one of the grandest races in western Europe, though he had not heard the last from his wife.

Chapter Nine

JAMES
AND
ALEXANDRA

T hings were changing once again for Jimmy Winkfield. No longer content with cleaning up in Russia and Warsaw, his Polish prince of the moment was pointing him toward the prestigious races of western Europe.

The other big change was Alexandra Yalovicina, an ample, handsome Muscovite, a good eight inches taller than James. She was about nineteen, and he was thirty and a black man in an all-white society. What her family thought was not recorded, but this was not going to be critical for a woman following her heart, and in Russia a young woman of nineteen was a woman.

Her family were not aristocrats, but they were military, which was as good or even better in this czar's Russia, where many of the highest-ranking regular officers were members of the court circle. They were also passionate horsemen who staged their own racing programs, especially at the czar's own track at Tsarskoye Selo, outside St. Petersburg, and who, of course, knew about the great jockey Winkfield. And when he had the time, Wink himself freelanced for the military, at one point riding and training horses for the Poliakoff stud farm, which bred horses for the czar's army. So it's likely that James and Alexandra met at a racetrack, where, indeed, he had met almost everybody he ever knew.

Jimmy Winkfield was at the top of his riding form at the Moscow Central Hippodrome when he met Alexandra. It was about 1910. Happily, she could ride. She sat a horse with a military bearing that had to delight the professional jockey. From an old picture, we know that on one wintry day Jimmy saw her astride a very dark horse, the mount's ears pricked because he understood very well that this little man knew horses. But for once the magnificence of the horse dissolved, as Jimmy focused on the rider. In an officer's hat and overcoat, whip in hand, well horsed, she hypnotized him. And she would soon transform him.

As it happened, Count Leo Tolstoy was eighty-two at the time and determined to escape the constant guilt he had felt living on his aristocratic estate while owning several others in the Volga Steppes. He wanted to die in solitude as a devotee of his own form of ascetic, pacifist Christianity, which rejected violence, the legitimacy of the church and state, and private property, and which already had become an established sect called Tolstoyism. But as everyone knew, the famous Leo Tolstoy had earlier been supportive of both state violence, as an artillery officer in the Crimean War, and of the lavishly expensive sport of horse racing.

Count Tolstoy could size up a steeplechase mare like a breeder, and after his novel *War and Peace* won international acclaim, he produced, in the almost equally successful novel *Anna Karenina*, one of literature's most memorable scenes of the sport—a military steeplechase at Tsarskoye Selo. Tolstoy gives the thrilling race no less than six pages. Jimmy's horse-loving girlfriend certainly must have read *Anna Karenina*, for it was Russia's most celebrated love story.

Like Alexandra's, Anna's love, Alexei, is a jockey—a steeplechase rider in the military. One day at Tsarskoye Selo came the

cry: "Mount!" Alexei Vronsky swung into his saddle aboard a beautiful dark bay, Frou-Frou, and awaited the start, a three-mile contest
with seventeen entries. It began with a problem that Wink knew
only too well. Tolstoy: "Three times the riders got into line but each
time some horse made a false start and they had to begin again. The
starter, Colonel Sestrin, was beginning to get impatient but at last,
at the fourth try, he shouted 'Off!'—and the race began.

"Every eye, every field-glass was turned on the parti-coloured
little group of riders while they were getting into line.

" 'They're off! There they go!' was heard on all sides after the
hush of expectation."

At the first jump, over a dammed-up stream, another mare fell
in front of Alexei Vronsky's mount just as she took flight. "Frou-
Frou, like a cat falling, made an effort of legs and back while in the
air and, clearing the other mare, sped on.

" 'Oh, you beauty!' thought Vronsky."

Frou-Frou was still in the lead at the most difficult jump, an "Irish
bank"—"an embankment with brushwood on top and a ditch on the
other side," which Frou-Frou could not see. "Giving a thrust from the
ground, she surrendered herself to the impetus of the leap, which carried her far beyond the ditch. Then, in the same rhythm, without effort and without changing feet, Frou-Frou continued her gallop.

" 'Bravo, Vronsky!' "

But at the last obstacle, a yard and a half water jump, which
Frou-Frou "cleared as if she did not notice it, flying over like a bird,"
Vronsky made a terrible mistake, dropping back into his saddle in-
stead of keeping up with Frou-Frou's pace.

"All at once his position had shifted and he knew that something horrible had happened. . . . Vronsky was touching the ground
with one foot and his mare was sinking on that foot. He had
scarcely time to free his leg before she fell on one side, gasping
painfully and making vain efforts of her slender, sweat-soaked neck
to rise, and began fluttering on the ground at his feet like a
wounded bird. Vronsky's clumsy movement had broken her back."

Perhaps it reminded Alexandra of a story James had told her
about a three-year-old named McChesney.

Under Alexandra's tutelage, Jimmy Winkfield, richer and more famous than the vast majority of Russians and Americans, began to look the part. One day, Moscow's new couple—James and Alexandra—went to a photographer's studio, and James effortlessly dominated the portrait with his irresistible new charm. He had always been a natty dresser, but now, thin and thirty-something, he exuded a prosperous insouciance in a neat wool suit, tie, and high-collared white shirt with French cuffs.

There was only the faintest trace of the weakening right eye. Standing, Jimmy folded his arms against the back of Alexandra's tall chair, his legs crossed casually like a dancer's, one powerful hand displaying a cigar in fingers that resembled thick bolts from working bridle bits for fifteen years. Alexandra reflected their mutual love and confidence, a quiet smile on her generous lips as she sat, as demurely as she could manage, in a white-collared, satiny dress, her large hands folded in her lap.

Wink expanded into western Europe in that 1910 season. He still rode in Russia (winning five of his nine Russian starts and in the money all nine times!), but during the late spring and summer he was based with Lubomirski in Vienna, Austria. Crossing the border into Germany and Hungary, he was often reunited now with top American jocks, all in flight from racing's problems at home, and he also encountered world-renowned riders from England, Australia, and France. Their gatherings in Europe on the eve of the First World War made this one of the most illustrious eras in sporting history.

Wink's new employer, Prince Stanislaw Lubomirski, teamed him with a superb trainer, Antoni Zasepa, who had worked in Poland with the American jockeys Tony Hamilton and Johnny Hoar. Antoni and Wink clicked. Zasepa adopted the American emphasis on intense preparation, and Wink exercised both his eye for horseflesh and his knack for making minor adjustments to produce major race horses. A Polish writer described the team this way:

> Zasepa . . . knew the horses in his care very well and was able to prepare them better than anyone for the upcoming

race. Jockey Winkfield was not only a terrific tactician and technician, but he also had a rare talent: he always really knew "what was in the horse" and how good the horse was.

In their first year together, Winkfield and Zasepa conquered the prestigious October Mares Race and the Prix Von Marchfeld, both at Vienna. And Wink suddenly found himself in the company of many former colleagues from home, among them Walter Miller, Joe Notter, Willie Shaw, and Mickey Miles, all white, of course, and the ex-jockey Fred "The Flying Dutchman" Taral, who had switched to training in Germany. With bushy eyebrows arched over laughing eyes, Fred was a comforting sight for Wink. Taral had gone head-to-head with all of Wink's black idols in the 1890s, but he'd always been friendly with them. With the Dutchman around, all the jocks, white and black, got along.

One season Fred went back home to recruit some good jockeys for Germany, only to find there weren't any left. Racing was about to be shut down completely in the Big Apple, and it was lying prostrate all over puritanical America. Taral contrasted the scene with Europe:

> The very best days of racing in the United States were never like conditions as they are in Europe today. The sport is universally popular. There are no spectacular betting men like "Pittsburgh Phil" [real name: George Smith] or men of that type. Everybody bets a little.

Wink and the other Yanks enjoyed seeing one another again. Wink was a big surprise to the Germans, since they had virtually no black compatriots, and the journalists never failed to identify him as black, or as the Germans usually put it, *farbige*, or "colored." But it was less threatening to be identified as black in Europe than in America, where the mere fact of being black could be dangerous. And there was news in 1910 that things were about to get worse at home. On the Fourth of July, of all days, boxer Jack Johnson was back, and this time he destroyed the great white hope Jim Jeffries. The country erupted, the headlines in Portland's *Sunday Oregonian* summing it up: CRUSHING DEFEAT OF WHITE HOPE, BLACK PRO-CLAIMED CHAMPION, RACE RIOTS BREAK OUT AFTER FIGHT. Other headlines across America:

THREE KILLED IN VIDALIA (Georgia) . . . OMAHA NEGRO
KILLED . . . TWO NEGROES SLAIN . . . BLACKS SHOOT UP TOWN
. . . HOUSTON MAN KILLS NEGRO . . . NEGRO SHOOTS WHITE
MAN . . . NEGRO HURT IN PHILADELPHIA . . . OUTBREAKS IN
NEW ORLEANS . . . POLICE CLUB RIOTING NEGROES . . . MOB
BEATS NEGROES IN MACON . . . 70 ARRESTED IN BALTIMORE

Jack Johnson and Jimmy Winkfield were very similar yet very different. Both were famous—one at home, one abroad—though Johnson was much more so. Both were athletes. Both were black men who had reached the peaks of their sports. Johnson had a white wife, and Jimmy a white girlfriend (and a black wife back home). On the other hand, they were also not alike. Johnson weighed twice as much as Wink and was more than a foot taller. The biggest difference was in their personalities. Johnson was known for going out on the town and "carrying on" and for driving fast cars. Wink had to get up too early in the morning for that—not that he would have done it anyway.

Word of the race riots at home reached the American jockeys by the time they gathered in the paddock at the great German spa Baden-Baden. On August 27, Jimmy Winkfield was warmly applauded along with the five white boys as they paraded to the post in the legendary Grosse Preis von Baden. A world away from the riots back home, Baden-Baden was nestled in a steep valley of the Black Forest, a few miles from the French border. The town was immensely proud of its crowd for the annual race, including all manner of European royalty, literally following in the footsteps of the spa's previous patrons, Queen Victoria and Czar Alexander I, artists and writers, including the now repentant Count Tolstoy, and assorted American heirs and capitalists on holiday. These, actually, were Wink's kind of people. From his Kentucky Derby moments in the sun, from performing for the elite from Saratoga to St. Petersburg, the young man from Chilesburg was simply used to it: he felt comfortable with these people.

In town he could saunter by the Friedrichsbad, where men and women still bathed naked together, something that wasn't happening in Chilesburg; the fabled casino, where not too long ago the ladies painted on the ceiling had looked down on Fyodor Dostoyevsky losing his money; and the Trinkhalle, where second-century Roman occupiers had their horses sip the natural hot sulfur springs to cure their rheumatism. Things changed, but slowly, in the little state of Baden-Württemberg—the visiting Mark Twain said that in these baths you could lose track of time after ten minutes and lose track of the world after twenty.

But when Winkfield arrived, Baden-Württemberg was at last in the final few years of its own, recognized royalty. Germany, of course, had its great king, its emperor, Kaiser Wilhelm II, but Baden-Württemberg had its own "little king," as he was known by the Germans. This was Grand Duke Frederick II, who would abdicate at the end of World War I in favor of a popularly elected state legislature, but not before Wink got a very good look at him. Wink had never witnessed anything like the little king's arrival with his little queen, the grand duchess, in their splendid carriage, and their operatic procession up to the royal loge. What American could sparkle like the little king? If any Yank could, it would have been Wink's old rival, the diamond-decorated Winnie O'Connor.

And now Wink's heart leapt, just as it had when he ran into Tony Hamilton six years earlier. Suddenly, here was Winnie, too, grabbing the little king's attention as he won the first race of the day, in which Wink did not ride. And Winnie wasn't through yet.

O'Connor had won this Grand Prix three years earlier, with the grand duke watching, and after that race, the little king had jokingly asked him how much fine Württemberg beer he had been drinking. If he had asked that on this day, the answer would have been a lot, probably, because Winnie had ballooned to 130 pounds, 25 pounds heavier than Wink. Heavy as he was, though, O'Connor had designs on a repeat in the Grosse Preis. He was not going to be stopped again by the black jockey who had beaten him in the Kentucky Derby. After all, what nicer trinket could be added to Winnie's laurels than a second Grosse Preis and the 100,000-mark, or $25,000, purse, about equivalent to the richest American event that season, the Futurity at Saratoga. And Winnie had a lot of help: his trainer was Fred Taral. The other four jocks Wink was up against were among the world's best, too, including England's Joe Childs and Australia's Frank Bullock, both multiple winners of the great English classics.

Yet they were all upstaged—little king, nobility, aristocrats, wealthy tourists, renowned jockeys, all mere earthlings—by a visitor from another world. It was a gigantic airship that materialized in the bright sky above the trees by the paddock. As the fans came to, they realized this vision was the work of Baden-Württemberg's crazy old count, who lived at Friedrichshafen down on Lake Constance, on the Swiss border. The seventy-two-year-old fool had stashed a team of mad engineers in his barn to perfect his folly and test it over the lake, where it couldn't kill too many people. The locals had a great old time making fun of the whole bunch of them.

The fool's name was Count Ferdinand von Zeppelin.

At twenty-five, von Zeppelin had sailed to America during the Civil War, fought with the Union in the Battle of the Potomac, then joined an expedition to the headwaters of the Mississippi. On the way, he stopped in Minnesota and made his first ascent in a balloon. Eureka! Over the next few decades, he explored the intoxicating possibilities of lighter-than-air flight and tested his first airship in 1900, covering nearly four miles in seventeen minutes. But what Jimmy Winkfield saw on that clear August day was even more important, for it was now, in 1910, that Count von Zeppelin began offering, for the first time in history, commercial airship travel. The Grosse Preis von Baden, arguably the most prestigious horse race on the Continent, was the perfect place to promote this phenomenal new travel by airship, or, as everybody in Germany was already calling it, by "Zeppelin-Ballon."

With his weak stomach for sea travel, Winkfield might have wondered: could they get this thing to fly to New York? Would he still throw up? A lot of fans, though, were worried about something more important—their lives. So-called "non-rigid" airships could become deformed or fold in on themselves in less than perfect weather. And on the count's first test flight, his ship had bent in several places. Within another four years, thirteen zeppelins would have crashed. But this was a crystal day, and the count's latest Zeppelin-Ballon had an innovative rigid frame made of aluminum. Said one relieved witness:

> The majestic ship descended from the hills beyond the racetrack and passed gently over the poplars near the paddock. It was greeted with a loud hurrah and waving of handkerchiefs.

Filling the sky over Winkfield's head, the airship was more than 400 feet long, lifted by more than 400,000 cubic feet of hydrogen gas, and driven by two Daimler engines with rotating propellers. We have no record of what Winkfield—or, for the matter, the thoroughbreds in the paddock—thought of this monster, but the count's employees were no longer the laughingstock of Baden-Württtenberg. Before long, they would be serving wine and sandwiches to twenty-four passengers per ship on zeppelin flights between major German cities.

Though transatlantic airship travel was still a decade away, the zeppelin would soon be capable of one-thousand-mile flights and would be aggressively promoted as a contribution to international travel and peace, which saddened its elderly German inventor. He thought of it as a bomber, which indeed it would be in World War I. The count would still be alive, though barely, when the most famous zeppelin, the *Hindenburg*, burst into flames and crashed at Lakehurst, New Jersey, in 1937, killing thirty-six people. Von Zeppelin would die in 1938, in his one hundredth year. And the otherworldly airship above Jimmy Winkfield's 1910 Grosse Preis von Baden would turn out to be the great-granddaddy of the Goodyear blimps that would hover over America's most prestigious sports events in the future. As they said in vaudeville, how could a horse race top that?

The 1910 Grosse Preis attracted an international field of six stunning horses. Three were German: one of Kaiser Wilhelm's colts, piloted by Frank Bullock, and two Taral-trained horses, under Joe Childs and Winnie O'Connor. Two entries were Austrian, two French, and one—Wink's—Polish.

They got a fast start in the mile and a half, with one of the French colts, Carlopolis, leading, Wink's Ksiaze-Pan holding second to the final turn, where Carlopolis ran out of gas. There wasn't much to it. Wink charged down the stretch unchallenged to win by an easy length and a half. Winnie was dead last.

Prince Lubomirski beamed as he accepted the beautiful gold cup from the grand duke himself. If Wink had never seen anything quite like this little king of Baden-Württemberg, the little king and all his Germans had rarely seen anything like this black jockey. Decades later, a German history of the ancient Grosse Preis von Baden, inaugurated in 1886, would pause to note: "The 1910 race was not without a touch of the *Exotik*, with the colored jockey Winkfield winning the prize."

What no one knew was that the world's fate was being vaguely conceived in Vienna, where a young Austrian named Adolf Hitler resided at the moment, hard by the railroad tracks and the Northwest Station, and where Wink was also based. Hitler had been living in Vienna since 1908 and would stay into 1913; Winkfield would be based in Vienna during the five-month-long racing seasons of 1910, 1911, and 1912.

Unlike Hitler, the thirty-year-old black jockey with the profitable habit of finishing in the money made the news occasionally in Vienna—in late October of 1910 he had been second behind the former American but now English star Danny Maher in the Austria

Prize Stakes. The twenty-one-year-old wallpaper hanger did not make the news. Rejected by the Academy of Fine Arts, Hitler was hawking his watercolors as postcards or pictures for frame makers' displays—and hanging that wallpaper. Like Jimmy Winkfield's St. Petersburg, his Vienna was a fast-growing imperial capital of some 2 million people, but Wink's work did not allow him much time to take in either the sights that young Hitler was painting—the street scenes and monumental government buildings—or Vienna's great circular artery, Ring Boulevard, with its famous cafés.

Winkfield's workplace was the Freudenau Race Course, on the banks of Vienna's other great artery, the Danube. It was certainly an appropriate spot for Wink. Flowing east—the only major river in Europe to do so—the blue Danube traced both his recent past, from Baden-Württemberg's Black Forest all the way across southern Germany to Vienna, and hinted at his future beyond Hungary and Romania to the Black Sea. Freudenau was one of the Danube's countless lovely stops, the end of the tree-lined Hauptallée on the west side of Vienna, which before and after the races would be filled with the scions of Vienna's two Rothschild branches—those of Albert and Nathaniel—the first Rothschilds Wink would be bumping into.

Wink was not the only American influence on Austrian racing. For the past fifteen years, American stable owners and trainers had been introducing doping to England and the Continent. At last, in 1910, the year Wink started at Freudenau, an Austrian, a Professor Fraenkel, responded to the American threat by inventing the single most important weapon against doping: the saliva test.

Wink's showing in the 1910 Austrian derby out at Freudenau had been ghastly. When he finally came home from somewhere down the Danube to end up sixth out of seven horses, it may have ruined the lives, or at least the weekends, of bettors who had put the family beer money on Wink and his colt, Kosarz. A lot of them probably needed to see Vienna's most famous doctor, for Jimmy Winkfield and Adolf Hitler's Vienna was also Sigmund Freud's Vienna. Indeed, they would have done well to put up a sign at the betting windows: "If your problem is Freuduenau, see Freud." Upon entering Freud's thickly furnished, Victorian-style parlor, the piece of furniture one noticed first was the couch. Covered with a throw resembling a Persian rug, it was raised at the left end so that you didn't lie in it, but rather sat, while stretching out your legs and explaining to Dr. Freud just why—for example—you did not instead bet the family savings on the brilliant three-year-old Rascal, who hit the wire more than ten lengths ahead of Wink.

Unless Winkfield kept the story to himself, he never plopped his own 105 pounds on that couch. If he had, given everything he was up against, the world's only great black jockey probably would have given the world's first psychoanalyst a heart attack. But yet another Viennese resident of Wink's day did go see the Freudians, as the doctor and his disciples were called. This was the slippery Leon Trotsky, who had escaped the czar's Arctic prison even before he got there. When Trotsky and his thirteen fellow convicts were given a rest stop at the small town of Berezov, Trotsky had faked an attack of sciatica and was allowed to remain behind. Assisted by a local peasant, he slipped out of town. Trotsky hiked for days, nearly five hundred miles across snowy expanses, until Siberian tribesmen provided him with a deer and a sleigh. In the Ural Mountains, he posed as a member of a polar expedition and eventually was given a horse, which he rode to the nearest railroad station. It was almost as formidable a trek as one that Jimmy Winkfield would later have to make.

In Vienna, where Trotsky established a little socialist newspaper, his assistant had a nervous breakdown and went to Freud's disciple Alfred Adler for psychoanalysis. Trotsky himself began going to the Freudians' meetings, but he apparently never met Freud. And neither met the watercolorist.

The world's only great black jockey and the future führer of Germany's Third Reich lived in even more separated Viennese worlds. Hitler was broke. Winkfield was making money right and left. For instance, on August 4, 1910, at Kottingbrunn, Austria, having already scored two firsts and a second on Lubomirski's Ksiaze Pan, Wink brought him in second again, in a stakes race worth

23,000 kronen. The next day, back in Vienna, a destitute Hitler told police that a partner had stolen his watercolor *Parliament*, which he claimed was worth 50 kronen, or more than two months of his rent in a city men's hostel.

When Winkfield won the Grosse Preis at fabulous Baden-Baden later that month, Hitler could only read about it, though the non-racetracker Hitler would have been more interested in the fly-by of the Zeppelin-Ballon. It horrified him. Lighter-than-air flight was unnatural, he would insist, pointing out that nature had not equipped a single bird with a bladder. And just as Wink began to think of the even richer German Derby, an Austrian court ruled that Hitler—parentless like Winkfield—had to give his entire orphan's allowance of 25 kronen a month to his minor sister Paula, because Adolf had at least some income.

In Freudenau's better boxes and stables—where most of the European owners and trainers spoke English—Winkfield could not have missed the buzz of what one newspaper called "anthropological politics." This was the constant theorizing not about the horse races but about the human races and their proper roles in the world. It was the talk of Vienna and, for that matter, much of Europe. Wink himself was Exhibit A—such an object of curiosity that, as he would later recall, many wanted to touch him—though he confounded the fashionable theories by outthinking the white jockeys and trainers and winning so often. One constant theme of the Viennese chatter was anti-Semitism. While Wink casually talked horses with his Jewish baron, Hitler devoured the anti-Jewish screeds of the Pan German movement, especially in its newspaper *Alldeutsches Tagblatt*, and the writings of its "philosophers," whose messages occasionally touched on Winkfield's world. The Pan German press frequently quoted the English-born Austrian resident Houston Stewart Chamberlain, who proposed "selective breeding":

Once you have recognized the miracles selection can achieve, how a race horse or a dachshund or an "exuber-

ant" chrysanthemum is gradually bred by carefully eliminating all inferior elements, then you will also recognize the
efficiency of the same phenomenon in the human race.

A no more intelligent but even more influential "intellectual,"
Otto Weininger, who had killed himself in 1903, still guided the
thoughts of young Hitler and other Pan German zealots. Writing
of "Negroes" and "Mongols," Weininger said that "anthropologi-
cally the Jews seem to be somehow related to both" and that none of
them, nor women either, should be "emancipated." Of course,
Hitler himself had no hope for black people becoming part of any
German nation, not that there were many black people around.
Claiming he was shocked that his Pan German friends thought
they could "Germanize" the Austrian Slavs, he said, "Germanization can only be applied to soil and never to people." His friends
thought Germanization simply meant convincing or forcing others
to accept the German language, Hitler said. "Yet it was a scarcely
conceivable fallacy of thought to believe that a Negro or a Chinese, let us say, will turn into a German because he learns German
and is willing to speak the German language and perhaps even give
his vote to a German political party. That was a *de*-Germanization
and the beginning of a bastardization and a destruction of the Ger-
manic element."

How the Pan German horror in Winkfield's Vienna—the open
attacks on Jews; the adulation of the recently deceased anti-Se-
mitic mayor and Hitler idol Karl Lueger; the race riots and attacks
on Vienna's Czechs; the Pan Germans' adoption of a political em-
blem, the ancient swastika; and the unseen reading and writing of
the watercolorist—how all this and parallel developments in Germany would end no one could know. But Winkfield listened to the
voices of Vienna—he had picked up some German over those three
long racing seasons, and the epithets, insults, and anger often
needed no translation anyway, or they got one from Wink's friends.
They could also be heard occasionally in the English that was com-

mon at Freudenau. As an outside observer—even as a victim—
Wink would have a better understanding of the ending than most
when it came.

At the close of Jimmy's 1910 season in Austria-Hungary and
Germany, Alexandra welcomed him back to Moscow for the winter. Along with the rest of Russia, she must have noted the dramatic
passing of Count Tolstoy on October 28. Still intent on dying in
solitude, the old man had left his wife and his estate and boarded a
train—to where, nobody would ever be certain. A few days later, the
author of *Anna Karenina* contracted pneumonia and died at a railroad station in the town of Astapovo. He was survived by a thousand fictional characters for readers to keep track of, but it was Tolstoy's Anna, with her steeplechase jockey/lover, who must have
resonated with Alexandra.

The two triangles, or troikas, if you will, in which Alexandra
and Anna were caught were hardly parallel. There is no record at
all, for example, of whether Alexandra knew about Edna, or Edna
about her. And in the Tolstoy story, it was Anna who was married
and her husband who did not know. So to put it mildly, there were
many differing details in the two tortured triangles, and yet both—
the lone Alexandra, her James, and Edna Winkfield on the one
hand, and the lone Alexei Vronsky, his Anna, and her husband on
the other—were tales of love and deceit—yes, deceit almost certainly by Jimmy as well—and fraught with the cruelest pain,
whether it was suffered now or delayed. Alexandra may have felt the
stab yet again when she read of the secret Anna was keeping from
her gentleman jockey. Tolstoy:

" 'Shall I tell him or not tell him?' she thought, looking into
his calm, caressing eyes. 'He is so happy, so full of his races, that he
would not understand properly, would not understand all the gravity of it for us.' "

Alexei Vronsky pleaded with Anna to tell him:

" 'I can see something has happened. Do you suppose I could
have a moment's peace, knowing that you have some trouble I am
not sharing? Tell me, for God's sake!' he repeated imploringly.

" 'Yes, I should never forgive him if he did not realize all the gravity of it. Better not to say anything. Why put him to the test?' she thought, still staring at him in the same way and feeling his hand which held the leaf trembling more and more.

" 'For God's sake!' he repeated, taking her hand.

" 'Shall I?'

" 'Yes, yes, yes . . .'

" 'I am with child,' she whispered slowly."

On January 4, 1911, in Moscow, Alexandra gave James a son. As James was still married to Edna, he presumably had not married Alexandra as well. They named the boy George Winkfield, after both Jimmy's older brother and a much-loved nephew, Gus's son. At least Jimmy would have a few months in Moscow during George's first spring, and with racing scheduled only three days a week in Russia, he would have plenty of time off for Alexandra and George. Maybe it was his happy, if unconventional, family life that helped him to a sensational record that season: twenty-six starts, with nine firsts, eight seconds, and four thirds.

By summer he was based in Vienna again but constantly riding the rails. He was the star of Russia one moment, Austria the next, then Hungary and Germany. He won the Russian Oaks at Moscow (for the fourth time), the Austrian Oaks at Vienna, and the Hungarian St. Leger at Budapest, which was in its golden age of racing, luring the world's best riders.

On another sortie across the border into Germany, Wink set out to top his Grosse Preis von Baden, one of the highlights of his life, but what he got was one of the strangest receptions of his life. It happened on June 25, 1911, at Hamburg, home of the premier fixture on this nation's racing calendar, the German Derby. Among the swells on hand were Baron Gustav von Springer, known in the press as *der reichste Mann der Donaumonarchie* (the richest man in the Dual Monarchy of Austria-Hungary), and Prince Thurn-and-Taxis, who was perhaps *der reichste Mann im Deutschland*, his family's control of European postal systems dating back to the Middle

Ages. And the equine swells included two colts from Kaiser Wilhelm II's government-run stud, Graditz.

But when Wink joined the procession of horses and riders to the starting line, thousands in the stands saw something they had never seen before: a black man. Indeed, millions of other Germans across the country had never seen a black man. Of course it was hardly the first time that, merely by showing up, Wink had educated northern Europeans; on this afternoon, however, thousands also burst into laughter, which surely confused him.

What they found funny was the name of his colt, Monostatos, which was also the name of the Moor in Wolfgang Amadeus Mozart's last opera, *Die Zauberflöte* (*The Magic Flute*). In that beloved work, Monostatos shows the world to confront its silly prejudices as he sings, sarcastically, "I must forgo love because a black man is ugly. . . . Dear, good moon, forgive me: a white skin has seduced me! White is beautiful, I must kiss her."

In fact, it wasn't the first time German racing fans had seen the four-legged Monostatos, who was owned by one A. von Schmeider. He was a strong colt, and last season, Winnie O'Connor up, he had won the race just before Wink's Grosse Preis von Baden. It wasn't the least bit unusual, either, to name a horse after an opera character. Right here in the parade to the post was Chilperic, namesake of a figure in Wagner's *Der Ring des Nibelungen* and owned by the plutocrat von Springer. Here, too, was Pantagruel, not an operatic but a literary colt, named for a gargantuan figure in the satires of François Rabelais. As Wink might have noted, this was a highly cultured crowd, not some yokels who named their horses after another bum from Chicago. What amused the fans was not the idea of naming a horse after an opera figure, but the fact that Monostatos was piloted by Monostatos. Also on that afternoon, Jimmy Winkfield found himself incorporated into European culture in another way. A Berlin reporter casually referred to him as "another Austrian professional . . . the negro Winkfield." After all, he was based in Vienna.

With *The Magic Flute* tinkling on in the happy minds of the fans, Wink prepared himself to add the 125,000-mark German

Derby to his other derby triumphs, from New Orleans to Moscow. And as the dozen riders waited for the webbed barrier to fly up, his "straw-yellow jacket," noted one writer, "stood in stark contrast to the jockey's black face." A false start—a second try—and they were off. The horde stormed past the grandstand for the first time, a colt named Mirage chased by Monostatos and Pantagruel, with Chilperic behind them. The order held past Hamburg's first turn and down the backstretch, with Mirage opening a two-length lead over Monostatos, to the Horner Bend, the turn on the side of the track facing the suburb of Horn. But as the grandstand crowd peered through their binoculars toward that final bend, they could see the flash of straw yellow advancing steadily, then taking over and leading the pack into the top of the stretch. They started screaming,

"*Der Neger gewinnt.*" "The Negro is winning."

Then, as if fired from a pistol, the reddish brown Chilperic shot toward Monostatos under the Aussie Bernard "Brownie" Carslake, a ghost of a jockey, almost a headless horseman. Nobody ever caught Brownie eating, and his swordlike nose and beady black eyes receded into a narrow bony face. He had no presence at all. What you could make out of him looked like death, and made you feel like it, too. Brownie and Chilperic grabbed the lead.

"*Der Neger* strained every fiber in his body," said a Berliner. "There was a murderous finish over the last 100 meters, neck and neck. At one moment Chilperic went in front, then Monostatos," but then bony Brownie again, back and forth, until, at the finish, it was Chilperic winning the 1911 German Derby by a length and a half!

Rising to their feet, thousands of Germans gave a thunderous ovation to both Brownie and Wink as they made their way through the crowd to weigh out. The details were carefully reported in the *Berliner Tageblatt*, the newspaper that the lonely watercolorist in Vienna and the radical Pan-Germans despised because it was edited by the brilliant Theodor Wolff, who happened to be a Jew. Wink's effort was so thrilling that years later it would make the official history of the German Derby. It could be added to his amazing series of in-the-money finishes in various derbies on two continents, from his two first-, one second-, and one third-place finish in the Kentucky Derby to this second and a third place in the next German Derby.

While under contract to his prince of Poland, Winkfield free-lanced for other stables, among them Germany's biggest, owned by Baron von Oppenheim. Famous across Europe, the baron's Schlenderham stud farm near Cologne featured renowned sires like Galtee More, brought over from Russia, and produced far more winners than Kaiser Wilhelm's government-run Graditz stud. However, the baron did have one pathetic colt with odd looks and a bulky gait—a colt Wink thought he could fix by riding him more aggressively.

"He looked like he could run if anybody ever got him goin'," Wink said.

But at first the baron wouldn't let him. He was afraid the colt was just plain talentless and that if Winkfield rode him, people would bet him anyway—"I was gettin' pretty famous over there by then"—and afterward be angry about losing their money. But Wink persisted, and soon enough Oppenheim gave in. As usual, the colt started poorly and it looked like the baron's fears would be real-ized. The colt was Oppenheim's Dolomite. It was Sunday, August 13, 1911—two months after the Derby—in Cologne, Germany. The Rhineland Breeders Stakes for two-year-olds. The bettors were right to be interested in the black jockey. He had nearly captured the derby and he had just won the Rhine Prize for all ages two days before. So why was Oppenheim worried?

"At the start, the field was 15 lengths up the track before I could get this colt movin'," Wink recalled. "Then we get to the stretch, and I give him a cluck or two, and off we go. He run so fast the others never see us. We win by eight lengths." The chart would show it was six lengths and the third colt another two behind.

So Wink had delighted yet another powerful owner. Like everyone else, the Jewish Oppenheims, of course, were unaware of what lay ahead.

In that 1911 European season, the black jockey had been spec-tacular. In addition to his Russian wins, three major stakes victories in Austria, and two in Hungary, he blitzed the German courses to capture twelve, or 40 percent, of his thirty starts. And he was listed as an assistant trainer with Zasepa, an auspicious sign for a jockey who wanted a future beyond his riding years. After all, he had a family to support, or rather, two families—Alexandra's and Edna's.

He caught another feminine eye that season at Budapest— eleven hours down the Danube, eight by rail. The black jockey was quite the star there, and a sweet little girl named Clara—she couldn't have been more than seven—couldn't take her eyes off him. What a nightmare that would turn out to be. But Wink didn't notice anything quite yet.

What a sweet, triumphant spring and summer—but not back home, where Edna was suing for divorce. Having moved out of his East Third Street house, she was living over on Race Street, named for the ancient local track. And now she formally charged that Winkfield had abandoned her sixteen months earlier—back on that day in February 1910 when he walked out. Of course, Jimmy had taken off countless times, but for work. After their marriage in 1900, he was always leaving for long periods. Edna had understood this was the gypsy way of horse racing; besides, he always brought back plenty of money. She had even spent a couple of seasons with him in Russia, but now, it seemed, he wanted to stay away forever.

Edna was granted the divorce in that summer of 1911. Winkfield made the arrangements from Europe beforehand, via wires to his lawyer. No details have surfaced about any alimony, but as incomplete Kentucky court records and later developments in Winkfield's family would indicate, Edna's property rights, claims for support, and maintenance were all settled out of court, properly, amicably, and generously—it was the way Wink did things whenever he could.

His arrangement with Alexandra was now at least partially regularized by his divorce, and later family tradition would have it that he married Alexandra, though the record of it may not have survived those turbulent times. Common-law marriages were also not unusual. Jimmy Winkfield's work record, however, would survive, albeit buried in the racing and newspaper archives of Russia, Poland, Germany, and Austria-Hungary. With his divorce final, he got back to his job. And he was still unstoppable, once again crisscrossing national borders and riding victoriously across northern Europe in 1912. He won eleven of twenty-nine in Russia and five of eight in Russian-controlled Warsaw, for a 43 percent win record. The Winkfield-Zasepa powerhouse captured the Oaks at Moscow for the fifth time, the Henckel Memorial at Vienna, and the Agricultural Ministry Stakes at Budapest.

And a new figure popped into his life, yet another Armenian petroleum tycoon, based in Russia and apparently just as rich as Mikhail Lazareff. After striking it big at his oilfields on the shores of the Black Sea, young Leon Mantacheff had begun operating his own stud farm in France, and in December 1912 he was a sensation at the famous thoroughbred auctions in Newmarket, England. Spouting money as he outbid buyers from all over the world, among them the czar's own, he bought seventeen horses for a total of 20,100 British pounds—or $107,000. It was more than two and a half times what the czar's envoys spent and more than 8 percent of the record total that Newmarket rang up that fall. "This, however, by no means represents his influence on the sales," reported Britain's *Bloodstock Breeders' Review*, noting that even Mantacheff's unsuccessful bids still pushed up the prices for other buyers. "Roughly speaking, it may be said that his presence put from 15,000 pounds to 20,000 pounds into the pockets of British breeders which they would not have got otherwise."

By late in the 1913 season, Winkfield was riding full-time for Leon Mantacheff in Russia. As the new moneybags on the scene, Mantacheff openly challenged his fellow Armenian, Mikhail Lazareff, for supremacy on the turf. "There is a fierce rivalry between the two," the *BBR* reported. "As we stated last year, Mr. Mantacheff derives his splendid wealth from oil. May his wells continue to gush and so add to his prosperity!" Mantacheff's runners earned the equivalent of 25,000 pounds in Russia that season, the British review reported. It was second only to Lazareff's winnings of 37,000 pounds.

Another Yank, Eddie Dugan, joined the boys in Moscow. It turned out he and Wink had a lot to talk about, if they ever got time. They would certainly have a lot of time—in fact, a desperate need—for each other later. They had both worked for that damn Sam Hildreth. After Wink had ridden Hildreth and his colt McChesney into the history books a decade ago, the old hick kept on rising, wound up training for August Belmont II, and hired Dugan as Belmont's main contract rider. Eddie won the 1908 and 1911 Preakness Stakes and the 1909 Belmont Stakes. Then, as American racing collapsed, Belmont let him out of his contract to ride for the Rothschilds in Germany. Now Eddie had left the Rothschilds to ride for Lazareff in Russia. In fact, he was out for a Preakness-Belmont-Derby triple crown, except his own third jewel would be the All-Russian Derby, which indeed he delivered to Lazareff in 1913.

At the end of that year, Wink's new boss was off to Newmarket again as he expanded his racing operations to include France and England. Mantacheff more than doubled his purchases of the previous December, to nearly 50,000 pounds—or more than $260,000. One of his few defeats at the auction was at the hands of the American John Sanford, of Amsterdam, New York, who outbid him for a mare.

Chapter Ten

WINK'S
WORLD WAR I

O n June 28, 1914, in Sarajevo, Bosnia, a Serbian nationalist named Gavrilo Princip shot and killed Archduke Franz Ferdinand, heir to the Austro-Hungarian throne. This would soon prove to be the first shot of World War I. On the next day, in Moscow, Jimmy Winkfield's mount Galust cantered onto the soaked track at the Hippodrome.

Wink was trying for a triple in the fabled All-Russian Derby, which he had won in 1907 and 1908. It was worth 50,000 rubles ($26,600)—much richer than that year's running of the original Derby at Epsom Downs in England; nearly three times the value of the Kentucky Derby; 50 percent more than America's richest, the Futurity.

Fantastically tricked out carriages and newfangled automobiles crammed the highways down from St. Petersburg, the czarist capital, to Moscow, the provincial metropolis, whose political importance was only a shadow of its future self. The pedestrian lines to the Central Hippodrome backed up for what seemed a mile, and the new pari-mutuel machines were starting to swallow more than 60,000 rubles for the day. The czar's government had designated it a holiday to celebrate the thoroughbred horse industry, and high above the track, in their flag-draped loges, Russia's social and military elite were dressed as if for a coronation. Which indeed it also was: the crowning of the great colt Galust, the "black maestro" Jimmy Winkfield up.

The charismatic Wink—reporters everywhere in virtually all-white northern Europe consistently called him the most "interesting" thing in sight—was a lone star in Russia, a superstar, as they would say later. But as his former employer the multimillionaire Mikhail Lazareff now told his own jockey, a brilliant Russian rider named Hatisov:

"Keep in mind, Hatisov, that great jockeys have lost the All-Russian Derby at one time or another, even Winkfield." Lazareff instructed the boy: "Do not rush. Ride calmly. You have an assistant, Dugan, on Flying Boy."

Eddie Dugan was riding Lazareff's other entry. The year before, he had handed Lazareff an unprecedented seventh All-Russian Derby, but for this one the tycoon was turning Flying Boy into a rabbit. He should take the lead, making the others wear themselves out chasing him, while Hatisov's mount, MacMagon, saved himself for a powerful, unbeatable finish. In Russia, as in America, it was an old ploy. Would it happen?

Wink paraded Leon Mantacheff's Galust up and down the stretch before what would be the last great battle between the two oil tycoons of the Russian turf.

As usual, the old ploy didn't actually happen. The designated jockey, in this case Eddie, hated the idea of taking the lead and sacrificing himself. So a colt with the whimsical name of Bob led to the old judge's tower at the first turn—from a distance, it looked like a water tower to a lot of Moscow's non-racing fans—with both Wink and Hatisov holding off, then opening up in a fierce backstretch duel. Wink collared the tiring MacMagon on the far turn, had him measured down the stretch, and, as they neared the wire, got Galust up to win Wink's third All-Russian Derby by a length. It was also a victory for Mantacheff's new trainer, I. D. Vadomski, who would one day save the tycoon's future.

The fans went wild, everybody once again shouting that Wink was the greatest jockey around, said one reporter—"an opinion seconded in Vienna," where Wink still rode occasionally.

Jimmy Winkfield became a modern media star as, for the first time, several pictures of him in Mantacheff's silks were splashed across one leading sports publication. He's a picture of confidence, his huge hands on his hips, in front of the giant columns of the Hippodrome entrance. By then, Winkfield was rolling in Mantacheff's oil and racing money, his latest contract having landed him a salary of 25,000 rubles (13,300 1914 dollars) plus 10 percent of all purses. His cut of the Russian Derby alone came to more than $2,000 for two minutes, forty-one and a half seconds of work. It was far more than top athletes at home were making.

Mantacheff had an advantage that helped keep Winkfield in rubles. Under the rules, Russian-born horses were allowed to carry less than the generally better bred English-born horses, and Mantacheff capitalized on it. Unlike other Russian stable owners, he could afford to send his broodmares to England to be mated with famous sires, then bring them home to foal. The high-class babies were thus Russian-born, if only technically, and got the very helpful weight allowance in races. Given the quality of Mantacheff's "Russian" stock, it was no surprise Winkfield rode over a hundred winners in 1914, his best year in Russia.

Meanwhile, as tens of thousands of Russians embraced "Dj Winkfild" (as they spelled it, because they pronounced it "Djames"), he thought of home, where racing, nearly wiped out by the anti-gambling movements, was finally on the mend. He also remembered that the black jockeys who had competed at the top of the sport for two centuries were gone forever. Except for one, who wasn't even present: Jimmy Winkfield. But life was becoming frightening in Russia again, too. After the Spanish-American War, the Russo-Japanese War, and the would-be Revolution of 1905,

World War I was the latest "interference" with Wink's quest for normalcy.

Within a few months of the Archduke's assassination by the Serb nationalist, the world—the world where Jimmy Winkfield had found his livelihood—turned into a massive, blood-drenched game of dominoes. And unlike most Americans at the time, Wink had some understanding of the parties involved and what was going on since he had worked in several of the countries affected.

With Germany's acquiescence, Austria attacked Serbia. Russia was waiting for something like this, a pretext to expand its influence in the Balkans after its defeat in the Russo-Japanese War. The czar's government declared its support of Serbia, "a kindred land," and mobilized against Austria and Germany. Germany then declared war on Russia, which immediately invaded East Prussia and the Austrian territory of Galicia. Finally, the war would engulf France, Belgium, and England, but the United States maintained its neutrality, for now.

In the fighting between Nicholas II—the caesar, or czar, of Russia—and his cousin Wilhelm II—the caesar, or kaiser, of Germany—Russia's troops suffered terrible reverses, and Nicholas tightened his repressive rule, further choking off civil liberties. But it was his German-born empress, Alexandra, and her advisor, the monk Grigory Yefimovich Rasputin, who became the leading figures in the empire, even in military matters. Rasputin derived his great personal power from his relationship with Alexandra, who had fought mental illness since she and her husband learned their son was a hemophiliac. As the struggle of backward, agricultural Russia against advancing, industrial Germany appeared ever more hopeless, Rasputin thwarted any attempts at reform.

But the crazy monk was hardly against entertainment—surrounded by the women of Nicholas and Alexandra's court as well as military wives and prostitutes, he was even more sexually than politically active—and apparently agreed that the one thing that must be preserved during the war was the racing season. Not that this was unusual in a war. In the American Revolution, the British revived racing in Brooklyn, where the occupation troops even staged a contest that included women jockeys. In the Civil War, just after the battles of Vicksburg and Gettysburg, the first thorough-bred racing season at Saratoga opened to huge crowds.

In the midst of the wartime festivities at Russia's racetracks, an even more famous black American had materialized out of nowhere. It was the world heavyweight boxing champion Jack Johnson. He had fled America to escape jail time for violating the Mann Act by transporting one Belle Schreiber across state lines, from Pittsburgh to Chicago, for immoral purposes. The judge said he gave Johnson a year in jail rather than just the usual fine because, as "one of the best-known men of his race," he would thus serve as an example "among his people." Americans would be debating the case into the next century. Johnson failed in his plan to set up box-ing exhibitions in Russia, but he did get an unscheduled bout, when a drunk and a dozen soldiers on leave set upon him on a street in Petrograd. Jack later said he knocked out three of them before the police arrived. He was kicked out of the country, but not before attending a party where he met a huge bearded man who, according to one account, "smelt strongly and ate and drank voraciously." It was the czarina's friend.

VOZVRASHENIYE GOSUDARYA IMPERATORA—RETURN OF HIS IM-PERIAL MAJESTY, read one headline on Nicholas's dramatic return from the front to St. Petersburg, or rather, Petrograd. Nicholas had decided to change the German name to its Russian equivalent. But his return was very nearly upstaged by the All-Russian Derby in Moscow on that same June day in 1915. The surprise was that Mantacheff won this derby with Grey Boy and not his better colt, Prometheus, ridden by the jockey whose nicknames included the "black miracle-worker."

Indeed, Mantacheff won almost everything in sight that year. Mikhail Lazareff had died, and, as if ordained, this understudy Ar-menian oilman rose immediately to the top of the winners' list in Russia and the buyers' list in England. As Mantacheff bested the amount spent at Newmarket by Lazareff's widow that December,

Madame Lazareff did Mantacheff an unintentional favor. Unable to manage it herself, she turned over the Lazareff stud farm, with its fifty-five impeccably bred broodmares, to the czar. It considerably enhanced the Crown Stud, but this government breeding operation was not a major force on the turf, certainly not like Lazareff's, Lubomirski's, and Mantacheff's. So by shutting down the Lazareff breeding farm, which had constantly furnished her husband with future top racers, Madame guaranteed his rival a long residence at the top of the winning lists.

The czarist racing authorities ignored the war as best they could. Russian racing, insisted the sport's leading international mouthpiece, Britain's *Bloodstock Breeders' Review*, was meeting "with unexpected success," and the fans were betting more than before the war. "There have been sporadic outcries against the continuance of racing in these days of stress and difficulty, but the Russian Government turns a deaf ear to all such blathering." Winkfield, however, was taking no chances. As he had done earlier when he assumed some training responsibilities, he began to branch out, hooking up with a business partner to open an ice-skating rink in Moscow, which was quite popular. He was looking ahead.

And he was moving in ever higher circles. A snapshot caught him with a couple of well-to-do cronies out on the town, Winkfield as always the snappiest dresser, in a summer suit and vest, a bow tie, and a neat white hat with a black band. Five- or six-year-old George is at his side in a sailor suit, already well above Wink's shoulders, his face a lot rounder, very much the son of his tall, plump mother. Wink took a suite at Moscow's National Hotel, with a valet, and caviar for breakfast, although the hotel registry hasn't been recovered to show whether Alexandra joined him. It was quite common for top jockeys to have valets, not only in Europe but in America, to take care of clothes and other personal needs and to track appointments, schedules, and itineraries. Wink had not had one back home, but at the moment probably no other jockey in the world was living quite as high as he. As he said later, "I was at the top of the tree."

One day he returned to the hotel to find his valet, a young man named Vassily, in front of the mirror. Vassily was trying on Wink's clothes and cape, twirling his diamond-encrusted cane, and talking to himself. "One of these days I'll be rich, and I'll have clothes just like these." Wink, more amused than anything else, just said, "What are you doing?" Terribly embarrassed, poor Vassily began to apologize profusely, but Wink understood what it was like to be on the outside looking in.

The ambitious Jimmy Winkfield's social climbing peaked in Russia when he ran into Baron Vladimir. The genealogy of Vladimir deMinkwitz sparkled with a long list of baronetcies dating to the sixteenth century. This latest baron was a spirited little man who had only five inches on the five-foot-tall Jimmy. He sported a neat, gray goatee, a twinkle, an aesthetic turn of mind, and a taste for adventure in the big-thinking field of public works. Born in St. Petersburg, deMinkwitz had been doing well as a civil engineer— but no better than well—until he got one of those spectacular ideas that can change the commercial life of a country. The baron's idea was to build a rail bridge across a valley connecting western Russia with Siberia. The czar's government commissioned engineer deMinkwitz to do the job, but with what turned out to be a huge catch. A team of skeptical government engineers first had to inspect the terrain, the surroundings, and the local weather to see if it was too risky. It was, they reported, but the baron went back to the site, reinspected it on his own, and vehemently disagreed.

The czar's men insisted he was crazy but said he was free to finance and build the bridge himself; if he succeeded, he could "name his price." So the baron not only built the span to Siberia but personally tested it, starting a locomotive across it by himself. The story of the bridge would become a highlight of deMinkwitz family tradition, but with no date, location, or other details provided— except that the czar's government showered the baron with honors and rewards, including his own railroad car and free travel anywhere. The good life became a life of luxury.

Baron Vladimir and his French wife, Lydie, had two daughters. One, Elizabeth, was married to Paul Thiemann, owner of a chain of motion-picture theaters, which were all the rage in Russian cities. Beautiful and more than a bit eccentric, Elizabeth costarred at the Thiemann's large estate, with fourteen servants, a monkey who had the run of the mansion, and a snake, a literal, living boa that Elizabeth wore around her neck at parties. She and Paul had a son and a daughter, who were apparently considered less amusing than the pets.

The baron's younger daughter, named after her mother, loved horses, both to ride and to gamble on. Family lore would have it that Lydie was a familiar figure at the racetrack, meticulously keeping track of her bets, that she had an eye for human talent, too, and was a big fan of Jimmy Winkfield. According to the same family tradition, Lydie, with her father, even got to meet the famous Moscow jockey in the paddock. Whether that launched a courtship is not known, and in any event the handsome star was married to, or at least attached to, Alexandra.

It is quite possible that twenty-one-year-old Lydie was at the Hippodrome with the baron on that summer day in 1916 when the thirty-six-year-old American went for yet another All-Russian Derby. It would be Wink's fourth. By now he was in territory Ike Murphy couldn't have imagined. He had answered Ike's seven major derbies—three Kentucky and four American—with nine of his own: the New Orleans, Tennessee, two Kentucky, two Polish, and three Russian Derbies. The minimum value of the All-Russian Derby had been upped to 50,000 rubles (again, $26,600) for 1916, far more than any race in America.

It rained all morning and afternoon, until a dramatic cloudburst brought the storm to a close just before the derby. With his political pull, the little baron doubtless sheltered himself and daughter Lydie in one of the better loges. The czarist officer corps and aristocracy—among them a general representing the czar, the Russian militia commander, and the mayor of Moscow—focused their binoculars on the black American. The weather didn't dampen the bettors in the least as the handle—the total amount bet—hit nearly half a million dollars. Mantacheff nursed such great hopes for his colt, Macbeth, that he apparently filed a "declaration to win." This was common when an owner was entering two runners but wanted to build the reputation of one with an important stakes victory. The declaration allowed the rider of the other horse, in this case Tabriz, to pull him, hold him back, if necessary, to let the favored horse win. With no declaration, it would have been illegal to hold back the stable mate. None of this was any surprise to Wink; the practice was common in America, too.

And they were off, charging through the Hippodrome slop! The two Mantacheff colts dispatched the other four by the time they hit the homestretch, but then it took everything for Mantacheff's other jockey to hold back Tabriz as Macbeth sailed home by three lengths. It was victory number ten for Wink in a major derby at home and abroad.

It was only Wink's unfailing charisma that stood out at that 1916 Derby, said a sarcastic newspaper columnist. The field was dominated by "two horsies of the stable of the Eastern oil tycoon Mantacheff—who the hell is he?—and, on top of that, its rider, a negro, Winkfield, was by far more interesting than its four-legged winner, Macbeth." The Russian writer's prejudice was aimed more at the upstart "Eastern oil tycoon" than his "interesting" black rider, but it helps explain the bond between Wink and Mantacheff—both were outsiders—as well as Wink's earlier bond with Lazareff. The writer signed himself "Anonymous," a smart move when criticizing an institution like Russian racing, which was completely controlled by the czar's government, not that the czar himself was closely connected with it. He had not attended any of the four All-Russian Derbies that Wink won.

Two weeks later, Wink was in Nick's hometown, as he might have put it, where on four-year-old Grey Boy he won the Petrograd edition of the race in the czar's honor, the Emperor's Prize. It was yet another spectacular double for him, as he had won it in Moscow in 1907. But the czar and czarina were not out parading about the racetrack even close to home. Their profile had been lowered in the face of the war and what were growing whispers of a new insurrection. In the privacy of his Petrograd palace, Nicholas had accepted another enchanting Easter egg that spring from the jeweler Peter Carl Fabergé. It was for the czar's mother, the dowager empress Maria Feodorovna. This "Order of St. George Egg" was only three and five-sixteenth inches tall, which was the point, of course: it was the canvas of an exquisite miniature, a minuscule yet breathtakingly detailed portrait of the blue-eyed, red-bearded Nicholas. When his mother got up close to it, her son's untroubled pink face looked as though all was well in the land of the Romanovs.

But in December 1916, the growing panic of the court was exposed. Like everybody else in Russia, Winkfield had to be astonished by the event on the night of the sixteenth. Prince Felix Felixovich Yusupov, who had married the czar's niece, and a few others from the court circle invited the mad monk Rasputin to join them for a dinner in the lavishly furnished cellar of the Yusupov family palace in Petrograd. To keep the goings-on out of earshot, the grand duke Dmitry Pavlovich, a cousin of the czar, stayed upstairs, playing "Yankee Doodle Dandy" over and over on the gramophone. Downstairs, the forty-four-year-old Rasputin was treated to one of the twenty-nine-year-old prince's specialties, cyanide cakes, but there was a problem: he liked them. As the prince patiently waited for Rasputin to grab his stomach and keel over, the hungry monk simply declined to do so—until finally, when Rasputin suggested they go have fun with some gypsies, Yusupov shot him through the heart. The monk fell in a heap, and the prince and his friends all went upstairs.

Just to be sure, it was said, Yusupov went back down to the cellar. The wounded Rasputin, thrashing about on his feet, rushed the prince, then dragged himself upstairs after him and made it into the courtyard, where he was shot again by one of Yusupov's party. They threw the body from a bridge into the icy Neva, and it was soon ruled that the cause of death was not murder, but drowning. The royal gang had killed the much hated monk to calm the hungry masses, but it did no such thing, and it was too late for reform.

In early 1917, as goods became scarcer and prices soared even higher, famine loomed. It did not threaten the aristocrats, of course, but when merchants and artisans become poor, and the poor starve, the privileged would do well to watch out. And those who could did more than that: they got out. By March, as Wink waited in his plush hotel for the snow to melt from the Moscow Central Hippodrome, antigovernment riots and a general strike paralyzed Petrograd. When the garrison was turned out to quell the rioting workers, the troops—150,000 strong—instead joined the riot. The Revolution triumphed right there on the streets of Petrograd.

The workers and soldiers in Petrograd immediately began forming groups called soviets, which would spread throughout the country to run the military, railroads, and communications services. They began arresting the czar's ministers while mobs attacked other czarist officials in Petrograd. On March 14, 1917, a progressive bloc of liberals and one socialist from the Russian parliament, the duma, which Nicholas had all but stripped of its power, formed a provisional government. The next day, Czar Nicholas II, the last of the Romanovs, abdicated and was imprisoned with his family, first at Tsarskoye Selo, then in western Siberia. Everyone panicked. Wink saw people leaving Moscow en masse and others just wandering the streets.

They "were like rabbits in the woods," he said later. "They didn't know which way to go."

Baron Vladimir deMinkwitz knew which way to go. The baron rented a boat to send his wife and daughters across a river to safety while he stayed behind to tend to last-minute business. If Wink and Lydie had indeed developed a relationship by then, she must have thought she would never see her Jimmy again. The boatman pulled the boat onto the water with a rope; as the family hid under a canvas, some revolutionary troops passed by on horses.

"Look what's going on over there," one of the troops said. "Why don't you shoot and see if there is somebody trying to escape or something?" They opened fire into the darkness, killing the boatman. But they had no way to stop the boat, which drifted to the other side. Lydie, Elizabeth, and their mother were safe, and years later Elizabeth would hand the story down to her son.

The little baron finally got out of Russia by himself. He rejoined his family, took them on a roundabout journey through northern Europe, including Estonia, where his family reportedly had an interest in a textile plant, and finally stopped in London.

Leon Mantacheff got out, too. He had worked for the Russian Red Cross during the Great War, so he was no stranger to chaos, but this was like nothing he had seen. The rioting had already halted racing in Petrograd late in 1916, after Fabergé had presented the royal family with their last Easter egg and after Wink had won the last Emperor's Prize in honor of the now deposed czar. As the revolutionary rioters began to spread through the countryside, they raided the breeding farms, including one of the Crown Stud farms that had been formed from the widow Lazareff's gift, and Mantacheff's own stud. The *Bloodstock Breeders' Review* would report that the Mantacheff farm was ruined and all his horses stolen. "Mr. Mantacheff is a multi-millionaire, but there is little of his money this side of [Germany's] lines, and no near prospect of any coming from Russia, where all is chaos and confusion."

But people underestimated the small Armenian, as they often had. Mantacheff not only managed to escape Russia but saved much of his fortune by selling his oil interests to a syndicate, reportedly for more than 1 million pounds (5 million 1917 dollars). And his horses had *not* all been stolen by the revolutionaries. His chief trainer, I. D. Vadomski, smuggled some of the best ones out of Russia and into France—via the United States!—a secret shipment that remains untraced to this day. But for all of Mantacheff's past kindnesses to Wink, there was no way the escaping millionaire could have taken his instantly recognizable jockey with him as well.

The elegant James Winkfield, who had been enjoying his caviar breakfasts at the National Hotel, had to change his style, and quickly. Amazingly, the Moscow Central Hippodrome was still open—a sign of the priorities in the provincial metropolis—but now Wink threw out the carefully selected suits he always wore to the track and dressed down, something he hadn't done since he was a little boy in Chilesburg. He deliberately sought out old clothes and kept them dirty. If he'd dressed as usual, he would have been pegged as a rich man—the enemy—and thus subject to arrest or murder.

"Nobody bothered us so long as we stayed dirty and wore old clothes," he explained. "But if we'd ever dressed up, they'd have figured we was aristocrats." He had to remember to keep his fingernails dirty, too. What worker ever had a manicure?

Winkfield was still his old professional self, far more interested in what was left of Russian racing than in the lethal political chaos. By April 1917, Vladimir Ilych Lenin had arrived from his latest Swiss exile, determined this time not to be outmaneuvered by the returning Trotsky. Lenin took over the Bolshevik party and converted it to a hard-line policy: overthrow the provisional government, end the war, seize the land and means of production, and set up a permanent revolutionary government. Even in the midst of all this, Jimmy Winkfield's mind was not on politics. Bitter cold held Moscow in its grip well into spring, and Wink was worrying about the racing season, the horsemen, and the horses, which was perhaps understandable considering the description that Jack Keene had given of Russia's racetracks under winter's grip: "Winter is something terrific, and the frost goes twenty feet into the ground. The horses are kept shut up in steam-heated stables and not exercised. Fresh air is pumped in, and the vitiated air pumped out. Horses come out to commence the season fat and sleek as seals."

But they took their time. "The season didn't open till May 14," Wink said. "I remember in 1917 they had to push snow off the tracks for a race, then push it back on, so the ground didn't freeze overnight. And it would end early in October."

Less devoted people would remember that the racing season was not the only thing that ended in October 1917. Old Russia ended. Eight chaotic months after the workers' revolution in Petrograd, the Bolshevik leaders approved an armed insurrection to make Lenin's radical dreams a reality. On November 7, rebel workers and soldiers stormed the Winter Palace in Petrograd in what history would call the Bolshevik Revolution. The next day, Lenin famously told the assembled revolutionaries:

"We shall now proceed to the construction of the socialist order."

"Chittlin' Switch," the racetrack of Jimmy Winkfield's boyhood. Founded in Lexington, Kentucky, in 1826 and opened the following year by the Kentucky Association, it was the oldest American racecourse still operating in Wink's day. It closed in 1933. (Photo, circa 1900, by Robert Lee McClure. Courtesy Keeneland Library)

America's top jockeys gathered at New York's Coney Island Jockey Club at Sheepshead Bay in 1891. Several were Wink's heroes and competitors. Front row, left to right: Fred Taral, Tony Hamilton, Tom Kiley, Marty Bergen. Middle row: Ike Murphy, Willie Simms. Standing: Charles Littlefield, George Covington, Miller, Taylor, Shelby "Pike" Barnes, Billy Hayward, Chippie Ray, Lambley, Robert "Tiny" Williams. (Some first names not known.) (Courtesy Keeneland Library)

Wink aboard "the best in the West." At Memphis in 1900, twenty-year-old Jimmy Winkfield had just chalked up the first win for two-year-old Garry Herrmann, named after a Cincinnati businessman. They later set an American record for a mile and fifty yards. (Courtesy Keeneland Library)

Wink on the greatest horse of his day. At Chicago in 1901, Jimmy led the two-year-old McChesney into the history books with one blazing win after another. But it was also on McChesney that Wink had the worst crash of his life, and left the Chicago fans yelling, "Winkfield's dead!" (Courtesy Keeneland Library)

The tiniest jockey in American history—and one of the loudest, showiest, and best—was the Brooklyn-born Winnie O'Connor, who debuted at age twelve weighing forty-five pounds. Wink beat him in the 1901 Kentucky Derby, and they went on to compete across half the world. (Undated photo courtesy the author)

James "Diamond Jim" Brady (left photo) and Lil Russell at Saratoga. Both followed Wink's career in 1902. A little past her prime, the hefty American beauty queen and singer is seen in 1906 with the high-rolling gambler Jesse Lewisohn, who shared her company with his friend Jim. (Jesse is also seen at left, behind Jim.) (Photos courtesy the author)

Churchill Downs on Kentucky Derby Day in 1903 when Wink made his bid for a third straight victory in the Run for the Roses. At the time, the "twin spires" above the Victorian grand-stand—now one of the most celebrated landmarks in American sports—were just eight years old. The grand-stand dates from 1895, mak-ing it the second oldest major sports venue in America, behind Saratoga Race Course, which dates from 1847. (Courtesy Kentucky Derby Museum)

At the Saratoga races in 1904 were the tough ex-boxer and trainer John Madden (left), who blackballed Wink and sent him fleeing to Europe that year; the patrician stable owner and founder of modern Saratoga William C. Whitney (second from left); an unidentified man; and Whitney's son, Harry P. Whitney (right). (Courtesy the author)

Wink in Russia. Already a champion jockey in Russia and Poland at age twenty-four, Wink had this studio portrait made before he returned to Kentucky for the first time in 1904, partly in the hope it might get him a job at home. It is probably the best portrait ever made of Wink. (Courtesy Liliane Winkfield Casey)

Wink and Alexandra Yalovicina. They met in Moscow in 1910 and the next year had a boy, George. They separated around the time of the 1917 Bolshevik Revolution but remained friends. She later joined the Russian émigré community in France and lived near Wink until her death in 1934. (Courtesy Liliane Winkfield Casey)

"The Black Maestro" was one of Wink's nicknames in Russia, where he became the national champion. "The black miracle-worker" was another. He is seen here in front of the massive columns of the Moscow Central Hippodrome after winning the 1914 All-Russian Derby, one day after an assassin in Sarajevo fired the first shot of World War I. (Courtesy the author)

With this picture on its cover in 1921, a Paris sports magazine made Wink a star from the beginning. He had just won an important stakes race on two-year-old Despote at the Maisons-Laffitte course. Holding the bridle is trainer Alexander Bashkirov, who had been president of the Moscow racecourses under the czar. (Courtesy the author)

Jimmy on the boardwalk in Deauville by the English Channel, his favorite resort and one of his favorite racing meccas, where he won both the Grand Handicap and the Grand Prix in 1922. (Courtesy Liliane Winkfield Casey)

On France's "Big Red." In white silks with red armbands, Jimmy rode the magnificent Aldebaran to victories in 1923–when he also won the Prix du Président de la République on Bahadur. (Courtesy Ken Grayson)

Shoe polish for the WPA. In 1941, out of work and sixty-one years old, Wink shoe-polished his hair to look younger when he applied for a jackhammer job on the streets for Queens, New York. (Courtesy Liliane Winkfield Casey)

Great jocks and friends forever. Wink enjoys a reunion at the 1961 Kentucky Derby with fellow Derby winner Roscoe Goose. (Courtesy the author)

Wink, the trainer. Elegant as usual, Wink, first with Lydie, then with their son Robert, maintained a successful stable in France for four decades, though the operation was interrupted by the Nazis who seized his stables and confiscated thoroughbreds to ship back to Germany. (Courtesy Liliane Winkfield Casey)

Wink with his grand-children. Having settled again in France after the Second World War, Jimmy relaxes with Robert's son and daughter, Thierry and Betsy, at the old homestead in Maisons-Laffitte. (Courtesy Liliane Winkfield Casey)

Chapter Eleven

THE ODYSSEY

The revolutionary congress of November 1917 responded to Lenin's cry with a manifesto promising to liberate "the exploited masses of the population from all the slavery and all exploitation."

If earning a lot of money was being a slave master, Jimmy Winkfield had been making the most of it. But he had also seen the October Revolution coming, so in late spring, as the revolutionaries were making Moscow the new capital of Russia, its "black maestro" had decided to abandon it—and take a job riding for a Polish officer in Odessa, on the Black Sea.

Six-year-old George was going to be okay with his mother, Alexandra. Unlike the baron and his family, Alexandra and the boy were not of the nobility and thus were safe from capture or murder. But she couldn't risk joining her Jimmy on the road in the midst of the revolutionary chaos, and he couldn't protect her out there, either. As he left, she had no idea whether she would ever see him again.

Steeling himself emotionally, as he had been doing forever, Winkfield set out from Moscow. He would be back soon enough, when things quieted down, he figured, so he boarded the train with only a suitcase containing a couple of suits, his saddles, riding gear, and $1,000 in paper bonds backed by the czar. At least he wasn't completely alone: he had quiet, composed, ever-ready Vassily at his side. In America, these two would have made a highly improbable team, always together, the black man in charge, each somehow immune to racism. But in Russia, on both sides of the Revolution, they were just a successful jockey, who happened to be black, and his excellent valet, who happened to be white.

Their next base, seven hundred miles south, looked like a lovely slice of the French Riviera, and indeed this stretch of the Ukraine's Black Sea coast was dubbed the Russian Riviera. Its jewel was Odessa, a splendid grid of broad, shady avenues, especially Nicholas II boulevard, and palatial villas, especially Nicholas II's. And now it was the last refuge of Russian and Polish racing. In 1915, when the German army had threatened Warsaw, all the best Polish racing stock had been shipped to Petrograd and Odessa. Later, all the other race horses that had not already been stolen by the Bolsheviks, sold out of the country, or permanently secreted on farms were dispatched to Odessa, too.

The czarists holding out in beautiful Odessa—royals, nobles, plutocrats; men, women, and children—were dreaming that Lenin and his Bolsheviks might fail. Even in revolutionary 1917, when Winkfield arrived, the Odessa racing society staged an amazing eight hundred races over ninety-four days with three hundred horses. Still beyond the bombs and guns, it even ran its own Odessa Derby, which in effect was the All-Russian Derby. It was worth 40,000 rubles, or $15,800, a bit more than the recently revived Kentucky Derby. The derby of that revolutionary moment brought out the best jockeys of the czar's Russia: Jimmy Winkfield, Eddie Dugan, the top Russian boys Michael Laks and a rider named Magdalinsky, and an excellent French jockey named Lemuel.

In the Odessa paddock, Wink admired the star colt, Liege. One of the finest in Europe, he was beautiful, fast, and smart; unfortunately, he was not Wink's mount. Or maybe it was not so unfortunate, for like some of the very best colts everywhere in the world, Liege could not bear to see a horse pass him. He was happy as long as he hogged the lead, but when another horse did slip past him, even by a couple of feet, he would simply quit fighting and surrender.

In the 1917 Odessa Derby, Michael Laks on Liege enjoyed a two-length lead into the backstretch. Then, as Laks would specifically remember, he heard somebody behind him working the whip. And now he actually felt, or thought he felt, his pursuer's "hot breath." Laks glanced around. "In a white jacket with a two-colored sash across the shoulder is the black Winkfield."

With every stride now, Wink's mount is stretching his head almost to what Laks called "the imaginary line at Liege's eye level, the line that no horse should cross." A combination of Liege's brains and heart and the jockey's talent takes over, and with every threat from Wink's horse, said Laks, "I turned up the power, working with my hands [on the bridle bit] and heels. There is no need for the whip. I hardly raise my hand with it when Liege speeds up, guessing my intentions." Liege breaks free.

But they are back at him at the top of the stretch. Wink, also disdaining the whip and knowing Liege's weakness, charges on—desperate to put a head in front of Liege.

"The frightening noise of the chase reaches my back," said Laks. "I do not let him cross the critical line"—and Liege wins in the last little corner of the czar's Russia where they could still pretend to have an All-Russian Derby. But it is not the last Wink will see of this animal.

The rich hung on in their villas and at their racetrack three miles south of town while, in Odessa itself, turmoil became the status quo. Not that the city was new to chaos. Nobody in Jimmy Winkfield's day had forgotten one of the most memorable episodes of the 1905 workers' insurrection, the mutiny on the Russian battleship *Potemkin*. Like anyone else, Jimmy himself could now dance down the majestic Richelieu Steps—there were twelve flights, each with twenty steps—from Nicholas II boulevard with its sweeping view of the harbor down to the docks. It was from down below that Odessa's own workers in 1905, emboldened by the *Potemkin* suddenly flying the Red flag in the harbor, repeatedly charged up the Richelieu Steps to launch their own revolution against the czar—only to be repeatedly massacred by the czar's cossacks descending from the flights above. The *Potemkin* mutineers failed to come to the workers' rescue. Some six thousand were killed. In a few years, scenes of the workers fighting with czarist soldiers on the steps would become the centerpiece of director Sergei Eisenstein's pioneering film *Potemkin*.

As a strategic port, the main gate to the Black Sea and the Mediterranean beyond, this Ukrainian capital had been occupied by foreign armies many times over the past century, and in the closing months of World War I the city government had been changing virtually every other day—from Ukrainian to Bolshevik, then to German, Austrian, Ukrainian Nationalist, and White (czarist) Army administrations. From the Ukrainian countryside came new reports of pogroms, with an outfit called the White Guard accused of killing hundreds of thousands of Jews in the midst of the Revolution.

The racing colony had been under the control of a remarkable Polish horseman since 1915, when Poland started sending its racing stock there for safety's sake during World War I. This was Frederick Jurjevich, who had single-handedly raised racing at Odessa to an unusually high level, considering the circumstances, then held it together through the bloody fighting of the contending local forces. "He negotiated brilliantly with each and every government," a Polish historian wrote, "using all sorts of means—requests, persuasion, bribery and threat." He fought against the requisitioning of horses, persuaded the authorities to allow breeding, and maintained a fine racing schedule, with the totalizator—the pari-mutuel betting machine—as the club's only source of income.

But Jimmy Winkfield was never farther removed from home, where not even the imprisoned czar nor the rising Bolsheviks were at the top of page one, and with good reason. In response to Germany's continuing warfare on neutral shipping and its reported designs on the United States itself, Congress had declared war on Germany in April 1917. In July, General John J. Pershing, appointed to command an American Expeditionary Force to France, cabled home from Paris asking for at least 1 million men, adding this chilling additional information: "This estimate would give practically half million men for trenches." He wanted them in France in less than a year, by May 1918.

Jimmy Winkfield's Odessa was another world. There, thanks to Jurjevich, yet another racing season went off without a hitch in 1918. With the czar and his family under arrest, a brave horseman named Ryszard Zoppi, who had managed the czar's Crown Stud, had been trying to keep the Moscow Central Hippodrome open. "In 1918, there were at the Moscow racecourse about 180 horses, including the best class animals," he said. "I had 12 horses in training there. At that time, I was trying to arrange with the Bolsheviks to allow racing to be resumed at Moscow, but failed.

"In July they arrested me. I, however, managed to escape. . . . All other owners had to flee also. The Bolsheviks nationalized all horses, but allowed them only 3½ lbs. of grain, so of course racing them was out of the question. What has happened to the horses since I left Moscow I do not know."

Zoppi eventually caught up with Winkfield and the others at Odessa, bringing his royal racers with him. He even got there in time to win the 1918 Odessa Derby, with a colt named Horoscope, who, like Liege, would later give Wink and the rest of them even more to remember. The czar and his family were not so lucky. In Odessa, Winkfield heard the startling news that on the night of July 17, 1918, Nicholas II, whose riders and horses he had met on the great race courses of Russia, had been executed along with his empress, Alexandra, and their five children in the cellar of a house at Ekaterinburg, in the Ural Mountains. The next day, the Bolsheviks threw a number of other Romanovs down a mine at Alapayevsk. Winkfield's czarist friends, their be-ringed fingers crossed, went ahead with plans for yet another season.

In the early spring of 1919, the Odessa racing society's funds were running out, yet the icebreakers were at work again on the Black Sea and Winkfield and the members counted on the coming season's handle to keep them going. The world war had ended with Germany's surrender on Armistice Day the previous November, so perhaps a new day would arrive at Odessa, too. They were dreaming. The good times on the late czar's Russian Riviera were over. The czar's Russia lay in ruins. And, as the Allied leaders prepared to meet at Versailles in France to redraw the map of war-ravaged central Europe—which would mean dismembering the great Austro-Hungarian Empire, both of whose capitals, Vienna and Budapest, had known the star jockey Winkfield—the Bolsheviks surveyed their own map and dispatched a force to capture strategic Odessa. It was in the hands of a small French buffer force called the Interventionist Army. The French officers relaxed by popping out to the little *champ de courses* on the edge of town to lose a few bets on Wink and the others.

The Bolshevik forces reached Odessa the first week of April and sat on the northern edge of town. Winkfield must have thought: I escaped them in Moscow—now they've caught me again. It was nothing personal. All across town, down by the port, along the coast, and especially around the gingerbread racetrack, murder by the Bolsheviks was in the air, and every former czarist and every horseman contemplated his apparently brief future. On Thursday, April 3, 1919, the Odessa newspapers ran a series of communiqués from the French command saying there was no danger, that everybody was safe. Nobody believed it. The French buffer outfit would be no match for the Bolshevik forces, which would find plenty of support inside the city. But most in the racing colony were too paralyzed with fear to think or do anything. Not Winkfield. Sitting on a cot in his stable, Jimmy thought things over and, as he later recalled, he first said to himself:

"This ain't no longer a fit place for a small colored man from Chilesburg, Kentucky, to be."

But he also remembered worrying about the 260 or so thoroughbreds—and was damned if he would leave them "to be eaten like hot dogs by the Reds."

On Friday, the French command changed its mind and announced an immediate evacuation of the city. As cannon fire began to rumble above the town, nearly everybody panicked. Not Frederick Jurjevich. His mind concentrated by the Bolshevik noose, he had been thinking like Winkfield. Finally, though seriously ill, Jurjevich exploded into action, organizing an immediate evacuation of the entire colony on foot and hoof—men, women, children, and their entire blueblood herd—to begin what could be an impossible 1,100-plus-mile trek to Warsaw. They would not take the shorter, direct route out of Odessa, northwest along the tiny village roads all the way to Poland, but instead would begin with a 300-mile detour, following the main road straight west then south to Bucharest, the Romanian capital and the nearest city with a rail connection to Warsaw. There they could put the women and children aboard a train and attempt the remaining, still impossible 800 miles on foot and hoof.

If Jurjevich could actually pull it off, with an assist from Winkfield, it would be the most dramatic movement of race horses in history—even more extraordinary than the many equine evacuations to escape the British in the American Revolution. The old slave trainers, jockeys, and grooms had played a major role in those events. One goal of the murderous British cavalry colonel Banastre Tarleton was to capture valuable thoroughbreds, most of them in the hands of slaves, who kept them safe and on a few occasions were freed for it. Once, when a groom in South Carolina repeatedly refused to tell Tarleton where a famous imported English racer named Flimnap was, even after being told it would cost him his life, the British strung him up on a tree in front of the house and left him to die. When they were gone, the servants ran out, revived him, and shipped Flimnap on their early equine underground railroad to a safe house on the North Carolina–Virginia border. There were similar rescues during the horse-farm raids, both Yankee and Confederate, in the Civil War.

In the darkness down by the Odessa racecourse, Winkfield and the others—owners, trainers, jockeys, stable hands—moved silently among the stables. Now and then, Liege or Horoscope or another champion reared and bucked and squealed. A natural leader since his adventurous days with Bub May, and now a veteran of world crises, Jimmy Winkfield took charge along with a stubborn Polish horseman named Jaworski and with Ryszard Zoppi, who as one of the late czar's managers was a very wanted man. Everybody pitched in—Vassily, Eddie Dugan, the Russian exercise boys—as they brought up the supply wagons, water wagons, and hay wagons. Winkfield and the other leaders selected their personal mounts for the march ahead.

At six o'clock, as a Ukrainian dawn broke over the frigid sea, Winkfield and the others started out of the Odessa stables. Along the port road, they formed a monster queue of some 260 race horses and their wagon train, the frail Jurjevich at their head aboard one of the most magnificent animals of Europe, the 1917 Odessa Derby winner, Liege. There was no question of escaping via the eastern, Asian route; it went nowhere and would only trap them in a few days in the isolated Crimea, making them easy prey for the Bolsheviks. They were returning to Poland. They would take the European route—again, not directly northwest to Warsaw but across the southwest tip of the Ukraine, then little Moldavia, and into Romania.

As thirty-nine-year-old Jimmy Winkfield rode out of the city that had been his latest home away from home, it was already going up in flames, the Bolsheviks now terrorizing the population to consolidate their control. Winkfield and his cohorts passed burning depots on the port road, walking the herd through smoke and soot as the cannon fire continued in the town, which frightened these civilians but which also told them they were not the first priority of the Bolshevik army and its local guerrillas. Winkfield and the others picked their way past corpses of other horses and broken military vehicles. Reaching the chemical storehouse at the end of the road, Winkfield knew that Odessa, for him, was over.

Behind him, the Odessa racetrack's sooty flag waved above a

mountain of fire and smoke. The roof over the three-story grand-stand and the bleachers in front of the finish line burned brightest. If Jimmy had time to think of anything as he peered through the black gusts, it was of eight-year-old George, safe with his mother. He must have thought of Alexandra, too, although after Moscow she had begun to fade from his mind, the way Edna had. Ahead was his newest challenge, the trek with a herd of nervous, hungry race horses across more than a thousand miles of eastern Europe's post-war wasteland to Warsaw, which was itself starving in the wake of the world war and was now also threatened by the approaching forces of Russia. In Moscow, the old Bolsheviks and other revolutionaries had forged a new Communist party and a new Red Army as well.

A little farther along, where the road left the port behind, Winkfield's band joined with their protectors, a Polish army lancer regiment under French command. The old road took them across the Ukraine's southwestern border into the deserted country of Bessarabia, heading west for one hundred miles before turning south along the Danube. The Danube! Only Jimmy knew its whole story, and his. As he rode south, the river flowed north before turning toward the Black Sea. Along the way, villagers mistook them for Bolshevik troops and opened fire, but Winkfield and the gang marched on, living off the country when they had to, buying and begging what food and hay they could. Many Romanians took these nomads for gypsies and refused to give them food or help. They were good Catholics, this band of Polish soldiers and mostly Polish horsemen, so at this time of year, even under these conditions, there were things they would not eat.

"Once, we come upon this cow," Winkfield said later, "but it was Lent, and no one would eat her." The cow wasn't home free, though. "We drive her along for 20, 30 miles, trying to get her to Easter. We finally swapped her for a pig and ate him on Easter Sunday."

From the Danube, it was another one hundred miles west to Bucharest, where they put the women and children aboard the train to Warsaw. They had wasted few thoughts on sacrificing their thoroughbreds, abandoning them to get on the train. They would never do it. These were horsemen. They started out again with their exhausted menagerie; the next long leg was even more impossible than the first. Winkfield and the others and their herd would walk those additional 800 miles all the way to Warsaw. They started north, first skirting the Transylvanian Alps, whose young glacial peaks shot straight up from the earth—you could walk up to them—unlike the worn-down mountains of Jimmy's Kentucky, which were the result of much earlier glaciers and had to be approached across miles of gradually rising foothills, mountain country.

Did Jimmy or someone think of Hannibal? How they had heard, in their childhood, of the Carthaginian general setting out from Spain in the second century B.C. with an army of some forty thousand, including saddle and pack horses and some elephants, and traversing a western range of the Alps? It was better not to think of old Hannibal. He had run into blizzards, landslides, and attacks from mountain tribes, and he had lost some fifteen thousand men. Still trudging northward, Winkfield's fugitive band and their horses hugged the foothills of the Carpathian Mountains before finally crossing back into northern Ukraine.

They aimed to pick up the broad Dniester River, bearing northwest again as they followed it upstream toward the Carpathians before turning north-northwest into Poland. But the supply wagons broke down, and with no hay or grain, the horses had to survive on green grass. Wink struggled to accept it as a few of the thoroughbreds died and were butchered and eaten.

"In the crazy mud and in the rain that froze on us," the Polish horseman Jaworski recalled, they struggled to the river, which there was at its average width of five hundred to seven hundred feet. They had planned to ford the Dniester from Owidiopol to Akerman but found the designated crossing blocked by heavy, slow-moving traffic—the river was an important artery for shipments of grain and other crops, cattle products, and lumber to the Odessa region—and the next crossing, near Bielajewka, was hopelessly blocked as well. The horsemen and their herd struggled on, looking for a rail bridge that supposedly stretched across the Dniester River Cove, at Karolina and Bugaz. They had long since discarded the fantasy that they were escaping the Bolsheviks with Russia's best horses, just brought to peak form for another season. Now the only question was how many, if any, might survive.

"They squealed and fought with each other," Jaworski said. They were not used to a starvation diet of poor grass and forced marches and the military discipline of marching in line.

It was already dark. The French and Polish commanders sent back word to set up night quarters near the road. "You could not see your own horse," Jaworski remembered. On their backs, under the stars they couldn't see, the two jockeys, Wink and Eddie, had buckets to talk about if they could stay awake. Old Sam Hildreth, for one thing. Though Hildreth was jealous of the easier life top jockeys had in the old days, he bragged that he paid them well, up to $1,000 a month plus bonuses.

"I don't remember that!" the two-time Kentucky Derby winner might have shouted into the Eastern European void.

And the Belmont Stakes victor: "I can remember that money; I just don't know where it went." Dugan, who had been a poor newspaper boy in California, never could hold on to all the money Hildreth paid him. Laughing, Wink might have imitated Eddie's little-boy voice: "It just slips right through my fingers somehow, Mr. Hildreth. I don't know how to save." Which is exactly what Sam remembered Dugan telling him.

Did Eddie tell Wink about Sam's teaching him how to save? Sam withheld his earnings, paying him only enough to survive on, then handed him $10,500 at the end of the season. Before Eddie took off for California to ride at the winter meetings and buy his poor mother some presents, Hildreth bet him $100 that he hadn't learned anything, that he'd return with less than he set out with. Dugan took the bet—and came back broke. Hildreth gave him $300 to get down to Belmont's training operation in South Carolina.

Wink heard a scream: a mare giving birth. He squinted through the flickering light from the bonfires across the camp and saw that they were in the middle of a wheat field, by a cemetery wall.

"Suddenly, we got terrible news," said Jaworski. The horsemen's leader, Jurjevich, had turned for the worse and was extremely ill. "Everyone grabbed his own horse by the bridle and ran over to see Jurjevich, asking 'What next?' "

Nobody knew.

At dawn they dragged their horses through the sands of the cove until they reached a clearing and the rumored bridge. Staggeringly high over the water, it was swinging in the middle, its pathetic wood planks moaning in the morning. Winkfield watched as the daring Jaworski tied his mount, Konwent, to a cart and started to lead him across the bridge. But one of the officers told him it would be better to lead the way with the late czar's horses, and they all held their breath as Jaworski brought the once-pretty Horoscope, prize of the late czar's Stud, onto the bridge. The 1918 Odessa Derby winner was followed by a few gigantic stallions who looked like they were carrying the stable boys by their collars.

Winkfield stepped around the vicious screws that stuck out of the planks and pierced the shoes of some of the others. Another horseman, very sick, was lashed to his mount but fell onto the planks and was carried the rest of the way. Jaworski saw himself dying on this bridge, far from his loved ones. "We thought of others, in despair." But the performance of the civilians—Winkfield, Jaworski, Zoppi, Vassily, Dugan, the sick Jurjevich—stunned the French and Polish officers watching the crossing. "The army men looked at the scene in awe," as Jaworski put it.

What the soldiers didn't know was that Winkfield and the others were not completely untrained civilians but among the greatest horsemen of their day, used to moving between racetracks hundreds of miles apart. Being flat broke again wasn't really a surprise for some of them, certainly not for Dugan. The broken-down bridge landed Winkfield and company on a small island, where, utterly spent, they collapsed for two days but had nothing to eat. "People kept falling asleep, their mouths full of sand."

Just as death seemed a distinct possibility, they returned to the march and made it to Kizil, a rich village of German settlers who saved them, at least for the moment. Their cadaverous thoroughbreds found meadows of fresh grass, devouring what their shrunken stomachs could hold while the Germans fed Winkfield's party hominy, eggs, and cornbread. For a minute, it was almost like home to Jimmy, and it bolstered them all for their next march, to the town of Czernowitz, "where the first sparks of hope arose."

The French commander assembled everybody in a field—and brought tears to many when he announced that they were at last standing on Polish soil. The tears were not only for their arrival in Poland but for their arrival in a free Poland. With the end of the war, the republic of Poland had been declared the previous November and a new government installed.

But the march wasn't over. The fugitives from Odessa would have to make the final trek in battle formation because Poland was actually still at war—under attack by the new Soviet Russia's Red Army along Poland's frontier with Galicia, on the northern slopes of the Carpathians. Proceeding in rigid battle formation was taxing for 105-pound Winkfield, but less so for this professional rider, who surely remained horsed most of the way, than for the others. It was strenuous as well for the constantly hungry horses—"the only feed we could find was in the ditches"—but it imposed the discipline that allowed the strange horse train to move fast. Then came the moment that thirty-nine-year-old Jimmy Winkfield could never forget.

On June 29, three months out of Odessa, "at the head of our exhausted and filthy horses," said Jaworski, "we at last entered Warsaw." Aboard the emaciated Liege, the equally frail Frederick Jurjevich led the convoy along rain-washed Nowy Swiat Street to the old Mokotowski Race Course. There, Winkfield, Vassily, Jurjevich, Jaworski, Dugan, Zoppi, and all the rest collapsed together. It was a stunning conclusion to the most epic exodus in sporting history.

Jimmy was back at the racetrack where, one revolution and one world war earlier, as a newly arrived American, he had won the Warsaw Derby and launched his international career. The march from Odessa would become known in Polish history as "The Odyssey," yet Wink wasn't waiting around for history to tell him what he had just done. In a matter of weeks, the Mokotowski track swung open its gates, and some of the Odyssey survivors were on the card. Indeed, the 252 surviving thoroughbreds—eight hadn't made it—now became the foundation of a new Polish breeding program.

In midsummer of 1919 the last of the great black jockeys rode before another conquering American hero. The name of the horse and the result are lost, but on this particular day it didn't matter. Until then, Wink had been basking in the warmth that the Poles obviously felt for him, not only as their former champion but as an American, because of the enormous U.S. war-relief program. And on this August day, the brilliant organizer of that relief effort to thirty European countries actually appeared at the Warsaw racetrack. Herbert Hoover, director of the American Relief Administration, was given a deeply moving reception.

Fifty thousand poor children from Poland's soup kitchens, from five to twelve years old and dressed in rags, came by trainloads to thank their benefactor, the future American president. For hours, the line of hungry but happy children marched down the homestretch where Wink himself had once pounded his way to victory. The irrepressible kids danced past the finish line in front of Hoover's box—laughing, chattering, and squealing, each carrying a little American flag and a little Polish flag. Thousands of adults, Winkfield likely among them, were moved to tears. Hoover even saw tears running down the face of the French military commander, so overcome he had to leave the grandstand after telling Hoover: "There has never been a military review of honor in all history that I would more like to have for myself than that which has been given to you today."

It was yet another moment Jimmy Winkfield would have trouble explaining to the folks back in Chilesburg. And there had been so many of them. Now, at last, as he watched Hoover and thought of America, it was clearly time to move on—to find a slower, more appropriate career for an aging athlete, something like that skating rink he had owned in Moscow.

In 1920, Wink heard from an old friend. It was Leon Mantacheff, who had a surprise for his old jockey. He wanted him to come ride for him—in Paris. There is no record of how high Wink jumped.

It was only now that he was really leaving Russia—the land he had called home for a decade and a half—since the Polish capital had been under Russian control when he arrived. He felt no particular warmth for the czar's dictatorship, and his life and work had shielded him from the terrible poverty and persecution that had accompanied it, even the pogroms, of which he knew nothing. In his own world, he was his own man. He had seen poverty and injustice at home, but once he left the Bluegrass, life had been about personal survival. He looked at Russia through blinkers, like some of his mounts, his object to win and survive. He cared about the government and the country only to the extent that it affected him, and to that extent he liked it. It had made him rich—and free.

"Before the Revolution, that was a good country," he said later. "And I never had to pay no income tax." He added, "There was no prejudice at all in Russia, not a bit. I would have stayed but for the Revolution."

He had taken out almost nothing tangible—a bit of cash, a few diamonds, the worthless Russian bonds. But memories, yes. The sweetest. The victories: the three Emperor's Prizes, the two Empress Prizes, the two Warsaw Derbies, the four All-Russian Derbies. His triumphant invasions of Germany and Austria-Hungary. Back in Russia, life couldn't have been any better for him as a jockey. Those had been the best years of his life, at least so far. And in one sense he wasn't leaving Russia. He would be reunited with his old friend Mantacheff, from their giddy days. He would be in a calmer place. And he could find out what had happened to Alexandra and George.

Chapter Twelve

AN AMERICAN
IN PARIS

Jimmy Winkfield had gone to bed in the skeleton of a capital that was Warsaw and had woken up in Paris. The wonders began. He soon found himself out at the hilltop Saint-Cloud Race Course, with its 185 acres of lawn and breathtaking views of the French capital, the most remarkable of which was the guy standing in front of him. It was Lucien Lyne, his boyhood neighbor.

In the past two decades of a life amazingly parallel to Winkfield's, Lyne had gone from being one of the nicest kids in the Bluegrass to the 1902 American Derby winner to the highest-paid American jockey abroad and back to a struggling Bluegrass boy again. Now, on the third of July, 1921, Lucien was on top once more in the most beautiful city in the world, and in the famous Prix du Président de la République. You can almost hear Wink and Lucien laughing it up, each thrilled to see the other and to be in the company of an old friend who knew how to pronounce *Chahlsburg*.

Had Wink heard? Lucien was about to sign with a reigning

king, Alfonso XIII, who was expanding the facilities at Spain's racing capital, San Sebastián.

Lucien had certainly heard about Wink's riding against Russia's king, the czar, and escaping from the Bolsheviks. Wink had held on in Poland, riding when he could at the old racetrack there, until getting the job offer from his old boss, Leon Mantacheff, in 1920. Records haven't survived to show whether Winkfield said good-bye to starving Warsaw right away or waited until the spring or summer of 1921 to board the train for Paris—or where Vassily, his faithful valet from Moscow to Odessa to Warsaw, was at the moment. But when Wink got there, he saw a lot of vaguely familiar faces and heard a lot of very familiar voices.

More Russian fugitives had arrived in the permanent, continuous tide of world refugees for whom France was a safe haven, just as America was to others. Few Americans other than that Yank refugee from Russia Jimmy Winkfield were aware of France's role, whereas the French people themselves—the funds were raised by popular subscription—had magnanimously acknowledged America's similar role with their gift of the Statue of Liberty, marking the centennial of American independence and finally dedicated in 1886. But to countless foreign millions, and often to exiled governments, Paris was France's Statue of Liberty, "the City of Light" at the end of their political tunnel, whether they had come from Europe, Asia, Africa, or Latin America.

In Jimmy Winkfield's Paris, one of the highest-ranking Russian refugees was the grand duke Nikolai Nikolaevich, whom the empress had forced out of power as a threat to his uncle the czar, but as Wink would also have confirmed, Nikolai was nothing when it came to furnishing gossip for the Parisians. The juiciest Russian was Prince Felix Felixovich Yusupov, who back in Russia before it was the USSR had shot the mad monk Rasputin. From the day the prince hit Paris through the next five decades, one of the town's more interesting whispers would be the tale of how that man on the corner almost did not murder Rasputin. Oh, and that wasn't half the stuff Jimmy could tell his new friends about those days.

The prince wound up in a plush building in the chic 16th *arrondissement*, but *la vie parisienne* wasn't so easy for many of the high-born Russians. Long on memories and short on employable skills, some famously wound up as broke but proud *chauffeurs de taxi*, like the cabbie who told a visiting Soviet Commissar, "I will never accept a tip from a Communist."

But not Leon Mantacheff—not yet, anyway. In fact, Mantacheff was suddenly the biggest-spending horse owner in postwar France, buying nine yearlings in the 1920 sales at Deauville, then crossing the Channel in 1921 to Newmarket, where the auctioneers were happy to see him alive and even happier that he was buying again. He picked up eleven of their broodmares.

"The return of Mr. Leon Mantacheff was pleasing to all," swooned England's *Bloodstock Breeders' Review*. "He has sold his big oil interests in Russia to a syndicate and apparently settled down in France, where last summer he was lavishing money on yearlings."

And then there was Mantacheff's American coup. Those Russian horses that his trainer Vadomski had smuggled to the United States had been brought to France in stages and still in secret—how many and their ages were not known. With his American contraband, his French yearlings, and his English mares, Mantacheff began happily upgrading his racing and breeding stock at his new empire just south of Deauville.

Ah, and all the love stories in the saga of the Russian exiles, a chapter that has never been told because sometimes it's just, well, too beautiful—and, of course, because it's a Russian chapter, tortured. There was the latest love story of Pablo Picasso, a year younger than Jimmy and already famous. He had been through his Blue, Rose, and Cubist periods when he took a job in Rome as a designer for the Ballets Russes of Sergei Diaghilev, who, along with many other artists and intellectuals, had departed Russia after the would-be Revolution of 1905. In Rome, in 1917, thirty-six-year-old Picasso went head over heels for the umpteenth time, his latest weakness being Diaghilev's thirty-year-old dancer Olga Koklova, who, of course, was soon immortalized in oil. Upon returning to Paris the next year, Pablo and Olga decided to marry, but the Revolution had turned Olga into a stateless person, so the police subjected Picasso and his dancer to endless police inquiries, collecting character references from the painter Georges Braque and the art dealer Ambroise Vollard before the marriage was officially sanctioned.

And then there was Jimmy's love story. The elegant Baron Vladimir deMinkwitz and his family had beaten Jimmy to Paris and were now discovering a charmed life in exile, though, of course, not nearly as well oiled as Leon Mantacheff's. The baron had been reunited with his wife, Lydie, and daughters Elizabeth and Lydie in northern Europe after their escape down the river from the Bolsheviks. They stopped off in Estonia, where they had a significant investment in a textile plant in addition to whatever funds deMinkwitz had been able to sneak out of Russia. Then the little family holed up in London, at the Royal Court Hotel on Sloane Square. At the police station, the sixty-three-year-old baron did a much better job than most of the other transients filling out their identity cards. Alongside the space where they would paste his ID photo—the picture of a happy escapee: eyes atwinkle under a neat bowler, white mustache and goatee neat as a razor—the designer and engineer printed his name in proud, artistic caps with strong serifs that looked like a Russian typeface—MINKWITZ—and affirmed his baronetcy by adding the "de" after "Wladimir." The deMinkwitzes had made it to London by October 1919, three months after Jimmy had reached Warsaw. They may well have crossed the Channel and joined the rest of exiled Russia in Paris before Jimmy arrived there in late 1920 or early 1921.

As might well be expected, the baron's pampered daughter Elizabeth and her German husband thought they would feel much more comfortable among the wealthy exiles in the south of France, so they went directly to sunny Nice, on the Riviera. Daughter Lydie, however, was staying put with her parents and was thrilled to learn that Paris had horse racing, and plenty of it, all around the edges of the City of Light. She just couldn't wait to start laying her rubles—no, francs—on these French nags. And not only that, as she would soon discover, they had her jockey hero. Alongside the Winkfield family tradition that Lydie, accompanied by the baron, had met Wink in a paddock at Moscow before the Revolution, and that they had begun at least a slight friendship in Russia, runs another and opposing tradition: that they did not meet until Lydie got to France. But whether it was in those fading days of old Russia or in this roaring decade that was dawning in Paris, Lydie and Jimmy doubtless first laid eyes on each other at the one place that was for each, and especially for both of them together, a paradise: the racetrack. If love bloomed first in Paris, it may well have happened in that 1921 season, when Wink was riding at Chantilly as early as June.

His old Lexington neighbor Lucien Lyne did not finish in the money at Saint-Cloud on that afternoon before the Fourth of July, 1921, but Wink was a different story. He paraded to the post for the Prix Quo Vadis, the race just before the Prix du Président de la République, on an unfortunate-looking Mantacheff three-year-old called Adry. Europe's most fashionable fans enjoyed Saint-Cloud's unobstructed start-to-finish view of the track all the more as Wink transformed the homely youngster into a fireball—shades of Mc-Chesney—over the mile-and-three-eighths-plus, chasing two of the top jockeys in France, George Bellhouse and Jack Jennings. And he nearly caught them, finishing behind Bellhouse for the third-place money.

Though he did not have a ride in the Prix du Président, Wink reappeared in the day's finale, the Prix Sea-Sick—French racing authorities resorted to fashionable English in naming a number of their stakes races, and Sea-Sick was perfect for the unseaworthy Wink. He was on two-year-old Suzon and up against not just a couple of the best riders in France but *the* two best, the aggressive Englishman George Stern and the modest American Frank O'Neill. Seeing O'Neill was yet another miracle in the international revolving door that was the life of America's top jocks. It was Frankie whom John Madden had yanked off The Minute Man and fatefully replaced with Winkfield at Saratoga. On this after-noon, they were nearly twenty years older. Wink could not catch Stern on the favorite, Ra-Ra, but he edged out Frankie by a short head for second.

Then, as Lucien went off to work for the king of Spain, Wink continued his attempted conquest of Mantacheff's new country, France. In less than a week, he succeeded beyond Leon's dreams, although not on a racetrack. A news photograph turned Jimmy Winkfield into a cover boy for the top racing magazine, *Le Sport Hippique*. It showed him on two-year-old Despote, who had just won a one-thousand-meter sprint at Maisons-Laffitte, outside Paris. Here was this newcomer, elegantly erect, atop the dark, spec-tacularly beautiful colt with a bright facial flash. The rider is iden-tified only in the article inside. What turned this minor race into a cover was that it was won by a black jockey. Wink was a curiosity in France, just as he had once been the *Exotik* Moor in Germany and the black maestro in Russia. The editor's choice made sense, of course: here is the world's only great black jockey.

Also unidentified on the cover, and looking down, the whim of the shutter hiding his glum face under a squishy golf cap, was Alexander Bashkirov. He was more than a champion trainer; he was the former exalted president of the Moscow racecourses. But now he was training for Leon Mantacheff in France and working with Winkfield. Apparently there had been a revolution.

The caption introduced the French public to Despote's owner, Leon Mantacheff, the new power on the French turf. He was tak-ing his empire on the road, which meant touring the world's most stunning constellation of racetracks around a single city. The seven Paris-area venues were Saint-Cloud, Auteuil, and the celebrated Longchamp, all on the edges of the capital, and Enghien, Le Trem-blay, Maisons-Laffitte, and Chantilly, ten to thirty miles out. The last two racetracks' towns also served as regional training, stabling, and residential centers for horsemen. From Maisons-Laffitte and Chantilly, thoroughbreds were taken to a different track every day.

Chantilly, thirty miles from Paris, was the more aristocratic of the two—"a high place of elegance," a brochure bragged—with large, lavish accommodations. Wink doubtless decided he approved of the place—again, his kind of people—after making one of his first French appearances there back in June. He had finished tenth among a world who's who of twenty-one jockeys in the Prix de Diane, which was won appropriately by one of the Rothschild barons, in this case the playboy Maurice, whose cousin Edouard's son Guy had a small mansion at Chantilly, modestly furnished with ten guest rooms and three gardeners. Chantilly also boasted a technical advantage. Workouts there were timed furlong by furlong—a good teaching tool for apprentice jockeys, instilling alertness at the gate and knowledge of pace. Being clocked every eighth of a mile "taught us to be keenly on the alert to get away the instant the flag fell," remembered the English star Steve Donoghue, who was based there in his youth, "then, knowing that our times would be clocked, each rider learnt to pay great attention to the speed shown by every other animal in the gallop as well as his own."

But Mantacheff, whose Paris home was on the chic avenue Kléber, a stroll from the Place de l'Étoile, stabled his horses at Maisons-Laffitte. Twelve miles out, it was by far the more popular center and in many ways more steeped in the sport. "The best tailor in the village specializes in making jockey silks," noted one charmed writer. With its facilities for all sorts of other sports, notably boxing, and a theatrical as well as horsey crowd, Maisons-Laffitte had a lot more flair and fun than Chantilly. It was a year-round Saratoga. A few years earlier, Winnie O'Connor had spent time there, hanging out at the Café de La Station with the celebrated boxer Georges Carpentier. Hard-working Frankie O'Neill lived there now, starting each day with a punishing training routine that kept him at the top of the winners' list. And Jimmy Winkfield would soon introduce Maisons-Laffitte to a new concept: a black resident. For now, though, he found temporary lodging in Paris.

After his star turns at the track in the bubbling and boiling

St. Petersburg of 1905 and later years and his stays in the glittering cultural capital of Vienna from 1910 through 1912, Winkfield
was again ensconced in one of the world's most exciting cities. His
work would not permit him to spend a lot of time investigating
Paris by night, but whenever he could, he might have grabbed
Lydie deMinkwitz and dropped by the Café du Dôme to be ogled
by the likes of Olga and Pablo, and Kiki, the artists' model. Or
Gabrielle "Coco" Chanel, who was about to introduce a perfume
she would call her No. 5. Or the music-hall sensation Maurice
Chevalier. Or the writer Jean Cocteau, whose world intersected
with Wink's because, like Picasso, he had been working closely with
the exiled Russian ballet people—and on top of that, he had been
born in Maisons-Laffitte.

The trend in bars was to cater to the homesick, especially the
latest Russians and Americans in Paris. Hard as it was to play and
ride, some jocks did drop in on the American joints, without their
wives or girlfriends, of course. Around five, Frankie O'Neill, the
clean-living St. Louis boy, would walk into a place like 5 rue
Daunou, which was about to be rechristened Harry's New York Bar.
It was one of the extremely rare joints in Paris where anyone cared
about American sports news—definitely the place to go to discuss
Babe Ruth and his current prodigious swatting.

As Harry's ads in the English-language Paris *Herald*, the bible
of Americans in Paris, advised:

"Just tell the taxi driver sank roo doe noo."

Frankie had only to open the door to become the center of
attention.

"Hello, Frankie, have a drink with us!"

"Say, Frankie, are you going to win the Grand Prix?"

But Frankie wasn't having much to drink. Like Jimmy Winkfield, he had been a jockey for nearly a quarter of a century, and
also like Wink, he knew you couldn't drink your way to the top.
O'Neill led an extremely comfortable life at Maisons-Laffitte with
his wife and three children—a reminder to Jimmy that he had a
son, now ten, left behind in the Revolution; that he had lost touch

with Alexandra, too (or at least no letters or telegraphs or records of attempts to get them past the new Russian authorities have surfaced); and that he had a fourteen-year-old daughter, Ida, whom he had adopted with Edna, left on the other side of another kind of divide. So many pieces of himself left behind. And Kentucky, too—maybe the biggest piece.

Unlike the passionately American Jimmy, who thought of Kentucky all the time, Frankie didn't have strong yearnings for home. Neither did Winnie O'Connor. Winnie was still around—though now he rode over fences as a steeplechase jock since he was too fat to ride on the flat—and he found Paris impossible to resist. The Brooklyn-born O'Connor said,

> The guy who sprung that line about all good Americans going to Paris when they die must have had race horse riders in mind. Paris may not be the racing center of the world, but it comes close to being a jockey's paradise. It was like heaven for me for many years.

And for Frankie, too: "I like France," O'Neill told the *Herald.* "I think it is a wonderful place to live. Every winter I go to St. Moritz with my family for a rest, and then we come back to Paris."

For all their passion for Paris, though, Harry's American bar was Frankie and Winnie's kind of place, a tiny crush of Yanks in their white shirts, throwing back martinis—a way to go home again without having to go there. But it was not Wink's kind of bar. Neither were the older oases that lured American business travelers and tourists, such as Maxim's, Ciro's, and the Café de Paris. But a few black alternatives were starting to appear, thanks to the popularity of jazz among a thin slice of the French, an intellectual slice who quickly became more knowledgeable about jazz than Americans.

One black American *boîte de jazz* was the Tempo Club on the rue Fontaine in Montmartre, opened in 1921 by Joe Boyd of Vicksburg, Mississippi. Back home, a new wave of blacks was fleeing the South, which was in the grips of the revived Ku Klux Klan, and Boyd was one of the tiny number who had made it this far, where they actually found something like freedom. Billed as a "social retreat for the many jazz artists in Paris," the Tempo Club also got the occasional American tourist struggling up Montmartre to the Eglise du Sacré-Coeur. But Joe's big, secret attraction was something else. "African golf," the white guys called it in the Twenties. Craps. The *Herald* on the Tempo Club: "The tuneful saxophone and traps, so conspicuously active in the front room, were only an accompaniment to the more subtle melodies of rattling 'bones' in the inner shrine."

Like Winkfield, Boyd had gone another step in departing from tradition: he had married a white woman, which, as Jack Johnson could have told you, too, was not a popular thing at the time. Wink also liked a little gambling, and if he stopped by the new Tempo Club in the off-season, he had to love it. This was illegal gambling, but this was also Paris, and Joe did fine until one spring night when, according to the *Herald*, a gang of masked men came in "on one of the rare occasions when Mrs. Boyd, a white Englishwoman, was present. Mrs. Boyd was severely beaten and stripped of her jewelry by the masked men, who made their escape." Whether the motive was robbery or a settling of gambling accounts and in part racially motivated because she was married to a black man was not known, but the outcome was tragic: Mrs. Boyd died of her injuries.

Jimmy may have joined Lydie and her parents and Mantacheff, too, at the hot new Russian places springing up to greet the refugees from the Revolution. After all, he had spent much more of his adult life in Russia than at home, and there were many more Russians than Americans in Paris. With his Russian friends and contacts, including Baron Vladimir and Mantacheff and his trainer Alexander Bashkirov, Winkfield knew this, but the other Americans in Paris didn't. They liked to think they were the most important foreign presence and tended to believe the usual estimate of forty thousand Yanks in Paris at the height of the Roaring Twenties. Then the American Chamber of Commerce did an actual count, which found only fifteen thousand (admittedly loud) Yanks in the city and suburbs, whereas the Russians, who had been arriving since the 1905 near-revolution, totaled sixty thousand. The Americans were behind even the British, at thirty-five thousand, and way behind the Italians, who numbered one hundred thousand.

Jimmy's Paris à la Russe featured Russian music at many of the formerly French cabarets on Montmartre. When one place, Mariettes, which had opened as a French restaurant a year before, suddenly changed its menu to southern Russian and its name to Caveau Caucasien, a rival Russian restaurant sprang up across the street the very next night. One can easily imagine the exuberant revelers dropping by one or the other—Picasso to please his Olga, or Cocteau with the Diaghilev flock, or the prince who murdered Rasputin or even the grand duke Nikolai himself. Some of the Russians who couldn't afford the caviar worked there instead as entertainers. At Mariettes, the performers included former officers of the czar's armies and beautiful women who everybody was sure had been princesses. Of course, Jimmy Winkfield must have been greeted as warmly by the Russians as O'Neill was at Harry's, especially by the former czarist officers who had made more than a few rubles off Wink at the Hippodrome. They could talk about the changes—in horse racing and in the country.

By now the Communist Party, which had succeeded the Bolsheviks and absorbed most of their leaders, had figured out that horse racing was popular in its new "Union of Soviet Socialist Republics," so the government reintroduced it. It was bringing big crowds back to the Hippodrome, although few of the exiles would ever see its towering columns again.

Another American in Paris was infatuated with Russia, though it was hard to imagine Wink making the scene with her. San Francisco–born dancer Isadora Duncan was busy inventing modern dance. She had established a school in Paris, and then, having fallen in love with the Bolshevik idea of a workers' revolution, she left in 1921 to set up another school in the new Soviet Union. While Winkfield had fled a Moscow racked by the failed dictatorship of the czar and the arrival of the Bolshevik dictatorship, Duncan discovered a Moscow in even worse shape, gripped both by the bloodthirsty Communists who had taken over and by a terrible famine. The modern dancer didn't understand any of this, but within a year of her arrival in Moscow, her Soviet hosts had figured out one thing. In a 1922 item that made Russians in Paris gulp, the *Herald* reported:

> Wishing to get executions over before the celebration of the Bolshevist Jubilee on November 7, the Commissariat for Justice at Moscow has ordered the revolutionary tribunes to complete the formalities of prosecution in all cases involving capital punishment before that date, the fifth anniversary of the Russian revolution.

Maybe Wink gulped, too. Would they have executed a black American aristocrat?

Jockeys needed to be home early. Old Winnie would even claim years later that it was the morning training, not the drinking, that eventually ruined him physically, although it's easy to question that logic. When Winkfield got up early to check in at Mantacheff's stable and work a horse at Maisons-Laffitte, he would see Frank O'Neill out there, too, but not on the track. On the neighboring roads. On foot. In the morning, wearing a wool sweater and heavy pants over a rubber suit over wool underwear, Frankie walked seven miles, in sunshine or rain, hot or cold, on all kinds of roads. And he kept it up, switching to horseback in the afternoon, from the first of March to the first of November.

Jimmy Winkfield, on the other hand, always had an easier time keeping his weight down. His morning work over, he would head out to that day's racetrack. The calendar was the first big difference he noticed about French racing. American stables traveled from one long "meeting" of several weeks to another long meeting along a circuit of tracks, such as Chicago, St. Louis, Louisville, Nashville, New

Orleans, and others on the western circuit. The Russians, too, had long racing seasons at one city before they loaded their horse vans and moved to another. But the French stables based their operations at a single training center, Maisons-Laffitte or Chantilly, and commuted every day to a different track. A fan in Paris would pick up the morning paper to find out where they were running. On a typical summer Wednesday, one might read at the top of the racing news:

The Week's Calendar

Today, Chantilly   Saturday, Le Tremblay
Thursday, Saint-Cloud   Sunday, Maisons-Laffitte
Friday, Chantilly

Once Winkfield got there—wherever "there" was—he would run up against a difficult adjustment. It wasn't so much having to switch from one course to another almost on a daily basis. All the courses were about the same, except for Saint-Cloud, where they sometimes ran counterclockwise, as in America. Also, as in Russia, all the courses were turf, which in the racing world means grass.

But the problem was their size.

"I was used to mile tracks," Winkfield said, "and around Paris they was all a mile and a half. The stretch went three-eighths. I would always want to go out too soon. I was stubborn, I guess; I always rode that way, and I wasn't fixin' to change now."

But one fine day he was perched at the post on one of Mantacheff's charges, waiting for the start. The start came, the horses went, and Wink was still perched at the post—until he finally got his mount going. "I figured I had no chance." So he took it easy. "I relaxed and just let that horse gallop to the three-quarters pole." And he was happily surprised to see the horses ahead of him start to fall back. "We were goin' a mile and a half, and by the time we got half a mile from the finish, I was movin' up."

This was learning on the job. Entering the stretch, he saw that his horse had plenty left. At the final furlong, he stepped on the gas. "You know, I almost won that race. Lost by a head, and after that everything was all right. I learned to stay back, let the other horses break the wind, then I would come in the last eighth."

On another afternoon, at beautiful Longchamp in September 1921, he was riding at a neat 114 pounds, with gear, in one of the most prestigious handicaps in France, the Omnium Stakes. His mount was Mantacheff's deceptively clunky looking Adry, the horse Wink had been bringing along all summer with the considerable help of a familiar trainer. The latter was I. D. Vadomski, Mantacheff's last trainer in Russia, the man who had spirited Mantacheff's horses away from the Bolsheviks via a secret shipment to the United States and then to France.

Making short work of it, Wink left Frankie O'Neill two lengths back on the American industrialist A. K. Macomber's Black Larry. Once again, the win made Mantacheff even happier than he could have expected. For the second time in four months, it landed his jockey and colt on the cover of *Le Sport Hippique*. Now somebody to be reckoned with, Wink was named in the caption, along with the proud owner. Wink looks a little thinner and drawn in the photo, the long season telling on him. But those magazine covers said more about Wink's charisma than they did about his record for that first full year of racing in Paris.

At the end of 1921, the hard-training, thirty-seven-year-old O'Neill led the French winners' list with 118; forty-one-year-old Jimmy Winkfield managed only 29, still good enough for fifteenth among 144 jockeys. Of course, Wink had always known it was about more than that; it was also about winning good races like the Omnium and about those cover pictures of Mantacheff's ponies.

"*Le blackman.*" It took a year on the French turf for that nickname to start appearing in the leading French daily *Le Figaro*, which certainly stole it from the bettors. "*Je joue le blackman.*" Variations on that line had been mumbled by countless fans since the first day Wink appeared on the Paris turf. Instantly recognizable and with talent to back it up, he had them betting the jockey, just as they had in America, Russia, and Germany. The world's only great black jockey stood out.

No white jockey back home—not even the legendary Earl Sande—had ever rubbed shoulders in a society like this. But Wink had been observing the rich for years—at the Kentucky Derby, at Saratoga and the New York tracks, at places like Moscow and Baden-Baden—and he was ready for the regulars in Paris. Among them, in the week of the 1922 Prix du Président de la République, were the Aga Khan; Lord Derby, for whose ancestor the world's most famous horse race had been named in 1780, the year it was first run at Epsom Downs; the usual slew of the Rothschilds, those robber barons who were real barons, too; a clutch of counts; and a top-hat-ful of American plutocrats. This time, though, neither the forty-two-year-old Winkfield nor three-year-old Bahadur were up to the job, finishing fourth.

A few weeks later, a July storm drowned thousands of Parisians taking the train or motor cars to Maisons-Laffitte. Mantacheff was trying for his first prestigious win in the 100,000-franc Prix Eugène-Adam. Winkfield already knew the town, since Manta-cheff trained there, but he was liking it more and more. An ancient Roman settlement nestled in thick woods along the Seine, it had been developed in 1818 by a banker named Jacques Laffitte. He turned it into a forested resort, full of country homes for the wealthy, the rising class of professionals, and artists who were no longer struggling. With its broad avenues, it was reminiscent of Paris, and it paid a grand tribute to Laffitte's idol, with its Place Napoléon shooting off twelve boulevards named for major events in Bonaparte's life. The town tipped its hat to Old Russia, too, with its Avenues of the Moscovy and Nicholas II.

And on one of their better days, the gods had made it a horse town. Laffitte himself established racing here; then Eugène Adam, first president of the French Sporting Society for the Encourage-ment of the Breed, bought part of the racetrack and preserved it as an important fixture of French racing. Wealthy English and Amer-ican sportsmen came running, joining an ever increasing tribe of athletes and artists, though the most famous of the latter was still hometown boy Cocteau. Georges Carpentier had some of his first fights in Maisons-Laffitte. And by the 1920s, it embraced a cheering section that a town brochure proudly described as "many cocottes and courtisanes"—loose women and high-class prostitutes.

More than anything else, though, Maisons-Laffitte was celebrated for the racetrack's spectacular final run along the Seine. Just short of a mile and a quarter, it rivaled Newmarket for the title of longest homestretch in the world. The track had a wonderful country charm, too, with its haystacks in the infield, its six old men in blue tamping down the turf after each race with long wooden mallets, and its high-steepled, red-and-green Tudor grandstand reminding fans of the gingerbread house in *Hansel and Gretel*.

On July 23, Leon Mantacheff's best colt, Bahadur, cantered to the post for the Prix Eugène-Adam. This time the Yank Georgie Bellhouse was aboard, while Wink was on a lesser prospect named Gaurisankar. This one was not only not as good as Bahadur, but he had a terrible temper—unless, one reporter noticed, he was accompanied on his travels "by his chosen companion, a woolly little lamb. He will kick up a fuss in his box, which keeps the whole stable awake unless the lamb curls up for the night." It had been on a recent outing in which Gaurisankar had run poorly that the trainer Bashkirov discovered the value of a mascot. "The lamb took luncheon from the tender green shoots along the fence." When the race was over, "the lamb ran out to meet its 'pal' and led the breathless horse back to the stables, turning to regard him now and then, as much as to say that it was sorry luck had been against him."

But the lamb hadn't done much yet for Gaurisankar, who was fourteen to one for the approximately mile-and-a-quarter (2,000-meter) feature. As the entries paraded by the serious bettors—a mass of light fedoras with black hat bands jammed in front of the stand—the bettors still liked Frankie O'Neill's Algérien. And it was Algérien, Bahadur, and four others who fought for the lead from the start until King Karol, under the Aussie Frank Bullock, pulled ahead. Wink finally caught him and was the first to peer down that famous, endless stretch. Feisty George Stern, on Zariba, made a go at Wink as they passed the parking lot jammed with the latest motor cars, but it was hopeless. Stern was almost standing in his stirrups, uncharacteristically surrendering, while Wink was bent in two, his crouch tighter than ever even as he won by an easy two and a half lengths. He had handed his ecstatic old Armenian boss his first major victory in their new country.

The sun broke through, lighting the blaze on Gaurisankar's face as he stood for the winner's picture, meek as a lamb, his rider beaming. Wink looked seven feet tall in the colors he had flown from Moscow to Paris: white jacket, red armbands, red cap, and belt. He had just become a permanent hero in Maisons-Laffitte, which was about to become his latest home away from home.

Chapter Thirteen

KINGS, QUEENS, AND WINK

S he looks like a hooker," somebody mumbled, "a cocotte."

The outraged former Mrs. Frank Gould, née Kelly, started across the floor toward the mumbler, a rich Parisian stable owner named Raymond Bamberger. In a foul mood anyway after her ugly divorce from an heir to American robber baron Jay Gould, she wound up and slapped Bamberger across the face. A solid, head-turning slap. Other evening jackets joined in, turning it into a full, cuff-linked brawl. The casino's waiters cleared the dancers from the ballroom, but it wasn't so easy pulling apart the dozen or so who were fighting.

It was four in the morning on Saturday, August 26, 1922, at Deauville. In town for the Grand Prix de Deauville, Jimmy Wink-field's next big race, were the shah of Persia, the king of Spain, the queen of Greece, the Aga Khan, and Winston Churchill (six years older than Winkfield). And it wasn't over at the casino. After order was restored the first time, Mrs. Gould, still flushed with anger, her hair falling into her face, attacked the same man again, belting him with another wicked slap. This time Bamberger kept his temper, but the other men started fighting again—until the orchestra, their jazz horns blaring, marched onto the floor between them, drowning their shouts and clearing the floor for good.

That afternoon, among the beaches, boardwalks, and parasols of the grand resort, the divorcée was nowhere to be seen. As for Bamberger, he and Lady Idena Gordon were at the track, and this time it was Monsieur Bamberger who looked funny, the news report noting "a red mark on his face."

Every August, racing moved to beautiful Deauville, on the English Channel, just as in America it moved to Saratoga Springs, where Wink had failed to catch on two decades earlier. The resemblance between the two spas ended there. Deauville was Saratoga all right, but with an ocean and a monarch or two thrown in. This August, one of the crowned heads on the scene was old Lucien Lyne's boss, Alfonso XIII of Spain, although he was actually crowned with his usual green felt hat, and he had left Lucien behind. *Le grand départ*, as the French called their mass escape from airless Paris, had shifted the entire racing circuit to the west, so that this week's calendar read:

Today, Deauville, Dieppe	Friday, Pont-l'Évêque
Wednesday, Caen	Saturday, Deauville
Thursday, Deauville	Sunday, Deauville, Dieppe

Deauville was the heart of this sea-air circuit, and this day brought the young Alfonso (thirty-six years old) to its emerald green racecourse for the first time, along with that virtual king the Aga Khan (forty-five years old). Leader of an Islamic Ismaili subsect called the Nizaris, most of them in India, the Aga Khan would have to be described in the jazz speak of the day as just as cool as Alfonso. A regular at both French and English tracks, he was fast developing one of the most valuable racing stables in the world, with the help of American trainer William Duke.

No jockey in America had ever ridden in front of as fancy a

mob as the one watching the band of Yanks in the Deauville paddock: Wink and four of the top six jockeys in France that year—
Frankie O'Neill, Matt MacGee, Guy Garner, and Georgie Bartholomew. If these jocks were impressed by the glittering crowd, the
crowd was equally impressed by this collection of some of the most
accomplished race riders in the world. Among them were two
American winners (O'Neill and MacGee) of the most prestigious
of all stakes races, the Derby at Epsom Downs; the Englishman
Steve Donoghue, one of the jockeys of the century; and tough old
Georgie Stern plus a couple of their French colleagues.

Nobody thought twice about the obvious: that the black American rider in the group, mixing easily with royalty and France's upper
classes and the best of his peers, could not have found steady work in
America. Wink was riding as well as he ever had. A European said
of him, "On the ground . . . Winkfield was a perfect gentleman. But
in the saddle he was a demon."

In that day's renowned Jacques le Marois Stakes, the biggest
threat to Wink and Gaurisankar was Stern, on Zariba. Georgie had
adopted the American crouch early on, and it had paid off: he had
been the top rider in France for years. He still had it, too. He had just
won the Prix du Jockey Club (the French Derby) for the sixth time
in twenty-one years, the Prix de L'Arc-de-Triomphe the year before, and the Grand Prix de Paris three times; he was eighth in
France's latest annual table of winning jockeys, compared to Wink's
fifteenth. As he got older, mean old Georgie resented the American
jockeys and took their success as his own failure. It was said of him:
"He was extremely good, extremely rough, and at his best and
roughest when riding to beat Americans." And this time he had
an extra motivation: revenge for his embarrassing two-and-a-
half-length loss to Wink in the big Prix Eugène-Adam at Maisons-
Laffitte.

The 1,600-meter (just short of a mile) Jacques le Marois feature
came down to Wink versus Georgie in the stretch, with Wink
ahead on the outside. A few meters short of the finish, Georgie
moved Zariba up, but Wink had no intention of letting him by.

He rolled Gaurisankar right into Zariba. Stern reached out, pushed away Wink's whip hand—and won by a head, reversing the Eugène-Adam. Wink filed a protest. He not only was rejected but also drew a warning from the judges for interference. The incident got a lot of coverage, some of it biased.

"In this kind of sport," the magazine *Le Sport Universel Illustré* commented, "Stern should be able to return a couple of blows against the *nègre* Winkfield." *Nègre.* Like the German he had heard, *der Neger Winkfield*, it was hardly as offensive as the word *"nigger"* in English. In Europe, and especially in France, considered by some the least racist of European countries, the slur lacked the edge it acquired in the mouths of Americans. Parisians used it casually, even tried to raise it to an art term with their costumed annual *fêtes nègres* or *bals nègres*. Oh, it was still a slur. The words shouted at Winkfield at the Kentucky Derby gate twenty years earlier—"You little nigger!"—could be translated perfectly as *"P'tit nègre!"* But this was one of the rare times *nègre* was used against him in the French press.

Leon Mantacheff certainly didn't blame Winkfield for the loss. There were two big races ahead. If Wink could take the lesser one, the Grand Handicap de Deauville, with the four-year-old Bomarsund, he and Mantacheff would have earned their wonderful seaside "vacation" and seen their Eugène-Adam victory confirmed, their place in French turf history assured. But Wink would have to face Frank O'Neill, the leading rider in France, on the favored Despard, and also Steve Donoghue on Fisticuff.

Meanwhile, times were changing. On Wednesday, three days before the Handicap, Donoghue boarded not a horse or a ship but the latest way of getting around, an "aeroplane." He flew from a little airstrip outside Deauville to the Hurst Park racecourse in England, rode a horse named Granely, then flew right back to Deauville. Two days later, on Friday afternoon, race goers at Hurst Park once again looked up and saw a small plane circling over their heads. It touched down right on the track, and a little man jumped out and ran for the jockeys' quarters. It was Steve again. The modern, airborne athlete was born. This time, Steve rode a horse named Soldier Song to victory for Lord Woolavington and was scheduled to take off right after the race for Saturday's 1,600-meter Grand Handicap de Deauville.

On Saturday morning, the Stars and Stripes flew from an American yacht in the exquisite little harbor at Deauville. It was a good omen for all-American Wink, but an even better sign was that Donoghue had been delayed in England and had to be replaced on Fisticuff by Charlie Hobbs.

From the start, the field of nineteen in the season's second biggest race ran in a crowd—until four moved up: Fisticuff, Frankie's Despard, a colt named Holyhead, and Bomarsund's stable mate Despote, who had helped make Wink a cover boy the year before. Fisticuff looked like the winner heading into the stretch, but out of nowhere came Wink and Bomarsund, picking off horses—Despard, Despote, then Holyhead—and beating Fisticuff by a neck. As for those who thought Wink could not have handled Donoghue on Fisticuff, they would get a partial answer two days later that would give French fans an occasion to compare these two stars, who met often enough at Deauville that summer. And the two had much in common.

Not all jockeys loved horses; for many, they were merely animals, tools for making a living and maybe getting rich. But Jimmy Winkfield not only loved them, he needed them. He once said, "If you took me away from them, I would die."

And Steve Donoghue said, "I love horses with all that is in me. Some people think of them as animals—I think of them as my friends, my greatest friends."

Winkfield had only to touch a horse, said a French jockey who saw him do it, and the horse would calm down. And as for Steve, "If the horse tries to fight for his head," the English rider George Duller commented, "Donoghue will lean over and give him a reassuring pat on the neck, or, dropping his hands, will take his ear. The effect is magical. The mount becomes calm and tractable immediately."

Wink and Steve each got an extra helping of courage, too. The attack on Winkfield in the Chicago "race war" and his spill on Mc-Chesney, when fans thought the jockey was dead, had hardly slowed him down. Steve proved his courage as a kid on the tiny tracks in the south of France, less than three-quarters of a mile around and all sharp turns. "Unless a jockey was entirely without fear," Steve said, "he was useless on these courses."

Yet love and courage were not enough. Skill was the sine qua non, and Steve had the edge here in at least one department: hands. Winkfield had huge, obviously powerful hands, which many might think an advantage. In fact, it is usually a disadvantage. A jockey wants small, flexible hands, his most important physical tools, to communicate directly with his mount, especially by manipulating the bit. "Underpinning the entire Donoghue method," said one expert, "were those exquisite, God-given 'hands' with which he could instill . . . confidence into the most timorous animal, or master the most fractious beast." Once doctors even X-rayed Steve's hands to search for some quality not possessed by other humans.

If Jimmy did not have Steve's hands, the two men did share the almost indispensable qualities of world-class jockeys as listed by future American champion Bill Shoemaker: "balance, intelligence, the ability to switch the whip from one hand to the other and back again, making the right moves most of the time, and a rapport with horses."

"Come on, Steve!" was the cry heard everywhere in the 1920s. Steve came on, all right. He had already won four Epsom Derbies, and before he was done he would add two more. He ran into Wink in a race two days after Deauville's Grand Handicap. Most of the crowd was behind Steve and Fisticuff, at odds of 100 to 95. Wink's mount, Despote, was a long shot, nearly 9 to 1, just the sort of dismissal that always inspired Wink.

On that Monday afternoon, as Wink held Despote back, Steve found himself battling Georgie Bartholomew's Sister Anne most of the way—until Wink at last made his move. Despote pounded down the stretch, catching Steve and Fisticuff in the last jump to beat them by a neck in "a rattling finish," as one paper put it.

"Capitally ridden by J. Winkfield," it said of Despote. But neither Despote nor Bomarsund nor even Gaurisankar was Wink's pride and joy just then. "I guess the best of the lot was Bahadur," Wink said, and with that runty three-year-old he prepared for the biggest race of the season, the Grand Prix de Deauville.

There was a bit of tension in the buildup to the event, set for the last Sunday in August. For one thing, Thursday produced a depressingly dull crowd. A couple of barons Rothschild, Henri and Robert. Herbert Pulitzer, of the American publishing family. Nothing much else. The pickings were so slim for the gossip writers that the *Herald* even mentioned the wives of two jockeys, albeit the top two in France, the Yanks Frankie O'Neill and Matt MacGee, probably because Frankie was such a favorite with the *Herald*. And other Americans were making waves again.

The message of America's Prohibition era had run smack into the French theory that the customer was always wrong, and it would be decades before many European restaurants offered free water, figuring they'd sell fewer drinks if they did. Some rich Yanks were actually boycotting Deauville because they couldn't get any water. At one supper room, an American made a major fuss over it, first offering to pay the price of champagne for a bottle of water, to no avail, then storming out.

But the Grand Prix on Sunday afternoon brought the big money back to the track. And the three kings—Alfonso XIII, Shah Ahmad of Persia, and the Aga Khan—were there too, not to mention assorted Indian and French princes and English lords and ladies. Alfonso appeared for the first time in a straw hat, like the regular guy that all the jockeys said he was.

The stars Jack Jennings, Steve Donoghue, and Jimmy Winkfield rode to the post in the opening five-furlong sprint and finished in that order, with Wink a length and a half back. In the second race he was back on Gaurisankar, but Donoghue beat him by a length. Wink was finishing in the money, but that wasn't the idea.

And then they were off in the biggest sporting event in the world before the most glittering audience in the world, the

2,600-meter (1.6-mile) Grand Prix, with a purse of 132,500 still-war-battered francs, or $16,600 (1922 dollars). Wink's Bahadur was in the front pack around the first turn and into the backstretch, where his stable mate Haroun Al Rashid took the lead, though they were still pretty much bunched. Wink rated Bahadur beautifully, biding his time, moving up slowly, progressively passing O'Neill on Algérien, then Haroun at the top of the stretch. Then Wink made his big move, pulling Bahadur away from Haroun and putting him into a hard drive for a grandstand finish. It was as if the boy from Lexington drank an extra shot of energy from the chance to conquer all in full view of the three kings. In the final meters, he held off a half-hearted challenge by Grillemont under Georgie Stern, who this time couldn't get close enough to reach out and bat Wink away. Wink won by an indisputable length and a half.

It was his most prestigious prize yet in France, before the most impressive audience of his career. He went on to finish his best-ever French season by advancing from fifteenth to seventh place among 293 jockeys. With 50 wins, he was well behind Frankie's spectacular 136, but then so were the second- and third-place George Bellhouse and Matt MacGee, with 75 and 74, respectively. Moreover, the latter three Yanks, who had already been riding in Paris for more than a decade and were sought after by all the stables, could get a virtually unlimited number of mounts, whereas newcomer Wink rode mainly for his Russian. To chalk up 50 wins in those circumstances was nothing short of astounding. Tack on the fact that Jimmy Winkfield had been through one attempted and one real revolution and an 1,100-mile escape. And that, at forty-two, he was four years older than Frankie and had to feel like it.

Those Deauville moments were magical—sharing with Bashkirov, his fellow refugee trainer, and Mantacheff, his fellow refugee owner, the applause of the most beautiful resort in the world. On occasion, Lydie and her parents may have taken the train out from Paris as well, because by now, as would soon be evident, she and Jimmy were a couple in love, doubtless with a lot more winning than losing days at the track behind them. For Jimmy, certainly, those moments by the Channel had launched a love affair with Deauville, one that Winkfield would pursue for years. It showed in a photograph taken a little later. In a striped knit sweater, shirt and tie, white pants, white shoes, a Cheshire smile on his face, Wink strolls down the boardwalk—an elegant portrait of success and happiness that would not have been possible in his beloved America, where neither success nor happiness was available to a black jockey.

There was plenty of racing at other European venues in the 1922 season—on the Spanish coast, for example, four hundred miles south of Deauville as the gull flies, at King Alfonso's six-year-old race track in the resort city of San Sebastián. Two Sundays after watching the Lexington black boy parade to the post in the Grand Prix de Deauville, King Alfonso watched the Lexington white boy Lucien Lyne parade to the post in the inaugural Gran Premio de San Sebastián. At 500,000 pesetas, or more than $32,000 (1922 dollars), it was the most valuable race in Europe. And the king's colt Ruban won it, thanks to a well-timed ride. So Lucien had his own Gran Premio to match Wink's Grand Prix. On Tuesday night, Alfonso staged a dinner for Lucien and the rest of Ruban's team that far outsparkled the banquet his father had thrown for him when he first left to ride abroad in 1903. The king surprised everybody by announcing that the Gran Premio would be doubled, to 1 million pesetas, or $65,400, about the same as America's richest races at the moment: the Kentucky Derby, the Preakness, and the Futurity.

On that same Tuesday, Wink turned up in Yorkshire to become the first (and last) black American in one of England's five classics, the St. Leger, an English Triple Crown jewel at that. The classics were the Derby at Epsom, the St. Leger, the 2000 Guineas, the 1000 Guineas, and the Oaks. The first three were the Triple Crown, a term coined in England before America used it on such hat tricks as New York's Metropolitan, Brooklyn, and Suburban Handicaps and, much later (1930), on the Kentucky Derby, the Preakness, and the Belmont.

Jimmy Winkfield was riding in the hoofprints of a role model.

Willie Simms, who had introduced the shocking American seat to England, had had it a lot harder than Wink. As an English historian wrote, the sight of a black rider taking the horse Eau Gallie to the start of the Crawfurd Plate in 1895 induced racist ridicule. Ultimately, the hatred was too much for Willie to endure, and he returned to America to resume his winning habits. A few years later, white Americans succeeded in England, with Tod Sloan winning twenty of his forty-eight outings and erroneously receiving the credit for introducing the American crouch. Now every jock in England crouched, though still to the disgust of their upright fellow citizens.

Several of the best jockeys in the world joined Wink in the Doncaster paddock. They included his old rivals Steve Donoghue, Frank O'Neill, and Matt MacGee, the latter having picked up the mount on Gaurisankar when Wink signed to ride Bahadur. It rained all night, of course, and drizzled through the day, so some of the bluebloods stayed away, but the joint was packed with miners and other laborers in the tens of thousands. A herd of twenty-four went to the post. Wink hoped Bahadur's small size would give him an advantage, allowing him to sneak around, but the miners made him a hundred to one.

The start was frightfully reminiscent of Wink's drenched Futurity years earlier, when he and Highball broke poorly from a lousy post on a sloppy track and rallied to get fifth. This time Wink and Bahadur weaved through misty horses to outrun their odds but still did no better than fourth, six foggy lengths back. Lord Lonsdale's Royal Lancer got the win. Of course, fourth left Wink an also-ran, but it summoned up something said of Simms's arrival at the start of the Crawfurd Plate: "Simms silenced the mockers in the time-honoured way: he won. In his slipstream toiled the cream of English jockeyship." A quarter of a century later, Wink did not win, but in his wake at the famous St. Leger struggled the cream of English and Americans-in-Paris jockeyship. Donoghue was sixth; others peering through the rain at the rear ends of Wink and Bahadur were O'Neill on the second favorite, MacGee on Mantacheff's

Gaurisankar, Guy Gardner, Joe Childs, and the all-time top Aussies Brownie Carslake and Frank Bullock, all of whom Winkfield had seen in other countries and other times. The *Telegraph*:

"They arrived like a lot of crows coming home at eventide."

When Jimmy came home to Paris from drenched Doncaster in that fall of 1922, his life was about to change. He knew he was in love, and he was ready to do something about it.

[*Chapter Fourteen*]

MARRIAGE
AND DIVORCE

O ne day in October 1922, a stable hand was walking Maurice de Rothschild's filly Sheherazade around the Maisons-Laffitte paddock. Something spooked her. She reared, buck-jumped, and fell on her head, fracturing her skull. Rothschild's people had her destroyed. Wink was horrified.

But he could not let it distract him, any more than he could be distracted by the fact that he was getting married to Lydie the next day, a Saturday. Happily, the wedding did not threaten to be the big interference with his schedule that the Russo-Japanese War had been, or the would-be Russian Revolution of 1905, or World War I, or the Bolshevik Revolution. For one thing, they were running at Auteuil that Saturday, which meant that all of the races would be conducted over jumps, and Wink never rode in hurdles or steeplechases. Piloting a horse at top speed in a full field was dangerous enough; he didn't need to add jumps to the equation, unlike Winnie O'Connor and others who had gotten too fat to make the flat-racing weights. Jimmy Winkfield still could.

So Wink had his wedding day off. It worked out nicely for the bride, too. The day off would give her more time to plan their Sunday bets—that was her department—and to get ready for Sunday's big race featuring France's horse of the decade. Pierre Wertheimer's two-year-old Epinard, or "Spinach," had already won five straight.

On October 21, 1922, in a quick Russian Orthodox ceremony in Paris, Lydia deMinkwitz, originally of Moscow and daughter of a baron, married James Winkfield, originally of Chilesburg and son of a farmer. With that, they started handicapping Sunday's races. But if Jimmy and Lydie were obsessed with big-time racing and small-time betting, the baron was not: he was too creative for that. So, chuckling away, the former engineer-architect set out to design Lydie and her beau a wedding gift, a dream of a house by the thickly wooded park in Maisons-Laffitte.

The bridegroom, however, was perhaps not chuckling away. It had been five years since he left behind his first Russian love, Alexandra, and their son George. Given everything that had happened to him, it felt like five lifetimes. Those painful moments when their faces would swim into his memories were almost certainly becoming less frequent, less intense; Alexandra and perhaps even George had receded into the backstretch of his mind.

On the day after the wedding, Wink did not have a mount in Epinard's event but was riding in the second feature, the Prix Delamarre, in which he had a fair chance on Mantacheff's three-year-old Haroun Al Rashid, or so he and his bride thought. For Wink, fair chance meant certain victory, and he figured his honeymoon would be in the winner's circle at France's most prestigious racecourse. Not so plain and simple, after all. Always at its best on Sunday, Longchamp welcomed the silk-hatted Aga Khan, Prince Murat, some barons Rothschild, Jacques Hennessy of the cognac Hennessys—once again, Wink's people. Yet for some reason, the bridegroom couldn't put it together that day. Maybe the wedding had thrown off his timing. Although the Prix Delamarre was swept by three Yanks, Wink wasn't one of them, and he failed to get on the board in his other race. Epinard had a better afternoon, winning his sixth straight.

Shortly after getting hitched, Winkfield decided to go home again. Unfortunately, Lydie couldn't go with him, and he would later say this was because she was Russian. What she was, however, was a stateless person, one of many newly arrived in France, where being stateless meant you were hopelessly entwined in the Napoleonic bureaucracy—for thousands of Russians, it might as well have been Bonaparte's revenge for the terrible winter of 1812. There had been that other recent case involving a Spaniard and his Russian bride—Pablo Picasso and the dancer Olga Koklova—whose stateless status had caused all sorts of police inquiries into their wedding plans. It had not helped that the police also considered the would-be bridegroom an anarchist and, worse apparently, a general troublemaker.

So one month after his marriage, Jimmy Winkfield made his way alone through the chic transatlantic crowd at Cherbourg on the Channel. On the docks of New York, this fashionable figure would have been on every other passenger's mind—exactly how did he get the money?—but he attracted no unusual attention at Cherbourg as he boarded the SS *Olympic*. Built by Britain's White Star and Dominion Line in 1911, she was the biggest liner in the world, with room for 2,700 passengers. She was magnificent, but she had a past: she'd been a troop ship in the First World War, and that was not half of it. Winkfield was sailing on the *Titanic*'s sister. It had been only ten years since that great ship went down to the bottom with more than 2,220 aboard, some 1,513 losing their lives. If this made him more seasick than usual, he could take comfort from the fact that ocean liners now sailed with certain advantages resulting from the *Titanic* inquest: enough lifeboats for everybody, lifeboat drills, a full-time radio watch, and an international ice patrol. As he drawled his vital statistics for the *Olympic*'s clerk, Winkfield chopped about two years off his age, giving his birth date as April 12, 1882, his age as forty. He had good reasons. A younger son-in-law might please the deMinkwitzes. More important, it might please Mantacheff and other stable owners as they sized up available talent. As for April 12, that was also Alexandra's birthday.

Disembarking after an uneventful six-day passage, he felt the eerie quiet of West Side Manhattan. Midtown was sleeping off Sunday night's Irish rioting against Britain's authority over the Irish Free State. As Jimmy could have explained to the French, but doubtless figured it would be hopeless to try, America's problems weren't only about African-Americans. Here, for example, were the Irish-Americans. The rioters had taken the sticks holding banners and smashed them over policemen's heads. The women among them had attacked the police, tearing their uniforms and scratching their faces until the cops gave up and became spectators. The demonstrators burned King George in effigy, somebody turned in a fire alarm, and when the firefighters got there, the demonstrators had turned on them, too. Said one newspaper: "The reserves of the West Forty-Seventh Street Station were literally kicked to a frazzle and thoroughly looked the part."

It was a few long blocks from the Hudson River pier over to Eighth Avenue, where even the world traveler Jimmy Winkfield was startled by what he saw—the largest structure ever built for railroad travel, Pennsylvania Station. It hadn't been there the last time he had come home, in 1909. Designed by New York's high-end architectural firm McKim, Mead, and White, and opened in 1910, this 500,000 cubic feet of granite had replaced some five hundred buildings between Seventh and Eighth avenues, from 31st to 33rd streets. Having checked himself when he saw it from the outside, the five-foot-tall Jimmy doubtless walked in as if he owned the joint, smiling at the idea that he actually did, in a very real way, because this was his America. Of course, any other human would have been humbled entering the 277-foot waiting room intended by McKim, Mead, and White to suggest the Roman Baths of Caracalla and the Basilica of Constantine, not that anybody had ever heard of them, and supported by 650 steel columns. But Jimmy had been the hero of the mammoth Moscow Hippodrome, where, unlike McKim, Mead, and White and most other Americans, he had been bathed in the applause of tens of thousands. He must have thought that Pennsylvania Station was just right.

This was the gateway to the South. The Pennsylvania Railroad was the logical line to the next gateway, Baltimore, and then on to the next, the Queen City of Cincinnati, where he would have to change from the Pennsylvania to the Cincinnati, New Orleans & Texas Pacific. This put him on what railroaders called "the Queen & Crescent Route," New Orleans being the Crescent City, or as its first leg was known, the Chattanooga line. God, Jimmy loved this country, its railroads, all that geography—if only he could stay. So the trip was simple as could be: from Pennsylvania Station to the dear old Chattanooga line, and home sweet home.

> *Pardon me, boy*
> *Is that the Chattanooga choo-choo?*
> *Track twenty-nine*
> *Boy, you can give me a shine*
> *I can afford*
> *To board a Chattanooga choo-choo*
> *I've got my fare*
> *And just a trifle to spare.*

Oh, this former shoeshine boy had more than a trifle to spare, and he was just the one for a shine; he always traveled high-class—hadn't he just come over on the sister ship of the *Titanic*? It would be another two decades before the ditty "Chattanooga Choo-Choo" would be introduced in the movie *Sun Valley Serenade*, but the lyrics would catch the reality of Jimmy's day.

> *You leave the Pennsylvania Station*
> *'bout a quarter to four*
> *Read a magazine and then*
> *You're in Baltimore*

Jimmy could leave Pennsylvania Station not about a quarter to four—though that departure time would have the distinct advantage of rhyming with Baltimore—but at five sharp to catch the Pennsylvania's famous FFV, its "Fast Flying Virginian," and read that magazine before he hit Baltimore. The other travelers would surely have taken this rich American hero of Europe for a railroad porter and asked him a question or two, and half the time he would have answered if he could, with a big smile, but he wasn't carrying their bags. Dinner in the diner, nothing could be finer, then a sleeper for $4 above the $18 for the whole 828 miles to Cincy— arriving there just twenty-four hours after he left New York. Here he could call on his brother William, eighteen years his senior, whose home overlooked a splendid bend of the Ohio, but more than likely he just jumped on the Cincinnati, New Orleans & Texas Pacific Railway for the 82-mile run down to Chittlin' Switch, as some still liked to call Lexington and the old track, though the track was abandoned now. Once he got there, Jimmy might have been tempted to sit tight on the Chattanooga choo-choo a moment more, cross the 280-foot High Bridge, with its three spans over the Kentucky River and that cliffside cave down there, where Daniel Boone once hid out, to see sister Bettie's family in Danville. It was just another 34 miles. But he didn't do that, either.

The old track right across from the railroad station said it better than anything: he was home in Lexington, at last. The family's famous baby found his survivors as comfortable, and comforting, as ever and, given the hand America had dealt them, were making the brave best of it. Typically proud, indomitable, accomplished Winkfields. Jimmy's brother Samuel had been described in the *Lexington Leader*'s charmingly racist "Colored Notes" as "one of Fayette County's substantial colored farmers" and brother Charles's son Robert had become a doctor in the Ohio state capital of Columbus. Moses got his name in the paper for assisting on a Colored Reception Committee at John Madden's Hamburg Place, next door to Chilesburg—as if his younger brother James had never double-crossed the lord of the estate, and as if Madden had not responded by trying to destroy James's livelihood. There had been family deaths. Brother Gus's wife Laura. Their daughter Sarah. Sam's son Andrew.

And, especially, sister Rachel. Twenty-three years older than James, she had been a mother to him. She and her husband, James Dancer, had been there to welcome him back to Lexington after he'd been "away with the horses." On the afternoon in Chicago when the fans thought Winkfield had been killed in his fall on Mc-Chesney, Rachel was the relative the newspaper mentioned. She had been dead eleven years ago now, but oh, how her memory tugged at him. And all the more because he was supposed to have gone home for the funeral. "Mrs. Rachael Dancer Parker, one of Lexington's best known and most respected colored women died at her residence, 553 East Third Street," the paper had said. It was going to be a magnificent funeral, with the magnificence of love such as only big families like the Winkfields could provide. "The pallbearers will be Mssrs. Gus, Samuel, William, Charley, and Hegakiri [a mangling of Hezekiah], brothers of Mrs. Parker." And then: "Mrs. Parker was a sister of Jockey Winkfield, now in Russia, and the body will be deposited in the vault until the arrival of her brother, which will be in about three weeks." In other words, a few days before Christmas 1911. It would have been perfectly normal; he had come home for Christmas in 1904, 1905, and 1909, and per-haps he had even wired them that he would be there for Rachel, or would try. Exhausted as he was by his incredible 1911 season out of Vienna, he could overcome the obstacles to such an undertak-ing—his family had given him the strength to resist everything but them. Still, it would have been awful for Alexandra and eleven-month-old George, whom he had already left behind for the whole season—terribly unfair, or so he must have been trying to convince himself even now, a decade later.

The Winkfields would have welcomed Lydie, but white Lex-ington would not have, nor would anyplace else in America if they'd known she was married to a black man, no matter how accom-plished. Nor was Winkfield himself all that welcome anymore. Winner of the first Kentucky Derby of the new century, he was also the last black jockey to have won it, an honor he would wear, posthumously, into the next century. Henceforth, black riders would not even ride in the Derby—with two exceptions that proved the rule. Just the previous year—1921—the Run for the Roses did have one black rider, its first since Jess Conley had come in third in 1911. Henry King came in tenth. It was more telling that the second-place finisher was named Black Servant (Planet won it). The second exception proved the rule, too, because it didn't happen until seventy-nine years later when Marlon St. Julien was sixth on Curule.

Visiting Lexington's old course, a backwater now, Wink could make out some of his old friends and heroes in the mist over the track, with all its buried batteries and stories. Every old track has its mist, chock-full of ghost riders, but especially this one on Race Street, the oldest in America. Some weren't all that ghostly, though. Willie Simms, the black star who had taught the English how to ride, though they would never admit it, was alive and well and training. So was Monk Overton, whose eighth and last Derby had been Wink's first. And Tiny Williams, whom Wink and Alan-a-Dale had driven into Churchill's sand in the 1902 Derby.

What stories Winkfield could tell them now, how he had survived the world war and a revolution and managed to become the world's only great black jockey. But he was always looking ahead; it was one of his secrets. Looking ahead, too, was crazy Jack Keene. Wink had to scratch his head when he saw that Keene was actually trying to build that limestone racetrack he had dreamed about. He even had his own quarry on his property now. For the past seven springs, when the days were still cool and the grass was turning blue, his black workmen had been hauling the limestone up Jack's soft, sweet hill outside Lexington, piling stone on stone, stopping whenever the money ran out, then starting again when his race horses brought in more cash. And the workers showed no signs of stopping. Wink was always trying to tell people things but couldn't because they wouldn't understand, so this time he might have just thought to himself: Jack Keene has got to be crazier than Count von Zeppelin.

On his visit home, Jimmy could drive out one of the pikes to Hinata Farm to see the horse everybody was talking about, a red chestnut, ready to retire. This was Man o'War, and sure as hell not that sorry Man o'War Wink had ridden in New York nineteen years ago. This one was racing's representative in what people were already sensing was some kind of golden era in American sports, the age of Ty Cobb and Babe Ruth, Gene Sarazen and Walter Hagen, Helen Wills and Bill Tilden, Jack Dempsey and Gene Tunney. Big Red had launched a new era of the turf with his stupefying, record-busting twenty-and-one record in 1919–20. In his only defeat, an overanxious starter at Saratoga had sent the horses off with Man o'War actually facing the wrong way. He still had lost by only half a length, the most notorious defeat in racing history. Man o'War would be the horse of the century, and Jimmy Winkfield was one of the very few men in America qualified to compare him with the best in the world. He could have ridden him, too, right then and there by the turnpike, if the stud groom, John Buckner, would have let him. But he couldn't have ridden him in a race, because one of the world's top riders of all time was the wrong color in his own country.

The plain fact was that if Winkfield were to stay in America, he might wind up as one of what Sam Hildreth, then at the peak of his career, called "the little darkies in the stables." Or he could become another Beaut, who took care of field glasses that the forgetful rich left in the Saratoga clubhouse. Beaut had developed an ingenious method of surviving. If a horse had an unbeatable lead down the stretch, Beaut would slip into a room off the clubhouse porch, where he stored his collection of racing colors. Then he would reappear, all smiles and draped in the winning hues to show the victorious stable owner that he had backed his horse all along. It got him big tips from the guffawing owners. On the day when Richard Wilson's Naushon was a cinch to win the Saratoga Special, Beaut, of course, prepared to don the Wilson yellow silks with green chevrons. As it happened, though, Hildreth's Novelty stole the Special. Just after Novelty crossed the finish line, Hildreth peered through the clubhouse window to see Beaut frantically tearing off Wilson's colors and replacing them with the Hildreth black jacket and white sash. Sam gleefully confronted Beaut, who quickly explained that he wasn't disloyal, that all the talk about Naushon had simply confused him, that he was a Novelty man from the start. In the general hilarity, Beaut got an even bigger tip than usual. This was not Winkfield's idea of a job.

And if he could ever bring Lydie over, the strange new wagering system at the big New York tracks, where Wink would have been working most of the time, or looking for work, would not have been her idea of how to bet, either. With their 1908 antigambling law against soliciting or recording bets in a fixed place, New York governor Charles Evans Hughes and the antigambling forces had wrecked the industry and shut it down completely in New York in 1911 and 1912. But the tracks had reopened in 1913, and now Hughes was at last in a place where he could do no harm: President Warren G. Harding's cabinet, as secretary of state. And the bookmakers went to ridiculous lengths to sidestep the Hughes law with a system called "oral betting." Wink learned that in these, the "Oral Days," as racetrackers would call them with appropriate solemnity and disgust, a bookie could not solicit but could quote odds to anybody who asked. The inquirer could then write his bet on a slip of paper, hand it over, and pay or collect the next day—or as Damon Runyon, the best reporter to hit the racetracks since Nellie Bly, described it:

> It is against the law, of course, to make book on horse races in New York State, so gentlemanly gentlemen stand around in convenient spots and permit you to hand them slips of paper on which you might note your theory of a race. You pay off, or collect, as the case may be, the next day.

Thus, in response to the antigambling "crackdown," the bookies wandered openly around the tracks as they pleased, listening to and accepting pieces of paper from the public. "You crazy Americans!"

Lydie would have joked to Jimmy. Financially speaking, the Oral Days of America's biggest sport really were crazy. Many of the bookmakers operated on a shoestring and were unable to pay off.

"I've got $3,000 in cash," one bookmaker moaned at the end of a season, "and $100,000 in paper."

As for the public, an expert said, "bettors welched for an estimated $250,000 a year," and the system led to more gangland killings. In one Runyon story, a bookie warns a losing bettor named Frankie Buzzsaw that if he doesn't ante up, he'll break his legs. Frankie makes a fine decision: he'll kill himself, in Saratoga's ancient United States Hotel. He ties the antique rope fire escape to his neck, jumps, and the rope splits. Frankie lands on the leg breaker, who chases him all the way to Mechanicsville. Somehow missed by prize-winning historians, the Oral Age would last twenty-six years, until 1934, when the Hughes law would be repealed and the bookies, with their little stands and chalkboards, were welcomed back with open wallets.

Jimmy really wanted to stay in America. But his stateless wife could not go anywhere easily, and he had to make a living, which he just couldn't do at home. Seven months after sailing from Cherbourg, Wink was back on a horse at Longchamp, towering above the silk hats as they awaited the premier race of the season, the Grand Prix de Paris. Even with European currencies flattened by what seemed the endless aftermath of war, this 1923 Grand Prix was worth 530,000 francs, or $86,620, to the winner, a full third more than America's richest, still the Futurity. Four prancing steeds drew the elegant carriage that brought the president of the Republic. Joining President and Madame Alexandre Millerand in the tribune, along with other ambassadors to France, was the American envoy, Myron Herrick, a staunch Republican, who was witnessing something he could not see at home, a black American competing at the top in professional sports. This could be uncomfortable. What if Winkfield embarrassed Myron by actually winning a race in front of the French president and ambassadors from all over the world?

Winkfield and Herrick were hardly the only Yanks on hand. Several American heiresses were at the sides of their poorer but nobler foreign catches. Fashion-plate Wink appreciated the imaginative getups the ladies had pulled on: an amazing amount of lace—lace capes, frocks, hats, belts, kilometers of the stuff. Wink walked Bahadur through the crowded paddock and onto the turf. Only a couple of minutes later, in the event just before the Grand Prix, the grandest sports crowd in the world watched Wink and his colt put up a tough fight to finish third. He was not booked in the big race, but in the second feature he was aboard the magnificent Aldebaran, a big red very reminiscent of the one in that blue field back there in Lexington, Man o'War himself. Up there on Aldebaran in Mantacheff's white with red armbands, Wink looked slim and fit, at once wise and youthful. Racing on or near the lead the whole time, he judged the pace perfectly and brought Aldebaran across the line first. Two lengths ahead of the brilliant Jack Jennings, six ahead of Georgie Bartholomew. Beautiful horses were good for him, and Wink rode this gorgeous three-year-old to the stars that burning summer. They had triumphed a month earlier at Longchamp, beating out Matt MacGee on a Rothschild entry, and they would help open the Deauville season with a big win over yet another Rothschild.

Six days after the Grand Prix, Winkfield was in his most prestigious race yet, the Prix du Président de la République. The other important Yank on hand was his good old boy and neighbor Lucien Lyne, who had done nothing in the Prix two years earlier, when Wink had run into him at Saint-Cloud. Lucien was still riding for King Alfonso down at San Sebastián. What a double-railed arc they had traced.

Wink winning the Kentucky Derby when Lucien was a kid.

Then, in that prep for the American Derby, Lucien on the horse next to Wink, watching him going down for the count— "Winkfield's dead!"

The white boy given a grand dinner as he leaves to ride in the king's England. Wink braving the ocean alone to ride in the czar's Russia, the kaiser's Germany, the archduke's Austria.

A jobless Lucien forced out of England. Wink fleeing the Bolshevik Revolution.

Lucien rising again in Spain. Wink back up in France.

And what a matchup today. Talk about déjà vu. They are at Saint-Cloud again, on the southwestern edge of Paris. And just like old times, it's the black Lexington boy against the white Lexington boy. The king of Spain against the former king of Armenian oil. Ruban, winner with Lucien of the Gran Premio de la España, against Bahadur, winner with Wink of the Grand Prix de Deauville—competing now, on the last Saturday of June, for the 1923 Prix du Président de la République.

They're off! Wink sat at the rear of the pack, his only company the dangerous George Stern, who hated him, on Zariba. George was more than ever out for revenge again, since Wink had beaten him in last year's big Prix Eugène-Adam and Grand Prix de Deauville.

As Wink and Stern both hung back, two of the favorites, Sir Gallahad and Niceas, unaccountably opened a duel. Several lengths ahead of the rest, they battled it out madly, exhausting themselves as if it were a match race across the Saint-Cloud grass. As if it were a mere sprint instead of a grueling 2,500 meters, just over a mile and a half. They finally fell back, of course, while Wink and Stern moved up to show them where you're supposed to duel it out— into the last turn, at the earliest, and down the stretch.

It was here, too, that homeboy Lucien made his move, and with the king's horse joined old Wink and Stern in a bunch. Fewer than ten meters to go. Royal Ruban, paying for his long trip from Spain, weakened slightly, but there was no daylight between the three. As the finish line approached, Wink literally bent himself in half while furious Stern lost his cool and was nearly standing. Wink's beautiful, conditioned little Bahadur flew across the line, half a length ahead of Zariba, three-quarters of a length up on Lucien and the king's Ruban. No little scrap of paper survives to show how Madame Winkfield did, but certainly not bad, as her husband paid five to one.

Wink, the lifelong money rider, had just added the Prix du Président to his endless tape of cash register receipts. Mantacheff, of course, was ecstatic. His two-legged and four-legged gushers had spouted another $40,000-plus and got their pictures back in the papers, in the *Écho de Paris* and the *Le Sport Universel Illustré*. In his white silks, catching the full sun, and brilliant red cap and armbands, Winkfield is more than confident. He's aloof now, every inch the champion, as the compact, reddish brown Bahadur is led past a crowd of men in derbies and ladies in top-heavy hats. He seems to be where he belongs—on top. Nearby, the regal, muscular Ruban provides a sad contrast with his thin, pale rider. But it will not be the last Lucien will see of his Chilesburg neighbor.

The next morning, *Le Figaro's* royalist turf writer, who signed himself Lebasi, could only insist that Ruban's performance was "more than honorable. If he had won, if his royal proprietor had honored the event with his presence, what an ovation!"—but the king had not shown up to encourage Lucien. Still, revenge was in the air. Ruban would race again in Paris in two weeks, in the Field Marshals Stakes.

It was a *bleu, blanc, et rouge*—as the French say: blue, white, and red—Fourteenth of July. Mostly red hot. A blistering Bastille Day up there on Saint-Cloud's shadeless hilltop for the running of the Field Marshals Stakes. It was not, strictly speaking, a rematch, because Bahadur was not running. But it was nevertheless a chance for revenge, because King Alfonso's Ruban now took on another Mantacheff racer, Bou Jeloud. The Paris *Herald's* pick: the king, of course. Madame Winkfield was offered five to one on the combined stable entry of Bou Jeloud, with Wink riding, and Gaurisankar, Stern up. But why were these two so coldly regarded? For one thing, lamb or no lamb to calm him down, Gaurisankar was better at shorter distances than in a 3,100-meter, or nearly two-mile, marathon like this. And Bou Jeloud was better on softer tracks.

It was not much of a race. They got off at a mild pace, Wink holding the lead unchallenged until the stretch, where he had to shake off Guy Garner on Mazeppa II, then Stern on stablemate

Gaurisankar. He did, taking it by three-quarters of a length. Alfonso, absent again, was spared seeing Lucien and Ruban finish fifth. Once again, the mere fact that Wink was black interested some, as it always had. *Le Figaro*'s turf writer said of the dull race: "It was only *le jockey nègre* who really attracted attention." Lebasi also polished off his previous nickname: "*Le Blackman* got along very well with Bou Jeloud."

Lydie and Jimmy's schedule worked out nicely in the fall of 1923. It was just as smooth as the year before, when they had gotten married between racing days. This time, when the flat races gave way to jumping at Auteuil and Enghien and to trotting at Vincennes, it gave them time together. It also gave Lydie a chance to concentrate on having her first child. On November 21, in the elegant 8th *arrondissement* of Paris, surrounded by her loving family and with the assistance of a midwife, Lydie gave birth to Robert.

Jimmy Winkfield's life was changing. At forty-three, he had slipped from seventh to twenty-first in the jockey ratings, with five Yanks above him, though that still put him way up there among 314. He was not the most famous, either. That honor still belonged to the Irish-American Frankie O'Neill. Winkfield once again started to think seriously about becoming a trainer. Maybe it had been the trip home the year before and seeing his old friends there that had brought the idea to the fore. Maybe it was the birth of another son, or the new house on nine acres, which the baron had built for them in Maisons-Laffitte. After all, he already knew how to train from doubling as assistant trainer for Prince Lubomirski's stable. And he'd learned so much working for Bub May and Lazareff and Mantacheff, even in the horrendous evacuation from Odessa and the march to Warsaw.

But now it was time for the 1924 Grand Prix de Paris, frustratingly unattained by Jimmy Winkfield and Leon Mantacheff throughout their illustrious careers. A field of twenty went to the post, owned by such luminaries as the Aga Kahn, a couple of unavoidable barons Rothschild, and Joseph E. Widener, one of the rich American stable owners who had finally seen that racing was sometimes bigger and better in Paris. In addition to the usual VIPs in the best boxes—the president of France, the shah of Persia, the Ras Taffari (ruler of Ethiopia), the queens of Greece and Serbia, and American socialites (a few Vanderbilts, Mrs. John Wanamaker, Mrs. Benjamin Guggenheim)—was virtually the entire U.S. Olympic team.

The 366 Olympians had crossed the Atlantic in the SS *America* and boarded special trains to Paris for the 1924 Games.

And with that, Jimmy Winkfield was no longer the only top black American athlete in sight. "De Hart Hubbard, the colored athlete from the University of Michigan, who is America's hope in the broad jump, wandered out of the station alone," one reporter noted, "and immediately lost himself in the crowd."

The American Olympians at the track on Grand Prix day seemed touched with gold without even competing for it. On his arrival, Johnny Weissmuller, the swimmer, was "surrounded by a bevy of girls from the *America*," one paper said. He would become Hollywood's Tarzan. On the very night Jack Kelly, an Olympic rower, checked in at his lodgings outside Paris, a short-circuit touched off five fires in the village next door. They would burn for three hours, spread to several houses and kill two firefighters—but would have been even worse had it not been for Jack Kelly. An electrician by trade, he and fellow athlete William Hapgood sped to the rescue, cutting the wires from the burning buildings and entering several of them. They searched for victims through the flames and smoke and rescued two Frenchmen, saving their lives. Jack Kelly just took over, directed the cutting of all the live wires leading into the village, "thus shutting off all possibility of further outbreaks." The front page headlines said, ATHLETES STOP VILLAGE BLAZE/ TWO AMERICAN OLYMPIC MEN WIN FIRST LAURELS IN ROCQUEN-COURT FIRE.

It wasn't the first, or last, time that the French would show how much they loved American heroes. And if that weren't enough, Jack Kelly, the electrician/rower, would one day get to be the father of the actress and princess, Grace of Monaco.

With the headlines the boys from home were getting, how was

that other American in Paris, a twenty-five-year-old journalist by the name of Ernest Hemingway, going to get any of the precious publicity he was so often ready to die for? The American athletes were all over the papers when a little gossip column called "Latin Quarter Notes" mentioned that young Hemingway had just put to bed the latest *Transatlantic Review* in the absence of editor Ford Madox Ford. Hemingway, it said, had finished two books so far, *In Our Time* and *Three Stories and Ten Poems*, which, it added snottily, "show the influence of Ring Lardner and Sherwood Anderson yet still contain much original material and here and there evidences of genuine imaginative power." Hemingway was beginning to learn the horror of having his work fall into the hands of frustrated newspaper people. So with the Ford job done, and having paid his dues several times over—as an ambulance driver in Italy during the First World War, he had joined the Italian infantry and been severely wounded—Hemingway wasn't going to subject himself anymore to the drunks at the *Herald*. Just as the golden boys from the SS *America* were arriving, Ernest Hemingway left the Latin Quarter and "hied himself to Spain."

Out at Longchamp, America's innocent young Olympians found a way—they hoped—out of the outrageous restrictions of their amateur status, which did not allow them to bet on the horses: their coaches formed a separate betting pool for the bunch of them. The Olympic Committee wouldn't throw out the whole team, would it? But even the non-racing fans among the Olympians could see that Mantacheff's entry in this Grand Prix, Transvaal, was a ridiculous long shot, 120 to 1. Yet in an equally ridiculous blanket finish, meaning it was so close you could throw a single blanket over the bunch of them, the outsider actually got up in the stretch to win. Leon Mantacheff—the poor, or rather rich, refugee from Russia—had won his prize of a lifetime, and it catapulted him to number three on the stable owners' list, behind Edouard de Rothschild and another rich Armenian, just ahead of the Aga Khan.

The deliriously happy jockey? Robert Ferré, a former steeplechase rider.

Jimmy Winkfield was on the sidelines. A few days earlier, Mantacheff had turned Transvaal over to a new trainer, a Frenchman named R. Wallon—"a hard worker and a young man," said *Le Figaro* after the race, "but one who was, especially, lucky." The winning rider "was also lucky because normally, if there hadn't been the divorce, Winkfield, *le jockey nègre*, would have ridden Transvaal."

"Divorce?" It was certainly a proper term for Wink's shocking sudden split with his fellow escapee from the Bolsheviks, his partner through victories in two All-Russian Derbies and all those triumphs in France.

It was a cold business call. Even though Winkfield had won on Transvaal in a minor race a month earlier, the old owner and the new trainer now simply preferred Ferré, who, after all, had leapfrogged Winkfield and risen to eighth on the winning list the year before. And in a sport dominated by all those foreigners, the up-and-coming Frenchman was also popular with the public. Looking hard at the facts, Mantacheff concluded it was time for everybody to admit it: Ferré was the better jockey now.

The break was not only cold but complete. Winkfield didn't become Mantacheff's second jockey—not a role Wink could easily have accepted with his seven-foot ego. He just walked away from the stable that he personally had helped turn into a gold mine over the past dozen years and through such tumultuous times it felt like a century. Walked away—and fought back when the top French racing moved to the coast.

It was the most glamorous Deauville season he and Lydie had ever enjoyed, thanks to a lightning visit by the prince of Wales, the future Edward VIII of England, and—more important to him—future husband of the American divorcée Wallis Simpson. The thirty-year-old prince dumped 100,000 francs at the tables and spent a day betting and losing on every race (not Wink's fault: he didn't ride that day). And in the royal glow, an outrage at Deauville gave Winkfield his first taste of revenge against Mantacheff, whose head was still swelled from winning the Grand Prix. The Armenian now hired Wink's fellow American, Guy Garner, who was leading the jockey standings, to ride Bou Jeloud in a Deauville feature. Guy finished fourth. Mantacheff was furious and even found the courage to tell the American star that it was a terrible ride. But he underestimated Guy, one of the white boys who had ridden at Lexington back in Wink's day. Guy snapped back.

"The next time he runs, you can ride him yourself!"

This was just what Winnie O'Connor had told John Madden in Brooklyn all those years ago, but it had never happened at the world's most regal resort. Even madder now, Mantacheff went straight to the stewards, who fined Guy 300 francs for rudeness to an owner. Aware of both Guy's and Wink's popularity, and worried about a jockey rebellion, the authorities posted a notice of the fine so that all others would think twice about ganging up on Mantacheff.

Meanwhile, Winkfield had no trouble getting mounts. He rode for a French duke one day, the American sportsman Frank Hitchcock the next, a French baroness on another day, and another rich Frenchwoman the next. But his sweetest revenge, indeed one of the most satisfying days of his life, came on the Feast of the Assumption, a splendid, sun-gorged holiday that reminded everybody that Deauville was the most beautiful racecourse in France. "Everyone was at the races today," a reporter noted, which meant the usual royalty, American playboys, and, as Winkfield noted with considerable interest, Leon Mantacheff.

Riding at 113 pounds, he was off on a long shot, Perle d'Or (Golden Pearl), in the opener, a claimer for three-year-olds, just short of seven furlongs. He had plenty of competition from the likes of Garner, Matt MacGee, and Georgie Bartholomew—and the rider who had replaced him at Mantacheff's stable. But Wink had the horse right there, and it was Perle d'Or. He won by a good length and a half, beating out such owners as the Aga Khan and Edouard de Rothschild. And the winning owner? The Paris *Herald* broke the story:

"The meeting opened with a big surprise. Mme. L. deMinkwitz's Perle d'Or, ridden and trained by J. Winkfield, winning the Prix de Dozule."

Neither Mantacheff nor Ferré had any wins that day.

So move over, Leon Mantacheff. Now Wink's mother-in-law, a Russian baroness in her own right, was a stable owner, too, albeit on a very modest scale. And Jimmy Winkfield was listed as an official trainer, which he had always known was his long-term destiny. He had decided he could operate his own racing stable at the highest level of international competition. Besides his considerable winnings and savings to date, he had the backing of Baron Vladimir deMinkwitz, whose investments reportedly included a textile plant back in Estonia.

A French trainer claimed Perle d'Or from the baroness for 21,000 francs. Baronne deMinkwitz also had a two-year-old named Basilique that Winkfield rode twice that season, though Basilique failed to finish in the money. Wink slipped in the jockey ratings that year, to thirty-ninth (fifteen wins) against Ferré's sixth (forty-eight victories), but at age forty-four he still had his moments, such as the day later that autumn when he won at Saint-Cloud and left Ferré in the dust. As it happened, though, he could not ride the following day because the races were at Enghien, which meant only hurdles and steeplechases. Besides, he and Lydie were having another baby.

Liliane arrived with the help of a midwife on October 21, 1924. Her betting parents wondered at the numbers. Jimmy Winkfield was born on April 12 (or so he was claiming these days) and married on October 21. His son Robert was born on November 21, daughter Liliane on October 21. A lot of 1s and 2s in there. If life was a horse race, Mr. and Mrs. Winkfield had the best post positions. And they were off to a fast start for the rest of their lives. Because Baby Liliane greeted *tout le monde* in the beautiful new house designed by her grandfather at *45 bis* (45-A) *avenue Églé* in the nicest little horse town on the Continent: Maisons-Laffitte, France.

Chapter Fifteen

JOSEPHINE
AND FRIENDS

The curtain rises. A Mississippi levee. Riverboats. Black women in bandannas.

A farm girl enters on all fours, hair slicked down, rear in the air.

The black band bursts into "Yes, sir, that's my baby!"

She rises, breaks into a Charleston, kicking out her legs, slapping her bottom to the music, spinning like a top.

It's an electric moment—Josephine Baker's debut on October 2, 1925, at the Théâtre des Champs-Elysées in Paris. The French had never seen anything like it. Some loved it, others were horrified, but at that moment she became the world's most famous black dancer. She was nineteen years old.

If Jimmy Winkfield had been at the theater that night, he might have been disgusted, as reserved and refined as he was in public. But the *Revue Nègre* made Josephine Baker a symbol of the French Roaring Twenties. And as she became less of a buffoon and more of a sultry singer and dancer, he had to love her new theme song, "J'ai Deux Amours" ("I Have Two Loves"), which continued: *"mon pays et Paris,"* or "my country and Paris." To any French person, it meant one's province and Paris, but to an American, and especially to Jimmy, it meant only one thing. America and Paris. The title that the all-American troupe gave its show, *La Revue Nègre,* might raise eyebrows today, but it would now translate most accurately as "The Black Revue." And it was hardly as dubious as the title of the first all-black musical that had hit Broadway a few years earlier, *Shuffle Along.*

The second notable Yank to arrive in Paris around this time had never been to America. He was a mere boy, not beyond his early teens, on the day he crossed the threshold of 45 bis avenue Églé in Maisons-Laffitte.

It was George, Wink's first son!

When Jimmy recovered, which took more than a moment, he could clearly see himself in this lighter replica—the round face, soulful eyes, strong mouth. Even with his touch of jowly Alexandra, and those pointy ears that looked like taxi doors, he was going to be one handsome young man. Born in the Muscovite January of 1911, George could hardly have been brought along on his father's adventures that year or the next, when Wink extended his amazing list of stakes performances in Germany and Austria-Hungary. The little boy had seen more of his dad through the next five years, when Jimmy had collected two more All-Russian Derbies and was the toast of Moscow. But when the Revolution sent Wink to Odessa, George would not see his father again for almost a decade.

And there was Alexandra, too! By the midtwenties, mother and son had made their way to Paris in the latter stages of the Russian flood. They had moved to Maisons-Laffitte, taking lodging with Alexandra's sister Vera Braun, in an apartment above a training stable, where Vera's husband was the foreman. It was on the avenue de la République, very near where Jimmy and Lydie lived; indeed, Vera and Lydie soon became very close friends.

Alexandra was a little over forty and terribly ill—mentally ill, according to one report, albeit a highly unreliable newspaper report, which said she "went crazy" and had to be "institutionalized." It would have been tragic, of course, if true, but hardly shocking, considering the craziness all around poor Alexandra in her last years at home: Russia's mad old rulers, its horrendous losses in the war, a terrible famine, the power-drunk new rulers who were—hard to believe!—even worse than those they replaced, and the frequent and then permanent absence of her James. Her James, who had another, irresistible life on horseback, almost as if this were his art, and it had to come first. Did not Picasso's art come first, before Jacqueline, before Olga, before any of the models and marriages that kept falling by the wayside? Was that how Alexandra was supposed to see it? And his Edna, whoever she was, before him? Was that what she got, too—an artist? And this Lydie, how would this new one see it? Would his art come before her one day, too? Whatever questions were raging in Alexandra's mind, there would be no documented evidence of any divorce from James. Or for that matter of any marriage, with her at least.

Certainly, George seemed to harbor no hostility toward his neighbor, his father. Having lived through the Revolution himself, George knew that his father, with all his high aristocratic connections, was a natural enemy of the Bolsheviks and had had no choice but to flee—yet he must have thought, "Couldn't he have taken me with him?" Now the teenager was thrilled to be reunited with his dad, dying to follow in his footsteps. He would be the future trainer Jimmy Winkfield's first jockey! And what a perfect way for Wink to hang up his own tack: tutoring his son as his successor. Indeed, it helped him forget his divorce from Mantacheff.

The Mantacheff split was not all that was easing Winkfield out of the saddle, nor was his continued slippage in the jockey rankings. His right eye was getting worse by the season. A surviving studio portrait from that time shows him in silks with a high white collar, confident and handsome as ever. His cool left eye and straight nose fix you, but the right eye doesn't; it is dilated to see what it can, which was less and less.

Yet here at last, direct from Moscow, was Wink's response to his decline: his re-creation of himself. George hit Paris at least by May 1926, when he was fifteen, and it took only a season for his old man, putting him through his paces on the Maisons-Laffitte training track, to get George to the races. Winkfield was actually doing his son a bad deed, and he knew it. He knew that rushing a would-be jockey was wrong—he even said so. He knew how valuable it was to be around the stables to observe riders and horses and pick up the tricks, but he couldn't wait. Of course, whether George was being pushed too hard or not, the boy had it a lot easier than the old man did back there with those tough white men, Bub May and Pat Dunne and John Madden. So George now became a student in a veritable college of horse racing, the superb training facilities of Maisons-Laffitte, which allowed the exercise boys and other "students" to meet some of the top race horses of France, not to mention their riders.

This college even had a "student union"—the jockeys' recreational club, one of the world's first. Racing towns are often lucky because their stable owners like to give something back to the place that gave them a life. And the finest gift that Winkfield's fellow jockey Jack Jennings gave to Maisons-Laffitte was this jockeys' rec. "In his more youthful days," Winnie O'Connor said about Jennings, "he was pretty tough, used to swear and drink and be cynical, until he was dangerously injured by a fall. The man of God who called on him said, 'Jack, I'm afraid you're not going to get well.'

" 'If I do get well,' said the little jock, 'I'll do something for my fellow riders.' "

"He got well and gave up profanity, drinking and cynicism. With his own money, he built a completely modern jockeys' club house at Maisons-Laffitte. It has shower baths and everything to make life homelike and comfortable for riders. Liquor is barred, but all other drinks and all kinds of food are served at cost."

The club was less important to pupil George than to real jockeys like Wink, who could use it right now to keep in shape, and it would be copied quickly in America—by Saratoga, for example, and the Fairgrounds Race Course at New Orleans. Saratoga's new rec had a distinguishing feature. "There are two sides to the recreation unit," the local newspaper explained helpfully, "everything being double—one for the white boys and the other for the Negroes. This is due to the preponderance of southern Whites at the track." It did not occur to the newspaper that there was also a very large group of southern Blacks there, but in the wrong jobs—grooms, stable boys, hot walkers, exercise boys—and on the wrong side of that wall.

Professor Jimmy Winkfield's teaching focused on overall horsemanship. He was very qualified; while other professors' curricula vitae may have noted their stints at Harvard, Yale, and Princeton, this one's included multiple Kentucky Derbies, Warsaw Derbies, All-Russian Derbies, the Grosse Preis von Baden, the Prix du Président de la République, and others.

"The biggest difference I see in the riders of today and those of my time lies in riding judgment, particularly in ability to judge pace," the professor said. "All the old riders were great judges of pace and were willing to wait for their openings instead of trying to ride over the field."

He mentioned a recent day at the races when "all the jocks rode out of the gate exactly the same way whether the race was for a half-mile or a mile and a half. And they continued to ride hell-for-leather for the first quarter, when they really should have been thinking about saving something for the last quarter. All that day I saw only one jockey who had anything resembling a firm hold in the first eighth of the race, and he won it."

He told of the lesson he had learned in that 1903 Kentucky Derby on the eerily named Early. "That was one time I failed to rate a horse properly," recalled Professor Wink. "I made my move at the three-eighths pole and went to the front at the quarter. My horse tired in the stretch and the winner, Judge Himes, caught me in the last few jumps." And the lesson stuck—because his mistake had cost him the honor of tying Ike Murphy's Kentucky Derby triple.

In 1927, George Winkfield made his debut as a professional jockey—though as an apprentice rider, or what back home was called a "bug boy," the bug being the asterisk in the program that noted the rider's apprentice status, which meant that his mount was allowed to carry five pounds less than the required impost. In the last race of the last afternoon of that long 1927 season—on November 12, on Saint-Cloud's airy hilltop—George could look down the stretch and see that he was not going to get on the board, but he could also look back proudly on an acceptable first season. While the old man devoted more time to training and registered only fourteen wins in the saddle that year, George was just behind with twelve, a solid start. Father and son were each ahead of Matt Mac Gee and even Frankie O'Neill. But George's dozen was not enough to move him beyond his apprenticeship to journeyman status—that would take thirty wins. So Daddy took out his pen.

Unlike a lot of his fellow Americans back home, Daddy even had his own letterhead. In the upper left, a beautiful thirty-six-point italic *J. Winkfield* announced the sender, over his avenue Églé address and his Maisons-Laffitte telephone number (just 542 in those days of fewer phones). Under it, on the first of February 1928, he filed a written application with the "Société d'Encouragement," this being the official shorthand for the society's full title, which continued "*pour l'Amélioriation des Races de Chevaux en France*" (for the Improvement of the Breed of Horses in France). The surviving letter, in French, appears to have been written by Lydie, who was, after all, the business end of the operation, but it was signed by said James Winkfield. And the application was not for the famous jockey himself but for "*mon apprenti Georges Winkfield*" to ride for another season—1928—as an apprentice, with the helpful weight allowance again.

At seventeen, George was coming along off the track, too. He was dating nineteen-year-old Denise-Marthe Valdois, a girl from the provinces who worked at the Café Féder, across the street from his father's house. Madame Féder's café was heaven, one of those places you find in every horse town worth its salt, where jockeys, trainers, and stable help gather round for an aperitif, tell lies, and talk about the races. Jimmy and George both wasted a lot of time there—Wink's favorite drink was vermouth and cassis—and

Jimmy's neighbors Frankie O'Neill and Jack Jennings, and old Lucien Lyne, who wound up retiring here, were doubtless no strangers to Madame Féder's, either. Wink stood out, but not for his color, though he was the only black person of note in Maisons-Laffitte.

"Everybody knew my father," Liliane would recall. "My father was the only African-American in the whole town—well, eighteen thousand people, that's not many people." Another who was a young witness to those lazy moments at Madame Féder's would remember, "They had respect for him. I never heard anyone saying something bad about him being black, American, or whatever."

What people seemed to like most about him was his quiet class. It was no big deal, really, nothing special. He simply enjoyed the company at Madame Féder's. He sipped his drink slowly, and if he had a bite to eat, or something to say, whatever it was, he took his time, and he smiled a lot. He liked to see other people smile, too. People felt good around him.

And to Denise, the country girl working at Madame Féder's, the promising seventeen-year-old jockey whose father was always the quiet center of attention looked very good, too. She could make a future with him.

On May 21, 1927, another American touched down in Paris. Holding a helmet for dear life, he was rushed by a mob of twenty-five thousand Parisians who flooded Le Bourget Airfield. Charles Lindbergh had just made the first solo transatlantic flight—a thirty-three-hour, thirty-two-minute hop from Long Island. Guards rushed him into an office at the far end of the field, where somebody offered him a seat.

"Thank you, I have been sitting," he said.

Myron Herrick, the American ambassador, was supposed to meet Lindy at that office, but security was so tight that a guard wouldn't even let the ambassador of the United States in. The distinguished and, incidentally, racist ambassador would later say this incident reminded him "of a darkey butler who was calling out the names at a reception in San Francisco. Three guests arrived together, and one of them said, 'Announce Mr. Bean, Mr. Pease, and

Mr. Oyster.' The darkey looked at him a second and said, 'You can't fool me, I bin at this business too long!' "

After his arrival that night, the rosy-cheeked twenty-five-year-old aviator brought the official greeters back to earth again when they explained they would drive him into town to stay at the ambassador's residence. "I want to go over to my ship first," Lindy told them, "and shut the windows. I left them open, and they will not know how to put them in."

You wouldn't have known it from low-key Lindy, but it was the most exciting moment of the decade in Paris. The moment he landed, Josephine Baker stopped her show to make the announcement. "*Bonne nouvelle!* Ladies and gentlemen, Charles Lindbergh has arrived!" she told the audience. Then some friends took her to a chic restaurant filled with others celebrating Lucky Lindy. An American, sitting near Josephine, called the waiter over and said, "At home, a nigger woman belongs in the kitchen." Baker later remembered that the waiter replied, "You are in France, and here we treat all races the same." As for her own reaction, she said, "I thought if the floor could open up and swallow me, it would be a blessing."

Lindy certainly surprised Ambassador Herrick when he got up at 4:30 in the morning, drove back out to Le Bourget, and got his plane up in the air again. It was his way of relaxing. Herrick wasn't the only one who was astonished. At the airfield, he said, Lindbergh "sailed out once more in the air, doing some terrifying stunts. The people at Le Bourget, especially the French pilots who understood what was going on, were extremely frightened at seeing him do these hair-raising tricks in the air. . . .They made repeated signals for him to come down, but he either did not see them or did not choose to interrupt his enjoyment. I have an idea this was the happiest morning of his stay in Paris."

Wink, who loved his work, too, would have understood. And he certainly got the main point of Lindbergh's accomplishment: he'd soon be able to get back home to Lexington in no time. Of course, neither Jimmy nor Josephine would have forgiven Lindy's later open admiration of Adolf Hitler.

For now, Jimmy Winkfield was doing extremely well in Maisons-Laffitte, as was Lydie, his business partner and owner herself of an occasional racer. Next to the house, the baron had built a stable for them, with twenty-nine box stalls. This horseshoe-shaped stable framed a closely cropped lawn circled by a gravel cooling-off path. Opposite was the house, with a balcony overlooking the stable, where Lydie could watch the horses come and go to the training track and cool out after a workout; a keen horsewoman, she was always looking for signs of stress in their racers. Best of all, the horses didn't have to be vanned to the track. Avenue Églé was two blocks away, an easy walk.

The house was a white stucco fantasy, with burnt sienna roof tiles, two dormers on the third floor, Lydie's Queen Anne balcony on the second, and a bay window under it on the first. By now it was home to eight: Jimmy, Lydie, the baron (his wife had died in 1926), little Robert and Liliane, and, on the third floor, the cook, maid, and chauffeur. Jimmy wasn't there a lot. He exercised many of the horses himself and always had quite a few to train. While Jimmy did the actual training, hiring local boys to help with the physical work, Lydie handled much of the mental work. She kept the accounts and made many of the business decisions, following developments in French racing and helping Jimmy pick out spots—appropriate races—for their horses. Should this filly be racing this far this early in the year? Is this horse ready for this level of competition? Does this one need a longer layoff, or has she been off the track too long already? Is the mare ready—is she healed? Could he be a jumper? Can she beat the boys?

Only twelve miles from Paris, and yet it was a lovely French country life, and rather like Kentucky. "Every other road was a dirt road, for the race, for the horses, for going to the track, or going to the exercise track," Liliane would remember. "You were close enough to go to Paris, or Versailles, or any of the other racetracks, or shopping in Paris. . . . But it was nice because it was a small town, small community, and everybody knew each other. You were not surprised when you would see a horse running away—you know, he had thrown a jockey off, or the exercise boy off his back, and the horse would run wild, you know, and everybody would try to catch it."

Winkfield not only had survived his divorce from Leon Mantacheff but had mended relations and even rode for him occasionally. But now Mantacheff was fading, unable to come up with a string to match the redoubtable Gaurisankar, Bahadur, Bou Jeloud, and Haroun al Rashid. His stud operation wasn't turning out so well, either. Gaurisankar, the horse with the lamb, did little as a sire. He did make future stud books, though. Thoroughbred owners are such fanatical researchers that, into the twenty-first century, a discussion of a certain racer's ancestors would lead all the way back on the female side to Gaurisankar, then forward again to his filly Pasiflore III, whose future female relatives would be bred to such American legends as Native Dancer, Bold Ruler, and Tom Fool. This wonderful stuff did nothing for Leon Mantacheff, however.

Winkfield was training virtually full-time. His jockey wins dropped to five in 1928, two in 1929, and two again in 1930. In the latter year, however, he saddled an impressive twenty-one winners as a trainer. He ranked thirty-seventh on a list of more than two hundred trainers with at least ten wins. In 1930, at age fifty, Wink gave up race riding once and for all. The oldest jockey performing at that level in Europe, he retired at twice the age most riders did. By his estimate, he had ridden more than 2,300 winners. His record stretched across two continents and was written in languages that the fans back home would have found exotically incomprehensible. Retracing Winkfield's American record and his startling career in six other countries—in chronological order: Poland, Russia, Germany, Austria, Hungary, and France—confirms a singular point. After Jimmy Winkfield and the other leading black jockeys were forced out of their sport in their own country, he alone was able to forge a brilliant international career. Unable to become the number-one jockey in America or even to take his shot at that dream, he had become the winningest jockey in the czar's Russia and Poland as well as one of the best of his day in Germany and France.

No other American athlete had represented his country for so long and so spectacularly abroad. And even though, as a black jockey, he would have been unwelcome—not officially banned, but extremely unwelcome—in America, he still carried high the banner of his country. Unlike the spectacular Irish-American rider Danny Maher, who became a British citizen, Jimmy Winkfield was a plain, permanent Yank, treasuring his American citizenship. He had named his first son George, not the Russian equivalent *Yuri*, and his first daughter Lillian, not the French *Liliane*, even though the rest of her family and Liliane herself adopted the French spelling. It never occurred to Jimmy Winkfield to become a Russian or French citizen. He had said once that he was doing so well in Russia, he would have stayed had the Revolution failed, but he would not have given up his American citizenship. Liliane would remember that very well.

"Apparently, it never occurred to him, early in Russia during the czar's period, or afterwards in France, to become a Russian or French citizen?" she was asked.

"No, he said he would never change his nationality, that he was positive . . . "

"Why not?"

"Because he loved Kentucky. Kentucky was his home. The United States was his country, and so he said he would never change. He had been offered to change, become a French person, and he said, 'No.' He would always be an American. . . . And then he always said he was going to die and be buried in the United States."

Would he be laid to rest at home? A very premature question. His career in racing was certainly not over, and neither were his troubles. For one thing, George's own career as a jockey wasn't turning out as well as planned. He was getting too tall—Alexandra's revenge—and with more size came more dieting to make weight.

Starvation didn't appeal to George, and he became frustrated with the whole enterprise. Then he got sick and had terrible headaches: tubercular meningitis. After those encouraging dozen victories in 1927, he won nine in 1928, four in 1929, and none in 1930, the year his father won two and quit for good.

Chapter Sixteen

WINKFIELD SHOT; WINKFIELD STABBED

Clara-Béatrice Haiman was a sweet little thing of six or seven when she saw the black jockey at the Alag Training Center, the main Hungarian racecourse, outside Budapest, back in 1911. In that land, he was an exotic wonder, one of the stars of the dual monarchy—and a monarch himself in the equestrian world of Clara's father, a trainer who once hired Wink to ride for him. Clara could never get close to him, of course. He was impossibly busy, sweeping some of the biggest races in her country—the Hungarian St. Leger, the Biennal Zuchtrennen (Biennial Breeders Cup), and the famous Ackerbau-Ministeriums (Agricultural Ministry Stakes). But she never forgot him.

In her twenties, Clara-Béatrice Haiman came to Paris as a part-time student at the Sorbonne. Later, if you could believe her, she became a correspondent for Hungarian newspapers. The French police didn't believe her. They didn't think she had a real job at all, and they ordered her out of the country in January 1930.

Clara declined to leave. She hid out in Paris, switching hotels, until one day, she again ran into the black prince of her girlhood at the Maisons-Laffitte racetrack. He was still the most elegant man in sight and would be the handsomest, too, once she got him an eye patch. She later claimed he had invited her to dinner, then to an apartment. "I didn't really know what I was doing—I became his mistress," she said. "He gave me tips on the horses, and I made a little money."

According to Clara, Winkfield set her up in the Hôtel des Mathurins on the rue Victor-Massé, but when she told him she was pregnant, he ended the affair. She said he did pay the expenses of the clinic where, in May 1931, she gave birth to a boy, but then he cut her off. She went after him, going out to his house in Maisons-Laffitte at various times and making terrible scenes outside.

Clara's life began to fall apart. She ran out of money and gave up on trying to get work. The hotel kicked her out that fall. One day she stashed the baby at a home for abandoned mothers, bought a revolver near the Gare St. Lazare, and headed for Maisons-Laffitte. She got off the train and started walking to the avenue Églé, firing the gun into the air several times to test it.

It was dark. Winkfield was in the stable. He saw a figure approach and recognized Clara. They started arguing. In less than a second, Clara pointed the revolver at him, Wink raised his left arm to cover his chest, and Clara pulled the trigger. The .35-millimeter bullet headed directly for his heart. Instead, it hit his elbow.

Wink ran out to a neighbor's stable. George, who had heard the shot, rushed to his side. A doctor gave Wink first aid and had him transported to the Saint-Germain-en-Laye hospital, where they listed his condition as not serious. Clara turned herself in to the Maisons-Laffitte police.

It was the talk of Madame Féder's that Monday night. Then, around 3:00 Tuesday afternoon, George arrived at the café, his head swimming with the horror of the night before. He had been having his own problems. The headaches that wouldn't stop. The dwindling of his jockey career. And he was fighting with Denise, his girlfriend who waited tables at Madame Féder's. She later said they had become lovers because he promised to marry her, and that he went so far as to present her with one of Lydie's rings to back it up. But then, she claimed, he started getting "brutal" and once even tried to strangle her. She told him it was over. So that afternoon after his father was shot, George, too, had had it with a woman. He confronted Denise at Madame Féder's and told her to return Lydie's ring.

"I'll give this ring back to your aunt," she told him, "but I won't give it to you."

With that, the press reports said, George started slapping Denise around. She retreated to the kitchen, he followed her, and she grabbed a knife and stabbed him. Bleeding from the left side, George was taken to L'Hôpital des Jockeys in serious condition. One report said Madame Féder's kitchen knife had perforated a lung.

It didn't help George's and his father's reputations that neither would contest the women's stories or even file a complaint against them. The Winkfields didn't want this kind of publicity, but their nonresponses helped lead the newspapers to believe the women. A couple of scandal sheets claimed that in the throes of the Russian Revolution, Jimmy had never divorced Alexandra, that "the jockey would thus be a bigamist," and that this was why they didn't want to press charges: "He and his son would reportedly prefer not to get the law interested in their affairs."

But proud Lydie did file a complaint, charging Clara-Béatrice Haiman with wounding her husband and with weapons violations, and it sent Haiman to jail. And thanks to Lydie's loyalty, Jimmy survived the scandal. In the following year, he coolly continued his winning ways and rose to thirty-fifth on the trainers' list, with twenty-three wins. George wasn't doing as well. Even the serious Le Figaro published the rumors that he had been "brutal" with Denise and had threatened her several times. With his career over, he was ill equipped to handle the negative attention, but under Lydie's leadership, the Winkfields embraced him all the more.

One day in 1932, another extraordinary visitor reached 45 bis avenue Églé. It was Lydie's utterly ravishing sister, Elizabeth Thiemann. She had presided over the Thiemanns' Moscow estate with her bulldog, live boa, monkey, and film-making husband, and according to family tradition had escaped with Lydie on the boat during that terrifying revolutionary night and eventually had made her way to Nice, on the French Riviera. And finally, almost miraculously it seemed—everything Elizabeth did seemed miraculous—here she was today, with a miraculous gift for her less glamorous but not forgotten sister. No, not at all forgotten. And indeed two gifts, right here: Elizabeth's daughter, Irene, born in Moscow in 1915, and son, Yuri, born in Nice in 1925. Although the children's last name was Thiemann, Yuri's real father was a certain Arcadia Guadagnini, who was German and who had been Paul Thiemann's best friend in Nice. As Elizabeth could have explained, it was all wonderful.

Elizabeth and Paul had divorced, Elizabeth was about to make a trip to Italy, and would dear Lydie please take the children? Elizabeth never gave people much of a choice. The children were so much for her to handle, and although she wouldn't have told Jimmy, Lydie would have known that Elizabeth had a new problem. It was called the Great Depression, it had started in America, and it made the children, like everything else in France, a tad expensive.

France's 1920s, roaring though they were, had been much worse than America's. France had never recovered from the First World War—indeed, has not to this day. It lost 1.3 million men, the future husbands and fathers and, yes, defenders of the nation. Another 7 million were wounded. Many entire small towns were in ruins. The economic damage was incalculable. This half-destroyed country's war debt to the United States alone was at least $5 billion, and many of the French were suddenly turning against Wink's fellow Americans out of their fury at having to pay such a steep price. Of course, the cost of war was affecting everyone. The United States itself was currently recovering from the 1932 march on Washington by seventeen thousand desperate vets demanding that Congress make payments on their so-called bonds, or promissory notes, for their war service.

Future "social historians" of the French 1920s, those wonderful
Années Folles (Crazy Years), would one day resurrect the shining
stars of the day—Gertrude Stein, and Hemingway, and Josephine,
and Coco Chanel, and Jean Cocteau, and Pablo Picasso—but would
be blind to the combined burdens of ordinary French citizens' lives:
their government's mountainous budget deficits, skyrocketing taxa-
tion, Germany's defaults on reparations payments, France's eventual
partial payments on the jaw-dropping American debt, the spine-
less franc, inflation that soared so high prices were a sick joke—
and the vast, immeasurable psychological torment of national de-
featism. Those Crazy Years had been a fun time, all right. But the
richest of the rich had sailed above the disastrous decade and gone
to the races, and with his contract with Mantacheff and his free-
lancing for his counts and dukes, Wink had ridden above it, too.
Over prostrate Paris—over Longchamp, Saint-Cloud, Chantilly,
Maisons-Laffitte—flew a glittering Pegasus, Jimmy Winkfield up.

So, in contrast to America's Great Depression—which had begun with the shock of the 1929 stock market crash, with the American dream of owning one's own home giving way to the reality of
breadlines and soup kitchens as unemployment tripled to more
than 13.7 million in a year—France's 1930s would be less of a
shock. Life merely got worse. In 1932, the year before President
Franklin D. Roosevelt began the long recovery at home, France
came close to complete bankruptcy as Germany ended its reparations payments. To that was added the decline in the tourist trade
because of hard times abroad and the difficulties of competing in-
ternationally with the devalued American dollar and British pound.

The rich still raced, though. In one of their favorite places, the
little horse town of Maisons-Laffitte, Lydie and Jimmy trained
enough of their horses and did well enough with a few of their own
to stay above water, if just barely most of the time and getting
dunked now and then. With Clara-Béatrice Haiman out of the picture and Jimmy's head straightened, at least for the moment, and
Lydie making damn sure that it was, and with the addition of Elizabeth's "gifts," *45 bis*, in a way, defeated the hard times. For, by luck,

Jimmy already had the American dream, though there surely wasn't a home in America like this one.

The Winkfield house was a literal Tower of Babel, which actually comforted Jimmy because he had grown used to hearing a lot of different languages in his travels. The languages of this house now were four. First, Lydie and Jimmy spoke French with the children, with Marianne, the cook, and with Tante ("Aunt") Jeanne Daloz, who had been the deMinkwitzes' French tutor in Russia.

They spoke Russian with each other, a compliment to Wink's ability to slip by in any tongue, especially if the issue, as usual, was *"Na kogo ty stavish v Tret'ey?"* ("Who do you like in the third?"). They also spoke Russian with the baron, with Ivan, the chauffeur, and with Vera Braun, a constant visitor who was very close to Lydie.

Winkfield had picked up a bit of German during his three long seasons in Vienna from 1910 through 1912, as he toured the racecourses of Austria-Hungary and Germany, working for such German-speaking plutocrats as Gustav von Springer and Baron von Oppenheim and their staffs. He could try out phrases on Marta, the maid, whose mission to teach the whole Winkfield household German was doomed to failure.

The fourth language was rarely heard at all in the Winkfield house. But English was still Jimmy's best language by far and, although he liked to encourage the notion that he was an amazing polyglot, his only really good one. He basked in his Kentucky drawl with his Yank and English buddies whenever he ran into them, which was all the time—at the Paris tracks, at Madame Féder's, and when they dropped by his stable.

As any visitor could see, *45 bis* was a full house. Under its red-orange tiles, the third floor belonged to the servants Marta, Marianne, and Ivan. As of 1932, the second floor harbored seven people in four rooms. Jimmy and Lydie in the master bedroom. Nine-year-old Robert and seventeen-year-old Irene, Lydie's niece, each with a separate room. And three sharing another bedroom: Tante Jeanne, eight-year-old Lili, and seven-year-old Yuri, Lydie's nephew.

On the ground floor, the French *rez-de-chaussée*, were the baron's room, the living room, and the kitchen, where Marianne presided as that rare bird in France, a terrible cook, though everybody loved her crêpes. Just off the dining room was Wink's holdout, a bright sitting room with a leather chair, a desk and telephone, and a samovar, one of the accents that made *45 bis* not only a small villa but a *dacha*. Another Russian touch was the fact that Wink, who had been introduced to the land of vodka two decades ago but survived by staying off the stuff, now had fun making his own, jazzing it up with orange and lemon peels.

Another of Wink's holdouts was the cellar, with an incubator next to the coal furnace. He had finally found a relaxing hobby—raising chickens—which sent him back to Chilesburg whenever he wanted.

And where was the missing member of *45 bis*? Although he lived with his aunt Vera, Jimmy's son George came by all the time. Lili idolized her handsome older brother, and George returned her love, tossing her over his shoulder and teasing her. They would organize bicycle races, with Lili and Robert and Yuri peddling furiously to a tree, only to find George jumping out to douse them with a bucket of water.

Away from the house—at the racetracks—Lydie and Jimmy had box seats to the strangest chapter of that era, and one of the most disastrous for the country—all the fault of another stable owner. It had begun in the late 1920s with a scam on the impoverished French public. Actually, there had been a series of con jobs that shocked the public, though they would not have tricked any member of the savvy race-going public, certainly not a Lydie. There had been Louis-Lucien Klotz, a prominent politician who had been one of the signers of the Versailles Treaty, not to mention the French minister of justice. A passionate horse player and gambler, he wound up in the headlines for passing bad checks.

Much bigger was stable owner Serge Alexandre, alias Sacha Stavisky. He was born in Kiev of modest Russian Jewish parents, who had emigrated to France at the turn of the century, either in the wake of the pogroms under Czar Alexander II or those of his grandson, Nicholas II, the czar of Winkfield's early Russian days. Starting as a minor gambler and gangster in Paris, Stavisky hit it big with a stock-brokerage swindle and around 1928 began buying newspapers, theaters, and a racing stable while collecting police officials, publishers, and politicians as friends. Getting himself named official agent for municipal bond sales in cities like Orleans and Bayonne, he wound up selling bonds, mainly to poor people, with a face value of some 500 million francs, though largely worthless. This went on for six years. Lydie and Jimmy and the rest of France did not hear about it until the press exposed the scandal in January 1934—and the police tracked down Stavisky in a villa in the Alpine resort town of Chamonix.

Trapped, stable owner Stavisky committed suicide or, in the version that many French people accepted, was "suicided" by the police, French being, as one Parisian wag observed on the fate of a similarly cornered criminal, the only language in which "suicide" is a transitive verb. Actually, the investigation showed that when police found Stavisky with a bullet hole in his head, they simply let him lie on the floor for more than an hour while they went about whatever they had to do and the con man slowly expired. But it hardly ended there. Because of Stavisky's political connections and the scope of the fraud in the midst of the national depression, tens of thousands of protestors took to the streets over the next month, wild fights broke out between extremists on both the left and right and the police, with twenty people killed and more than two thousand wounded.

As a direct result of "L'Affaire Stavisky," two successive French governments would fall. No history of France would ever be able to ignore that con man's biggest scam. In the wake of the economic disaster that already gripped the country, it helped pave the way for the rise of a coalition government of the left, dubbed the Popular Front, which would immediately nationalize a number of major industries, including banking, coal, and, especially, armaments in the face of the growing threat of a resurgent Germany. The virtual

political civil war of those years and the strain of a massive over-
haul of industry made that threat all the more terrifying.

Here was Wink's wider world, a world he knew far better than
most people on earth:

◆ In 1933, in the depths of the German depression, the ma-
jority Nazi Party has selected Adolf Hitler as chancellor of
Germany. Suddenly, the failed watercolorist from Wink's
Vienna days is a direct threat to *45 bis*.

◆ In this same year, the vast empire that Wink conquered as
the black maestro, from Warsaw to Moscow to St. Petersburg
to Odessa and back, is gripped in yet another famine. And
in the dictatorship of Joseph Stalin, who succeeded Lenin on
his death in 1924 and has now dealt with Leon Trotsky, the
young revolutionary from Wink's St. Petersburg and Vienna
days. Trotsky has been deported and is now on his way to
yet another exile, in Wink's Paris.

◆ In the midst of the Spanish depression, with its strikes and
riots, the royal from Wink's Deauville and Paris days, the
sporting King Alfonso XIII, has been deposed and exiled by
a new republican government—but now that government
faces a rebellion by General Francisco Franco—and civil war.

This was Wink's world. But at least for now, on avenue Églé, the
polyglot pleasures of the pretty white house and the shrieks of Lili,
Robert, and Yuri that accompanied George's bucket of water
drowned out the headlines. But then silence drowned out the
laughter when the long-suffering Alexandra died in 1934. Even
sadder was George's death the following year at age twenty-four.
The headaches inflicted by the tubercular meningitis had never
ceased. George's condition deteriorated, and he died in June at the
L'Hôpital des Jockeys, where he had been taken four years earlier
after Denise had stabbed him. It was at least a tiny consolation to
his dad that the death certificate listed George as "Jockey."

"It was a very traumatic experience," Lili recalled. "I remember that because he was Russian Orthodox . . . you cannot keep the body long, because there was no embalming. I went there with my mother and my father, and my brother, and I had to tell him good-bye, and they said, 'You go kiss him.' And I've never forgotten the feeling to kiss a cold body. And that really bothered me for a long time, especially because I was very close to him. . . . It affected me so that I wouldn't go see a dead person—even after, in this country."

The cold crept into *45 bis* and into Jimmy's relations with his children. He had never been very good at communicating with them—if he was going to survive at the top, when was he ever to find time? On top of that, what language was he supposed to use? But those were just polite excuses: there were deeper reasons for his failure to bridge that terrible distance to his children's hearts.

He had been orphaned as a child, and the only surrogate father to come along, when he was eighteen, was Bub May, or Bub's father W. H., the two of them gruff, business-first characters. He had certainly never had a role model for fatherhood. He just did-n't know how to do it. And as if the transition from jockey to trainer and stable owner hadn't always been difficult to pull off, he was struggling more than ever now in France's version of the Great Depression. Jimmy and Lydie were preoccupied by just try-ing to make ends meet.

Finally, there was that wall that Alexandra had run into, the wall that often blocks a man or woman of the highest achieve-ment—an unparalleled artist, a world-class athlete, even a former one isolated by his ideals or his memories—from his loved ones. His achievement, his art, becomes his priority, his only real concern. In the coming century, America's Ray Charles would be remem-bered for remarking, "Music to me is like air—like the air you breathe. I can't live without it." From the beginning, the very best jockeys, like other athletes, have been viewed as artists as well. Even in the Deep South of 1902, the *New Orleans Daily Picayune* had been forced to put aside any prejudice and label the newcomer Jimmy Winkfield "the Black Artist" who had won their city's derby.

Artist? How else to sum up the sublime human talent that again and again could lead race horses to their highest performances? Another rider who was called an artist was Britain's legendary Steve Donoghue, whom Wink had known and, by the luck of a day, beaten at Deauville. For Donoghue, his relationships with his horses—his instruments, his palettes—were more important than those with humans. To quote him again: "I love horses with all that is in me—I think of them as my friends, my greatest friends." Jimmy Winkfield himself, talking with a reporter, would anticipate Ray Charles, saying of horses, "If you take them away from me, I would die."

Of course, history and the world have often been shaped by creative geniuses whose first loyalty was to their art, music, business, or profession, and who, as a consequence, were not model husbands or fathers. In this case, it was the children who suffered from their famous father's inattention; Lydie didn't, or at least not as much. Alexandra had been forced to figure out her place among his priorities—which lonely place would be a distant second, or third after George—or perhaps she never did figure it out. But Lydie understood her husband's first priority, and by some miracle, it was also one of her priorities. What fabulous luck for the two of them, because this strong woman would never have stayed around otherwise. From the beginning, from back in Moscow, she had adored the races, the horses, the pageantry, and especially the betting. Women always had, though the male historians of the sport, of course, never noticed. Lydie, particularly, had been such a happy girl at the Hippodrome, tossing the baron's rubles on that black maestro's horses—unless they weren't any good. She was no sentimental fool about this American. She understood him as an artist, as Edna, and Alexandra, and perhaps Clara, never had, but it was very lucky for him that she, too, loved the game.

Beyond his riding years, Winkfield's mysterious ability to connect with horses seemed to get better and better. Take the wicked Parvenez. Because they weren't terribly well bred, most of the

Winkfield horses had been gelded and thus, unlike potential sires, could be raced until they were much older. But the frightening brown Parvenez was the exception. He was a stallion and mean as hell. Wink was the only one who could feed him. The manger was at the far end of the stall, and to dump the bucket of oats in it, you'd have to walk by that scary animal. Nobody else was crazy enough to do it, but when Wink walked in there, nasty Parvenez would just nuzzle and lick him.

Winkfield's talents were similar to those of a trainer back home, Tom Smith, who at the time was handed a colt named Seabiscuit. Wink understood better than anybody the publicity campaign being managed by Seabiscuit's owner, Charles Howard. As Seabiscuit headed for his 1938 match race with War Admiral, it was the story of an owner powered by the loss of a son, like Winkfield; of ancient clever tactics by "Silent Tom," such as calming a horse with farm animals, the way silent Jimmy's lamb had calmed Gaurisankar; of a jockey's horse-whispering talents, like Wink's; of the terrible disadvantage of a jockey being half-blind, again like Wink; and of a fabulously rich owner—unlike Wink.

As Jimmy Winkfield mourned his first son, other distractions besides work pulled at him. French racing's black American star helped lure other stars. One time he saw Bing Crosby at the racetrack. Bing was one of the leaders of California racing, a member of the board of the new Santa Anita racecourse, so he and Wink could talk about American racing. Others would come out to Maisons-Laffitte to see Wink. There was a movie producer, L. L. Lawrence, who had a small string trained by Wink. There was Wink's friend the Aga Khan. They had been at the top of French racing together for more than a decade and had neighboring stables in Maisons-Laffitte. The Aga Khan's son, Aly Khan, who later married the actress Rita Hayworth, rode for Wink in a "gentleman's race" featuring owner-jockeys.

Josephine Baker visited *45 bis.* Wink may not have been a fan when she first hit Paris, but he admired the later, more sophisticated

Josephine. How could he not? She loved horses, and she had a thing for jockeys. Her second husband—she was still an impoverished teenager then—had been a small-time jock. "Like Josephine," as her biographer would point out, William Howard Baker "had the trained reflexes of someone who has command of his body." In Paris, Josephine rode her own horse, Tomato, in the Bois de Boulogne and appeared in promotional events at the tracks. In a mock race at Le Tremblay, her fans exploded when they saw La Baker, impossibly long and tall, take the lead from the crouching little champion Henri Semblat. When she visited the Winkfields, she spoke English with Jimmy and French with Lydie. Eleven-year-old Lili was very impressed, of course, and didn't miss a thing; she noticed that Josephine was "very effervescent," spoke with her hands—beautiful hands—and was "very European-acting."

Bill "Bojangles" Robinson was another guest. The celebrated dancer had worked as a racetrack stable boy in Washington, D.C., and was a renowned gambler, so he and Jimmy had plenty to chew over. Nobody could have understood better than Jimmy a certain weird talent Bojangles had. He could run backward and had supposedly set a world record of 8.2 seconds over seventy-five yards.

There was the tenor Roland Hayes, the first black man to win acclaim in America and Europe as a concert artist. A son of former slaves, he had moved from Georgia to Tennessee in 1900, a year before Wink captured the Tennessee Derby, and had gone on to a stunning career abroad. When Hayes returned home, his foreign successes allowed him to get the recognition, professional management, and promotion he had never found at home, something Wink could fathom only too well.

And there were the guys from home who needed a buck, especially in these hard times. Phil Chinn, a Kentucky colonel who knew Wink from way back, had been on a horse-trading trip to Berlin when he ran into Jimmy on the way home. Chinn was amazed. Suddenly, the black kid from down the pike, from that little nowheresville called Chilesburg, the one who was so stupid he had taken on Big John Madden and been run out of American racing—suddenly, he was the toast of Paris.

"All the Americans in Paris went to the races, of course," Chinn said later. "They would lose their money and lay for Winkfield. They would hit him for a five-spot for supper. I suppose he fed an average of ten Americans a day over there. He was a man with a heart."

Chapter Seventeen

CHICKENS, RABBITS, AND NAZIS

His famous friends could not see it, but the cold that George's death brought to *45 bis* seeped deeper into Jimmy's heart, where he closed it off, the way he had defeated so many other hurts. Lydie, too, had pains to forget. But instead of trying to heal themselves in a life with the children, they ignored them, outdoing even the French upper classes in ensuring that the kids were seldom seen and certainly not heard.

Robert, Lili, and Yuri were not allowed to take meals with the family until they were twelve or thirteen. "We ate separately," Liliane remembered, "either upstairs in our rooms or in the kitchen with the cook, so we did not have much contact, discussion, either with my mother or my father. We were raised by a governess and my grandfather."

Robert had the best deal. He was going to be the next Jockey Winkfield, so his parents included him as they planned their races and went to the racetracks, leaving Lili and Yuri behind. Even before George showed up in Paris a decade earlier, Jimmy had taken his infant son to the tracks and introduced him around, especially to the horses. And Robert did have a lot of the qualities of a professional jockey, notably a deep love of the sport, a willingness to train hard, and a fierce determination to succeed. Plus one that had nothing to do with all that. "Robert had a golden heart," his admiring cousin Yuri, who was two years younger, would remember. "He was my best buddy."

One day near *45 bis*, Robert and a bunch of his friends were all riding the same bicycle, when it fell over. Robert was buried at the bottom of the pile, where he had a huge grin on his face as he almost suffocated. Yuri never forgot that happy face under all those squirming bodies; to him, that was Robert. Yet it was a fragile heart, and would break over the smallest thing. Robert was constantly arguing about everything, never giving in on the slightest point— exactly the opposite of his outwardly diplomatic father, who hid it all, except on the day Robert took the watch.

It was around the time of the 1936 Olympics. Jimmy's heart swelled as he heard that Jesse Owens, a son of sharecroppers, had won four gold medals in Berlin—in the 100 meters, 200 meters, long jump, and 4 × 100 relay—turning Hitler's display of Aryan superiority into a showpiece of Aryan ignorance, just as Jimmy himself had done to the Pan German movement's racism in the Austria and Germany of 1910 through 1912. In those years—even as the young watercolorist tried to picture a future white German world, Winkfield's accomplishments, prominently displayed in the popular newspaper that Hitler seemed to hate most, the *Berliner Tageblatt*—Jimmy Winkfield had been in a very real sense the first Jesse Owens. But who knew this, except the quiet, speechless Jimmy Winkfield? For Robert and Yuri and the other kids in Maisons-Laffitte, this very exciting moment that came only every four years was a chance to play their favorite new game. "Olympics!"

Robert got hold of the gold stopwatch his father owned so he and Yuri could time themselves as they ran Olympic events, just like

Jesse Owens. Jimmy showed up, and when he saw that Robert had his precious watch, he went into a state of shock. His face turned gray. He got the horse whip.

Robert had no idea what the watch meant to his father. He had no way to know that just as Hitler's Olympics would remind Wink of his days in Austria and Germany, Jesse's stack of thick, gleaming medals, validated by stopwatches, would turn Wink's thoughts to his own gold, won two decades earlier in Russia and which Robert was now treating like a plaything. Like it was nothing—instead of an eternal prize, possibly the very watch that Wink had accepted before the applauding tens of thousands at the Hippodrome after winning the 1908 All-Russian Derby. That watch was, in a sense, Wink's whole life, and could bring all of those memories flooding back. Of course, Robert might have known some of this if his father had merely bothered to tell him, if the lonely man had not completely closed himself off. And then the father, too, might have learned something—that Robert, his son, was more important than the stupid gold watch.

Wink came back with the horse whip. Robert ran, but his father chased him.

"I think he hit Robert on the leg a couple of times," Yuri said. "Robert was hurt. I know he was hurt. . . . He limped for a while."

Lili was eleven that summer—and Jimmy's favorite, though you would hardly know it from the way he held himself back. "I really was closer to my grandfather first and then my father second, but it was limited. We were left at home. It was our grandfather who looked after us—my mother and father were at the racetrack. My father would do something with me, would take me to town to get the newspaper or something, or get the bread, but it was never really . . . really sitting down to talk until I was married."

Despite being in the racing business with his wife, Jimmy shared the common belief among horsemen that the backstretch—the stables and training area—was no place for women. Every summer when they went to Deauville, Jimmy and Lydie took Robert to the track and left Lili playing on the beach with Tante Jeanne. As a result, Lili said, "I wasn't too crazy about horses. I was kind of afraid." Her adored, and adoring, grandfather tried to help. He had Lili make cards for her father's stalls, with the names of the horse and owner and the owner's colors—in the case of the horses that Jimmy himself owned, purple and black. The baron taught Lili to ride a little, and she had an old horse she would ride in the park, the "forest" next to *45 bis.*

But Jimmy loved his daughter more than it showed. She was the one, not Robert, whose future he wanted to ensure by sending her to the United States. "My father always told me that he was going to send me to America to get my education," Liliane said. Yuri agreed: "They knew that if she stayed there [in Maisons-Laffitte], she would never be somebody."

Yuri got the worst deal. Dumped in Maisons-Laffitte by his whirlwind of a mother, Jimmy's nephew never found real surrogate parents. "I was never loved like a true mother and a true father with a real home," he said, still hurting after all these years. "I know that many times Tante Lydie would go and buy clothes for Robert and Lili and wouldn't buy clothes for me. I was just getting passed-down things. One day I didn't have any shoes and had to wear my sister's shoes going to school. Everybody was laughing at me, of course."

Jimmy's chicken-raising hobby kept him in touch with his inner Chilesburg, but Yuri did much of the work, and it was mean work for a twelve-year-old. For one thing, Jimmy showed him how to kill a chicken, Chilesburg-style. Under his uncle's close surveillance, Yuri laid the bird on the ground and drew a line in front of it. "The chicken, for some reason, would not move." Yuri closed his eyes, swung an ax at the neck, missed, did it again, and lopped off the head. As the chicken ran away, Yuri screamed his own head off.

Another day found him holding a rabbit by its back legs, Jimmy ordering him to hit it on the neck with his hand. Although he wasn't sure it was dead, Yuri cut it, drained the blood and took out the heart. Uncle Jim, as Yuri always called him, had more orders: hang up the rabbit; cut around the hind legs; push the skin all the way down to the head. Yuri then cut around the head so the skin came all the way off. He stuffed the skin with straw and hung it to dry until the furrier came to buy it. Now Yuri amounted to something.

All of this gentleman farmer's work was very important to Jimmy. Not only did it get him back to Kentucky even faster than Lindy could have, but in his deadly serious directions to Yuri, you could see Jimmy's own love for the everyday labor of his Bluegrass boyhood. It was his anchor. And his contribution to the family's survival when things got tight, matching, if only symbolically, his father-in-law's contribution in putting a roof over their heads. It might have made more sense for Jimmy to teach these things to his son or daughter; after all, they were both a little older than Yuri, and it would bring them closer to him. But Robert was too good for it, Robert was for business, and Lili was a girl. So he used Yuri.

Even on those days when Jimmy got close up to Yuri for almost an hour, instructing him in his chores, the boy never felt love. Of course, Yuri had not known much love in the household of his sophisticated parents either, before he was dumped in Maisons-Laffitte. But he wasn't the only one. What Yuri could not understand as a child, of course, was that his uncle had had almost the same problem. He had been the last of seventeen children—the first, born in 1855, twenty-five years his elder. He was raised by extremely busy, older parents—George and Victoria had been at least in their forties when Jimmy came along—and was orphaned before he reached his teens or shortly thereafter. His older siblings had been there for him, and all his buddies around the stables, but like millions of others growing up in a predominantly white society, he had not experienced much love outside the immediate black community and had perhaps known even less as a lone black ranger in Europe. He was not a man bathed in love.

One day Jimmy, Lydie, Robert, and Lili all piled into the Model T to go to the local movie house. Yuri, naturally, was left to do the dishes. As he was scrubbing, his older sister, Irene, who was working at the time, showed up and asked why he didn't go with the family. "Well, they had chores for me to do."

Irene helped him finish and said, "Let's go, I'll take you to the movie." They sat right behind Uncle Jim and Aunt Lydie—a speck of justice that Yuri would savor for the rest of his life.

But Irene, who turned twenty in 1935, scored big points with Jimmy. "She had the britches," Yuri said. "They just clicked; they were talking one to one." She proved him wrong in his ridiculous theory about keeping women from the backstretch. Irene not only walked the thoroughbreds at *45 bis*, she exercised them on the Maisons-Laffitte track. That was all you needed to win over Wink: a talent for horses. With Irene, it also helped just being in Maisons-Laffitte, where there was plenty of support for the idea of women jockeys. A few years before, the town had organized the first modern official races for women riders.

Toward the close of the decade, many in France—Jimmy Winkfield among them—were only vaguely aware of Nazi Germany's threats across Europe. Germany started its illegal rearmament in 1935, reoccupied the Rhineland in 1936, and declared an *anschluss* (union) with Austria in 1938. That was the year Britain, France, and Italy caved in to Hitler's demand that Czechoslovakia's Sudetenland be ceded to Germany. And it was later in 1938 that another Winkfield came to France.

It was Jimmy's niece Martha. She was the daughter of his late older brother William, who had taken Jimmy in for a time in Cincinnati after their parents died. On a tour of Europe with two friends, Martha Winkfield Bush and her husband stopped off at *45 bis*. They really liked fourteen-year-old Lili. Having no children of their own, they offered her the chance to stay with them in Cincinnati and go to school there. At last, as the Nazi threat loomed larger every day, it seemed Lili was going to escape. As it turned out, though, Jimmy hadn't gotten the necessary papers from the American embassy, so Lili didn't escape after all. She stayed put.

By late that autumn, no one could have been unaware of the threat. On the nights of November 9 and 10, 1938, Nazi mobs in Germany, Austria, and the Sudetenland attacked Jews in the streets and their homes and destroyed more than seven thousand Jewish businesses. Ninety-six Jews were killed and hundreds injured. At least a thousand synagogues were burned. Thirty thousand Jews were arrested and sent to concentration camps. It was the Nazis' first public physical attack on the Jews—the Night of the Broken Glass, or Kristallnacht, after the shattering of the shop windows— the beginning of the Holocaust.

Among Winkfield's friends, those two nights radicalized Josephine Baker, reminding her of racist attacks on her when she had performed in Germany a decade earlier. She set off on an anti-Nazi campaign that would propel her into the French Resistance. As for Jimmy, the worsening news radicalized his family plans. "My father wanted to make sure that I left France at the time, before the war, so that I would be protected and not be exposed to soldiers," Liliane recalled.

Not long after March 1939, when Hitler invaded the rest of Czechoslovakia, the required papers and passport for Lili's departure were ready. "That was all hush-hush," Yuri recalled. "They were packing the bags and said, 'We have to go.' They just packed the bags and left." Jimmy took Lili to Le Havre on the train. She embarked, alone, on the HMS *Britannica*, which stopped in Southampton, then sailed for the unknown land of her father. Sad as it all seemed for Yuri, it was anything but for Lili.

"I was happy to leave," she said. "It was not a very close knit family." Besides, her American flag–waving father had assured her it would be wonderful, that she would get that education and start a new life. "America was like a dream for a lot of people," Liliane said. "It was an adventure." On the high seas, she ventured into the great ship's library, discovered a trove of French books, and dove in. "I read all the books I couldn't read at home—Emile Zola's books," which passed for X-rated at the time. Jimmy Winkfield had pulled it off. He had sent his little girl to America. Now he would have to deal with the Nazis.

Eight weeks after Lili left Maisons-Laffitte, Hitler invaded Poland. The Allies, Britain and France, declared war on Germany. World War II had begun, although for France, actual fighting was still nine months away. Jimmy's household had other problems. His father-in-law suffered from extreme gout and a weak heart. He had already amassed all of his memories and did not need to throw in another world war with Germany. His adopted France had been at war for a month when Baron Vladimir deMinkwitz died in the white stucco house he had built for his Lydie and her husband. It was a month and a day before his eighty-third birthday.

Jimmy's beloved niece, Irene, the rare one who actually loved horses, was suddenly gone, too. At twenty-four, she vanished without telling anybody. She could not advertise the fact that through her father—Elizabeth's divorced husband Paul Thiemann—she was a German national. But in her flight through southwestern France, she had to produce her *carte d'identité,* and at Perigueux she was arrested. The authorities threw her into one of their "assembly centers" for German nationals, the French version of the American concentration camps soon to be created for Japanese-Americans. An American reporter, Eric Sevareid, never forgot the prisoners in one of the French camps:

"They stood beside their double-decker wire pallets, their eyes fixed upon my face, their eyes peering out of their long, matted hair from dead faces white as chalk."

Irene's Aunt Lydie, who had taken her in, and Uncle Jim, who understood her love of horses, had no idea where she was.

As Jimmy's loved ones disappeared before his eyes—Lili and Irene gone, his father-in-law dead—he sought consolation in another love. Perhaps it was the terrible loss of those three, perhaps it was the looming Nazi threat, perhaps it was an enduring passion for an old flame, or all of those pressures at once, but in January, 1940, at age 60, Jimmy indulged in an affair with an Englishwoman in the racing community. Whether Jimmy wanted it to end or not, the Nazis were about to cut this relationship short, but not before it produced results.

Chapter Eighteen

THE NAZIS
VERSUS WINK

I t was Sunday, April 7, 1940—a beautiful spring afternoon for
the opening of the season at Longchamp, the most fashionable racecourse in Paris, and a proud papa gave his sixteen-year-
old son a leg up in the paddock. Chantepoulet—Singing Chicken—
was the name of the horse, and Robert the name of the Winkfield
riding him.

Although Robert didn't have enough horse to catch the winner over the 1,400 meters, a little over eight-tenths of a mile, he
did manage second by a length in the field of fourteen. At long
last, Wink again had a son in the game. What war? The Winkfields
were mostly in denial, although Wink had taken the precaution of
sending Lili to America.

Other foreigners were taking other precautions. Wink's fellow
Parisian Pablo Picasso, for one. Francisco Franco's troops had captured Madrid the previous August, ending the Spanish Civil War,
and Franco, who had assumed dictatorial powers as El Caudillo
(the Chief), was openly sympathizing with Hitler. Where did the

Spaniard Picasso stand? To anyone who knew him, it was obvious—how more obvious could it be than in *Guernica*, the mural that captured the horror of the German air attack that Franco had requested on the Basque town of Guernica and that had hung there for all to see at the Paris Exposition of 1937? Still, in that April of 1940, when those who were carrying passports of pro-German states were automatically under suspicion, Picasso felt he had to make it even clearer where he stood. Besides, his beloved Spanish republicans had lost, and now his second home was threatened: he must make it his first home.

So, on the Wednesday before Robert climbed aboard Singing Chicken, Picasso—in a move that would not be revealed until 2003—wrote to the minister of justice, applying for French citizenship. If he were a French citizen, no one, he thought, would be able to question whose side he was on. As he would soon learn, he was wrong.

Out at exquisite Longchamp, those enjoying the really remarkable spring weather and still in denial along with the stable owner Jimmy Winkfield and his son Robert were their colleagues in the business, the famous Jewish stable owners—the Rothschilds, the Wildensteins, Pierre Wertheimer, all having a lovely time. After all, although the Allies had been officially at war since Hitler invaded Poland in September, it was a strangely low-key business—the Parisians called it a "phony war," a *drôle de guerre*—with the Germans and French only exchanging occasional artillery fire, with little effect.

Even the French and English military officers in Paris made it to the races in large numbers, along with American and British civilians and ladies vying to get their spring hats in the papers. On the pretty afternoon when Robert came in second, the lady whose hat got in the *Herald* could thank the fabric flower petals that were stuck on it. THIS HAT'S IN BLOOM, cheered the headline.

Denial, indeed, was everywhere. "Hitler will never really go to war," said the American heiress who collected modern art to the earnest young reporter in Paris. "He is not the dangerous one,"

Gertrude Stein told Eric Sevareid. "You see, he is the German ro-
manticist. He wants the illusion of victory and power, the glory
and glamour of it, but he could not stand the blood and fighting involved in getting it. No. Mussolini—there's the dangerous man,
for he is an Italian realist. He won't stop at anything." One month
later, the headlines marched toward Paris.

May 11, 1940: REICH INVADES LOW COUNTRIES, LUXEMBOURG.

May 12: BATTLES RAGE OVER 300-MILE FRONT/DUTCH HOLD
FIRM.

May 13: The eighty-four-year-old sports editor of the *Herald*,
Sparrow Robertson, more in denial than anyone in town, announced:
"Race meetings in England, as in France, have been banned for the
time being." The French army took over Wink's stable, quartering
troops and two hundred horses on his property, though the stable had
only twenty-nine stalls. Thus, what remained of Jimmy Winkfield's
training operation, founded in his last few years as a jockey, came to
an end—or was at least suspended. There would be no record of
whether he sold his last few horses or turned them over to the French
army. But the French soldiers taking over the stable and moving into
the house at *45 bis* did share their food with the Winkfields.

May 19: FRANCE STOPS NAZIS ON ARDENNES CANAL/INVADERS
WIDEN POCKET TOWARD WEST/DEFENDERS ABANDON BRUSSELS,
ANTWERP.

May 20: Sparrow: "Racing, which was banned in England owing
to the present unsettled conditions, has resumed again in a meeting held in Manchester on Saturday." Stubbornly hunkering over
his typewriter in his office off the Champs-Elysées, the curmud-
geonly four-foot-eight Sparrow tapped on: "Horse racing . . . pro-
vides a means of relaxation which is deeply appreciated, especially
so during these troubled times."

May 22: RACING NAZI UNITS REACH ARRAS, AMIENS/AS PLANES
WREAK RUTHLESS DESTRUCTION/BRITISH BATTLE FIERCELY NEAR
CAMBRAI.

May 29: LEOPOLD [OF BELGIUM] CAPITULATES TO GERMAN
ARMY/BELGIAN PREMIER SAYS NATION FIGHTS ON.

June 4: The Germans launched their first serious bombing raid on Paris. Millions fled their homes, heading south with one thought, as one refugee recalled: "The Germans are coming!" Robert and Yuri dashed next door and found their neighbors gone, the house empty, dinner on the table. All over town, people were leaving on bicycles, on foot, in cars. Across the street, Madame Féder tore off in a horse and buggy. Sirens. Distant explosions. Hysterical traffic. Josephine Baker was in one of the southbound caravans of cars, motorcycles, bicycles, baby carts, pedestrians. Though the Americans were not yet at war with the Germans, the Nazis posed a special threat to a black woman. She made it three hundred miles to Les Milandes, her estate in the Dordogne, where she hid Free French volunteers. But the fugitives did not include Jimmy Winkfield. He remembered Germany. Did he hear the crowd in Hamburg cheering their Moor? Did his mind's eye fix on Baron von Oppenheim, his celebrated Jewish employer?

Jimmy Winkfield had already done his escaping, enough for a lifetime. He outraced the racists who blocked his livelihood after John Madden blackballed him. He outraced the Bolsheviks from Moscow to Odessa and across eastern Europe. He couldn't manage another escape all by himself. If he and what was left of the Winkfield family couldn't get help, they would have to sit it out.

June 12: The *Herald* printed its last issue—only one page, the reverse side blank except for a few advertisements, the front-page headline reading, GREAT BATTLE FOR PARIS AT CRUCIAL STAGE.

June 13: Nazi forces poured into the suburbs. By one police count, 4 million of the 5 million people in Paris had fled.

June 14: The Nazis captured the City of Light and staged a mammoth parade down the Champs-Elysées.

Within days, people began returning to their homes and shops, including Madame Féder and her boyfriend, who found the chaos of coming home as bad as leaving. The boyfriend got shot, hit in cross fire. Many had no place to flee to anyway, and within a month, more than half the businesses were open again in Paris. In newly occupied Maisons-Laffitte, machine-gun emplacements marked off some of the horse paths. *Stuka* dive-bombers, which had softened the French defenses, flew over the racecourse. Along the streets grew *la Plante Verte*, as the residents called the German soldiers in their green uniforms.

The Green Plants paid a visit to *45 bis*. Hitler's policy of confiscating French art and other "cultural goods" had been extended to include racing stables, and the Germans were looking for thoroughbreds. This was hardly unprecedented in war. In America, black grooms and jockeys had helped hide race horses from the British during the American Revolution and from rival armies in the Civil War. Now the Nazis were stealing sires, broodmares, and promising yearlings, especially from Jewish owners. Inside Germany, they seized the top horse farm in the land, the Schlendahl stud of the Oppenheims, Wink's old employers. In the USSR, too, the Germans seized the leading breeding farm and its entire herd. This was the Voskhod Stud, founded after the Revolution; all the other Russian studs were taken over as well. In France, one stable owner, Madame de Bonand, lent her *nom de course* and colors to Ralph Strassburger, a Jewish American who had thoroughbreds in France, so the Nazis wouldn't confiscate them. Another owner, Gabriel Brun, did the same for Jean Stern.

On the day the Nazis arrived, they found Yuri there, alone and scared to death of the big open military car filled with German officers. Where are your horses? they asked the frightened Yuri. And where are the other horses at Maisons-Laffitte?

Wink was at a neighboring stable.

Yuri was amazed that the Germans knew the names of the owners and their prized racers. Little did he know that the hour had come for Hitler's favorite horsemen, the Munich racecourse operator Christian Weber and Weber's protégé, the SS officer and recent top steeplechase jockey Hermann Fegelein, and for the rest of the Nazi racing establishment. A member of Hitler's original tiny band of Nazis, Weber had risen to become one of the kings of the Nazi turf, his Munich course featuring a race appropriately called the Braunes Band von Deutschland, or Brown Ribbon of Germany. It was in this Nazi spectacle in 1936 that the undefeated German Derby winner Nereide met Corrida, the two-time winner of France's Prix Arc de Triomphe. Something of a rematch of the First World War's enemies, by equine proxy, it turned Hitler's Olympics into a double-bill. With the European world watching and the racetrack's proud owner in his box, the German horse won.

But now Christian Weber and his fellow stableowners would do more than defeat the French champions: they would steal them. Perhaps consulting with his jockey protégé Fegelein, who was currently rising fast in the SS ranks, Weber wound up with a list that included the French stallions Téléferique, Biribi, and Crapom, who would all be sent straight to Weber's Isarland Studs farm. For immediate training, he would grab the yearling Lotse, unaware that this French colt would become his best, destined to run (but not win) the 1943 German Derby.

The world would later learn of the Nazi confiscation of art from French museums and private collections, but little would be heard of the thefts of fabulous racers by Hitler's horsemen. Weber didn't even get the best of them. Other German owners stole great champions, among them Marcel Boussac's four-year-old Pharis II, the French horse of the decade, winner of the 1939 Grand Prix de Paris and the Prix du Jockey Club (also known as the French Derby). Hitler had stressed the importance of stealing the Rothschild art collections, but while his art experts raided those treasures, his horse experts got, among many others, Edouard de Rothschild's great stallions Bubbles and Brantôme.

Where are your horses? the German officers with the big car asked Yuri.

He told them there weren't any here, that the French Army had pulled them out.

The Germans left, but shortly afterward they met Wink himself. It was, at last, the confrontation whose seed had been planted on that day in 1911, when "*der Neger*"—in the straw-yellow silks that the *Berliner Tageblatt* thought contrasted so remarkably with his black skin—startled Germany by nearly winning its celebrated

Derby, and surely outraged young Hitler and the bookie Weber. Like many Germans back then, one or two of the officers now arriving at Wink's doorstep still might not have seen a black man, though now they might spot a few of the Africans fleeing France, not that they were likely to greet them very heartily. Indeed, France's deployment of African colonial troops—notable the brilliant Senegalese marksmen—in the First and now this Second World War both outraged Hitler (who called it a Jewish plot) and made their fellow black man, Jimmy Winkfield, even more welcome in France.

The Germans told Wink they were going to quarter soldiers and horses on the property—so that if the earlier French takeover had meant that Winkfield's training business was over, these new German occupiers confirmed it. And they turned out to be much worse than the French army. One day, Wink saw a German officer trying to push a horse into a stall that already had others in it. The horse balked. The German started beating the animal.

Wink couldn't stand it. He picked up a pitchfork and started for the officer, who pulled a gun.

"I'm an American, don't shoot!" Jimmy said in German.

And the officer stopped hitting the horse.

But the pressure of that terrible year only increased. At midnight on October 30, 1940, Jimmy's affair the previous winter resulted in the birth of twins, a boy and a girl. Jimmy had now had five children with three women: his first Russian (and perhaps common-law) wife Alexandra, mother of George; his second Russian wife Lydie, mother of Robert and Liliane, and the woman with whom he had the twins. Of course, these do not include the unknown mother of Ida, whom he and Edna had adopted in Russia, or the Hungarian woman with a gun, Clara-Béatrice, who alleged that he had fathered her son in 1931.

No one ever questioned Jimmy Winkfield's all-conquering charm. But men asked: exactly what was it that attracted those women, especially as, in the later thirties, his looks were leaving in a hurry, his thin hair graying, his right eye squinting more than ever, his wiry frame in the midst of a disappearing act? So what was in the Winkfield charm? Could men copy it? Clearly the mere fact that, except for Edna and the perhaps admiring Josephine Baker, his known women had all been white had nothing to do with it: there had been few opportunities for him to meet black women in Europe.

New father Jimmy would not see much of his twins as infants because by February 1941 he had just about given up any thought of holding out at Nazi-occupied *45 bis*. As an always-proud U.S. citizen, he took his case to the American embassy and asked them what to do.

"Well," the brilliant official said, "we won't tell you to leave. But neither do we suggest that you stay."

Winkfield decided to leave. He got exit visas from the American Red Cross for himself, Lydie, and Robert, then went around to say his good-byes. He even visited his estranged partner in his glorious international adventures, who had done so much for him through their triumphs in Russia and France until "le divorce." By then, Leon Mantacheff was almost the cliché of those Russian refugees who had lost everything in the Revolution or, as in his case, after they got to France. The usual story was that they had all become taxi drivers, but Leon Mantacheff had met a different fate. Wink reported that his old friend was earning "a meager livelihood for himself washing cars—autos that only the Nazis are permitted to drive."

And Wink bid good-bye to old homeboy Lucien Lyne, who was also living in Maisons-Laffitte. Their friendship had soared like a double rainbow from the Bluegrass to the racetracks of America to Europe. The exiled king of Spain himself could have told you about both of them. Having watched the black Lexington boy win the Grand Prix de Deauville in the world's leading resort, in 1922, the king went home to watch the white Lexington boy win the world's richest horse race, the inaugural Gran Premio de San Sebastián. Lyne was Spain's top rider that year. After Alfonso was exiled in 1931, Lucien kept on riding through 1936. Although, like Wink, he was totally forgotten back home in America—never mind that he had captured America's two most important races, the Futurity and the American Derby, in 1902—Lucien's career ended with some startling statistics: a 25 percent win record in more than 7,500 races in nine countries.

Also like Winkfield, Lyne was well married, to Mildred de Neuter, daughter of King Alfonso's most famous trainer. As the two Lexington boys drawled their farewells, Jimmy was happy to note that Lucien was still in perfect health and very much in charge of his own training stable. Limited racing was resuming, and some of the famous French stakes races would be run throughout the war, although the Grand Prix would be moved to Auteuil in 1943 due to an inconvenience: the bombing of Longchamp.

On February 25, 1941, Yuri watched Uncle Jim, Aunt Lydie, and his "best buddy" Robert as they waited for a taxi outside the house. At fifteen, Yuri was being left behind again, this time with Tante Jeanne. He was not surprised. He was not an American, after all. His uncle was an American citizen who was quite properly being rescued with his family by the American Red Cross. And Yuri had never really felt accepted by his aunt and uncle anyway.

Yuri was in that limbo shared by more than a few other foreigners in occupied Paris. Once again Picasso was an example. The painter had been shocked—so shocked he would keep it a secret for the rest of his life—when the French police rejected his application for citizenship. When his police file was discovered more than half a century later, it would show that Picasso's public opposition to the pro-German Franco government hadn't fazed the French police, who were more upset that he had sent money to the Spanish republicans. This would-be French citizen couldn't win. The police said he had been an anarchist as far back as 1905, had not fought for France in 1914, "retained extremist ideas evolving toward Communism," was "a so-called modern artist"—and was "arrogant and stuffy" and not even friendly with his neighbors. "He should be considered suspect from a national point of view."

A few months after Uncle Jim, Aunt Lydie, and Cousin Robert left, as Yuri would brutally sum it up afterward, "My mother was in Italy, remembered she had a son, and sent for me." He joined Elizabeth in Mussolini's Turin, where he finally learned that legally he was a German, and thus Mussolini's ally. But Elizabeth didn't like the climate in Turin, and as usual she could do something about it because she had money—a German pension as compensation for the seizure of Thiemann family property in Russia. She took Yuri to San Remo on the Italian Riviera, where he got a job as a waiter at the famous Savoya Inn—but lived in fear that his German citizenship would be discovered and he'd be drafted for the German army. So one day Elizabeth went to the German consul and lied that her son wouldn't be a good soldier because he had syphilis. Since Yuri was a minor, she was allowed to renounce his German citizenship for him. "That's the only thing my mother did right!" Yuri happily recalled.

On the other side of the war, Vera Braun moved into *45 bis* with Tante Jeanne. And with their Red Cross transit visas, Jimmy, Lydie, and Robert made it safely across southwestern France and Spain to the Portuguese capital. A haven for spies and fugitives, Lisbon was a neutral beehive of international intrigue—international except for Communists, who were certainly not safe in the Portugal of dictator Antonio Salazar, Franco's ally. In his own peregrinations, Leon Trotsky would never have tried Lisbon. In fact, it had turned out Trotsky was safe nowhere: the previous August, Stalin's agents had shot and killed him in Mexico. But Jimmy's friend Josephine Baker, who had visited the Winkfields at Maisons-Laffitte, had just left Lisbon. She'd been eavesdropping there on diplomats and making notes in invisible ink on her sheet music; a French captain, slightly carried away, would declare, "the destiny of our Allies and consequently the Free French was written in part over the pages of 'J'ai Deux Amours.'"

Wink regaled the sophisticated Lisbon set with his stories of the czar's Russia, the kaiser's Germany, the emperor's and the archduke's Austria-Hungary. He had his personal concerns now as well, though—principally how to get the hell out of there. Resourceful as ever, he managed to borrow $800 from the American consulate for the family's passage to New York on a small boat. After seven weeks in the Portuguese capital, they sailed for the country Wink had not seen in two decades. Jimmy Winkfield was going home.

He arrived in New York City on April 30, 1941, with $9.

Chapter Nineteen

THE BACKSTRETCH

R ight off the boat in 1941, Wink's first stop was Sugar Hill.
It was the perfect spot, for a moment.
  Wink, Lydie, and seventeen-year-old Robert were taken
in by a Mr. and Mrs. Harcourt Tynes, who had met them on a visit
to France. The Tynes lived in that hilltop cube of Harlem, from
145th to 155th streets and from Amsterdam Avenue east to Edge-
comb Avenue, which offered just a taste of the same life-giving
spirit as prewar Paris.

  Dubbed Sugar Hill as early as 1919, for the "sweet life" of its
many well-to-do black residents, the cube was also home to many
black intellectuals, journalists, artists, musicians, and dancers,
wealthy and otherwise. *Ebony* magazine reported just before the
Winkfields arrived that Sugar Hill's household incomes ranged
from $3,000 to $7,000, which meant upper middle class. But rents
soared to $87 a month for five rooms, so everybody was taking in
boarders. Whether the Winkfields paid, or promised to later, or
were simply welcome friends, it wasn't for long. Jimmy Winkfield
was soon showing his startled czarist Russian bride a five-year-old
baby called the Triborough Bridge.

Take a look at that, honey.

Jimmy himself had never seen the Triborough, or half the other amazing sights of Babylon 1941. The thing about New York, as everybody said, was that every time you came back, half the sights weren't there yesterday. But Jimmy remembered a few that were still around. The first time he came, as Bub May's stable boy on Brooklyn's Coney Island in 1899, the cables of the mammoth bridge around the corner had been breathing the North Atlantic for only sixteen years. When, in 1904, he sailed home from Russia the first time—a twenty-four-year-old man of the world—the statue in the harbor was only eighteen years old. On his last visit, in 1922, the railroad palace, Penn Station, the size of which poor Lydie could not have even imagined unless she started thinking first of the Moscow Hippodrome of her girlhood, was eleven years old. They were all still there—bridge, statue, Penn Station.

But look what New York was pushing now, or take just one thing, since it dominated everything else. Looking southwest from the Triborough Bridge, you could see it shooting 102 stories up from the corner of Thirty-Third Street and Fifth Avenue. Exactly a decade old, it was 250 times taller than five-foot-tall Wink, who was sensitive to tall things; in fact, it was the tallest building in the world—and always would be, or so everybody thought, which should have been enough to prove to Lydie that New York was the greatest city in the world. But the budget-minded baroness would have noticed something else. The Great Depression was also a decade old, so the shiny Empire State Building's eighty-five stories of office space were only half rented.

And here, finally, was the new Triborough Bridge, which would take Jimmy, Lydie, and Robert out of the borough of Manhattan, either to Queens or the Bronx—thus, "triborough." It was not one span but a gigantic flying complex of three bridges and frightening as hell, not only to Lydie but to anybody with his feet on the ground. Like a vast construction from outer space, it hung perilously in orbit forty-three meters above the confluence of the Harlem and East rivers and Hell Gate Channel. And like the Empire State, like almost everything in America's cities, the Triborough reminded people of the Depression that President Roosevelt could not seem to defeat—because the bridge construction had begun on October 25, 1929, the very day the stock market crashed, then investors balked at funding it, and it finally took seven years to complete. From Harlem's main drag, 125th Street, the Triborough's lift bridge would take Jimmy and Lydie straight across the Harlem River to Randalls and Wards islands. Then it would connect with the Triborough's main suspension bridge—2,780 feet, or more than twice as long as the Empire State was high—from Wards Island to Queens.

The Winkfields moved to the other side of the bridge. Specifically, to Jamaica, in the heart of Queens. Jamaica was the very place where thirty-eight years earlier, toward the end of 1903, Wink had desperately searched for mounts amid a series of hammer blows to his livelihood—John Madden's hex, hard times and fierce racism at the tracks—that not only ended any hope he had of becoming America's leading jockey but forced him out of the country he loved. Now he was again desperately searching for work amid hard times for millions of Americans. And he was in the exact middle of it. If the Depression could be glimpsed through the narrow windows of the Empire State's empty floors, it was all over Queens.

But FDR was all over Queens, too: the borough was the biggest work site in the world, field headquarters for Roosevelt's emergency employment and relief agency, the Works Progress Administration. Of course, it was perfectly natural that Jimmy Winkfield should have a ringside seat on the century's worst economic crisis by far and FDR's historic initiatives against it. Never mind his merely athletic achievements, such as his back-to-back Kentucky Derbies; Wink had already had clubhouse seats at many of the most important moments of his century: the Russian end of the Russo-Japanese War, the 1905 "rehearsal" of the Russian Revolution, the First World War, the introduction of lighter-than-air flight, the Russian Revolution, the Paris of the Roaring Twenties, the Nazi invasion of France. He wasn't one to miss a global event.

Now he was smack in the middle of the century's latest crucible,

the Great Depression, and on the very battlefield where Roosevelt
had concentrated his WPA forces. In the world of politicians—of
compromise and half-measures—it was difficult even to imagine
the daring, the bravado, the supreme optimism of this Roosevelt
initiative. It was also a measure of the suffering of the American
people. FDR's outlay for the WPA in 1935 was an impossible
$4.8 billion, more than half of the entire federal budget. And an
enormous portion of it went to New York City—7 percent, or
$20 million a month. Why? Because nearly 7 percent of all Amer-
icans on relief lived in New York City; because the WPA's director,
Harry Hopkins, had worked in a settlement house in New York
City and had led the state relief agency; because Mayor Fiorello
LaGuardia, who had already coordinated many brilliant city and
private relief initiatives, enjoyed immense influence with Roosevelt
and Hopkins. And, not least, it would never be more obvious in
President Roosevelt's four terms that he, too, was a New Yorker.

Jimmy and Lydie could see that the WPA's crews had accom-
plished wonders across the city. They had built the FDR Drive in
Lower Manhattan, South Shore Drive in Brooklyn, 255 play-
grounds, five thousand acres of new parks, and many schools, hos-
pitals, clinics, and police and fire departments. They had torn down
5,500 old buildings to make room for new ones in the Williams-
burg section of Brooklyn and the Lower East Side of Manhattan.

But Queens, with nearly 20 percent of the city's territory, was
the bull's-eye of both the federal and city efforts. And one of the
driving forces had been the 1939–1940 World's Fair in Queens, on
the site of the old Corona Dumps along the Flushing River. Starting in 1936, WPA crews removed mountains of refuse and installed
water mains, sewers, and streets. The city expanded Jamaica Avenue, the borough's most important thoroughfare, and opened the
Independent subway in Jamaica. To make the world's fair—and
Queens—accessible to the world, the city's Triborough Bridge Authority simply threw up another bridge as if it were nothing, the
Whitestone, which crossed the upper East River from the Bronx
to Queens; then the city built the Whitestone Expressway and

Grand Central and Cross Island parkways; and finally the feds contributed LaGuardia Airport, at a cost of $43 million. Opened in
December 1939, it was the first airport in the United States built by
the federal government.

The winner of the All-Russian Derby and the Prix du Président
de la République, the trainer whose stable was next door to the
Aga Khan's outside Paris, never thought he'd be looking for relief
work with road crews in Queens. And he didn't, at first. When he
got back home to America, he figured he could find work at one of
the racetracks around Queens—Jamaica, Aqueduct, or Belmont,
just across the border in Nassau County. Hardly a month off the
boat and who should he run into out at Belmont but another Lexington homeboy, old Marshall Lilly? What Depression? Here were
these two Kentucky gentlemen of the old school—drinking each
other in, one more courteous than the other. Marshall's rainbow had
not spanned the ocean, but it had taken him to the pot of gold. He
was the most famous and possibly best exercise rider in the land,
working for America's top stable, Greentree, owned by Helen Hay
Whitney and flying the colors of one of her favorite gowns, pink
and black. Early every morning, sometimes before sunrise, Whitney
could be reassured that all was right in her world when she peered
across the fences to the far side of the training track and saw a hat
bouncing up and down. It was Marshall Lilly, in his trademark
derby. Wink called him "the honestest man who ever wore a hat."

Quiet Wink loved to listen more than talk, so he caught up
fast and soon heard that not all of his old friends were still out there
raising hell like Marshall. Everybody else, it seemed, was dead.
Gone were the other two great black jockeys, his role models.
Willie Simms, like Wink a two-time Kentucky Derby winner, had
died in 1927, at fifty-seven. Monk Overton, who made it into the
books by winning six out of six in Chicago back in 1891, had
wound up in a Chicago police court a decade later. It took six cops
to hold the little man, inspiring the headline JOCKEY "MONK" OVER-
TON IS INSANE. But Monk continued his career as a fine trainer
until he died in 1935 at sixty-five. Not only were Wink's idols dead,

but as the stable hands around the New York tracks could tell him, he had no successors: not a single black jockey had reached the level he had achieved in the first few years of the century.

But if he had gotten into New York just a year earlier, he could have visited old Bub May. Bub, who had given him his start and talked him into crossing John Madden, eventually moved to the Big Apple, changing his redneck nickname to the more respectable, Yankee-sounding Bud. John W. May died at Nassau County Hospital in 1940, at age sixty-nine, and was buried in Lexington. The only other American who ever held Winkfield's contract, Pat Dunne, had beaten Bub to the graveyard in Lexington, but his son Francis was carrying on the family racing tradition as an official at Aqueduct. Could the Dunne family save Wink again?

No. There was no work for Wink at the New York tracks, where nobody remembered him, with the possible exception of one or two wizened stable hands. What there was, when the Nazis had your house and you were stuck in Queens with no money, was street-repair work, and plenty of it. The WPA was repairing streets and highways that, if laid out end to end to make a single thorough-fare, would have taken the Winkfields out to Chicago and beyond. They totaled two thousand miles. But despite Wink's wonderful curriculum vitae—where had he won that gold watch?—there was enormous competition for the jobs: the WPA's New York City workforce ranged from 100,000 to 245,000 at various points, with up to 100,000 still trying to sign on. Nobody would care that one of the latter applicants had won Deauville's Grand Handicap and Grand Prix in the same season.

How, at age sixty-one, was Wink going to get a WPA job? He had hit bottom—again. But he hadn't been a quitter when the world was against him at age twenty-three. And now he had a secret weapon, which nobody knew about in America. The freedom he had experienced in Russia and France had made him even stronger, strong enough to ignore the few insults that people in those countries had occasionally sent his way. Once he got used to it, he had taken to European life comfortably and confidently. What was extraordinary about him now was that he could ignore the slings and arrows, whatever they threw at him, and prepare to re-invent himself yet again. So, in the Winkfields' little apartment in Jamaica, he began by shoe-polishing his gray hair black. Then he slipped into a broad-lapel suit that would have looked perfect any Sunday afternoon on the Champs-Elysées. He added the correct thin-striped tie and a knitted V-neck sweater. It was the old, perma-nent Winkfield elegance. It made him at least ten years younger—you can tell from a photograph—and it impressed the hell out of the WPA interviewer down the street. It didn't hurt, either, that Wink lied about his age, as he had when he took on the younger jockeys of Paris two decades ago; this time he must have taken a lot more than two years off. He got the job. It was the hardest thing he would ever do.

While Baroness Lydie toiled at a glove factory, Monsieur Jimmy manned a jackhammer to break up the cement in the streets of Jamaica. The last time he was here, nearly four decades ago, most of Jamaica's streets weren't even paved—so, he may have mused to himself, what was the point? One day, sixteen-year-old Lili came up to visit from Cincinnati—she hadn't seen them in three years—and she would remember her mother complaining that the shoe polish in Papa's hair got all over the pillowcases. Through the work-day, the actual, back-breaking toil on the streets, the jackhammer-ing, was especially tough on the muscles of an aging man whose life had been a long physical trial on a speeding horse. But nobody knew that. Nobody knew the little man out there in the sun had been the toast of St. Petersburg and Hamburg and Paris.

Amazingly, Wink wasn't the only old jockey around. Having squandered his fortune, Winnie O'Connor was making ends meet as a bartender next door in Brooklyn, telling stories to the Depres-sion drunks about the fabulous races he'd won all over the world. If they ever got together, Wink and Winnie could reminisce about their old battles, how Wink had beat him in the Derby, and the big ones they had both won in different years, the Graf Hugo Henckel-Memorial at Vienna, the Grosse Preis von Baden, the Grand Prix de Deauville. Winnie would die in a few years while holding down the bar job.

After five weeks in New York City, Wink made a quick trip home to the Bluegrass, and between family reunions he pulled off one of his publicity coups, just as he used to do when he was riding. He got himself a long interview in the Lexington paper, which reminded everybody that he was the "only colored boy alive who ever rode a winner of the Kentucky Derby." Naturally, it was picked up by the white boys down the street at the nationally circulated *Thoroughbred Record*, and the *Louisville Courier-Journal* interviewed him as the "last of the great Negro jockeys and only living member of his race ever to ride a winner in the Kentucky Derby."

It was in those interviews that Winkfield began his career of gilding the lily, embellishing stories of a career that hardly needed it and usually suffered from it—sometimes because he couldn't remember it all and other times because, well, he loved to tell stories. And the interviewers helped him. "He can speak French, German and Russian as well if not better than English," one paper raved, whereas it should have said something like, "He has quite a bit of broken Russian and French and a few notions of German and can speak English better than anyone."

The jobless Wink again proved himself an expert on his sport. He offered the *TR* a clear and simple analysis of his way with two-year-olds. As the paper reported: "He hustled them out of the gate in a hurry and then took a tight hold and saved something for the finish after the other boys had run their mounts limber." More important, Jimmy Winkfield had an explanation "for the alarming death and injury toll among modern riders," the *Courier-Journal* said. In those days, as Laura Hillenbrand would write in *Seabiscuit*,

riders suffered horrible injuries when dragged from their stirrups and under their horses' legs or when thrown forward, ending up clinging to the underside of the horses' necks while the animals' front legs pummeled their chests and abdomens . . . between 1935 and 1939 alone, nineteen riders were killed in racing accidents.

But not back in Winkfield's early days on the American circuit, and not now in Europe, Wink said. One reason for all the accidents in the United States, he explained, was that jockeys were rushed into their jobs. Trainers would push them into competition before they had any idea of safety.

A lot of them kill themselves before they really learn the fundamentals of riding. . . . They go out there riding with their heads down and don't watch where they're going. . . . They should learn first of all to watch where they're going. We rode crouched over, too, but we kept our heads up and our eyes open. When we saw that a horse ahead was lugging in or lugging out, we would estimate which way he was going and take up without losing much ground. And there weren't half as many as accidents.

Winkfield pointed out that Europe had fewer riding fatalities than America even though the fields over there were larger.

In 32 years of racing, I fell only five times. . . . The last time was in the French Oaks at Chantilly in which there were 19 starters. There was a five-horse spill on the track and one jockey was hurt, but my horse picked his way through the pile and I didn't get a scratch. That was one of the few near-serious accidents that I have ever experienced in thousands of races.

In Lexington, he got to work on his personal issues, too, or at least the main one: he was broke. And in debt. Like other stables in France, his training business had been losing money fast as the 1930s came to a close, and it vanished as the Germans arrived. So now he mortgaged his Lexington house for quick cash to live on, but if he thought that nationally circulated *TR* article was going to restore his name and fame and help find him a job, he was wrong. In fact, the reporter who copied the story from the *Leader* accidentally called him "Wakefield" throughout. So much for his stardom. Still, it was in this *TR* article that Wink offered that telling self-analysis:

He will probably remain in this country for some time to come, following his profession. . . . He has had a colorful and successful career on the turf. He is still active and healthy. What his future plans may be he isn't at all sure. He does want to remain close to horses, because, as he put it, "If you take them away from me, I would die."

It sounded like an obit, but not if you knew Jimmy Winkfield, who never gave up. It wasn't so much that he drove himself. He still moved at his gentlemanly pace, still spoke slowly, considering every word, and not because he was over sixty now. It was the way he was and always would be. He endured, like Kentucky limestone. And damned if he didn't have a lesson in limestone right in front of him.

When Winkfield saw it on his last visit home, two decades earlier, crazy Jack Keene's stone racetrack wasn't even half finished. But stubborn Jack had kept his workers hauling the stone from his quarry to his huge work site for another thirteen years, creating gigantic piles like some modern-day Stonehenge, until Keene's folly was "almost medieval in its vastness." It was still only half-finished and without a roof, when, in 1935, a group of Bluegrass horsemen finally adopted it as the site of something almost as singular as Jack's dream: a nonprofit racetrack, dedicated to preserving the sport in the heart of the Bluegrass, with revenues earmarked for educational and charitable purposes.

They called it Keeneland. It opened in 1936 and, because of its thoroughbred auctions, Keeneland Race Course became famous among horsemen the world over, which made world-traveling Jack especially happy, though with barely disguised pride he kept right on calling it his "stone barn." The man who sent Jimmy Winkfield to Russia would finally be struck down by a heart attack at the Fairgrounds racetrack in Detroit in May 1943, at age seventy-three, but his own racetrack would remain one of the sport's jewels into the next century.

Like Kentucky limestone, Wink was going to endure, too, and the life of the four-time All-Russian Derby winner improved slightly when at last he got a job in his beloved industry—as a stable hand. Doing anything with race horses beat the jackhammer. He landed the work through Robert, who had found a small job himself helping out and riding a few races in New York for the Bostwicks, a steeplechase family based in the fancy horse town of Aiken, South Carolina. As a steeplechaser, Robert was not about to bring back the vanished black jockeys; in fact, they had never been forced out of jumping. Steeplechasing's important minority of black riders had included Charlie Smoot, the national champion of the twenties, and Colonel "Not" Brooks, another star, who rode into the thirties. Robert wasn't a very good jumper, and sometimes he was terrified, his face freezing in fear in midair. But he was working.

In its first full year in the war, 1942, America staged about eighteen thousand horse races. Unprecedented throngs mobbed the tracks. Just a few miles from where Jimmy, Lydie, and their son lived in Jamaica, Belmont Park registered a record 51,903 fans on Memorial Day. They bet $2.1 million, also a record, and there were a number of million-dollar handles. The 1941 Triple Crown winner Whirlaway was back and on his way to smashing the half-million-dollar earnings barrier. Helen Hay Whitney's (and the fifty-something "exercise boy" Marshall Lilly's) Greentree topped the money list for the stables.

One June day, eighteen-year-old Robert Winkfield captured the third race at Aqueduct, a hurdle. So now both Winkfields had won in America. Robert rode at somewhere around 130 pounds, and the chart for the Bostwick family's Galley Boy read: "Start good from flag. Won easily." His father went with him a couple of months later when the Bostwicks took Robert up to Saratoga. It brought back memories for Wink: it was there that he had once rubbed shoulders with the most glittering names of racing. And there again was Robert, riding on a card with such stars as Eddie Arcaro, Johnny Longden, Conn McCreary, and Don Meade. But unlike them, Robert would almost certainly have avoided the jockeys' swimming pool because it had a wall separating whites and blacks. And Robert ended up in the sky again, too, jettisoned at the tenth fence by Mrs. Bostwick's Arms of War—but he did something else that saved the day for Wink.

Robert told the Bostwicks his father was good around horses, the understatement of 1942. That got Wink a job at their training track and stables down in Aiken for the winter. He left Lydie in Jamaica with some friends because he was not about to expose her to whatever southern hospitality awaited the white wife of a black man. One day down there, Pete Bostwick asked him:

"Say, Winkfield, you aren't by any chance the Winkfield who won the Kentucky Derby, are you?"

"Yes, suh, I win it twice, in oh-one and oh-two," said Jimmy in his horseman's grammar.

"Well, my goodness," Bostwick said, shaking the old man's hands. "Where have you been all these years?"

"Well, I tell you, Mr. Bostwick, I been around."

The U.S. Army now solved one of Jimmy's problems. He would no longer have to worry about his son's prospects. All that his American-citizen son wanted now was to join the U.S. Army so he could get back to France and see *45 bis*, his childhood home. It was easy to join the army in 1943. You sat around and waited until the draft board called you, which is what the Jamaica Selective Service Board did to Robert in May. Signing up, he told the army his home address was Hialeah Park, the famous racetrack in Florida, which may have been wishful thinking, since Hialeah was shut down that year because the air force was taking it over.

The army's statistics for Robert seemed especially relevant: five foot three and a half, 130 pounds, Negro, Jockey. In case any officers were unclear about it, "Negro" was defined in a report from the National War College:

As an individual, the negro is docile, tractable, light-hearted, care free, and good-natured. If unjustly treated, he is likely to become surly and stubborn, though this is a temporary phase. He is careless, shiftless, irresponsible and secretive. He resents censure and is best handled with praise and ridicule. He is unmoral, untruthful, and his sense of right doing is relatively inferior.

Officially, "Negro" meant that in this man's army, Wink's son was going to be denied a chance to serve in a combat unit. And "Jockey" translated nicely into his army job: light truck driver, which in Robert's case meant driving gasoline trucks to the white units. But Robert took things in his own hands and boldly assigned himself an additional mission: liberate Maisons-Laffitte. Damned if he didn't do it, too. Right after hitting Europe in the wake of the Normandy invasion, his unit found itself six miles from the old horse town. Robert went to see his captain.

"Would it be all right if I ran over there in a jeep?" he asked.

"Okay, just be careful. The Germans aren't completely cleaned out of that area yet."

Robert drove down the road and into town, where he saw a lot of his friends, who'd been living under the Germans for three years.

"I've come to liberate Maisons-Laffitte!" he told them, with a grin on his face. They had a little wine to celebrate. While he was there, Robert could have told old Lucien about Jimmy's visit to Lexington, and Lucien had a story or two himself to tell: he had trained the winner of the prestigious Prix de Diane, the French Oaks, under the noses of the Nazis, and to top that, in the year Robert arrived, he had been held in a detainment center by the Germans for a few weeks. It was turning into a pretty good party when an old neighbor ran up.

"You'd better unliberate fast," the neighbor said. "There's a German tank coming through the woods."

So the steeplechase jockey-turned-U.S. Army driver got out of Maisons-Laffitte.

On the other side of the war, the steeplechase jockey-turned-SS major general received an astonishing promotion. Never mind that Hermann Fegelein was illiterate and ignorant; on the contrary, those qualities perhaps suggested harmlessness and surely helped him as he was dispatched straight to Berlin to be SS chief Heinrich Himmler's representative to Adolf Hitler himself. Fegelein was stationed in Hitler's bunker, which was built deep under the Chancellery garden as a protective fortress, command post, office, and residence. Fegelein got even closer to the Führer by marrying Gretl, the sister of Hitler's mistress Eva Braun.

As Robert and his fellow GIs advanced into Germany and their Russian allies advanced into Berlin, clinical insanity advanced through Hitler's bunker. When President Roosevelt died on April 12, 1945, Hitler's propaganda minister, Paul Joseph Goebbels, got on the telephone to the *Führerbunker* shortly after midnight Berlin time: "My Führer! I congratulate you! Roosevelt is dead! It is written in the stars that the second half of April will be the turning point for us. This is Friday the thirteenth. It is the turning point!"

On April 21, the panicking Hitler ordered SS General Felix Steiner to counterattack the overwhelmingly superior Russians in Berlin's southern suburbs. Steiner declined, and Hitler became hysterical. In what historian William L. Shirer would call the greatest rage of Hitler's life, the Führer shrieked that this was the end, everyone was deserting him. Fegelein, the former jockey, got on the bunker's telephone and told his boss, Himmler, about Hitler's blow-up.

"Everyone is mad in Berlin!" Himmler shouted. "What am I to do?"

What he did was secretly ask Sweden's Count Bernadotte to advise the American commander, General Dwight D. Eisenhower, that he, Himmler, was taking over, and that Germany was ready to surrender. On April 26, Himmler's man Fegelein slipped out of Hitler's bunker, switched into civilian clothes, and headed for his home in the Charlottenburg district of Berlin. The legitimately paranoid Hitler noticed Fegelein's absence the next day, brought him back to the bunker, and had him thrown into the guardhouse.

Two days later, a courier brought Hitler a Reuter news dispatch revealing that Himmler was planning to take over and surrender the German armies to Eisenhower. Hitler exploded again. Himmler! His own "true Heinrich!" The Führer "raged like a madman," said a witness. His color turned bright red—"and his face was virtually unrecognizable." Fegelein was immediately brought from the guardhouse, questioned about Himmler's treason, accused of being in on it, then taken to the Chancellery garden and shot.

"Eva cried," remembered one of Hitler's secretaries. "Her sister was about to have their child." But Eva did nothing to save her brother-in-law. "Poor, poor Adolf," was all she said to someone next to her, "deserted by everyone, betrayed by all. Better that ten thousand others die than that he be lost to Germany."

Early on the morning of April 29, a Berlin city councilman was called to the bunker to join Hitler and his mistress of twelve years in matrimony, after they had sworn in the marriage document they were each "of complete Aryan descent." The bride signed her name "Eva Hitler."

That afternoon Hitler learned that in Italy—where Elizabeth and Yuri Thiemann now lived—his ally, the dictator Benito Mussolini, had been captured in Milan along with his mistress, Clara Petacci. The two had been executed, then hanged by their feet for all to see.

At 3:30 P.M. on April 30, Adolf Hitler stuck a pistol in his mouth and fired. Eva Braun, beside him, swallowed poison. The bunker's staff carried the corpses to the garden, doused them with gasoline and burned them, as Martin Bormann, who had been Secretary to the Führer, and Goebbels stood by and Russian army shells exploded around them.

On May 7, 1945, at Reims, France, Germany surrendered unconditionally to the Allies. The shooting and bombing stopped by midnight the next day, and in the final chaos of the war, Hitler's favorite horseman, Christian Weber, was killed by anti-Nazi insurrectionists.

Robert got out of the U.S. Army in 1946. That was an important year for his sister, too. Lili had more than fulfilled Jimmy's dreams for her. After graduating with honors from Walnut Hills High, a public college preparatory school in Cincinnati, then whizzing through Fisk University in Nashville in three years, with a major in social work, she married Edmund Casey, an equally brilliant student at Meharry Medical College, across the street from Fisk. For Papa Wink, Lili's American ride must have seemed like winning the Czar's Prize, the Grosse Preis von Baden, and the Grand Prix de Deauville all in the same afternoon.

By then, Wink was working for a few other owners besides the Bostwicks and about to prove—as he had when he first went to Russia and again when he first went to France—that it was hard to keep Jimmy Winkfield down. At age sixty-six, with his son at his side, he was going to climb all the way back to the top. Exactly how, he couldn't tell you. But he began to get a few training jobs on his own, and Robert soon joined him as a trainer for the same small stable, owned by one J. M. Siebel, who toured the mid-Atlantic tracks. Around 1949, that old Winkfield lightning struck.

Siebel picked up a gelding named Little Rocket. The unsung little horse rocketed Jimmy and Robert Winkfield to five years of sheer bliss on the Maryland–Delaware–West Virginia circuit. For the first time since 1905, when Jimmy came back from Poland and went down to Hot Springs, Arkansas, "J. Winkfield" was back in the American record books—as a trainer, with two straight wins for Little Rocket at Laurel, Maryland, in October 1949. A couple of weeks later, at Pimlico, Little Rocket added a third win. And two years after that, with seventy-one-year-old trainer Jimmy saddling him for one victory, trainer Robert for four, and five other times on the board, the Rocket had his best year, earning $9,100, a considerable sum. Good as the money was, Wink liked being back in the winner's circle even more.

The Rocket dragged the happy Winkfields over to Charles Town, West Virginia, where Jimmy gave a new boy named Bill a ride or two. The first time Bill rode onto the track, he saw five horses fall. Two days later, a horse tried to run off with him, then went down on its knees while Bill slid onto its head and shouted,

"What'll I do now?" But Wink could tell this kid couldn't be stopped—any more than the young Wink. Two decades later, in 1969, Bill Hartack would tie Eddie Arcaro for the most Kentucky Derby wins—five. Thirty-six years after that, entering 2005, Hartack and Arcaro would remain unchallenged for that distinction, the late Bill Shoemaker being the only four-time winner. The latter three would be among only twenty-two jockeys in 130 years to win more than one Kentucky Derby. Another would be Hartack's early booster Jimmy Winkfield.

At Delaware Park in 1953, as he waited for Robert to bring the little brown colt up across the border from Bowie, Maryland, Jimmy rediscovered his old black magic: manipulating the newspapers. He got himself into a column about how Eric Guerin had lost the Derby that month when the inferior Dark Star beat his fabulous Native Dancer by a head. The Lexington writer said it recalled Jimmy Winkfield's loss on Early, a half century ago to the day. "Just like Eric Guerin, he was beaten once in the classic while piloting the odds-on favorite."

The columnist went on:

> He's past 70 now and never in the limelight as the trainer of a modest string while he sticks to his boyhood resolve of spending the rest of his life with horses. Jimmy comes in [to Lexington] every year or so to visit two brothers, Mose and Hezzie Winkfield, and a sister who also continues to live at Uttingertown [as Chilesburg had been renamed], on the Royster Road, but except for a few relatives and a few old timers the feats in his heyday as a jockey have generally been forgotten.

A wire-service photo that ran with the column showed Jimmy in a golf cap and his trademark V-neck knit, with his bad right eye and that win-photo smile, the one Little Rocket would bring out. The Rocket was so good Jimmy and Robert were able to pay all their debts and even start saving money. And Lydie bet the hell out of him. In fact, it was the money from her bets on Little Rocket that blasted Jimmy, Lydie, and Robert right back to France.

Lydie went first, to get *45 bis* ready for her husband and son. Tante Jeanne had died a few years earlier, of lung cancer, but Lydie still had the help of Vera Braun, the sister of Jimmy's first Russian wife, Alexandra. Jimmy went the next year, actually planning to sell the Maisons-Laffitte house and then go back to the States. But when he got there, some of the owners he had trained for before the war got after him to stay. "And then my wife started in," he joked later. "She'd always wanted me to go back. And first thing you know, here I was again. I called Robert to come over and help me."

Robert didn't need convincing. Having tasted the racism of his dad's favorite country, he once told his sister, "I'd rather be a beggar in France than a millionaire in America." He had recently married a Washington, D.C., girl, Mary, and they had a child, Lydia. She followed him to France, tried to get him to go back, gave up, and returned by herself, remaining separated from her husband. Robert never did return to America.

Jimmy not only called for Robert to come over in 1953, but he also visited the woman with whom he had had twins. He had left when they were only five months old, so in effect the thirteen-year-olds had never seen their father.

The boy—another Jimmy—couldn't wait to tell *Papa* that he was going to be a jockey, too. Think of it: son George had so much wanted to be a jock, just like his dad, but he grew too tall; so had son Robert, but he grew too fat, and now here was the next junior jock—and a Jimmy at that. Wink had yet another chance to replicate himself!

But Wink, who had so encouraged George and then Robert to succeed him, was seventy-three now and not always so charming. Besides, he had never been good at emotional moments like this—they required you to open up, which required that you trust someone to love you—which was one thing for which Jimmy's life in a white world, in Kentucky and in Europe, had never prepared him. And, at long last, he was tired. How was he going to handle his responsibilities toward this new family, other than come through with some money whenever he could? Since when was love a requirement? Besides, the boy was getting chubby.

So when Jimmy, Jr., proudly announced to Wink that he was going to be a jockey, too, the five-foot father, according to a neighbor, looked at the burgeoning boy and snapped,

"You'll never be a jockey!"

And then he walked on by.

All around Maisons-Laffitte, everybody was dying on Wink again. He couldn't trade memories with Lucien Lyne the way he used to, because Lucien was terribly frail and increasingly deaf. Yet, even now, Wink could see a bit of himself in his friend, who was still warm and friendly and the perfect Kentucky gentleman. Lucien was sixty-nine when he died at Maisons-Laffitte in February 1954. No less poignant was Leon Mantacheff's exit. Here was another tale that most of Jimmy's America would have seen as the story of a white man and a black man, but which Jimmy, Leon, and France knew was just the story of two friends.

And what a story. The man who handed Wink a second lease on fame in the land of the czars, who saw him through Moscow's hardships during that earlier world war, who rescued him from Poland after the Revolution, who introduced him to the City of Light and to Gaurisankar, Bahadur, Aldebaran, and Bou Jeloud, had been forced to liquidate most of his stud and racing stable in Normandy. Yet Mantacheff had managed to return to racing briefly in 1947 to win the Prix Penelope with his filly Sylphide. Still, it was long over for him when he died in October 1954. Of course, Leon and Wink had suffered through their Parisian "divorce," but what an English obituary said of Mantacheff—that he was "peculiarly gifted with a serenity which enabled him to meet good and bad fortune with equal composure"—was exactly what you could have said of his once indispensable American jockey.

In his seventh decade, Wink himself was still going strong—or at least going. With Robert doing the heavy lifting, he re-created the family home and top-level racing stable he had founded on the avenue Églé, and in 1956 father and son brought most of the *45 bis* alumni together for a reunion.

And it was quite a reunion. Hard-working Yuri, Jimmy and Lydie's nephew, came from Italy, where he'd been living since the war. The Free French had bombarded San Remo, forcing fabulous Elizabeth and others into a hillside cave, where she insisted on staying for nine months. Then the GIs came in, chasing the Germans and Italian Fascists out, hiring Yuri for their kitchen, and finally taking him to Trieste as an interpreter. He married Gianna, a Trieste girl, and now, thanks to the U.S. National Catholic Relief services, they were on their way to America, stopping en route to see Uncle Jim.

Yuri's sister, Irene, traveled from her home in Nyons, Switzerland. She had contracted tuberculosis in that terrible French "assembly center" for German nationals but had survived and was back to regular exercising, walking all over Maisons-Laffitte the way she used to do on a thoroughbred.

Obviously, a picture was called for, and Gianna got a super shot. On the left: that strong businesswoman Lydie, looking a little tired and heavy, with her ankles paying the price, but also Russian-motherly and contented, with her arm in Robert's. Her grinning son is well over his 130-pound steeplechasing weight. Next, with his arm around his boyhood idol Robert, Yuri is smiling, too. At Yuri's height of five foot eight, his funny crushed fedora sits well above this jockey-sized family. Then Irene, the tiniest one but with the sleek form of an adolescence spent on horseback. She's arm in arm with the only other born jockey of *45 bis*.

A French neighbor from back then thought that Jimmy, with that eye and shriveled body, looked, well, ugly. But Wink had conquered such silliness a long time ago, and here, as always, he's showing the world how to dress, his fedora crisp, his trench coat belted, one famous large hand pocketed, the tie perfect. His thick glasses sport light-colored rims; his shoes and hat lift him a couple of inches. He is not looking at Gianna. People can look at him.

One thing about *45 bis* hadn't changed. "During dinner time," newcomer Gianna would complain, "they always spoke about horses, and that's all they talked about." But Wink had changed. He'd been transformed by his return to America and the little racetracks there, by the fun he'd had with Little Rocket. He had mostly—not completely but mostly—lost the cold, mean edge he had shown in France to young Yuri and sometimes to Robert. He had mellowed with age. No longer the unreachable star, the dictatorial businessman, the often secretly insecure black man in a white world, he was a relaxed, wonderful host to Yuri and Gianna. "He showed us where was *la piste*, the track," she said. "He took us all around and explained things to us." Vera Braun helped, presenting Gianna with two exquisite little glasses from Russia. It wasn't like old times at Maisons-Laffitte. It was a lot better.

That was quite a year, 1956. For one thing, it was the last year Jimmy Winkfield rode a horse. This was nothing spectacular, to be sure, but it wasn't a bad accomplishment, either, for a gentleman of seventy-six. It was also the last year Wink owned a racing stable, as he turned over the operation to Robert, although—to the son's constant annoyance—the old man stayed on as advisor. What did anybody expect?

The stable got much better. Robert expanded it to accommodate thirty-six thoroughbreds at one point. Father and son even opened what Wink must have dreamed of since Lazareff gave him a Russian understudy at the dawn of the century: a jockey school. Later, a European horseman recalled that Jimmy had been "especially popular with other riders who sought his advice frequently and to whom he gave it generously." And after that he had become an even more attentive professor to sons George and Robert and niece Irene.

So once again in his extraordinary career, Wink was "at the top of tree," to use his old Kentucky phrase.

The Winkfields' clients had a certain tone. Mildred Lyne, Lucien's widow and daughter of Spain's former royal trainer Adolphe de Neuter, was one of them. So was the wealthy Parisian painter Serge Poliakoff, who shared not only his thoroughbreds but many memories with Wink. Poliakoff's father had bred horses for the czar's army, and Wink had ridden and trained them and had known Serge as a little boy. Poliakoff's visits were wonderful reunions. One day, a magazine photographer took a picture of Wink tutoring Serge on the finer points of a thoroughbred, and as they stood in the beautiful manicured courtyard, you could see that both men were aristocrats. If anything, Poliakoff, in his late fifties, seemed to be the dowdy one in what looked like a Russian great coat, while Wink, in another perfectly creased hat, a cinched dark sports jacket, and a high-collared open shirt, resembled a drawing out of *Vogue Hommes*.

Of all the people Jimmy Winkfield met in France in those years, one stood out the most. One day in 1958, he took his daughter Lili and her daughter Yvette, who were visiting from Cincinnati, for a ride into Normandy, where they stopped at a small chateau. There they met a cheerful, round-faced, red-cheeked man with thinning black hair and an extremely prosperous air about him that matched his chateau. It was Vassily, Wink's old, faithful valet.

Poor Vassily, who had secretly admired himself in the mirror, ablaze in the black maestro's finery, who had been with him as Wink breakfasted on caviar in the National Hotel and piled up his All-Russian Derbies, who had survived Trotsky's and Lenin's revolution with Wink, who had escaped to Odessa with him, who was at his side during the horrendous trek through eastern Europe. Vassily, too, had made it to France, and now he was a millionaire industrialist with a factory, a bottling plant apparently, with lots of employees. He lived in Paris and had his own fancy clothes to try on in front of the mirror.

But Jimmy also bore a terrible burden in 1958. His wife died—his Lydie, who as a girl had fallen for the black maestro at the Moscow Hippodrome, who had helped steer his ride to stardom in Paris, who had run the money end of *45 bis*, who had stood by her man when that Hungarian woman opened fire and again when he fathered that boy and girl in 1940 (if and when she knew about it).

But Wink weathered the loss of Lydie, too, and in a way that lengthened his own life yet again. He began going back to America, wintering in Cincinnati with his Lili and her husband, the prominent Dr. Edmund Casey, and their daughters Yvette, Yvonne, and Amie. Best of all, he was right across the broad Ohio River from the real America, otherwise known as Kentucky. The Caseys' big house was only a few furlongs from one of Wink's old stomping grounds—Latonia racetrack, where he had won its derby, and Newport, where Bub May had sneaked him into a race even though he was suspended. His mind was always racing.

On a typical night in Cincinnati, Wink got the family playing poker, just the way he and Lydie had played *belote* back in Maisons-Laffitte, but this time with feeling. Then somebody—Lili or Edmund or one of the girls—said something mildly funny, and that was all it took. Wink burst into laughter and pulled out another stogie, a big fat, smelly thing like the ones Edward G. Robinson smoked in the movies. The grandkids loved him, and they carried on well into the night.

Those winter trips home gave him a chance to visit Winkfields in Kentucky, where naturally he also managed to get himself plastered all over the newspapers, which then forgot about him until he stopped by a year later to remind them. The *Thoroughbred Record* uncorked yet another gallon of reminiscences, from his first days as an exercise boy at the Kentucky Association track to his imminent departure for France, by air. "I get too sick traveling by ship, but I've crossed the ocean by air in comfort several times."

If Jimmy had always known how to manipulate Lexington's newspapers—the *Herald* in the morning, the *Leader* in the afternoon—they also knew just how to deal with him, as a harmless throwback to the older racist days. What the Lexington editors did not know how to deal with, as the sleepy Eisenhower fifties gave way to the awakening Kennedy sixties, was those young black residents parading outside the town's segregated lunch counters, hotels, and theaters. So they intentionally ignored one of Lexington's biggest stories in years, a story that affected the entire community—or they buried it deep inside the papers year after year, leaving the vast majority of their readers ignorant. Later, in the supposedly more enlightened 1980s, the editors would joke that that they should print this "clarification":

"It has come to the editor's attention that the *Herald* neglected to cover the civil-rights movement. We regret the omission."

Thus, to the good old white editors in Lexington, their noncoverage of the marches and sit-ins was still just a joke. It would be four decades after the protests started before the local newspapers' own racism would finally be exposed—by the then-merged *Herald-Leader* itself.

Wink's nephew Yuri had found his way to the Cincinnati area, too, and was still living a fantasy life of sorts. A perfect one for somebody who had missed out on a lot of love. He was a candyman for Kroger's grocery chain, supervising the concoction of jelly beans, gumdrops, and other dreamy confections. This allowed Yuri to send money to his mother, Elizabeth, back there in San Remo, but then things got tight and he had to stop. Elizabeth responded like her old demanding self, firing off threatening letters and warning Yuri that she'd hire a lawyer to be sure the filial support continued. Mother couldn't control him anymore, though. When Yuri and Gianna went back to Italy on a visit, she agreed to see him, but not his family, so Yuri refused to visit her. "Maybe she didn't want us to see her so poor," Gianna said charitably, then added, "because she never worked a day in her life."

Leave it to Wink to lighten the scene by adding a touch of old Chilesburg. One Easter, the old farmer showed his American family how to use the unused parts of a pig to make what the French call *tête-de-veau*, the Italians *testa*, and Americans, rather inelegantly, head cheese. It was delicious. But the fun visits to America would end in the spring, when he started dreaming of April in Paris. "When the leaves commence comin' on the trees, I want to get back to Maisons-Laffitte," he told an inquiring reporter. "I want to be with the horses."

As the 1960s got under way, *Sports Illustrated* followed Wink to France and gave him a huge boost, presenting the fabulous

Winkfield life story that had been summarized on occasion in the Lexington papers though never completely, never accurately, and, of course, never nationally. Now, with the help of Jimmy's failing memory and never-failing embellishments, *S.I.* came up with a very pretty, though still inaccurate, tale of Wink's life. It was not nearly as riveting as his true story, but at least it nailed *45 bis* and the old man's daily routine. The stables around the courtyard, the pebbled walking ring, the lawn and shade trees were lovelier than ever. The stalls were usually full. The stuccoed walls of the house the baron had built had faded to a comfortable faint tan, the red tile roof a warm brown. An old dog named Prince guarded the door.

The eighty-one-year-old master was "straight and lean as a riding crop." He should be: he got up at five o'clock every morning to supervise the training schedule.

"I do most of the work," Robert told the *S.I.* reporter, and he wasn't joking when he added, "He just tells me all the things I'm doing wrong."

When the morning workouts were over, Wink would sometimes grab a fork and help pitch hay, mostly just to show the stable boys how to do it. Then he'd "wait for lunch in the late morning sun," and after lunch he'd grab his battered binoculars and go to the races. How was the Winkfield stable doing at the races? Damn good, thanks to their five-year-old Françillon. She was nothing less than the best handicap mare in France, winner of the 3.5 million franc Prix de l'Élévage (Breeder's Prize), the highest honor the Winkfield stable ever received. That mare guaranteed Robert, as the trainer, a permanent place in French racing history, alongside his dad, the jockey.

Francillon had just won the Breeder's Prize again when the *S.I.* reporter showed up. She had started as a jumper, was switched to the flats because she had so much speed, and now Robert was thinking of switching her back to jumping. "I think she'll clean up as a steeplechaser," he said. Jumping was an area Robert knew much better than his father. Not that this stopped the lively octogenarian from demonstrating right and left that he was becoming a pain in the derriere for Robert.

"She's too good to jump," Wink snapped, shaking his head sadly for dramatic effect. "But you can't tell this Robert anything. All he wants to do is hurry, hurry."

But Robert had the last word this time, as his incredible Francillon went on to a third straight Breeder's Prize in 1961.

The *S.I.* article drew a response from an old reader. "For us Russian horsemen in the days before the revolution, the name Winkfield was like Shoemaker, Arcaro and Longden—combined in one," wrote K. I. Davidoff, a former captain in the czar's army.

Even in the 1960s, no black person in American racing could attain the status the Winkfields enjoyed in France. Yet Wink would never let go of America. He had never given up his citizenship. He was an American, and he had his permanent loves, like his family and Kentucky, and nothing was going to keep him from his winter trips home. He did worry, though, that his 1960–1961 winter there would be his last: the doctors had scheduled him for an operation in Cincinnati to remove a possibly cancerous growth.

"I could have had just as good an operation in Paris, but I knew I was going to die, and I wanted to die back in Kentucky," Jimmy said.

On that trip home, the dying Wink visited the scenes of his Bluegrass boyhood. Then suddenly, two weeks after leaving the Cincinnati hospital, he was downing pork chops for lunch. The cancer had turned out to be only a bit of ulcerated tissue on his small intestine that had blocked his digestion. The surgeon told Liliane, "Everything inside him is small, just like a child."

He was going to live, after all. So he started dreaming of a side trip. What the hell. He wrote to his closest surviving friend in Lexington, his nephew George, brother Gus's son, who was about Jimmy's age. The handwriting was exceptionally neat, the letters looking almost like italics, the lines as straight as Maisons-Laffitte's long stretch.

Dear George:

I have to come back to Lexington shortly and pland [sic] *to go to Louisville to see the Derby, which will be run the first of May.*

I mean the first Saturday in May and I may be in Louisville one
week before the race. My health is much improved. I have taken
on 5 pounds and my appette [sic] *is better. Take care of yourself*
and take it easy. Our working days are over. I close best wishes.
   Your uncle,
   Jimmie

Jimmy got an invite to the annual banquet of the National Turf
Writers Association a few days before the Derby. The *S.I.* piece was
doubtless what got him invited. "I never been back to the Derby since
I last rode there in 1903," the old publicity hawk had told the reporter.
And he slyly added, in the biggest sports magazine in America, "No,
I don't plan to tell anyone I'm comin' to Kentucky. My goodness,
they wouldn't remember me. Who can remember back 60 years?"

Chapter Twenty

You Can't Come In

In the early evening of the first Wednesday in May 1961, Lili and Wink drove out of Cincinnati, across the Ohio, and southwest down to Louisville for the National Turf Writers banquet. Lili couldn't wait to get there: they were having split-pea soup! Then, the menu said, prime ribs, baked potato, broccoli, tossed green salad, and a chocolate fudge sundae, but who cared about those other things? "I told my father, I said, 'I sure hope they have split-pea soup because I love split-pea soup!'"

They parked near the hotel, in the middle of downtown. The attractive thirty-six-year-old woman and her small, slightly bowlegged father got out and walked toward Louisville's most famous hotel, the richly paneled Brown. Wink set the pace, as usual, and it was slow, as usual, as if he wanted to savor every step. Once one of the world's fastest men on a horse, Wink had always taken his time doing everything else. Let the horses do the hurrying.

The Brown dripped Kentucky Derby tradition and a thick Mornay sauce, which was ladled onto its celebrated open-turkey sandwich, called the Hot Brown. Helped along by a good couple of tablespoons of butter, a half cup of melted cheese, and eight or so slices of country ham on top of the half pound of turkey, it was by far the most famous dish in Kentucky and the first thing people thought of when they walked in the door. Would they dare have a Hot Brown? White people. A black American couldn't just walk in the front door.

The doorman himself was black, Liliane remembered. "The doorman was very, you know, nice, polite, but he said, 'No, you can't come in, we don't allow you people to come in.'

"And I said, 'Well, we're guests of the *Sports Illustrated*.'

"So he said, 'Well, wait a minute.' So he closed the door, went, spoke to somebody, and he came back, and he said, 'No.'

"And I said, 'Well, I insist to speak to the person of the *Sports Illustrated*, who is here, I understand, for dinner.' So he went back upstairs. I could see the steps going up."

As they waited, there was a practical consideration. Wink needed food. "It would have been hard to drive back or to find someplace to stop to eat, you know, because he had to eat—it was past the dinner hour."

The doorman talked to somebody upstairs.

"So later on, he came back down and said, 'Okay, you can come in.'"

Inside, someone, apparently from *Sports Illustrated*, "came and shook our hand, but that was it," Liliane recalled. "Nobody said anything, except the waiter showed us the seat where my father and I sat down. And my father saw, next to him, or was it right across from him? . . . Roscoe Goose." Roscoe had been one of the Kentucky white boys who rode like hell to keep up with the Kentucky black boys back when he and Wink were coming up. "The Golden Goose" sure kept up. He was famous for his victory in the 1913 Derby, his mount Donerail paying the best price yet, $184.90, and setting a track record, which touched off a publicity blitz that helped save dying Churchill Downs.

"Roscoe saw my father. He said, 'Oh, little Jimmy!'—he called him 'little Jimmy'—'so nice to see you,' and all that, and they started talking, and my father told him why he was there.

"Roscoe said, 'For goodness sake, don't tell them your age because you look younger than I am.'"

Wink looked at the menu, saw the split-pea soup, and tried to cheer up Liliane. "Well, you got your wish." It didn't work.

Her father began to quietly work his way through his prime rib. While the other diners laboriously went about cutting theirs, putting down the knife to switch the fork to their right hands, switching back again to cut, and so on, Wink simply retained the knife in his right hand and the fork in his left, the European way, proceeding very slowly as always, enjoying it. Lili was still upset.

Roscoe was "the only person that talked to us the whole time," she remembered. "Nobody else said a word to either one of us." Roscoe's friendliness was more courageous than Lili knew. He'd been an adviser on yearling purchases to J. Graham Brown himself, the miserly owner of the hotel, who was said to hole up in his room, fixing moth holes in his old tuxedo by poking a pen through them and painting the white lining black so they wouldn't show through. But unlike so many others, Roscoe was not afraid of the multimillionaire, even if this one was a major stockholder in Churchill Downs and had been one of his wealthy employers. Roscoe had salted away a million himself from his training and advising.

"It was a nice meal, but you felt awkward," Liliane said. "You really felt, you know, that everybody kind of looked around but didn't say anything." She couldn't wait to get out of there.

Was it possible she was more upset about it than her father?

"Yeah, I was more upset because he was—he had just had this operation and he was recovering, and after, you know, the *Sports Illustrated* spoke so well . . . it was embarrassing."

Wink, on the other hand, handled it with perfect calm, and conquered all yet again. Three days later Wink and Roscoe sat together at the Derby and had a hell of a time under the Twin Spires. Both wore fedora hats and pin-striped suits and clutched binoculars. Jimmy smoked a long, thin stogie. The press stopped by and Wink entertained them, and the stories were picked up around the country, full of Wink's usual errors but the reporters didn't care. They wanted stories, and Wink had them.

"So much has changed," he sighed between puffs. "When I raced here, the sand! There was so much sand they had to push it away from the starting post. It was easy to get bogged down, and the first two or three steps were crucial."

He cheerfully supplied the reporters with His Greatest Moment in Sports, but it depended on when you asked. The *Courier-Journal* dutifully reported that it came "not as a Derby winner— but when he won Le Grand Prix du Président de la République. 'It was a big prestige race for the president of France,' he said."

To others, he gave the answer Americans wanted to hear: "I have received many thrills from racing in many countries, but I'll never forget the thrill of winning those two runnings of the Derby in succession." And he kept his good eye on the history books. "At least I was the only rider other than Murphy to put winners back to back in the race." It would take yet another dozen years for another jockey, Ron Turcotte, to match the feat, on Riva Ridge and Secretariat in 1972–1973 and a decade beyond that for Eddie Delahoussaye, the last rider to accomplish it, to ride home on Gato Del Sol and Sunny's Halo in 1982–1983. Wink would be one of only two to finish in the money every time in as many as four Derbies, Jimmy's two wins giving him the better average over his role model Lonnie Clayton.

Thoroughly enjoying himself in the box at Churchill, Wink named Bahadur as his best European horse. His best American horse? McChesney, though the colt nearly killed him. That fall in Chicago wasn't Wink's best McChesney story, though; he preferred the ones where he walked away rich.

It's 1901. McChesney has ripped off nine races like it was nothing, and his owner, John Ward, suddenly has a chance to unload him at a nice profit to trainer Sam Hildreth, but only if the colt looks good in his next one—seven-eighths of a mile at Worth, Illinois. At the track, Ward calls Wink over to him and says, "Now he can win easy if he just gets away good. You're a quick boy, and

I want you on him. And make him look good, boy!" The octogenarian was just warming up.

By some rare disaster, Wink and McChesney are left at the post. Yet they catch the others at three-eighths of a mile and will obviously win—but that won't be enough. To clinch the sale, the official chart has to say McChesney won easily. Wink has an idea.

"I held myself as if I was just sailing along with no urging, and kept my right hand clenched like the horse was under a hold. But what they couldn't see from the stands"—as Wink and McChesney came down the stretch—"was that with my left foot on the inside I was booting that horse in the flank!" He crossed the finish line three lengths in front, "winning easily," the chart said helpfully. "Anyway, Mr. Ward gave me $1,000."

Full as he was of his memories, he still had his nose for news, and he would combine the two to lecture the hell out of the sport and get it in the papers. It was "shocking and hard to understand," he whined, that his great pupil Bill Hartack, who had already won two Derbies, was missing today. "Bill rode for me in Charleston, W. Va., back in the late 40's, and I knew then that he would be one of the great ones. I think he's the best jockey in the business and I can't understand why he's not riding for someone." The Associated Press picked it up, thrusting old Wink into some more warm and comfortable headlines.

Wink cried as the crowd sang "My Old Kentucky Home." They watched some pretty good jockeys—Willie Shoemaker, Eddie Arcaro, Johnny Longden, a dozen others—parade to the post to the applause of tens of thousands, the same famous parade that Wink had joined four times. They watched jockey John Sellers and the brown colt Carry Back win the 1961 Run for the Roses. Wink would never see another Kentucky Derby. He would never need to.

If Liliane harbored the bitterness of that Derby banquet for a long time, it was understandable, but her father would never let it get to him. Would never let anything get to him. Far more than most humans, he knew how to patch up the past, often by patching up the present so that the past would not need repairing. This was one of his secrets with women, who couldn't help loving him, whether he was twenty or eighty. He stayed on in Cincinnati for a few weeks after the Derby, to rest up from his operation and the excitement of the Derby—and to take another side trip.

Some side trip. With daughter Lili at his side, the eighty-one-year-old gentleman paid a visit to his eighty-year-old first bride, not in Lexington, where they had started out all those decades ago, but in Jamaica, Queens. Edna Winkfield had moved there, at least by the 1950s, and probably earlier. But Wink's memories now were certainly not of his 1903 Jamaica, where John Madden's anger had changed his life, or of his 1941–42 Jamaica, where he jackhammered the streets—but simply of Edna. His sweet, gentle, adoring Kentucky Edna, who had married him in 1900, followed him to Russia in 1906, brought back their Ida in 1907, and divorced him in 1911. Whatever the precise terms of their separation, and of his support, he remained a good friend over the years, if mainly through correspondence and mutual friends. And Edna had kept the flame alive with a wedding picture of her and her Jimmy. They were the same loving couple now, plus six decades. To Lili, she appeared a bit, well, senile—perhaps it was what would later be called Alzheimer's disease—but it would be hard to imagine that Jimmy would stop loving any woman for that or any other reason, except maybe Clara-Béatrice, the Hungarian with the gun.

They were the same loving couple—but for Edna, add Jamaica. It wasn't the same lively community it had been during the war—with the life-giving help of Roosevelt's WPA until 1943—and just after. Like cities all over America, Jamaica had a new citizen, one that Jimmy himself had escaped when he left America: fear. Like millions of other Americans, Edna began locking her doors. And she kept right on locking them—every last one she could find in that frightening home of hers in that frightening city. If FDR had not died two years after the WPA ended, what would he have done about this new, undefined, nationwide threat—"fear itself?"

Edna went much further than everybody else in Jamaica. Jimmy noticed that she had locked her kitchen cupboard doors, too. Every single one of them. It would be the last time he would ever see her.

Jimmy flew back to Maisons-Laffitte, full of that amazing 1961

Derby experience and the memory of Edna. A few years later, by some miracle, another top jockey entered the family. Robert and Mary had divorced after a decade of separation, and Jimmy Winkfield's son now married the third best woman jockey in France. Jeanine Lefevre was the daughter of a French movie star, René Lefevre, who stabled some horses in Maisons-Laffitte. Wink could hardly have been more thrilled with his new daughter-in-law. Jeanine rode, Robert trained, and the two of them gave the delighted Wink two more grandchildren, Thierry and Betsy. In 1967, all of France, or at least French racing fans, celebrated the Winkfields as French racing authorities created a Winkfield Day at Auteuil Race Course. On top of that, one of trainer Robert's horses, Fandine, captured one of the day's biggest features.

"He paid 30 to 1, too," Wink bragged, never mind that Fandine was a mare.

He just couldn't make them out. In a "Dear Daughter" letter, he wrote to Liliane:

"My eyes are so bad can hardly see the horses."

But he still had it. A Parisian interviewer saw this Wink, at age eighty-seven: "crinkled silver hair, brilliant jet-black eyes, svelte, smiling, drawing on his cigarette-holder, deploying his suspenders, alert to everything."

The summer of 1969 brought a terrible shock. Billet de Banque, a horse owned by Jimmy, won a feature at Chantilly—and failed the postrace urine and saliva tests. The experts detected the presence of ephedrine, a stimulant. As trainer, Robert was automatically responsible, whether he had anything to do with it or not. The investigators questioned Robert and the few employees of the Winkfield stable, including a young man who had been fired a few days before the race, and all denied giving the horse the drug.

It would have been stupid, said Robert. "Even if the idea of doping a horse had ever entered my head, I would never have chosen a race at Chantilly. All trainers know quite well that at Chantilly and Longchamp all winners have to take a dope test."

And unnecessary, he added. "Billet de Banque was the press

choice for the race and was favorite at three and a half to one. It is never very intelligent to dope a horse. But it is even less so when that horse is the favorite."

And the horse showed no signs of it afterward. "Generally," Robert said, "when a horse has been doped it takes several months to recover. In the month following his win at Chantilly, Billet de Banque won two more races. In these circumstances, I still believe that the experts could have made a mistake."

But, in this first doping case in France in seven years, Robert was still fined 10,000 francs, the heaviest penalty ever imposed on a trainer or jockey in that country. Even though the fine did not mean he was found guilty—but was simply automatically responsible—it was, of course, hard on Robert. His father, at eighty-nine, was hardly fazed. After all, he could compare it with the Russian Revolution, two world wars, and being broke in Queens during the Great Depression.

As Jimmy found out the next year, living in France still had its advantages. In the winter of 1970–71, a Kentucky freelance journalist named Marjorie R. Weber visited Jimmy, Robert and his family, and Jimmy's second wife's sister Vera Braun, who lived with the Winkfields. Marjorie Weber surely told them how she'd heard that Roscoe Goose dearly hoped Wink would visit again and come by his house near Churchill Downs, so they could finish the conversation they'd begun at that Derby. But Roscoe, as it happened, had only six months to live, and it was not likely Jimmy would ever return home. Weber realized that, and to make sure her visit with the ninety-year-old jockey would be preserved for all time, she sent a report to a turf archivist. It perhaps said less about Jimmy than it did about America:

> Mr. Winkfield is a gentle, dear, elderly little man. They all have so much culture and fineness that it is difficult to think that . . . you know what I am trying to say . . . they are colored (they never use the word Negro) or partly so. I mean nothing vicious about this at all . . . please, believe me. We

loved them so much that, with the exception of Mr. Winkfield, who would not come downstairs to tell us goodbye, we
kissed them all goodbye. He had tears in eyes and so did
we as we hated to leave. But, as I told Robert, guests are
like fish in that after three days they begin to smell, so it was
really better that we stayed only a day and a half. Robert
drove us to the airport—an hour and five minutes one way
over ice and slush. We didn't want him to do it, but our pleas
were completely ignored. If Mr. Winkfield's life were a jig-
saw puzzle, the Derby would be only one small piece.

Wink may not have been up to saying good-bye that day, but
even at his age he wasn't hiding from reporters. A year and a half
later, on a day in May, another found him at *45 bis*, now ensconced
under lime and chestnut trees and perfumed by lilacs. And the
minute the reporter gave him an opening by asking about his first
race, Wink's mouth was out of the starting gate. This time, his version was closer to reality than the tale he had told *Sports Illustrated*
a decade earlier. He had even stopped lying about his age. Ninety-
two-year-old Wink on his first race:

> It was in Chicago in 1898. Though I was just an ap-
> prentice, I came in second out of 13 riders. There were four
> colored jockeys and I was in fifth place at the start. I cut
> across to fourth place, two horses fell down, and at the turn
> I was in third place, then I took the lead, but was caught in
> the finish.

He only left out how he wrought disaster by forcing his horse,
Jockey Joe, through a tiny rabbit hole, then crashing one horse into
another, finally finishing second behind one of the horses left standing—and thus showing the world who this stable boy named
Jimmy Winkfield was, and who he was going to be.

In 1973, he was still at it, advising yet another American visitor how to tell if a horse is ready to run by feeling his side and

flanks—"if hard and flexible, he can go to the post"—and what was still wrong with all those young jockeys:

They lack a sense of pace. They burn a horse out before he hits the stretch—then go for the whip. To be a great jockey, you have to have a stopwatch in your head. You keep your horse in hand until you're ready to take him out front—but you don't move out there until you're sure you can stay out there.

On the night of March 23, 1974, Jeanine—the younger jockey at *45 bis*—was giving her kids their baths. The ninety-three-year-old jockey upstairs insisted she give him one, too, but then fell asleep. He never woke up.

So Wink was never granted his profound wish to die in Kentucky. His as yet unwritten epitaph? He wouldn't want it to be anything heavy. Actually, maybe he would. But it should just try to capture the spirit that lifted him above all the troubles he saw, and outran.

"He was grateful and happy, even to the end," his daughter Liliane once said. "Patience and endurance were his assets. . . . He ate slowly, spoke slowly, and moved slowly. But he could *ride*."

NOTES

Chapter One

5   **they called it Chilesburg.** The author enjoyed a sunny day of Bluegrass hospitality and conversation in what is left of Chilesburg, but very little has been written about the place. You might look at Richard Chiles's obituary, "Died," *Kentucky Statesman*, Oct. 7, 1853, 3. On both Chilesburg and its successor, Uttingertown, see William Henry Perrin, ed., *History of Fayette County, Kentucky, with an Outline Sketch of the Blue Grass Region by Robert Peter* (Chicago: Baskin, 1882), 492, 499–501, and Robert M. Rennick, *Kentucky Place Names* (Lexington: University Press of Kentucky, 1984), 57, 302.

5   **Berkshire County, England.** On the first Winkfields and Winecas Field, try any number of Winkfield Web sites, including www.berkshirehistory.com, and David Nash Ford, *Winkfield Hamlets* (Berkshire: Bullbrook, 2000). Winkfield's daughter, Liliane Winkfield Casey, says George and Victoria had seventeen children. The last, Jimmy, would have been born in 1880, according to what Jimmy frequently told reporters and others when he was riding. The 1880 U.S. Census for Fayette County, Kentucky, does list a Marcus Winkfield, two months old, at the home, which suggests that Jimmy may have originally been named Marcus James Winkfield. Note that records of the Kentucky Bureau of Vital Statistics, the Lexington (Kentucky) Public Library, and the daily *Lexington Leader* recount events in the lives of Jimmy's siblings and other relatives over the years.

5   **that conflicted state.** It seems likely that George and Victoria set up house in Chilesburg sometime before the war. There are some inconsistencies in the U.S. Census reports, but it would appear that the Winkfields had their first child, Augustus, in 1855 and that, at the end of the war, in 1865, George was thirty-two and Victoria thirty-three.

6   **Chilesburg to Uttingertown.** Jimmy Winkfield was long gone when the hamlet was renamed for Sam Uttinger in the early twentieth century, but for good summaries of the many Kentucky hamlets named after white founders, see Rochelle Riley, "Land of the Free," *Louisville Courier-Journal*, May 9, 2000, C-1, and Valerie Honeycutt, "Saving Black Settlements," *Lexington Herald-Leader*, Feb. 24, 2001, A-1. Local historian David P. Spencer has done extensive research on Chilesburg and Uttingertown.

6   **The youngest was Jimmy.** Through his thirties, Winkfield indicated he was born about 1880, but as we'll see, in his forties he began to take two years off his age, apparently to improve his chances of getting hired to ride. He would make his birth date April 12, 1882, but there are no other records confirming this.

6   **had other ideas.** The blurry story of Winkfield's childhood has been told in some of his published interviews and contemporary newspaper accounts and also recounted by his daughter Liliane and granddaughter Dr. Amie Casey.

6   **ready for action.** The favorite ready-for-action Winkfield pose would be beautifully demonstrated when he was thirty-four and had just won the All-Russian

Derby in 1914, and then nearly two decades later by his son Robert, when a snap-shot seemed to transform Robert into his father as a child in the same pose.

7   **vice president of the United States.** Sadly, there is no recent history of the Ken-tucky Association track, one of America's earliest big sports venues, but see Don Edwards, "Park Brings Grandstand Feel back to Downtown," *Lexington Herald-Leader*, April 20, 1992, B-4. For a view of the track's successor, the Keeneland Race Course, which thrives on the old tradition, see William F. Reed, *Keeneland* (Prospect, KY: Harmony House, 2000), with essays by Edward L. Bowen, Jacqueline Duke, and William F. Reed, and poetry by Richard Taylor.

7   **boots were a mess.** Winkfield family tradition has it that Jimmy also lived with his brother William in Cincinnati for a time before returning to Kentucky to ride.

7   **They had begun as slaves.** The only history of the black jockeys is Edward Ho-taling, *The Great Black Jockeys* (Rocklin, CA: Forum/Prima, 1999). For their rise in New York, see Hotaling, "When Racing Colors Included Black," *New York Times*, June 2, 1996, Sports sec., 9. For Maryland, see Hotaling, "Black Jockeys Rode into History," *Baltimore Sun*, Feb. 6, 2000, C-1.

11   **They called him Honest Ike.** For more on Ike Murphy, see Hotaling, *Great Black Jockeys*, 239–76; Edward Hotaling, "Hall of Fame: Isaac Murphy," *Backstretch*, July–August 1999, 32; Betty Earle Borries, *Isaac Murphy, Kentucky's Record Jockey* (Berea, KY: Kentucke Imprints, 1988); and Peter T. Chew, "Ike and Wink," *The Kentucky Derby: The First 100 Years* (Boston: Houghton Mifflin, 1974), 33–40.

11   **The deal was off.** "Moving of the Pole," *Lexington Leader*, Nov. 5, 1901, 7. This was only one of several reports on this great scandal of the day.

12   **Lexington in 1893.** "The Opening Day," *Lexington Morning Transcript*, Oct. 17, 1893, 1.

12   **somebody else: manners.** A fine summary of Marshall Lilly's life, a study in mod-esty, manners, and great achievement, is Kent Hollingsworth, "A Man Who Knew Champions," *The Blood-Horse*, Nov. 24, 1975, 5152–57.

14   **changing whip hands.** Jockeys did indeed use spurs in those days, and as we'll see, Jimmy will soon be digging in his spurs in Chicago.

14   *Salvator, Salvator won!* Edna Wheeler Wilcox, "How Salvator Won," *Spirit of the Times*, July 12, 1890, 1082.

15   **famous colored jockeys."** The magazine was *Munsey's*, December 1900, 357.

16   **little chance at all."** The (Covington) *Kentucky Post* found the story worth page 1 on June 10, 1895. Jim Reis recalled it in "Blacks Once Held the Reins," *Ken-tucky Post*, Feb. 14, 1994, 4K.

16   **faucet pouring blood.** Across the broad Ohio, the white-run *Cincinnati En-quirer* blamed Thompson. Under the headline FISTS USED IN A HORSE RACE/TWO JOCKEYS FOUGHT EACH OTHER, it declared: "A more foolhardy and brutal exhi-bition of jeopardizing the life of a fellow jockey has seldom been witnessed than when he [Thompson] . . . smarting under the prospect of certain defeat, tried to knock Jesse Mathews off his horse or throw him over the outside rail." See *Cincinnati Enquirer*, May 18, 1899, 4.

17   **bluish in late May.** In recent decades, massive mowing earlier in the spring, along

with cropping by livestock, has wiped out much of the blue in the Bluegrass, leaving disappointed visitors wondering what all the talk about blue grass was about.

18   **Kentucky claimed the title.** Try to get yourself into a chair sometime with the rare and exquisite James Douglas Anderson, *Making the American Thoroughbred, Especially in Tennessee, 1800–1845* (1916; reprint, Nashville: Grainger Williams, 1946), and pause to learn more about Dr. Barry (97–98 and other pages). A product of Dublin University and a surgeon in the British navy, Barry wound up siding with the colonies and settling in North Carolina, then in Tennessee. Says Anderson: "The history of the grazing sections of Kentucky and Tennessee show [*sic*] such a close connection between [equine] blue blood and blue grass, it is worthy of mention that Dr. Barry, who brought Grey Medley into Middle Tennessee, also introduced blue grass; he blazed the way for the greatest agricultural specialty the Middle Basin has ever had—the breeding of thoroughbred horses. By this specialty has Tennessee been best known ever since she stopped producing presidents." We might blame the myth-making powers of Bluegrass for the fantasy of Anderson and other Americans that Tennessee produced three presidents, when in fact it has produced none. The three were two North Carolinians, James Polk and the famously impeached (but not convicted) successor to Lincoln, Andrew Johnson, and, of course, Andrew Jackson, over whom the two Carolinas have been feuding almost since he upped and left their vague border area. Celebrated Tennesseans, but Carolinians all.

18   **survival of black jockeys.** Bill Brummell, a great-great-nephew of Jimmy Winkfield descended from brother Gus, shared with me his theory that groups like the Ku Klux Klan largely avoided the Bluegrass because of its valuable horse farms. George C. Wright, coauthor with Marion Brunson Lucas of *A History of Blacks in Kentucky* (Frankfort: Kentucky Historical Society, 1992), agreed, telling me white vigilante groups did pretty much stay clear of the Bluegrass and the cities, such as Lexington and Louisville. Of course, as Wright added, "Whites in urban areas had their own, and very effective, ways of keeping blacks in check." See also George C. Wright, *Racial Violence in Kentucky 1865–1940: Lynchings, Mob Rule, and "Legal Lynching"* (Baton Rouge: Louisiana State University Press, 1990).

18   **pneumonia in his midthirties.** In addition to the above-noted sources on Murphy, see "Isaac Murphy's Death," *Thoroughbred Record*, Feb. 15, 1896, 79.

19   **making new friends.** The 1961 *Sports Illustrated* article cited earlier, and later sources that borrowed from it, said Winkfield took this first racetrack job not at Lexington but at Latonia, in the north of Kentucky on the Ohio River. However, the article contained a number of errors, and the old Lexington track, long forgotten when the *S.I.* article appeared, is much likelier. Indeed, an earlier report based on an interview with Winkfield said he got his start in Lexington. See Len Tracy, "Fifty-odd Years Scarcely Have Dimmed the Memory," *Thoroughbred Record*, Feb. 21, 1959, which says Winkfield "served his apprenticeship as an exercise boy at the old Kentucky Association track at Lexington."

23   **"the Big Apple."** FitzGerald was using "the Big Apple" for New York City by at least 1921 in his first *Morning Telegraph* column. He later told of having heard it first just before World War I, in an exchange between two black stable hands at the Fairgrounds Race Course in New Orleans: " 'Where y'all goin' from here,' queried one. 'From here we're headin' for the Big Apple,' proudly replied the

other." Since "apple" phrases were common all over the country and everybody knew horses loved apples, the stable hand probably did not coin it. It most likely had already been used by Winkfield's day among stable hands and also by New Orleans Dixieland bands, just as it would be bandied about later by jazz musicians in Harlem. Mary K. O'Donnell, a librarian at Skidmore College, led me to Barry Popik's research on this. Popik has tracked down FitzGerald's own accounts of how he picked up the term, notably in his *Morning Telegraph* columns "Around the Big Apple with John J. FitzGerald," Feb. 18, 1924, and "In the Paddock with John J. FitzGerald," Dec. 1, 1926. See also Gerald Leonard Cohen, *Origin of New York City's Nickname "The Big Apple"* (Frankfurt am Main: Peter Lang, 1991), and Barry Popik, "The Green 'Big Apple,'" *Irish-America Magazine*, January–February 1994, 1-A. Perhaps the latter article's title, a tip of the hat to the Irish-American FitzGerald, should have been "The Black 'Big Apple,'" a tip of the hat instead to the African-American stable hands.

25   **track at Roby, Indiana.** The Roby, Indiana, racing operation is partially described in an advertisement in the *Daily Racing Form*, Sept. 16, 1895, n.p.

Chapter Two

26   **Derby three races later.** Obsessed with numbers and time, racing people were among those who knew this was the final Derby Day of the century. They knew a century ended in a 0, not a 9, unlike the many who thought 1900 began a new century rather than ended one. Most humans would even miss the story of an entire new millennium, staging gigantic celebrations because they thought it began in 2000 rather than 2001.

26   **famous "twin spires."** Weep, fans at Fenway Park in Boston and Tiger Stadium in Detroit, which fail to get the honor of being America's oldest sports stadiums. They date from only 1912. Churchill's grandstand, with its pair of Victorian steeples, went up much earlier, in 1895, making it the second-oldest major American sports arena still in operation. It's interesting to note that Churchill's earlier grandstand was not torn down immediately; in 1896, the empty hulk loomed over what was suddenly the "far" side of the course. Our oldest major sports venue still in use? Saratoga Race Course, which dates from 1847. Its present grandstand went up in 1892, included elements from its 1864 predecessor, and was later much expanded.

27   **sales of "Kentucky whiskey."** Karl Baedeker, *The United States* (New York: Scribner's, 1909), 568.

29   **"Parade to the Post."** American bugle calls date to at least the Revolutionary War and were used in all branches of the military by the close of the Civil War. At Fort Larned, Kansas, "First Call" was summoning soldiers to formations as early as 1868. In American racing, there was no agreed-upon call to the post until the bugler F. A. Heckler introduced "First Call" at all the major eastern tracks in 1895, after some experiments with it at Monmouth Race Course in New Jersey. See also Tom Gilcoyne, "Q & A," in the quarterly of the National Museum of Racing and Hall of Fame, *Racing* 3:1 (Winter 1997): 9.

29   **down the fences.** Observers rarely had much to say about the black fans at any of the American tracks. But in 1896, it was noted that Churchill's abandoned original grandstand was deserted, "save for a few Negroes who sat there and took in the races from there." The same report said: "Although the colored man and brother

was not much in evidence as if there had been a free field, still there was quite a re-spectable number of Negroes in the grandstand and around the 'bookies.'" See "Ben Brush Wins the Kentucky Derby," *Louisville Commercial,* May 7, 1896, n.p.

31 **and 'Monk' beamed."** The best account of Monk's huge day is probably " 'Monk' Wins Six Races," *Chicago Tribune,* July 11, 1891, n.p.

32 **against Gibson particularly."** Some of the human Lieutenant Gibson's career is traced in Thompson Buchanan, "Intrenched [*sic*]," *Louisville Courier-Journal,* April 29, 1901, 1.

34 **¹⁷/₂₀ seconds faster.** Their speeds show how intensely the best young thorough-breds were conditioned in early spring to be brought to Derby form, to bring them to the edge of peak—so intensely that some trainers, then and now, have simply refused to do that to a three-year-old baby, keeping him in the barn instead.

35 **lead into his seat.** Collectors of Kentucky Derby trivia might be interested to know that only once has a horse ever been allowed to run over the prescribed weight for the Derby, which in modern times has been 126 pounds for colts and 121 pounds for fillies. This was in 1971, when, for reasons nobody at Churchill Downs can recall, Saigon Warrior carried 127 pounds—and came in twentieth and last. Canonero II won it.

36 **sport's motherland.** A good contemporary account of American racing's flight abroad is "Our Horses and Jockeys Abroad," *Munsey's Magazine,* Dec. 1900, 353–63.

Chapter Three

40 **other mainstream sport.** The best survey of African-Americans in sport is still *A Hard Road to Glory* (New York: Warner, 1988), by the late tennis champion Arthur R. Ashe Jr., assisted by three others. One might quibble, however, with Ashe's statement that in 1891 boxer George Dixon became "the first black man to hold an American title in any sport." Three years earlier, the black jockey Shelby "Pike" Barnes had become the first American rider to top 200 victories as he racked up 206 and won the national riding title. He won the title again in 1889.

41 **record for the distance.** This first race on Derby Day provided a good example of what could go wrong in that era before modern starting gates locked in the horses. First, a three-year-old just took off in the wrong direction, and when his jockey immediately jerked him back, the bridle broke. Then another colt broke through a gate. It took starter Curley Brown twenty minutes to line up the eight horses again. But when he sent them off once more, Lady Blue refused to budge, then crashed through a gate and headed back to the stables, costing another ten minutes. Network television would never stand for it. As those twenty thousand spectators suffered through all this on that 1901 Derby Day, a bunch of boys tried to catch a rabbit in Churchill's infield, an ancestor of modern baseball cats. They never caught the rabbit.

42 **jockey in the country.** As for the lightest professional jockey at that moment, it was one L. A. Jackson, at eighty pounds.

42 **determine the horse's odds.** Through most of the next century, the standard pari-mutuel bet would be $2. For the story of John Morrissey, the bookmakers, the

betting pools, and pari-mutuel operations at America's racetracks, see several references in Edward Hotaling, *They're Off! Horse Racing at Saratoga* (Syracuse, NY: Syracuse University Press, 1998).

43 **decorating his underwear.** For more on Diamond Jim Brady and the 1889 Derby, see Brownie Leach, *The Kentucky Derby Diamond Jubilee* (New York: Dial, 1949), 45, and Hotaling, *They're Off!*, 139.

43 **room was bare.** O'Connor found the pin remarkable enough to mention in his memoirs, but said nothing about it being embedded in his little chest.

43 **don't try it."** The newspapers provided the direct quotations used in racetrack passages.

43 **gates locked horses in.** Speaking of old tricks, one day before the Revolution, along the then-raging (later rechanneled and tamed) Roanoke River between North Carolina and Virginia, the young slave jockey Austin Curtis taught the veteran slave jockey Ned a thing or two. In the quick, two-horse, quarter-mile races of those days, the riders themselves were responsible for the start. They would turn their mounts in a circle until they were in line as they came out of a turn, then take off. On this day, Ned kept circling but refused to line up, because he knew that as it dragged on, Curtis's nervous horse was getting wound up and unmanageable. But Curtis finally forced the issue by intentionally letting his leg hang loose from the stirrup. It worked: Ned, seeing that leg hopelessly dangling, figured Curtis wasn't ready, and took off—to defeat.

44 **legs and clean stride.** A rider "shook up"—roused—a lagging horse by talking to him, working the bridle bit with his hands, or whipping or spurring him, often all at once.

46 **lies about it.** "The Negro," *Louisville Courier-Journal*, April 29, 1901, 1.

47 **piece of gold."** Terrell, "Around the World in 80 Years," *Sports Illustrated*, May 8, 1961, 73. Unless otherwise noted, this work's few direct quotations of Winkfield are from this long article, though many of the article's most important other elements are inaccurate, or never happened. Caveat emptor.

49 **record for the distance.** See the charts for October 2 and 3 in *The Daily Racing Form* (Chicago: Daily Racing Form, 1901), 483–84.

49 **many of those included.** See the "Jockeys' Mounts" listings in *Goodwin's Official Annual Guide to the Turf* (New York: Goodwin, 1899-1900).

Chapter Four

50 **his namesake here."** "Owner of Abe Frank Was/Certain of Colt's Victory," *Louisville Courier-Journal*, May 4, 1902, 3.

52 **each horse in the race."** Fitzsimmons also told Terrell in "Around the World" (78–79) in 1960: "They were horsemen in those days. A jockey would ride his mount in the morning and sometimes even cooled him off. So he knew his horse because he'd worked him. Now you have to lead a jockey to the horse he's going to ride, put him in the saddle, lead him to the post, and take him off when he's through. All a jockey's interested in these days is sleeping until noon and then going to some nightclubs after the race is over. They don't know anything about the other horses in the races." Studying each horse in a race is "what Winkfield apparently did in 1902. He was a professional."

52 **"Ride him good, Wink!"** It was the earliest appearance in print of Jimmy Wink-
    field's nickname.

53 **monster May Day.** Sam misremembered the year as 1903 in Samuel C. Hil-
    dreth and James R. Crowell, *The Spell of the Turf* (Philadelphia: Lippincott,
    1926), 144–49.

56 **years after the Derby.** He told the sand story to Terrell, "Around the World,"
    73–74.

61 **stalls, as I had."** Hildreth and Crowell, *Spell of the Turf,* 144–45.

62 **motion being perfect."** W[alter] S. Vosburgh, *Racing in America 1866–1921,*
    (New York: The Jockey Club, 1922), 183–84.

63 **Elias J. "Lucky" Baldwin.** For more on Lucky Baldwin, founder of Santa Anita,
    see George Waller, *Saratoga: Saga of an Impious Era* (Englewood Cliffs, NJ:
    Prentice-Hall, 1966), 207, 211; William H. P. Robertson, *History of Thoroughbred
    Racing in America* (New York: Bonanza, 1964), 112–28; Hotaling, *They're Off!,*
    121, 128, 133, 148, 227, and 243; and Hotaling, *Great Black Jockeys,* 253–55.

65 **was miraculously okay.** Indeed, McChesney was more than okay. After winning
    twelve of twenty-one races in 1902, he would pass into the hands of new owners
    and become America's best horse again in 1903, winning eight of fourteen. See
    Vosburgh, *Racing in America 1866–1921,* 183–84.

66 **more this year."** "Jockey," *Lexington Herald,* June 19, 1902, 8.

Chapter Five

68 **in all directions.** Winn tells his story in Frank G. Menke, *Down the Stretch! The
    Story of Colonel Matt Winn, As Told to Frank G. Menke* (New York: Smith and
    Durrell, 1945).

70 **hat over the crowd.** While what must be millions of hats are thrown in nineteenth-
    and twentieth-century literature, and especially journalism, and especially at race-
    tracks, someone back then pointed out that he never saw one thrown. They do
    cost money.

70 **"shriek[ed] with excitement."** "Judge Himes, Little Thought Of, Beats Early,
    the Odds-on Favorite, by Half a Length," *Louisville Courier-Journal,* May 3,
    1903, 1.

70 **responsible for the result.** "Judge Himes, Little Thought Of." ILL-TIMED RIDE BY
    WINKFIELD . . . is the subheadline.

71 **thousands on Early.** President William McKinley opened his first law practice
    in Canton, Ohio. An assassin shot President McKinley in Buffalo, New York,
    on September 6, 1901.
        The blood certainly didn't freeze in Wink that day. He was in the money
    all day with two wins, two seconds, and a third. A reporter noted, "His effort on
    Wain-A-Moinen was brilliant, and his ride on Cogswell was as pretty an exhi-
    bition of judgment as his mistake in the Derby was fatal."

72 **in the Kentucky Derby again.** Wink's daughter Liliane Winkfield Casey told
    me her father had spoken to her about the death threats. I spoke for several
    hours with Liliane and her daughter Amie in an interview in Cincinnati on Au-

gust 14, 2002. "He said that he was threatened," Liliane recalled, "that he should not ride, expect to ride, anymore in a Derby." I asked her how he phrased it. "Just was told that 'you better watch out,' that 'no nigger was gonna run in the Derby anymore,' and he better get out of the races, racing business."

72   **Fields vaudeville troupe.** Lil's life is amusingly summed up by Parker Morrell in his biography *Lillian Russell: The Era of Plush* (New York: Random House, 1940).

73   **money and gambling.** The most recent general history of the resort is Hotaling, *They're Off!*, the source of the Saratoga stories and quotations in this chapter.

73   **"about 400 miles."** The phenomenon of a booming Saratoga in the midst of the Civil War is covered in two chapters of Hotaling, *They're Off!*, 41–62.

74   **affairs of a continent.** For more of the context, see Hotaling, *They're Off!*, 85–87. See also Henry James, *Portraits of Places* (Boston: Houghton Mifflin, 1883), 324–37.

74   **water goes into you.** The old-time version was: "At one you go into the water; / At t'other it goes into you." Quoted in Hotaling, *They're Off!*, 65; and in the *Daily Saratogian*, July 28, 1865, 2.

74   **C-O-L-U-M-B-I-A.** Hotaling, *They're Off!*, 109.

74   **flaky fried potatoes.** For the story of how potato chips were invented at Saratoga, see the several references in Hotaling, *They're Off!*, 22, 37, 71, 80, 86–87, 178, 314.

75   **across the land.** Hotaling, *They're Off!*, 150.

Chapter Six

80   **news of Wink's Futurity.** The *New York World* and the *New York Times* provided some of the best coverage of the Futurity.

81   **odds in the big one.** O'Connor tells the story in *Jockeys, Crooks, and Kings.* (New York: Cape and Smith, 1935).

82   **boys off the track.** Charles B. Parmer, *For Gold and Glory: The Story of Thorough-bred Racing in America* (New York: Carrick and Evans, 1939), 150–51.

83   **howls of protest."** Robertson, *History of Thoroughbred Racing*, 183. See also Steven A. Riess, "Jamaica Racetrack," *Encyclopedia of New York City* (New Haven: Yale Univ., 1991), 612.

84   **send him to England.** For more on Lucien Lyne's coup in signing with James R. Keene, see the files of the *Lexington Leader*, especially "It's a Fortune," Oct. 19, 1902, 6; "Lyne Contract Is Signed," Oct. 25, 1902, 5; "Banquet to Lyne," Jan. 4, 1903; and "Horse Gossip," July 11, 1904.

84   **I never forgot it.** Sandford Lyne's concern for Ravello and her foal, sired in England by Collar, was justified. The colt, a big chestnut named Frank Gill, won four of nineteen at age two and five of nineteen at age three, the latter string including the Coney Island Jockey Club Stakes, the Withers, and the Travers. See Vosburgh, *Racing in America 1866–1921*, 195–96.

85   **James R. Keene at Carlsbad.** The files of the *Thoroughbred Record* are the best source for the various deals that sent America's top jockeys to Europe.

85 **showed it to Russia.** Sloan was brought to Russian-controlled Warsaw by Jan Reszke, who was not only a major Polish stable owner but a world-renowned tenor. Sloan introduced the American crouch to Poland (and thus Russia) in the spring of 1901 and was followed toward the close of that season by Hamilton. The crouch was so novel over there that one Polish writer thought Hamilton was merely "imitating" Cash Sloan, whereas many American jockeys, black and white, had been crouching for years. For a good summary of Polish racing at this time, see *Dzieje wyscigow I hodowli koni peinej krwi w Polsce (History of racing and breeding of full-blooded horses in Poland)* (Warsaw: PWRiL, 1970), especially the section on American jockeys and trainers.

86 **vast living room."** "J. O. Keene's Career As a Horseman," *Thoroughbred Record*, Sept. 10, 1921, 127.

87 **Jack was gone.** Jack Keene's checkered Russian career can be tracked in the frequent reports of the *Thoroughbred Record* and the *Lexington Leader*.

87 **you might think.** There was a well-known Irish Lad running in America at the same time, of the same age and also from an imported sire. He won the Saratoga Special and the Brooklyn and Metropolitan Handicaps for Harry P. Whitney and trainer John Madden. It was Lazareff's Irish Lad who first established Galtee More's reputation as one of Russia's leading sires.

88 **didn't kill it.** For more on Galtee More, see the Russian journal *Konnozavodstva (Horse-Breeding & Sport)* and several references in Roger Longrigg, *History of Horse Racing* (New York: Stein and Day, 1972).

88 **winning too much.** Indeed, the American trainer had been lavishly praised in Russia after winning the All-Russian Derby with Irish Lad. *Horse-Breeding & Sport* said Keene had "rendered great service to the Russian Stud by maintaining the glory of Galtee More." It added this unwittingly ironic note: "It is interesting to know what reward Mr. Keene will get for it."

88 **contract with Dunne.** The *Thoroughbred Record* would report in 1904 that Wink rode for Dunne "until last winter." See the *Record* of June 7, 2004. This would not have conflicted with Wink's Lazareff contract in November 1903, as that committed Wink only to ride in Russia starting in the spring of 1904. Another report said Wink at one point planned to ride at the Benning track in Washington, D.C., in the winter of 1903–1904.

88 **For 13,000 Roubles** "Papers Signed," *Lexington Leader*, Nov. 15, 1903, 1.

90 **via Jack Keene.** Lazareff likely assisted, through his man Keene, in arranging and financing Winkfield's first trip to Europe. Another good example of such careful handling of his valuable jockeys' travel and other arrangements will be seen a year later, when Wink returns.

Chapter Seven

91 **could learn Polish.** The chief sources for Jimmy Winkfield's foreign experiences, starting with Poland, are his comments in interviews; reports on the interviews; news coverage, including some photographs, as mentioned elsewhere in these notes; records of his races in several foreign countries; and interviews in French with his daughter Liliane and daughter-in-law Jeanine.

92 **world's equine population.** The numbers are from the writer Susanna Massie,

who came up with many other fascinating stats in an October 1989 series for *The Blood-Horse* magazine.

93 **entirely different program.** Russian racing is described in "Metropolitan Gossip," *Thoroughbred Record,* Jan. 31, 1903, 68, and J. O. Keene, "The Success of Yankee Turf Methods in Russia," *New York Illustrated Sporting News,* Nov. 28, 1903, 4.

93 **Warsaw Derby itself.** The Polish newspaper *Kurjer Warszawski* had a strong interest in racing, making it a fairly good source for the major Warsaw events.

93 **known all over the world."** "Horse Gossip," *Lexington Leader,* June 7, 1904, 7; see also "Late Turf News," *Lexington Leader,* July 11, 1904.

94 **Polish and Russian racing.** The princely Lubomirski brothers, who employed Cash Sloan, Tony Hamilton, and others, were Stanislaw, Stefan, and Wladyslaw, who owned the then-famous Kruszyna-Widzow Stud from 1896 until 1911, when Wladyslaw became sole owner. See the article, "The Team at Widzow before the First World War"—*Ludzie Widzowa wokresie przed pierwsza wojna swiatowa*—in the collection of the Polish Jockey Club.

94 **very important contests.** The files of the Moscow daily newspapers are among the better sources for Russian races.

94 **Hippodrome for the first time.** For brief introductory summaries of the world-renowned Moscow Central Hippodrome and a few of the more famous Russian equine traditions, see Kenneth Vella, "Ippica Nel Mondo,"www.brigliesciolte.it/giornale/articoli/kenneth01.htm and www.horse.spb.su/history/k12e.htm.

94 **leaped into the sky.** The Hippodrome's main building was destroyed by fire in the 1940s and rebuilt in the next decade.

96 **rings on every finger.** Hamilton's fall, his career, and other Americans' careers in Poland and Russia are touched on in "American Jockeys and Trainers in Warsaw," in *Dzieje wyscigow (History of racing).*

96 **had a few complaints.** Quoted, without naming the friend, in "Late Turf News," *Lexington Leader,* July 11, 1904, 7.

98 **21.6 win percentage.** Michael Laks described the life of Russian jockeys in a valuable memoir published in Moscow: "Three Colors of the Trade," *Sports Life* 8 (2002): 45–47, and 9 (2002): 34–35.

100 **managed to do well."** Terrell, "Around the World," 8.

101 **for Doc Allen.** See "Winkfield," *Lexington Leader,* Dec. 14, 1904.

Chapter Eight

103 **spend the winter here.** Coverage of the American jockeys' return home included "American Jockeys Home," *Kansas City Star,* Dec. 6, 1904; and "Yankee Jockeys Back in America" and "Jockey Winkfield Did Well in Russia This Year," *Louisville Courier-Journal,* Dec. 11, 1904.

104 **replication of celebrity.** United Press would be founded in 1907 and the International News Service in 1909. A brief summary of the early news syndicates can be found in Laurence R. Campbell and Roland E. Wolseley's old (there's a section called "Rewrite Man") but still serviceable *Newsmen at Work* (Boston: Houghton Mifflin, 1949), 42–43.

106 **in Hot Springs.** Wink's Hot Springs period can be tracked in the Little Rock *Arkansas Gazette* and the 1905 *Racing Form*.

106 **feared guard ever since.** Sir Bernard Pares, *History of Russia* (New York: Knopf, 1944), is superb on the origin of the Preobrajensky Regiment and its later use, starting on page 185. He points out the eponymous village's name meant "transfiguration," which is rather what happened to this palace guard as it became larger and more important over the centuries.

107 **organize for further action.** A fine portrait of prerevolutionary St. Petersburg—indeed a mosaic of portraits by some of its famous sons and daughters, among them Dmitri Shostakovich and George Balanchine—is Solomon Volkov, *St. Petersburg: A Cultural History* (New York: Free Press, 1995). Pares's extremely detailed *History of Russia* is also very helpful. The chief biographical sources used for that tumultuous 1905 in Russia were Ronald Segal, *Leon Trotsky* (New York: Pantheon, 1979); Robert C. Tucker, *Stalin As Revolutionary: 1879–1929* (New York: Norton, 1973); and Dmitri Volkogonov, *Lenin* (New York: Free Press, 1994), and *Trotsky: The Eternal Revolutionary* (New York: Free Press, 1996).

109 **Cambridge and Oxford."** Volkov, *St. Petersburg*, 147, quotes Nabokov indirectly.

110 **Cambridge and Oxford."** The diarist was a friend of the poet Mikhail Kuzmin, quoted in Volkov, *St. Petersburg*, 144.

110 **cemetery of Manchuria.** Quoted in Volkogonov, *Trotsky*, 35.

110 **rules us overboard!"** Volkogonov, *Trotsky*, 36.

112 **officer actually left.** Volkogonov, *Trotsky*, 41.

116 **G. Hamilton Keene** Radtke was second on the U.S. winners' list with 177 victories in 1905, and third with 196 in 1906. See *Goodwin's* 1905–1907 volumes.

118 **won by a black jockey.** Racing historian Charles Parmer wrote that Lee was "a quiet, courteous fellow, giving most of his attention to reducing, for that bête noire of jockeys, overweight, was threatening him." See Parmer, *For Gold and Glory*, 150–51. Combined with the dwindling job market for black riders, his weight problems might have pushed him off the track. But he did better than many afterward and, as late as the 1930s, was working as a trainer at the small stable of John O'Connor in Schuylerville, New York.

Chapter Nine

121 **great jockey Winkfield.** After the Russian Revolution, Tsarskoye Selo, meaning "the czar's town," would be renamed Pushkin.

122 **contest with seventeen entries.** Interestingly, Tolstoy describes one of the other seventeen jockeys as "coming along at a full gallop, crouching over his horse like a cat, in imitation of an English jockey." Tolstoy was writing *Anna Karenina* between 1874 and 1876, two decades before English commentators would be surprised by the American crouch, so the latter seat was presumably more extreme than the crouch of some of Tolstoy's English steeplechasers. It might be noted, too, that an English writer had noted some of America's black jockeys crouching over their mounts in the 1830s; see Hotaling, *Great Black Jockeys*, 111–12.

122 **and the race began.** If she's reading this, Oprah Winfrey must forgive the author for not using the translation she called for as her recent book club selection but

rather Rosemary Edmonds's excellent translation of L. N. Tolstoy, *Anna Karenina* (London: Penguin, 1978). The race begins on page 213.

124 **how good the horse was.** "The Team at Widzow before the First World War," 79.

124 **both at Vienna.** Good sources for the German and Austrian races are the daily files of the newspapers *Berliner Tageblatt, Berliner Taglische Rundschau,* and the *Berlin Sport-Welt.*

124 **training in Germany.** Taral trained for the dye manufacturers A. and C. von Weinberg.

124 **Everybody bets a little.** "Fred Taral in America," *Thoroughbred Record,* Nov. 23, 1912, 245. For more on this Hall of Famer, see "Success in Germany," *The Blood-Horse,* Jan. 5, 1985, 55.

125 **Grosse Preis von Baden.** Besides the standard newspaper sources mentioned above, see the brochure of the Baden-Baden racing association, Internationaler Club, *Internationale Galopprennen Baden-Baden: Ein kurzer Streifzug durch eine bewegte Geschichte* (Baden-Baden: Internationaler Club, n.d.), 17; also the Internationaler Club's 1910 racing manual for 1910, 648–49; and the race coverage by the local *Badisches Tagblatt.*

127 **in seventeen minutes.** The first airship to make a successful test flight was built by the French engineer Henri Giffard in 1852.

128 **in World War I.** As the old count intended, zeppelins bombed England in World War I but proved vulnerable to guns and storms.

131 **he slipped out of town.** Volkogonov, *Trotsky,* 94. He and Segal, *Leon Trotsky,* are the principal sources used for Trotsky's long Viennese exile.

131 **Alfred Adler for psychoanalysis.** Segal, *Leon Trotsky,* 96.

132 **bird with a bladder.** See Brigitte Hamann's *Hitler's Vienna,* translated by Thomas Thornton (New York: Oxford, 1999), 387, for more on this and an excellent summary of his 1908–1913 stay there.

133 **the human race.** Hamann, *Hitler's Vienna,* 203.

133 **should be "emancipated."** Hamann, *Hitler's Vienna,* 228–29.

133 **never to people."** Hamann, *Hitler's Vienna,* 323.

135 **she whispered slowly."** Tolstoy, *Anna Karenina,* 205.

135 **the German Derby.** In addition to the sources cited earlier for the story of this German Derby, see Internationaler Club, "1911 Chilperic: Abscheid von den alten Tribunen," *Internationale Galopprennen Baden-Baden: Ein kurzer Streifzug durch eiene bewegte Geschichte* (Baden-Baden: Internationaler Club, n.d.), 90–91.

136 **I must kiss her."** Emanuel Schikaneder, Libretto, *Mozart: Die Zauberflöte,* dialogue prepared by Peter Branscombe, 1991; *Neue Mozart Ausgabe Bareneiter,* English libretto, Capital Records, 1964; EMI Records Ltd. 1991, Virgin Classics Ltd., London, 1998.

136 **the plutocrat von Springer.** The family of Prince Thurn-and-Taxis might be called the Rockefellers of Germany.

136 **piloted by Monostatos.** The Mozartian star turn by Monostatos and his jockey was pointed out to me by German researcher Claudia Rong and is noted in "1911 Chilperic," 90.

137 **"The Negro is winning."** "*Neger*" is pejorative in German today. Its use in Wink's day could be translated as "Negro," according to Dr. Frank E. Wagner, language program coordinator at the Goethe-Institut in Washington, D.C.

137 **history of the German Derby.** "1911 Chilperic," 90.

138 **government-run Graditz stud.** Longrigg, *History of Horse Racing*, 197–99, 302.

138 **got him goin'," Wink said.** Again, unless otherwise noted, Wink's few quoted recollections are from Terrell, "Around the World."

139 **suing for divorce.** The official but incomplete file of Edna Winkfield's divorce papers are in the Fayette Circuit Court records at the Kentucky State Archives in Frankfurt.

140 **prices for other buyers.** The files of the British *Bloodstock Breeders' Review* are an excellent source not only for following news developments in British and Continental breeding but for learning important racing and other news.

141 **boys in Moscow.** For Eddie Dugan's racing records, see the 1908–1912 volumes of the *American Racing Manual*, published by Triangle in New York, and the running files of the Russian daily newspapers. See also Hildreth and Crowell, *Spell of the Turf*, 218–22.

Chapter Ten

142 **Austro-Hungarian throne.** While dedicated to Serbian nationalism, Princip was said to be an ethnic Bosnian acting with the knowledge of the Serbs.

144 **allowance in races.** For a different reason, a mare today might be sent to Kentucky to be serviced by an important stallion, then returned, say, to New York to foal. The high-class result could be then be promoted as a New York–bred, as was the recent Kentucky-conceived, New York–bred favorite Funny Cide.

145 **even in military matters.** The liveliest account of this monk, almost as politically active as he was sexually active, may still be Rene Fülöp-Miller, *Rasputin: The Holy Devil* (New York: Viking, 1929).

146 **the czarina's friend.** See Denzil Batchelor, *Jack Johnson and His Times* (London: Phoenix, 1956), 96–102, for this episode and Batchelor's entire account for the rest of Johnson's extraordinary life.

147 **was quite popular.** Wink's daughter Liliane Winkfield Casey has no details of the skating rink, except that he had mentioned it to the family.

148 **Russia with Siberia.** Yuri (George) Thiemann, nephew of Jimmy Winkfield and his third wife, Lydie deMinkwitz Winkfield, told the author the story of the bridge in an interview on February 12, 2003. Part of deMinkwitz family lore, the story also comes with no details on the scope of the project.

150 **in America, too.** "The declaration to win" would die out in the United States after World War II.

151 **land of the Romanovs.** The author got up close to this Fabergé egg in 2004 at

Sotheby's New York, which sold a farmer's dozen, including this and eight other Imperial Eggs, from the Malcolm Forbes collection, for more than $100 million. Snapped up by a Russian businessman Victor Vekselberg, to help restore Russia's heritage, they were all returned to Moscow for public display.

151 **not murder, but drowning.** This version is based on Segal's account of the murder in *Leon Trotsky*, 121–22. See also the longer, livelier, and opinionated ("a cowardly and treacherous murder") account in Fülöp-Miller, *Rasputin*, 344–68.

152 **last-minute business.** Elizabeth's son was Yuri Thiemann; again, the treasure of amazing stories from the lives of Jimmy Winkfield and his in-laws does not include such details of which river this was or which crossing point.

154 **the returning Trotsky.** Still a good biography is Robert Payne, *Life and Death of Lenin* (New York: Simon and Schuster, 1964).

154 **sleek as seals."** "Metropolitan Gossip," 68.

Chapter Eleven

155 **on the Black Sea.** The story of Jimmy Winkfield's move to Odessa was assembled bit by bit from reports in various Polish, British, American, Russian, and French publications (in that order of importance), which are cited in other notes and the bibliography, and from an interview with his daughter Liliane Winkfield Casey.

156 **jockey named Lemuel.** The Russian jockey Laks left an excellent account of this Odessa Derby in "Three Colors of the Trade."

158 **pioneering film *Potemkin*.** See Richard Hough, *The Potemkin Mutiny* (Englewood Cliffs, NJ: Prentice-Hall, 1960). As for Eisenstein's many innovations, they included panning a ship at rest, from bow to stern, to make it appear to be moving. *Potemkin*, completed in 1925, was Eisenstein's second full-length film. The first, *Strike*, from the year before, also dealt with workers who had fought the czarist government.

158 **during World War I.** A good account of the Polish role in Odessa racing is "Odessa, 1915–1919," starting on page 407 of *Dzieje wyscigow* (*History of racing*).

159 **men for trenches."** John J. Pershing, *My Experiences in the World War* (New York: Stokes, 1931), 1, 95.

159 **Moscow Central Hippodrome open.** Zoppi is quoted in the 1919 *Bloodstock Breeders' Review*, 210–11.

159 **a mine at Alapayevsk.** See Pares, *History of Russia*, 481.

161 **foot and hoof.** The Odessa racing community's escape and overland trek was told in an extraordinary report, much of it composed on the road, by a member of the expedition, Tadeusz Jaworski, in *Jezdziec i Hodowca* (*Rider and breeder*), no. 38 (n.p., 1926), 410. It was reprinted in *Dzieje wyscigow* (*History of racing*). It makes no mention of Winkfield. For the Jimmy Winkfield–Roy Terrell version, see Terrell, "Around the World."

161 **the Civil War.** For more on the role of slaves on horse farms in the Revolutionary War and the Civil War, see Hotaling, *Great Black Jockeys*.

163 **finish line burned brightest.** The photograph showing the grandstand in flames is from *Dzieje wyscigow (History of racing)*, engraving no. 243.

165 **Eastern European void.** Hildreth remembers Eddie in Hildreth and Crowell, *Spell of the Turf*, 218–22.

167 **exodus in sporting history.** A hint of it would leak out when Hildreth noted in his memoir (1926) that Eddie Dugan "went to Europe to ride and later barely escaped through the enemy lines," 218.

168 **deeply moving reception.** Hoover is moving in recollecting his visit to the track in *Memoirs of Herbert Hoover: Years of Adventure, 1874–1920* (New York: Macmillan, 1951), 359–61.

Chapter Twelve

170 **woken up in Paris.** Winkfield's going to bed in Warsaw and waking in Paris is not to be taken literally. He may well have boarded an overnight sleeper, something he was used to doing in his travels between racetracks all over the world, but neither his train tickets nor other documents have survived to show his travel dates.

170 **Prix du Président de la République.** The chief source for Wink's and other French races of this period, and for off-track developments, is coverage in *Échos de Paris, Figaro, Le Sport Hippique, Le Sport Universel Illustré, Le Temps*, and the European editions of the *New York Herald* and *New York Herald-Tribune* as well as the records in the *Annuaire de la Chronique du Turf* (Paris: Chronique du Turf, annual).

171 **escaping from the Bolsheviks.** As noted earlier, Lucien Lyne's continuing adventures were briefly noted occasionally in the *Thoroughbred Record* as well as in the publications listed in the previous note.

171 **did not murder Rasputin.** Rasputin's murderer was still the most fascinating resident of the 16th *arrondissement* in the early 1960s. Yusupov died there in 1967, at age eighty.

172 **eleven of their broodmares.** Also as noted earlier, Britain's *Bloodstock Breeders' Review* tracked the auction action at Newmarket.

173 **was officially sanctioned.** The details of Picasso's problems with the French police—then, earlier, and later—would be buried in the French police archives until the Nazi occupation of France, then transferred to Berlin, moved again in 1945 to Moscow, and finally returned to France after the collapse of the Soviet Union. See Alan Riding, "Picasso in Paris: A Suspect, Never a Citizen," *New York Times*, May 28, 2003, B1.

175 *Le Sport Hippique. Le Sport Hippique*, Oct. 1, 1921 cover.

176 **large, lavish accommodations.** The bragging about Chantilly is done, naturally enough, by the French racing association. See *Guide des hippodromes* (Paris: France Galop, n.d.), 20–21.

176 **and three gardeners.** The Rothschilds can be plucked one by one from the helpful family tree at the close of Frederic Morton's *The Rothschilds: A Family Portrait* (New York: Atheneum, 1962).

176 **as well as his own."** Quoted in Michael Tanner and Gerry Cranham, *Great Jockeys of the Flat* (Enfield, Middlesex: Guinness, 1992), 134.

176 **boxer Georges Carpentier.** Carpentier was in the news just then. In a historic encounter in Jersey City, New Jersey, he was clobbered by Jack Dempsey, to which Madame Carpentier, from her Paris apartment, responded with that Gallic talent for summing up things: "It is the victory of brute force!" See "Bruce Force Won," *New York Herald*, July 3, 1921, 1. As for Winnie, having regaled us with his often highly imaginary German adventures in his perfectly entitled memoir, *Jockeys, Crooks, and Kings*, O'Connor proceeded to his French recollections, some of which were excellent lies.

177 **Kiki, the artists' model.** Still among the better treatments of Paris when it sizzled are *Les Années Folles* (Paris: Denoel, 1956) and, in English, Billy Klüver and Julie Martin's illustrated *Kiki's Paris: Artists and Lovers 1900–1930* (New York: Abrams, 1989).

177 **sank roo doe noo."** Everybody called it the *Paris Herald*, but it was formally the *European Edition of the New York Herald*. Similarly, they would later call it the *Paris-Trib*, though by then it was formally the *European Edition of the* [merged] *New York Herald-Tribune*. The author is one of its alumni. A nostalgic account of it in Wink's day is Al Laney, *Paris Herald: The Incredible Newspaper* (New York: Appleton, 1947).

177 **the Grand Prix?"** The barflies' greetings for Frankie O'Neill are quoted in "Frankie O'Neill Is Accounted Most/Popular American in French Capital" in the July 4, 1922 edition of the *Paris Herald*. The piece was almost certainly written by sports editor Sparrow Robertson, Frankie's biggest fan.

179 **died of her injuries.** The assailants had not been caught as of six months later. See "Paris Court's Fine of Ex-Jazz King/Reveals Tragi-Comedy of Montmartre," *New York Herald*, Oct. 22, 1922, 1.

180 **inventing modern dance.** Still one of the most useful accounts of her life is her autobiography, *Isadora* (New York: Award, 1968), originally published as *My Life*.

183 **cover of *Le Sport Hippique*.** *Le Sport Hippique*, Oct. 1, 1921, cover.

184 **top-hat-ful of American plutocrats.** The Rothschilds were a major presence on the German, French, and English turf for decades. For their story, and a family tree, see Frederic Morton, *The Rothschilds: A Family Portrait* (New York, Atheneum, 1962).

184 **Prix Eugène-Adam.** "Chronique," *Le Sport Universel Illustré*, July 23, 1922, 224.

184 **more and more.** See *Guide Historique et Touristique de Maisons-Laffitte* and *À La Découverte du Parc*, both published by the Office de Tourisme at 41 avenue de Longueil, 78600, Maisons-Laffitte, France.

185 *Hansel and Gretel.* Maisons-Laffitte's groundskeepers and grandstand made it a favorite of David Alexander, who remembered it in *A Sound of Horses*.

Chapter Thirteen

187 **1922, at Deauville.** Two causes were reported for this historic battle of the Casino de Deauville. One was Mrs. Gould's impression that Monsieur Bamberger had said she resembled a cocotte, apparently without detailing what was cocottish, as

opposed to coquettish, about her. The other was that Bamberger, at the table of Lady Idena Gordon, overheard some nasty remarks about a portrait of the lady by the celebrated French caricaturist Sem. According to this account, Bamberger chivalrously attacked the remarker, a Monsieur de la Astoreca, who was busy dancing with Mrs. Gould, who hauled off and whacked Monsieur Bamberger. Exercising its always brilliant news judgment, the *Paris Herald* put this at the top of page one, along with the sinking of a French battleship that hit a reef in the Mediterranean, with three sailors missing. See "Fight in Casino Gives Deauville Exciting Topic," *New York Herald*, Aug. 27, 1922, 1.

187 **older than Winkfield).** Again, the Paris newspapers are the chief source for off-track developments: *Échos de Paris, Le Figaro, Le Sport Hippique, Le Sport Universel Illustré, Le Temps,* and the European editions of the *New York Herald* and *New York Herald-Tribune.*

189 **he was a demon."** Terrell, "Around the World," 73.

189 **riding to beat Americans."** Roger Longrigg, *History of Horse Racing* (New York: Stein and Day, 1972), 279.

191 **my greatest friends."** The chief source here for remarks by and about Donoghue and the other great jockeys of Great Britain and Australian is Michael Tanner and Gerry Cranham's superb *Great Jockeys of the Flat* (Middlesex, Eng.: Guinness, 1992), passim.

192 **rapport with horses."** Tanner and Cranham, *Great Jockeys of the Flat*, 9.

196 **induced racist ridicule.** Edward Hotaling, *The Great Black Jockeys* (Rocklin, CA: Forum/Prima, 1999), 198.

Chapter Fourteen

201 **travel, Pennsylvania Station.** See "The End of Penn Station" at www.forgotten-ny.com.

201 **31st to 33rd streets.** The demolition of the original Pennsylvania Station in 1964 was one of the horrors of that era's "urban renewal" movement.

202 **trifle to spare.** One site offering the lyrics is www.mamarocks.com/chattanooga_choo_choo.htm.

202 **reality of Jimmy's day.** "Chattanooga Choo-Choo," composed by Harry Warren, was nominated for an Academy Award in 1941. The movie *Sun Valley Serenade* starred such notables as Glenn Miller, Dorothy Dandridge, Milton Berle, and the ice skater Sonja Henie.

203 **before he hit Baltimore.** Because they were based on travelers' needs, the times and fares given must have been close to those available to Winkfield, though they are based on an earlier source, Baedeker's 1909 *United States*, q.v., 402, 578, 582.

206 **defeat in racing history.** The story of Man o'War, especially his Saratoga appearances, is told in Edward Hotaling, *They're Off! Horse Racing at Saratoga* (Syracuse, NY: Syracuse University. Press, 1998), 205–15.

206 **darkies in the stables."** Samuel C. Hildreth and James R. Crowell, *The Spell of the Turf* (Philadelphia: Lippincott), 205–6.

206 **method of surviving.** Hildreth and Crowell, *Spell of the Turf*, 179–82.

207 **the next day.** For more on "the Oral Days," see Hotaling, *They're Off!*, chapters 17–21.

208 **more gangland killings.** Hugh Bradley, *Such Was Saratoga* (New York: Doubleday, Doran, 1940), 300–301.

208 **the way to Mechanicsville.** Quoted in Hotaling, *They're Off!*, 230–31; and George Waller, *Saratoga: Saga of an Impious Era* (Englewood Cliffs, NJ: Prentice-Hall, 1966), 130.

Chapter Fifteen

218 **nineteen years old.** The chief source for Josehpine Baker is Lynn Havey's excellent *Naked at the Feast* (New York: Dodd Mead, 1981).

221 **by May 1926,** The Prefect of France's Seine et Oise Department issued George an ID card in May 1926, doubtless getting the details from his father, as the prefecture spelled Jimmy's birthplace "Charlesburg," which, of course, was how the proud Kentuckian pronounced Chilesburg.

221 **served at cost."** O'Connor, *Jockeys, Crooks, and Kings*, 214–14.

223 **the required impost.** In the United States, in recognition of female riders, "bug boy" has been supplanted by "bug rider" in recent years. The allowances vary by tracks and states. Traditionally, a single bug in the program indicated a 5-pound allowance, meaning that a horse with an impost, or required weight, of 123 pounds could carry 118 if the rider was an apprentice. But the system was and remains more complicated than that, allowing for multiple bugs. In New York State, a rider starts with a triple-bug (three asterisks), or 10-pound allowance, which he keeps until his fifth win. His status then drops to a double-bug in the program, or 7-pound allowance, which he keeps until he wins thirty-five more, or a total of forty. Then he gets a single bug, or 5-pound allowance until the first anniversary of his fifth winner, at which point he becomes a journeyman jockey. If he hasn't chalked up his fortieth win by that anniversary, the rider keeps the 7-pound allowance until he does, then becomes a journeyman—or gets out of the riding game because nobody wants to hire a jock who just can't seem to collect forty wins. Bug allowances are not given in stakes races.

223 **take thirty wins.** One of George's fellow jockeys in his final race, F. Hervé, scored his thirty-first victory that year and thus lost his apprentice allowance. In that last race with Wink Junior, though, his mount was also an also-ran.

224 **American, or whatever."** The witness was Lydie's nephew Yuri, or George, Thiemann, who commented in the above-referenced interview.

225 **business too long!' "** See T. Bentley Mott, *Myron Herrick: Friend of France*, chapters 42–45, available at www.lib.byu.edu. For a recent critical treatment of Lindberg, see Max Wallace, *The American Axis: Henry Ford, Charles Lindbergh, and the Rise of the Third Reich* (New York: St. Martin's, 2003).

Chapter Sixteen

230 **back in 1911.** The French newspaper reports would vary on the dates of Clara's birth and the first time she saw Winkfield. The more likely version was that she was seven when she saw the famous jockey during his big 1911 season at Budapest, when he won the Hungarian St. Leger, the Biennal-Zuchtrennen, and the Preis des Ackerbau-Ministeriums (the Agriculture Ministry Stakes).

235 **in the third?"**). To Saidamin Shamilov's translation for "Who do you like in the third?" Ed Lozansky offers the alternative *"Kto tvoi favorit v tretiem?"*

235 **Yuri, Lydie's nephew.** Yuri was forever mortified by this sleeping arrangement. "You slept in the same room with Lili and Tante Jeanne?" he was asked seven decades later. "Yep," he finally admitted. Gianna, his wife of forty-nine years, said, "Well, for goodness sakes, you never told me that." But Yuri may, in fact, have been switched to Robert's room when he got a bit older.

236 **alias Sacha Stavisky.** One of the better accounts in English of the Stavisky affair is William L. Shirer, *The Collapse of the Third Republic: An Inquiry into the Fall of France in 1940* (New York: Simon and Schuster, 1969), 204–30.

237 **a transitive verb.** A later usage of "suicided" surfaced after the death of Georges Figon, one of the characters in the Ben Barka affair, involving the murder of a Moroccan opposition leader, in the 1960s.

240 **my greatest friends."** Quoted by Tanner and Cranham, *Great Jockeys of the Flat*, 135.

241 **owner—unlike Wink.** See Laura Hillenbrand's *Seabiscuit* (New York: Random House, 2001).

242 **plenty to chew over.** Good summaries of the Bojangles story are "Bill 'Bojangles' Robinson," www.kathleenacademy.com/funzone/bojangls.html and, under the same title, www.imdiversity.com.

242 **a concert artist.** Roland Hayes's career is reviewed briefly in "Roland Hayes: Musician and Composer, 1877–1977," www.bridgew.edu/HOBA/Inductees/Hayes.htm.

Chapter Seventeen

245 **especially to the horses.** Many years later, a Parisian racing weekly would quote Robert as saying, "My first promenades, a few days after my birth, were in this [racetrack] setting. My father quickly took me to the stables, and the very first things I saw were on horses being trained." Unfortunately, most of this was probably in the reporter's head, because he went on to quote Robert as also saying there were about thirty horses in the stable, thus confusing 1923, when Robert was born during Wink's jockey period, with post-1930, Wink's training period. See Jean Heltey, "Champion des États-Unis et vedette dans la Russie des Tsars," *Dimanche Turf*, ca. 1965.

250 **beginning of the Holocaust.** A brief summary is "Kristallnacht," www.us-israel.org/jsource/Holocaust/kristallnacht.html.

250 **X-rated at the time.** In 1929, more than a quarter century after Zola's death and when Lili was five, a French critic still felt obliged to excuse the novelist's "crudity" by saying he was making up much of it. Zola could indeed make a train wreck sound sensual. To translate one scene: "The [locomotive], turned over on its loins, its stomach open, was losing its steam through torn faucets and broken pipes in sighs that groaned like the death rattles of a furious giant. A white breath came out of it, inextinguishable, rolling like thick cloud-wheels along the ground while from the furnace the fallen live coals, red like the very blood of its entrails, added their black fumes." (*La Bête Humaine.*) See E. Abry, C. Audic, and P. Crouzet, *Histoire illustré de la Littérature Française* (Paris: Didier, 1929), 624–25.

251 **white as chalk.**" Eric Sevareid, *Never So Wild a Dream* (New York: Knopf, 1946), 120–24.

251 **in January, 1940,** The date is based on the birthdate of the resulting offspring, as recorded in the French vital-statistics records.

Chapter Eighteen

253 **for French citizenship.** Riding, "Picasso in Paris," B5.

256 **taken over as well.** Susanna Massie, "The Soviet Turf," *Blood-Horse*, Oct. 7, 1989, 5466–69.

260 **in nine countries.** Among many other features, Lucien won the Premio Cimera, the Spanish version of England's classic 2,000 Guineas, no fewer than five times between 1921 and 1928; His Majesty the King's Prize, twice; and the Spanish St. Leger and the Gran Premio de Madrid.

260 **national point of view.**" When the Picasso file finally became public in 2003, the writers and Picasso experts Armand Israel and Pierre Daix commented, "France lost a celebrated man whom it could have been proud to have included among its citizens." As for Picasso himself, as Alan Riding pointed out, on Oct. 5, 1944, six weeks after the liberation of Paris, he joined the French Communist Party. See Riding, "Picasso in Paris," B5.

Chapter Nineteen

263 **wealthy and otherwise.** For those who can't remember New York in 1941, or any of the decades following, *The Encyclopedia of New York City*, edited by Kenneth T. Jackson (New Haven, CT: Yale, 1991), offers various glimpses. See especially the contributors Thea Arnold (Sugar Hill), Carol Willis (Empire State Building), Rebecca Read Shanor (Triborough Bridge), Jon A. Peterson (Queens), Vincent Seyfried (Queens and Jamaica), Barbara Blumberg (the WPA), Paul Barrett (LaGuardia Airport), and Jeffrey Kroessler (the World's Fair).

263 **taking in boarders.** See Obatunji McKnight, "Tasting Sugar Hill," www.harlemlive.org/community/harlemNtrans/.

264 **only sixteen years.** Wink may have stopped briefly in New York the year before, in 1898, when the Mays first took him to Chicago.

267 **the federal government.** LaGuardia was initially called North Beach Airport, but the name was changed soon afterward.

276 **It is the turning point!**" The last days of Hitler and Fegelein are based largely on William L. Shirer, *Rise and Fall of the Third Reich* (New York: Simon and Schuster, 1960), 1107–43. See also Albert Speer, *Inside the Third Reich* (New York: Avon, 1970), 517–44.

279 **more than one Kentucky Derby.** There were four triple Kentucky Derby winners entering 2005—Ike Murphy, Earl Sande, the retired Angel Cordero Jr., and the contemporary jockey Gary Stevens. Stevens could conceivably win two more, though it is extremely unlikely. Wink's group—the twenty-two winners of more than one Derby—includes such recent stars as Jerry Bailey, Kent Desormeaux, and Chris McCarron.

281 **And then he walked on by.** The neighbor would tell this story a half century later.

282 **staying for nine months.** Touchingly, "Elisabetta" would be honored by the Italians at the close of the war with the Military and Hospital Order of St. Mary of Bethlehem, the citation reading, "*Colta, distinta, vivace la Baronessa di Minkwitz e stata sempre dinamicamente interessata ai progressi della Cultura europea e di quella italo-francese in ispecie.*" Or: "cultivated, distinguished, vivacious, the Baronessa di Minkwitz always had a lively interest in the development of European, and especially Franco-Italian, culture."

286 *Herald-Leader* **itself.** The *Lexington Herald-Leader* broke the story on July 4, 2004. The *Herald* and *Leader* merged in the 1980s, and the paper is now part of the Knight-Ridder newspaper chain. See also James Dao, "40 Years Later, Civil Rights Protests Make Page One," *New York Times*, July 13, 2004.

Chapter Twenty

292 **wouldn't show through.** For more on Brown and a recipe, using Worcestershire sauce, for Hot Browns, see Lynn S. Renau, *Jockeys, Belles, and Bluegrass Kings*, (Louisville, KY: Herr House, 1995), 134–36. Irene Hayes, with the help of May K. Roberts, comes up with a few other Hot Brown recipes in *What's Cooking in Kentucky* (Ft. Mitchell, KY: T. I. Hayes, 1994), 93–94.

292 **his wealthy employers.** While his hotel directed blacks to the back door and the freight elevator, Brown enhanced his Brown Hotel Stable by hiring black trainers and advisers. He died in 1969.

296 **the day's biggest features.** See "Vainqueurs à 30/1" and Jacques Orliaguet, "Ambre Rose et Fandine," *Paris-Turf*, March 28, 1967, n.p., and J. J. Arsene, "La Vedette à Mme R. Winkfield," *Paris-Turf*, n.d.

296 **alert to everything."** Heltey, "Champion des États-Unis."

297 **ever return home.** Goose died on June 11, 1971, at age eighty.

298 **who he was going to be.** See Chapter 1 for the full account of wild Wink's first race.

299 **kids their baths.** Jimmy Winkfield would have been ninety-four when he died if his birthday were before March 23. When he cut two years off his age in France in the 1920s, he used the birthday April 12, but it has never been verified.

299 **He never woke up.** Marshall Lilly sent his regrets—and died the next year at age ninety.

299 **But he could** *ride."* Quoted in Greg Kocher, "A Jockey's Story," *Lexington Herald-Leader*, April 30, 2002, A1.

Selected Bibliography

Newspapers and Periodicals

Besides interviews with his family and the sporting archives of two continents, the principal sources on Jimmy Winkfield are the newspapers of his day. They took me back a century and to seven countries. Soon, we will have no newspapers at all, but if our doomed newspapers have been, in the happy phrase of *Washington Post* publisher Philip Graham, "the first draft of history," their remains, in whatever new form, will still serve as the first draft of the distant past, and an enormously valuable archive at that. Those below, for example, offered me a preliminary version of the Jimmy Winkfield story, one of the most extraordinary lives of any athlete anywhere.

Baden-Baden, Germany's *Badisches Tagblatt*; Berlin's *Berliner Tageblatt*, *Sport-Welt*, and *Taglische Rundschau*; *Baltimore Sun*; Chicago's *Daily News*, *Record*, *Tribune*, *Daily Tribune*, and *Times-Herald*; Cincinnati's *Enquirer*, *Post*, and *Post and Times-Star*; *Columbus Dispatch*; Covington *Kentucky Post*; Danville, Kentucky's *Advocate Messenger*; *Kansas City Star*; Lexington, Kentucky's *Herald*, *Leader*, *Herald-Leader*, *Kentucky Statesman*, *Morning Transcript*, and *Observer and Reporter*; Little Rock's *Arkansas Gazette*; London's *Daily Telegraph* and *Sunday Telegraph*, Louisville's *Commercial*, *Courier-Journal*, *Herald*, and *Times*; *Moskovskiia Vedomosti*; New Orleans's *Daily Picayune*; New York's *Daily Racing Form*, Illustrated Sporting News, *Sun*, *Times*, *World*; Paris's *Echo de Paris*, *Figaro*, *Matin*, *Temps*, *Paris Turf*; and Warsaw's *Kurjer Warszawski*.

And these weeklies, biweeklies, and monthlies: *American Turf Monthly*, *Backstretch*, *Blood-Horse*, *Bloodstock Breeders Review* (UK), *Business Review*, *Dimanche-Turf* (France), *Ebony*, *Goodwin's Official Annual Guide to the Turf*, *Louisville Defender*, *Ippica nel Mondo* (Italy), *Munsey's Magazine*, *l'Oeil* (France), *Players*, *Spirit of the*

Times, Sport Hippique (France), *Sports Illustrated, Sports Life* (Russia), *Sport Universel Illustré* (France), *Thoroughbred Record, Time, Turf, Field and Farm, Turf and Sport Digest,* and *Zhurnal Sporta* (Russia).

Books and Articles

A La Decouverte du Parc. Maisons-Laffitte: Office de Tourisme, n.d.

Alexander, David. *A Sound of Horses: The World of Racing from Eclipse to Kelso.* Indianapolis: Bobbs-Merrill, 1966.

The American Racing Manual. New York: Triangle. Annual.

Anderson, James Douglas. *Making the American Thoroughbred, Especially in Tennessee, 1800–1845.* Norwood, MA: Plimpton Press, 1916.

Arsene, J. J. "La Vedette à Mme R. Winkfield." *Paris Turf,* n.d.

Ashe, Arthur R., Jr., with the assistance of Kip Branch, Ocania Chalk, and Francis Harris. *A Hard Road to Glory: A History of the African-American Athlete.* New York: Warner, 1988.

Baedeker, Karl. *The United States, with Excursions to Mexico, Cuba, Porto Rico, and Alaska: Handbook for Travellers.* New York: Scribner, 1909.

Batchelor, Denzil. *Jack Johnson and His Times.* London: Phoenix Sports Books, 1956.

Borries, Betty Earle. *Isaac Murphy, Kentucky's Record Jockey.* Berea, KY: Kentucky Imprints, 1988.

Chew, Peter. *The Kentucky Derby: The First 100 Years.* Boston: Houghton Mifflin, 1974.

Duncan, Isadora. *Isadora.* New York: Award, 1968

Dzieje wyscigow I hodowli koni peinej krwi w Polsce (History of racing and breeding of full-blooded horses in Poland). Warsaw: PWRiL, 1970.

"FISTS/Used in a Horse Race/Two Jockeys Fought Each Other." *Cincinnati Enquirer,* May 18, 1899, 4.

Fülöp-Miller, René. *Rasputin: The Holy Devil.* New York: Viking, 1929.

Guide des hippodromes. Paris: France Galop, n.d.

Guide Historique et Touristique de Maisons-Laffitte. Maisons-Laffitte: Office de Tourisme, n.d.

Guilleminault, Gilbert, avec le collaboration de François Brigneau . . . [et al.]. *Les Années Folles.* Paris: Denoël, 1956.

Hamann, Brigitte. *Hitler's Vienna: A Dictator's Apprenticeship.* New York: Oxford University Press, 1999.

Haney, Lynn. *Naked at the Feast* (A Biography of Josephine Baker). New York: Dodd, Mead, 1981.

Heltey, Jean. "Champion des États-Unis et vedette dans la Russie des Tsars." *Dimanche-Turf,* ca. 1965.

Hildreth, Samuel C., and James R. Crowell. *The Spell of the Turf: The Story of American Racing.* Philadelphia: Lippincott, 1926.

Hillenbrand, Laura. *Seabiscuit: An American Legend.* New York: Random House, 2001.

Hollingsworth, Kent. "A Man Who Knew Champions" (Marshall Lilly). *Blood-Horse,* Nov. 24, 1975, 5152–57.

Hoover, Herbert. *The Memoirs of Herbert Hoover: Years of Adventure 1874–1920.* New York: Macmillan, 1951.

Hotaling, Edward. "Black Jockeys Rode into History." *Baltimore Sun,* Feb. 6, 2000, C-1.

———. *The Great Black Jockeys: The Lives and Times of the Men Who Dominated America's First National Sport.* Rocklin, CA: Forum, 1999.

———. "Hall of Fame: Isaac Murphy." *Backstretch,* July–August 1999, 32.

———. *They're Off!: Horse Racing at Saratoga.* Syracuse, NY: Syracuse University Press, 1998.

———. "When Racing Colors Included Black." *New York Times,* June 2, 1996, Sports sec., 9.

Hough, Richard. *The Potemkin Mutiny.* New York: Pantheon Books, 1961, c1960.

Internationale Galopprennen Baden-Baden: Ein kurzer Streifzug durch eine bewegte Geschichte. Baden-Baden: Internationaler Club, n.d.

Jaworski, Tadeusz. *Jezdziec i Hodowca (Rider and breeder),* no. 38, 1926, n.p.

Keene, J. O. "The Success of Yankee Turf Methods in Russia." *New York Illustrated Sporting News,* Nov. 28, 1903, 4.

Keeneland. Prospect, KY: Harmony House, 2000.

Klüver, Billy, and Julie Martin. *Kiki's Paris: Artists and Lovers 1900–1930.* New York: Abrams, 1989.

Kocher, Greg. "A Jockey's Story." Lexington *Herald-Leader,* April 30, 2002, A1.

Laks, Michael. "Three Colors of the Trade," (Moscow) *Sports Life* 8 (2002): 45–47, and 9 (2002): 34–35.

Laney, Al. *Paris Herald: The Incredible Newspaper.* New York: Appleton-Century, 1947.

Leach, Brownie. *The Kentucky Derby Diamond Jubilee, 1875–1949.* Louisville: Gibbs-Inman, 1949.

Longrigg, Roger. *The History of Horse Racing.* New York: Stein and Day, 1972.

Lucas, Marion Brunson, and George C. Wright. *A History of Blacks in Kentucky.* Frankfort: Kentucky Historical Society, 1992.

Menke, Frank G. *Down the Stretch: The Story of Colonel Matt J. Winn.* New York: Smith and Durrell, 1945.

Morton, Frederic. *The Rothschilds: A Family Portrait.* New York: Atheneum, 1962 [c1961].

O'Connor, Winfield Scott, and Earl Chapin May. *Jockeys, Crooks, and Kings: The Story of Winnie O'Connor's Life as Told to Earl Chapin May.* New York: Cape and Smith, 1930.

"Our Horses and Jockeys Abroad," *Munsey's Magazine,* Dec. 1900, 353–63.

Pares, Bernard. *A History of Russia.* 4th ed. New York: Knopf, 1944.

Parmer, Charles B. *For Gold and Glory: The Story of Thoroughbred Racing in America.* New York: Carrick and Evans, 1939.

Payne, Robert. *The Life and Death of Lenin.* New York: Simon and Schuster, 1964.

Perrin, William Henry, ed. *History of Fayette County, Kentucky, with an Outline Sketch of the Blue Grass Region.* Chicago: O. L. Baskin, 1882.

Reis, Jim. "Blacks Once Held the Reins." (Covington) *Kentucky Post,* Feb. 14, 1994, 4K.

Riding, Alan. "Picasso in Paris: A Suspect, Never a Citizen," *New York Times,* May 28, 2003, B1.

Robertson, William H. P. *The History of Thoroughbred Racing in America.* Englewood Cliffs, NJ: Prentice-Hall, 1964.

Segal, Ronald. *Leon Trotsky: A Biography.* New York: Pantheon, 1979.

Sevareid, Eric. *Not So Wild a Dream.* New York: Knopf, 1946.

Shirer, William L. *The Collapse of the Third Republic: An Inquiry into the Fall of France in 1940.* New York : Simon and Schuster, 1969.

————. *The Rise and Fall of the Third Reich: A History of Nazi Germany.* New York: Simon and Schuster, 1960.

Tanner, Michael, and Gerry Cranham. *The Guinness Book of Great Jockeys of the Flat: A Celebration of Two Centuries of Jockeyship.* Enfield, U.K.: Guinness, 1992.

Terrell, Roy. "Around the World in 80 Years." *Sports Illustrated,* May 8, 1961, 71.

Tolstoy, L. N. *Anna Karenina.* Translated by Rosemary Edmonds. Harmondsworth, United Kingdom: Penguin, 1978.

Tracy, Len. "Fifty-odd Years Scarcely Have Dimmed the Memory." *Thoroughbred Record,* Feb. 21, 1959.

"Vainqueurs à 30/1," *Paris Turf.* March 28, 1967, n.p.

Volkogonov, Dmitri. *Lenin: A New Biography.* Translated and edited by Harold Shukman. New York: Free Press, 1994.

————. *Trotsky: The Eternal Revolutionary.* Translated and edited by Harold Shukman. New York: Free Press, 1996.

Volkov, Solomon. *St. Petersburg: A Cultural History.* Translated by Antonina W. Bouis. New York: Free Press, 1995.

Vosburgh, Walter Spencer. *Racing in America: 1866–1921.* New York: The Jockey Club, 1922.

Wilcox, Edna Wheeler. "How Salvator Won." *Spirit of the Times,* July 12, 1890, 1082.

Wright, George C. *Racial Violence in Kentucky, 1865–1940: Lynchings, Mob Rule, and "Legal Lynching".* Baton Rouge: Louisiana State University Press, 1990.

ACKNOWLEDGMENTS

AS THE FINISH LINE FOR *WINK* KEPT RECEDING, LAURA HILLENBRAND, author of *Seabiscuit*, e-yelled at me:

"Run, Ed, run like Secretariat ran!"

Thanks to Laura.

Thanks, too, to Dan Rather, Douglas Brinkley, Jean and Charles Osgood, Lea Thompson, Henry Louis Gates, Jr., Susan Kidd, and Barbara Harrison.

Thanks to PEB, the famous artist of the turf Pierre Bellocq, who drew me word pictures of Wink's later years and of Maisons-Laffitte, the hometown they each adopted.

Thanks, especially, to Jimmy Winkfield's daughter, Liliane Winkfield Casey, who gave me a push out of the gate as we reviewed his life and career on two continents. To his son Robert's widow, Jeanine, a top jockey herself in France. To Liliane's daughter, the veterinarian Amie, and Robert's son Thierry. Wink rides on in the multilingual tales of his nephew Yuri Thiemann, better known as George around here. Did his wife Gianna interrupt their reveries in French, Italian, and English long enough that afternoon to serve us goodies from northern Italy? We were too busy laughing and missing the plane. It was a delight to recall our way back to Chilesburg, Kentucky, with Jimmy's great-nephew John Frye (sister Bettie's grandson) and his wife Helen and his greatniece Artemesia Winkfield Brummell (brother Gus's granddaughter) and her son Bill and grandson Billy.

I couldn't have the Winkfields in mind long before thinking of my friend Anne Butler, an authority on Kentucky genealogy and director of the Center of Excellence for the Study of Kentucky African Americans at Kentucky State University, and David P. Spencer, a keeper of Chilesburg memories.

Across the ocean that Jimmy braved in 1904, I thank all those of the little united nations—Spain, Romania, Austria, Hungary, Poland, Germany, Russia, France—who helped me document Wink's story for the first time. It is a saga told mostly in five languages. Monika Massalska, assisted by her husband Witold Massalski, unlocked the language that drowned Wink at his first European stop when a Polish dictionary was placed in his large hands. The secrets of his years under the czar were spilled by Zarema Mazaeva, Saidamin Shamilov, Elza Paskushova, Ed Lozansky, Zhena Yerukhimovich, Alexandra Costa, and Ivan Gnilosyrov. The dual meanings of the Austro-Hungarian dual monarchy's archives were simplified by Miodrag Milovanovics, of Sarajevo.

"Whenever the literary German dives into a sentence," said Mark Twain, "that is the last you are going to see of him till he emerges on the other side of the Atlantic with his verb in his mouth." In the case of Dr. Frank E. Wagner, he emerged with a trawler-ful of insights. Help here also came from Stefan Brunner, and Dr. David Morris. Enough already? Kurt Maier explained how New York Yiddish got this "already." *La langue de Molière? Pas de problème*, thanks to Marthe, with more tips from Lydie Stefanopoulos, Edith Bernard, and Monique and Jean Vincent.

My extraordinary, lifesaving research mentors included Elena V. Andryushenkova in Russia, Claudia Rong, and senior handicapper Harald Siemen in Germany, and Dominika Golaszewska and Jerzy Budny in Poland. Plus Tanya Mashchikova, Tom Leary, and David Siefkin in Russia, Olympiu Petry from Romania, Christophe Meran from Austria, and Michael Jirowec in Poland, and Georg Lang and Brigitte Habres in Germany. Monique and Jean got me started in France, where the glories of Franco-American friendship are personified by Anne and Hughes "Buck" Agnès. *Merci* to Guy Thibault, Jacques Marec, Elisabeth Forget Kurek, Duncan Alexander, Alexandra Dimitrov, Anne-Catherine Fleurot, and Jeanne Freud. Nick Higgins helped me cross the Pyrenees into Spanish racing. My British navigators, led by A. G. (Tony) Morris, were a thundering herd whose mere names needed translation: Brough Scott, Ultan

Guilfoyle, Owen Byrne, Graham Snelling, and Gwen Doeg-Smith. *Heureux qui, comme Wink, fait un beau voyage*, but he couldn't stop thinking about America. At Saratoga Springs, New York, where Wink rode in 1903 and assisted his son Robert in the 1940s, Francie and Tom Gilcoyne were my rescuers, along with John von Stade, Peter Hammell, Catherine Maguire, Dick Hamilton, Lori Fisher, Allan Carter, Beth Sheffer, Kitty Macica, and George Stojak at the National Museum of Racing. In and around the Big Apple: Barry Moreno at the Ellis Island Immigration Museum, Jane Schwartz, and Andrew "Ande" Brown IV. At Pimlico: Joe and Karin De Francis, Mike Gathagan, Rich Paul, Joe Kelly.

At Churchill Downs: John Asher, Tony Terry, and bugler Steve Buttleman. At the Kentucky Derby Museum: Lynn Ashton, Jay Ferguson, Chris Goodlett, Sandy Flaksman, Lisa Huber, and Angie Fleitz. At Keeneland Library in Lexington: Phyllis Rogers and Cathy Schenck. Also in the Bluegrass: Ed Bowen, Ken Grayson, Jan Marshall, Chris Doerge, Tony Moreno, Sharon and Jim Claypool, Laura Tucker, Gerald Smith, Mildred Bailey, Martina Hunnecke, Clest Lanier, Dr. J. Blaine Hudson, Aukram Burton, Jenifer Raisor, and Susanna Massie Thomas.

At my favorite track outside of Saratoga, the Library of Congress, were Zarema Mazeva (again), Grant Harris, Craig D'Ooge, Bruce Martin, and Harry Licht, and at the U.S. Army's Center of Military History, Dena Everett. At the National Sporting Library in Middleburg, Virginia: Peter Winants, Rob Weber, and Lisa Campbell. At the Public Library's Selima Room in Bowie, Maryland: Susan Stephenson. Major assists over the years have come from friends Denise Rompilla, Marylou Whitney, Jensen Barber, Gee and Wayne Wood, Erica and Douglas Rosenthal, Ulises Joya, Dr. Jon Wiseman, John De Marco, Robin Bledsoe, Mary K. O'-Donnell, Jim Walker, Edan Lichtenstein, and Sam B. Girgus.

I cannot imagine being blessed with a better editor than Jonathan Eaton, editorial director at McGraw-Hill Trade. It would take another book to set out Jon's invaluable advice to me, and one that would be well worth publishing. As a matter of fact, I hit the trifecta with editors. In Tristram Coburn I got a coach and a friend, and Tris hooked me up with editor Pete Fornatale, who has not only an unerring feel for narrative nonfiction but (as a horseman himself) a way with tales of the turf. Thanks to brilliant design and production manager Molly Mulhern, indefatigable publicity manager Ann Pryor, indispensable Nancy Dowling, inspiring project editor Ben McCanna, faultless copyeditor Shana Harrington, and the entire fantastic teams at McGraw-Hill in both New York and in Maine.

I am honored to be represented by Harvey Klinger of the Harvey Klinger Agency in New York City and grateful to Jenny Bent for her terrific work in the early stages.

Yannis A. Stefanopoulos was my superb assistant.

Luc and Greg were my terrific editor-trainers; Luc fiercely reining in much of the manuscript, Greg ready with the oats from Delmonico's.

Ed Hotaling
Washington, D.C.

INDEX

Abe Frank (race horse), 50, 52, 55
Adams, Eugène, 184–85
Adry (race horse), 174, 183
African-American Masons, 18
Aga Khan, 188, 193, 199, 212
Ahmad, Shah of Persia, 193
Alan-a-Dale (race horse), 51, 52, 54, 56, 57, 58
Alard Scheck (race horse), 43, 44
Aldebaran (race horse), 209
Alexandre, Serge, 236–37
Alfonso XIII, 171, 188, 193, 238
Algérien (race horse), 185, 194
Alldeutsches Tagblatt, 132–33
Allen, James M., 66–67, 101
All-Russian Derby: 1903, 88; 1904, 95–96; 1907, 115; 1908, 116, 246; 1913, 141; 1914, 142–44; 1915, 146; 1916, 149–50
aluminum horseshoes, 87
Aly Khan, 241
American crouch, 36–37, 85, 97, 196
American Derby, 11, 56; 1884, 59–60; 1902, 60–67; wins by black jockeys, 60
Anna Karenina (Tolstoy), 121–22, 134–35
antigambling movement, 75, 118–19, 207–8
anti-Semitism, 111, 132–34, 158, 250–51. *See also* Pan German movement; racism
Approval (race horse), 21
Arkansas Gazette, 106
Arnold, George, 49
Associated Press, 104
athletes: baseball, 12, 26, 30, 40, 206; boxing, 42, 118, 124–25, 146, 206; Golden Era, 206; Olympic, 213, 245–46;

public introductions, 30, 98. *See also* black jockeys; jockeys
Austin, Dale, 105
Austria, 129–34
Austrian Oaks, 135
Austria Prize Stakes, 129–30
Auteuil Race Course, 296
Avenstoke (race horse), 23–25

Baden-Baden, Germany, 125
Baden-Württemberg, Germany, 125–26
Bahadur (race horse), 184, 185–86, 193, 194, 196, 210–11, 293
Baker, Josephine, 218–19, 225, 241–42, 250, 255
Baldwin, Elias J. "Lucky," 63, 97
Bamberger, Raymond, 187–88
Barnes, Shelby "Pike," 14
Barry, Redmond Dillon, 18
Bartholomew, Georgie, 189, 209
baseball, 12, 26, 30, 40, 206
Bashkirov, Alexander, 175, 194
Basilique (race horse), 217
Batiste (black jockey), 67
Beaut (racecourse worker) 206–7
Belle's Commoner (race horse), 64, 65
Bellhouse, George, 174, 185, 194
Belmont, August, II, 17, 76, 141
Ben Brush (race horse), 44
Bennett, George C., 50
Berliner Tageblatt, 137, 245, 257
betting. *See* gambling
Big Apple, 23. *See also* New York City
Billet de Banque, 296–97
black jockeys: first to use

"American seat" abroad, 36–37; forced out of racing, 15–16, 36, 46, 204–5, 227–28; notable slave jockeys, 7–11; not forced out of steeplechasing, 273. *See also* jockeys; racism
Black Larry (race horse), 183
Black Servant (race horse), 205
Bloch, Henry, 87, 94
Bloodstock Breeders' Review, 140, 147, 153
Bloody Sunday (Russia), 106–7
Bluegrass, 17–18
Bly, Nellie, 75, 207
Boland, Jimmy, 32–35, 35–36, 106
Bomarsund (race horse), 190, 191
Bon Jour (race horse), 16–17
Booker, Henry, 68–69, 106
Boston (race horse), 9–10
Bostwick, Pete, 274
Bou Jeloud (race horse), 211–12, 216
boxing, 42, 118, 124–25, 146, 206
Boxwood (race horse), 76
Boyd, Joe, 178–79
Boyd, Mrs. (Joe), 179
Brady, Diamond Jim, 42–43, 62, 72
Braun, Eva, 276
Braun, Gretl, 276
Braun, Vera, 219, 261, 280, 283
Braunes Band von Deutschland, 256–57
Breckinridge, John C., 7
Breeders Stakes: 1908, 117; 1909, 117
Brighton Beach racetrack, 23
Brown, Curley, 43
Brown, Ed, 19, 77
Brown, J. Graham, 292
Brun, Gabriel, 256

Buckner, John, 206
Bullman, John, 61, 80
Bullock, Frank, 127, 185, 197
Burns, Tommy, 25, 67, 84
Bush, Martha Winkfield, 249
Buzzsaw, Frankie, 208

Café Féder, 223–24, 231–32, 255
Cahn, J. C., 29, 36
Calumet Farm, 91–92
Cannon, James, 92, 100, 101
Carlopolis (race horse), 129
Carpentier, Georges, 184–85
Carslake, Bernard "Brownie," 137, 197
Casey, Edmund, 278, 285
Caywood, Billy, 62, 92
Chamberlain, Houston Stewart, 132–33
Chantepoulet (race horse), 252
Chantilly, France, 175–76
Charles, Ray, 239
Charmante (race horse), 21
Chicago Daily News, 22
Chicago Record, 37
Childs, Joe, 127, 197
Chilesburg, Kentucky, 5, 6
Chilperic (race horse), 137
Chinn, Phil, 27, 47, 242–43
Chittlin' Switch racetrack, 7
Churchill Downs, 26, 292; fallen on hard times, 30, 52; record speeds, 34; revitalization, 68–69. *See also* Kentucky Derby
Cincinnati Enquirer, 60
Civil War, 5, 10; horse raids, 161; slave jockeys of, 7–11
Clay, Henry, 7, 17, 51
Clayton, Lonnie, 12
Coburn, Monk, 50, 52, 67
Colin (race horse), 117
Coney Island racetracks, 23
Coney Island Jockey Club, 13–14, 22, 79
Congress Sweepstakes, 41
Conley, Jess, 48, 205
Cornelius (slave jockey), 9–10
Corrida (race horse), 257

Corrigan, Ed, 19, 47
Count (race horse), 115
Courier-Journal, 28, 35, 40, 44, 58–59
Cresent City Derby, 52–53
Crown Stud farms, 115, 146–47, 153, 159
Cruzados (race horse), 63–64, 66
Curtis, Austin, 8
Curule (race horse), 205

Daily Racing Form, 48–49
Daloz, Jeanne, 235
Daly, Mike, 41
Dark Star (race horse), 279
Davidoff, K. I., 288
Deauville, France, 172, 187–95, 215–16
Delahoussaye, Eddie, 57, 293
deMinkwitz, Baron Vladimir, 148–50; arrives in Paris, 173; builds bridge to Siberia, 148; builds house for Winkfields, 199, 217, 226–27; death, 251; leaves Russia, 152–53
deMinkwitz, Baroness Lydie, 148, 152, 173, 217
deMinkwitz, Lydie. *See* Winkfield, Lydie
deMinkwitz, Elizabeth. *See* Thiemann, Elizabeth
Derbies, 59–60. *See also* American Derby; Kentucky Derby
Despard (race horse), 190, 191
Despote (race horse), 175, 191, 192, 193
Dolomite (race horse), 138–39
Donerail (race horse), 291
Donoghue, Steve, 176, 189, 190–91, 193, 196
doping, 88, 130; Billet de Banque, 296–97; saliva test, 130
Dr. Walmsley (race horse), 37–39
Drake, John, 63
Dugan, Eddie, 141, 156, 162; aids in horse evacuation, 162–65
Duke, William, 188

Duller, George, 191
Duncan, Isadora, 180–81
Dunne, Francis, 268
Dunne, Patrick, 47, 69, 71, 73, 76, 268

Early (race horse), 68, 69, 70, 71, 222
Eau Gallie (race horse), 196
Ebony, 263
Edward VIII, of England, 215
Eisenhower, Dwight D., 276
Ellison, Charles E., 62, 69
Emperor's Prize: 1905, 108; 1907, 114; 1916, 150
Empress Stakes, 111, 117
English Triple Crown, 87. *See also* Triple Crown races
Epinard (race horse), 199
Epsom Downs, England, 59, 103, 142
European racing: American crouch, 36–37; compared to American, 87, 97, 124, 181–82; native jockeys, 98–99; opportunity for U.S. jockeys, 83–84; tracks, 93; training techniques, 97; trotters, 95; weight regulations, 96, 144

Fairgrounds Race Course, 23, 221–22
Fandine (race horse), 296
Fegelein, Hermann, 256, 257, 276
Ferdinand, Franz, 142
Ferré, Robert, 214–15, 217
Field Marshals Stakes: 1923, 211–12
Firenzi (race horse), 14
Fisticuff (race horse), 190, 191, 192
FitzGerald, John J., 23
Fleischmann, Julius, 76
Flimnap (race horse), 161
Florizar (race horse), 33–34
Flying Boy (race horse), 143
Fraenkel, Professor, 130
France, 233–34. *See also* specific cities
Françillon (race horse), 287–88

Francisco, Franco, 238, 252–53

Frederick II, Grand Duke, 126

French Sporting Society for the Encouragement of the Breed, 184, 223

Freud, Sigmund, 130–31

Freudenau Race Course, 130

Frisbie, Frank, 94

Fuller, Grover Cleveland, 77, 81

Futurity Stakes: 1888, 13–14; 1890, 15; 1901, 81–82; 1903, 77–82

Galop (race horse), 116

Galtee Boy (race horse), 108

Galtee More (race horse), 87, 108

Galust (race horse), 142, 143

gambling: antigambling movement, 75, 118–19, 207–8; Canfield Casino, 75–76; craps, 179; oral betting, 207–8; pari-mutuel machines, 42, 158; "southern tip," 44

Garner, Guy, 189, 197, 215–16

Garrison, Edward "Snapper," 14

Garry Herrmann (race horse), 47

Gates, John "Bet-a-Million," 76

Gato Del Sol (race horse), 57

Gaurisankar (race horse), 185–86, 189–90, 193, 196, 211–12, 212, 227

George Arnold (race horse), 49

German Derby: 1911, 135–38; 1936, 256–57; 1943, 257

Germany: 1933, 238; Graditz stud farm, 136; Pan German movement, 132–34, 137, 245; Paris invasion, 253–62; WW II, 249–51. *See also* Hitler, Adolf; *specific cities*

Goebbels, Paul Joseph, 276

Goodwin's Official Annual Guide to the Turf, 49, 67

Goose, Roscoe, 13, 291–93, 297

Gould, Kelly, 187–88

Graditz stud farm, 136

Grand Handicap de Deauville: 1922, 191–93

Grand Prix de Deauville: 1922, 187–88, 193–95

Grand Prix de Paris: 1923, 208–9; 1924, 212–15; 1939, 257

Grand Union Stakes, 76–77

Gran Premio de San Sebastián: 1922, 195

Gravesend racetrack, 23

Great Depression, 233, 234, 265

Greentree stable, 267

Grey Boy (race horse), 150

Grillemont (race horse), 194

Grinstead, James, 12–13

Grosse Preis von Baden, 135; 1910, 125–29

Guadagnini, Arcadia, 233

Guerin, Eric, 279

Guernica (Picasso), 253

Haiman, Clara-Béatrice, 139, 230–31

Halma (race horse), 58

Hamburg Belle (race horse), 81

Hamburg Place, 62, 77, 203

Hamilton, Tony, 12, 14, 18–19, 85, 95–96; negative media characterization, 15

Haroun Al Rashid (race horse), 194, 199

Hartack, Bill, 278–79, 294

Hatisov (jockey), 143

Hawkins, Abe, 10

Hawthorne (in Chicago), 20

Haynie's Maria (race horse), 8–9

Hemingway, Ernest, 214

Heno (race horse), 61

Henry Burt (race horse), 38

Herald (Paris), 178, 179, 181, 193, 211–12, 216, 253–55

Herrick, Myron, 208, 209, 224, 225

Highball (race horse), 77, 80–82

Highland Lad (race horse), 33–34

Hildreth, Sam, 61, 63, 65, 141, 206–7, 293–94; Hildreth Day at Worth, 53; teaches Eddie Dugan to save, 165

Hillenbrand, Laura, 270

Himmler, Heinrich, 276, 277

Hinata Farm, 206

Hindenburg, 128–29

His Eminence (race horse), 40, 44–45

Hitler, Adolf, 129–30, 131–32, 238, 249–51, 276, 277; *Parliament* reported stolen, 131–32

Hoar, Johnny, 92, 94

Hobbs, Charlie, 191

Holtman, J. J. "Jake," 69

Holyhead (race horse), 191

Horoscope (race horse), 159, 162, 166

horse breeding in Russia, 89, 144, 146–47

horse evacuations: historical occasions, 10–11, 161; the Odyssey, 160–69

horse raids, 10–11, 256, 257

horseshoes, aluminum, 87

Hot Brown sandwich, 290–91

Howard, Charles, 241

Hughes, Charles Evans, 118, 207

Hungarian racing, 134, 135, 230

Ike Murphy, 63

Inventor (race horse), 51, 54–55

Irish Lad (race horse), 87–88

Iroquois (race horse), 33

Isarland Studs farm, 257

Jackson, Andrew, 8–9

Jacques le Marois Stakes, 189–90

Jamaica (New York) racetrack, 83, 265, 295

James, Henry, 74

Jaworski, Tadeusz, 162, 164, 165

Jeffries, Jim, 125

Jennings, Jack, 174, 193, 209; builds jockey's rec club, 221
Jersey Derby, 59
Jockey Club, Coney Island, 13–14, 22, 79
Jockey Joe (race horse), 19–22
jockeys, 7–8: "bug boy," 222–23; European, 97, 98–99; Europe offers opportunity for Americans, 92, 94, 105–6, 124; hands of, 192; health, 18; no future in U.S., 206–7; women, 249. *See also* black jockeys; white jockeys
jockey's rec club, 221–22
Johnson, Jack, 118, 124–25, 146, 179
Jones, Willie, 8
Judge Himes (race horse), 69, 70, 222
junk bonds, and "L'Affaire Stavisky," 236–37
Jurjevich, Frederick, 158, 162–69

Kaiserin Augusta Victoria (steamer), 113
Kaiser Wilhelm II, 126, 136
Karoli (race horse), 108
Keene, G. Hamilton, 116
Keene, James R., 86, 105
Keene, John Oliver (Jack), 154; alleged doping, 88; contracts with Wink, 85–90; limestone racing complex, 86, 205, 272–73
Keeneland Race Course, 272–73
Kelly, Jack, 213
Kenner, Duncan, 10
Kentucky: Bluegrass, 17–18; horse raids in, 10–11. *See also specific cities*
Kentucky Association racetrack, 7, 205, 285
Kentucky Derby, 59–60; 1875, 30; 1884, 11; 1890, 11; 1891, 11; 1900, 26–28, 32–35; 1901, 40–47; 1902, 50–59; 1903, 68–71, 222; 1961, 294–95; black jockeys forced out, 204–5; con-

secutive winners, 57–58, 293; Derby Day, 28; exceptions to May dates, 40; field sizes, 52; jockeys with most wins, 278–79; rose collar, 44; wins by black jockeys, 30; youngest winner, 12
Kentucky Post, 16
King, Henry, 205
King Karol (race horse), 185
Klodziak, Joseph, 97, 100, 101
Klotz, Louis-Lucien, 236–37
Knight, Tommy, 64, 65
Knights Templar, 18
Koklova, Olga, 172–73, 199
Konwent (race horse), 166
Koreshok (race horse), 116
Kosarz (race horse), 130
Kristallnacht (Night of the Broken Glass), 249–50
Ksiaze-Pan (race horse), 129, 131–32
Ku Klux Klan/kuklux, 18, 32, 71–72, 178–79

Ladas (race horse), 106
Laks, Michael, 98, 100, 156
Latonia Derby, 11
Lazareff, Mikhail, 87, 143; rivalry with Mantacheff, 140–41; stud farm given to Czar, 146–47
Lee, Jimmy, 117–18
Lefevre, Jeanine, 296, 299
Le Figaro, 183, 212, 215, 232
"leg up," 29
Lemuel (jockey), 156
Lenin, Vladimir Ilyich, 98, 154, 155
Lewis, Isaac, 12
Lewis, Oliver, 30
Lewisohn, Jesse, 72
Lexington, Kentucky, 7
Lexington Herald, 60, 66, 285; regrets not reporting civil-rights movement, 286
Lexington Herald-Leader, 286
Lexington (Kentucky Association) racetrack, 7, 205
Lexington Leader, 67, 89–90, 93, 203

Liaotung Peninsula, 96, 107
Liege (race horse), 156–57, 162
Lieut. Gibson (race horse), 32–34
Lilly, Marshall, 12–13, 34, 117, 267
Lincoln, Abraham, 42, 73
Lincoln, Bob, 73
Lindbergh, Charles, 224–25
Little Rocket (race horse), 278
London, S. P., 99
Lorraine (steamer), 117
Lotse (race horse), 257
Louisville, Kentucky, 27
Louisville Courier-Journal, 28, 100, 104, 270
Louisville Times, 28, 71
Louisville Tribune, 31
Lubomirski, Stanislaw, 94, 117, 129, 212
Lueger, Karl, 133
Lyne, Lucien, 13, 63, 66, 105–6, 174, 210, 259, 275; career statistics, 260; death, 281; goes to England, 84–85; meets Wink in Paris, 170–71
Lyne, Mildred, 283
Lyne, Sanford, 13, 84–85

Macbeth (race horse), 150
MacGee, Matt, 189, 193, 194, 197, 223
Mackay, Clarence, 11
MacMagon (race horse), 143
Madden, John, 62, 77–78, 79, 80, 81–83
Magdalinsky (jockey), 156
Maher, Danny, 36, 103, 129–30
Maisons-Laffitte, France, 176, 185; training facilities, 221
Man o'War (legendary race horse), 206
Man o'War (race horse), 83
Mantacheff, Leon, 140–41, 150, 175, 194, 214–15, 259; death, 281; escapes Russia, 153; in Paris, 172; sanctions Guy Garner, 215–16; smuggles horses to U.S., 153, 172
Marconi, Guglielmo, 80

Martin, Willie, 20–22
mascot companions for
  horses, 185–86, 241
Mathews, Jesse, 16–17
May, Bub, 22–23, 45–46,
  268; contract with Wink
  ends, 47; hires Wink, 19;
  hires Wink to ride Highball, 77–78, 83
May, W. H., 22–24
McChesney (race horse),
  60–67, 293–94; speed
  and physical appearance,
  48–49
McDowell, Maj. Thomas
  Clay, 51, 58
media portrayals: of black
  jockeys, 15, 35, 71, 104;
  of blacks, 59; racial focus,
  49. *See also individual*
  publications
Medley (race horse), 9
Miller, Walter, 124
Miss Bennett (race horse),
  38
Mitchell, Carroll (Carl), 25,
  86, 87, 94
Mokotowski Race Course,
  167–68
money rider, 11, 47
Monmouth Handicap, 14
Monmouth Park, 82
Monostatos (race horse),
  136–38
moonshine, 73
Morgan, John Hunt, 10–11
Morris, Green B., 76
Morrissey, John, 42
Moscow Breeders Stakes,
  85, 108, 117
Moscow Central Hippo-
  drome, 94–95, 114, 159
Munsey's, 36
Murphy, Ike (Honest Ike),
  11–12; death and funeral,
  18–19; discredited as in-
  toxicated, 14–15; "money
  rider" approach, 11;
  trainer, 97
Mussolini, Benito, 277
Myosotis (race horse), 16–17

Nabokov, Vladimir, 109
National Turf Writers Association, 289, 290–92
National War College,
  274–75

Native Dancer (race horse),
  279
Naushon (race horse), 206
negro: defined by National
  War College, 274–75;
  defined by Parkhurst, 46;
  defined by Parmer, 82
Nereide (race horse), 257
Neuter, Adolphe de, 283
Neuter, Mildred de, 260
New Orleans Christmas
  Handicap, 49
New Orleans Daily Picayune,
  53, 67, 239
Newport, Kentucky, 22
New York City, 263–67;
  dubbed "Big Apple," 23;
  Pennsylvania Station,
  201–3; racetracks, 13–14,
  23; Triborough Bridge,
  263–66
New York City Morning
  Telegraph, 23
New York Daily Tribune, 75
New York Times, 14, 15
New York World, 75, 77
Niceas (race horse), 210
Nicholas II, Czar, 87, 92,
  106–7, 115, 144–46,
  150–52, 159, 237
Nigger Baby (race horse), 20
Nikolaevich, Nikolai, 171
Notter, Joe, 124
Novelty (race horse), 206–7

O'Connor, J., 37–39
O'Connor, Winfield (Win-
  nie), 49, 103–4, 126–27,
  136, 176, 269; on Aven-
  stoke, 23–24; career
  highlights, 41–42; dia-
  monds, 42–43; move to
  England, 85; weight, 41;
  on Yankee, 81–82
October Mares Race, 124
Odessa Derby: 1917, 156;
  1918, 159
Odyssey, the, 160–69
Offutt, Maymie, 119
Olympic Games: 1924, 213;
  1936, 245–46
Omnium Stakes: 1921, 183
O'Neill, Frank, 80, 174–75,
  176, 183, 189, 193, 223
Oppenheim, Baron von,
  138; Schlendahl stud
  farm, 138, 256

oral betting, 207–8
Outen, Maria, 119
Overton, Alfred "Monk,"
  48, 205, 267; Kentucky
  Derbies, 30–31; records
  set, 31

Paget, Sydney, 77, 81
Palmer, Joe, 28
Pan German movement,
  132–34, 137, 245
Panic of 1893, 15–16
Panic of 1897, 82
Pantagruel (race horse),
  136, 137
pari-mutuel betting ma-
  chine, 15, 158
Paris, France: "City of
  Light," 177; German in-
  vasion, 253–62; racing
  season, 181–82, 188;
  Russian immigrants,
  179–81; society, 176–77,
  178–80
Parkhurst, Charles, 46
Parmer, Charles, 82–83
Parvenez (race horse),
  240–41
Pasiflore III (race horse),
  227
Pavlovich, Dmitry, 151
Pennsylvania Station, 201–3
Perkins, James "Soup," 12,
  17
Perle d'Or (race horse),
  216–17
Petrograd, Russia, 146, 152.
  See also St. Petersburg,
  Russia
Pharis II (race horse), 257
Picasso, Pablo, 172–73, 199,
  252–53; seeks French cit-
  izenship, 253, 260
Piggott, Joe, 92, 94
Pimlico Race Course, 82
Poland, 85, 167; horses, 158;
  postwar period, 168–69;
  Russian controlled, 93;
  the Odyssey, 162–69. *See*
  also Russia; Russian
  horses
Poliakoff, Serge, 283–84
Poliakoff stud farm, 121,
  284
Poniatowski, Prince, 43
potato chips, 74
Potemkin, 110, 158

Preobrajensky Regiment, 106–7
Pretoria (steamer), 115
Princip, Gavrilo, 142
Prix Arc de Triomphe, 256–57
Prix de Dozule, 216
Prix Delamarre: 1922, 199–200
Prix de l'Élévage (Breeder's Prize), 287–88
Prix du Jockey Club, 189, 257
Prix du Président de la République, 293; 1922, 184; 1923, 209–11
Prix Eugène-Adams: 1922, 184–86
Prix Penelope: 1947, 281
Prix Quo Vadis, 174
Prix Von Marchfeld, 124
Prometheus (race horse), 146
Pushkin, Alexander, 109

Queen's Plate, 51

racetrackers: America, 63, 74–76, 79; Europe, 94, 125–26, 135–36, 187–88, 193, 208, 213, 215–16, 241–43
racetracks: bugle call, 29; circuits, 20, 27; Early American "heats," 9–10; European tracks, 93, 182; Louisville, 27; Newport, 22; New York City, 13–14, 118–19; Paris, 175; "starters," 21; starting gates, 20, 21, 54
racing industry: effects of antigambling bills, 118–19, 207–8; expansion after Civil War, 13; financial hardship, 15–16, 36, 82, 141; historical effect of war, 145–46
racing tricks on the track, 11
racism: anti-Semitism, 132–34, 158, 249–51; Parkhust speech, 46; "characteristics" of black jockeys, 82; conflict between jockeys, 16–17, 37–39, 67, 69–72, 82–83; European compared to

U.S., 124–25, 190, 280; expressed through rough-riding tactics, 16–17, 37–39; Georgia race riots, 125; and interracial marriage, 179, 204–5, 274; in jockey rec club, 222; media role, 15–16, 35, 49, 59, 71
Radtke, Herman, 116
Rancho Santa Anita, 63
Ransch, Jerry, 85
Rapid Water (race horse), 76–77
Rascal (race horse), 131
Rasputin, Grigory Yefimovich, 145, 151
Reiff, Johnny, 36
Reiff, Lester, 36
Rhineland Breeders Stakes, 138–39
Richards, Joe, 92, 94
Riva Ridge (race horse), 57, 293
Roosevelt, Franklin D., 234, 265–66, 276
Rothschild, Albert, 130
Rothschild, Edouard de, 214, 216, 257
Rothschild, Maurice de, 198
Rothschild, Nathaniel, 130
Royal Lancer (race horse), 196
Ruban (race horse), 195, 210
Run for the Roses, 44. *See also* Kentucky Derby
Runyon, Damon, 207
Russell, Lillian, 72–73
Russia: antisemitism, 111; Bloody Sunday, 106–7; Bolshevik Revolution, 154, 156; Odessa, 156–61; Preobrajensky Regiment, 106–7; Russo-Japanese War, 92–93, 96, 99, 107, 110
Russian horses: breeding, 89, 144; Crown Stud farm, 115, 146–47; horse training, 87, 97, 154; number of breeds, 92; wintering, 154
Russian Oaks, 95, 108, 115, 135
Russo-Japanese War, 92–93, 96, 99, 107, 110

Saint-Cloud, France, 170, 182, 210
Salvator (race horse), 14
Sande, Earl, 184
Sanford, John, 141
Sannazarro (race horse), 43
San Sebastián, Spain, 171, 195
Santa Anita Race Course, 63
Saratoga Chips, 74
Saratoga Special Stakes, 76
Saratoga Springs, 20, 73–76; Canfield Casino, 75–76; famous visitors, 74–76
Scheftel, W. M., 77
Schlendahl stud farm (Oppenheim), 138, 256
Schmeider, A. von, 136
Schorr, Johnny, 43
Scoggan, Hiram, 33, 38
Seabiscuit (Hillenbrand), 270
Seabiscuit (race horse), 61, 241
Secretariat (race horse), 34, 57, 293
Serbia, 142, 144–45
Sevareid, Eric, 251, 254
Shaw, Willie, 124
Sheepshead Bay racetrack, 13–14, 23, 80
Sheherazade (race horse), 198
Sheridan, Phil, 59
Shirer, William L., 277
Shoemaker, Bill, 192, 279
Siebel, J. M., 278
Simms, Willie, 15, 36–37, 48, 85, 196, 205, 267
Simon (slave jockey), 8–9
Sir Gallahad (race horse), 210
Sister Anne (race horse), 192
six wins of six races in single day, 117–18
Sloan, Cassius "Cash," 36, 85
Sloan, Tod, 36–37, 84, 196
Smith, Tom, 241
Smoot, Charlie, 273
Spain, 171, 195, 238, 252–53
Spanish-American War, 19, 93

Spanish Civil War, 252–53
Sport Hippique, Le, 175, 183
Sports Illustrated (magazine), 286–89
Sport Universel Illustré, Le, (magazine), 190
Springer, Gustav von, 135
SS *America,* 213, 214
SS *Belgravia,* 101–2
SS *Cedric,* 103
SS *Olympic* (ocean liner), 200
SS *Titanic* (ocean liner), 200
St. Julien, Marlon, 205
St. Leger: English, 103, 195–97; Hungarian, 135
St. Petersburg, Russia, 108–11, 146. *See also* Petrograd, Russia
Stalin, Joseph, 238
starting gates: claptrap, 20; Maxwell machine, 54; webbed barrier, 21
Stavisky, Sacha, 236–37
Stein, Gertrude, 254
Steiner, Felix, 276
Stern, George, 174, 185, 189–90, 194
Stern, Jean, 256
Stewart, Charles, 9
Strassburger, Ralph, 256
Sunday Oregonian (Portland), 125
Sunny's Halo (race horse), 58
Suzon (race horse), 174
Sylphide (race horse), 281

Taral, Fred "The Flying Dutchman," 19, 42, 85, 124, 127
Telegraph, 197
Tennessee Derby, 40–41
Tenny (race horse), 14
The Don (race horse), 62, 69
The Minute Man (race horse), 77, 80–82
The Rival (race horse), 51, 55, 57
The Rush (race horse), 28
Thiemann, Elizabeth, 149, 173, 251, 277; leaves children at Winkfields, 232–33; refuses Yuri's visit, 286; sends for Yuri, 261

Thiemann, Irene, 233, 249, 250, 282
Thiemann, Paul, 148, 149
Thiemann, Yuri, 233, 247–49, 256–57, 260–61, 277, 282–83; relocates to U.S., 286
Thompson, Coley, 16–17
Thoroughbred Record, 38, 84, 104, 270–72, 285
Thrive (race horse), 29, 33–35
Thurn-and-Taxis, Prince, 135–36
Times-Herald (Chicago), 21–22
Tolstoy, Leo, 121, 134
trans-Siberian railroad, 96
Transvaal (race horse), 214–15
Travers, Saratoga, 51
Triple Crown races, 87, 103, 141, 195, 273
Trotsky, Leon, 110, 111–12, 131, 154, 238, 261
Tsarskoye Selo, Russia, 120, 121–22, 152
Turcotte, Ron, 57, 293
Turf Congress Handicap, 47
Turner, Nash, 51, 54–55, 57
Twentieth Century Stakes, 67
Tynes, Harcourt, 263

United States, enters WW I, 158–59
United States Hotel Stakes, 76
Unsightly (race horse), 24–25
U.S. Cavalry, 29
USSR, 180–81. *See also* Russia; Stalin, Joseph, 238
Uttinger, Sam, 5, 6

Vadomski, I. D., 153, 172, 183
Valdois, Denise-Marthe, 223, 231–32
Van Dusen, Clyde, 33–34
Van Meter, Frank, 40, 45
Vassily, 156, 171; aids in horse evacuation, 162–69; dreams of riches, 147–48; successful businessman, 284

Vosburgh, W. S., 61–62
Voskhod stud farm, 256
Vulcain (race horse), 53

Wachs, Fred, 285
Walker, Billy, 12
Wall, E. Berry, 72
Ward, John, 293–94
Warsaw Derby: 1904, 93; 1905, 108
Weber, Christian, 256, 257, 277
Weber, Marjorie R., 297–98
weight: European regulations, 96, 144; lightest jockey over, 41; weighing out, 35
Weininger, Otto, 132–33
Weissmuller, Johnny, 213
Wertheimer, Pierre, 199
Whirlaway (race horse), 273
white jockeys: force black jockeys out, 15–16, 36, 46, 204–5, 227–28; initially trail black competition, 13. *See also* jockeys; racism
Whitney, Helen Hay, 267
Whitney, William C., 62, 74, 76
Widener, Joseph E., 76, 212–13
Wilhelm II, Kaiser, 136, 145
Williams, Robert "Tiny," 18–19, 51, 55, 205
Wilson, Richard, 206
Winecas Field, 5
Winkfield, Charles, 203
Winkfield, Edna, 105; adopts Ida, 113; divorces Wink, 139; joins Wink in Russia, 113; later years, 295–96; marriage to Wink, 39; return to U.S., 115–16; separation from Wink, 119
Winkfield, George (Wink's father), 5–7, 248
Winkfield, George (Wink's son): arrives in Paris, 219, 220; birth, 135; career as jockey, 221, 222–23, 228–29; death, 238–39; ill health, 228–29; professional debut, 222–23; stabbed by Denise, 231–32

Winkfield, Ida, 113, 115, 119
Winkfield, James (Wink): aids in horse evacuation of Odessa, 162–69; appearance, 100, 123, 144, 153–54, 220, 282, 296; Billet de Banque fails saliva test, 296–97; birth of Clara's child, 231; birth of George, 135; birth of Robert, 212; business partner with Lydie, 226, 240, 246; buys ice-skating rink, 147; cancer scare, 288; career accomplishments, 227–28; carriage driver, 17; childhood, 5–7, 248; citizenship, 228, 288; claimed birthday, 200–201, 217; contract with May, 20, 25, 46, 47; contract with Keene, 85–86, 89–90; contract with Mantacheff, 140–41; contract with Lazareff, 89–91; contract with Lubomirski, 123, 212; contract with Patrick Dunne, 47; death, 299; death of Lydie, 284–85; ditches Madden for May, 77–82, 83; divorces Edna, 139–40; escapes Paris invasion, 260–62; eye affliction, 73, 100, 123, 220; family life at 45 *bis avenue Églé*, 234–35, 239–40, 244–51, 282–93; family reunion at 45 *bis avenue Églé*, 282–83; first European trip, 91–102; first race, 20–22, 298; gold watch, 116, 245–50; grandchildren through Liliane, 285; "greatest moments," 293–94; hobbies, 6, 236, 247–48, 286; horses first love, 220, 240, 272; injured riding Dr.

Walmsley, 37–39, 204; injured riding McChesney, 60–67, 204; jockey school, 222, 283–84; languages spoken, 234–35; last Kentucky Derby, 294; last time on a horse, 283; *"Le blackman,"* 183, 212; marriage to Edna, 39; marriage to Lydie, 198–200; media publicity, 35–36, 39, 99–100, 104, 232, 239–40, 270–72, 279, 285–86, 289–94; nickname "Wink" bestowed, 19; owner-trainer, 217, 234–35, 287–88; personality, 97, 224, 258–59, 299; rank as trainer, 232; relationship with Alexandra, 120–23, 135, 155; relationship with Clara, 230–31; returns to France after war, 280–84; reunion with Edna, 295–96; rides Early, 69–72; rides Monostatos, 136–38; separates from Edna, 119; siblings, 5–7, 203–4, 249; split with Mantacheff, 214–15, 227; as trainer, 97, 212, 222, 240–41, 270, 298–99; transition to trainer, 226–28; weight, 48, 131, 181; wins on Perle d'Or, 216–17; winters in U.S. with Liliane, 285; works for WPA, 267–69
Winkfield, Jeanine, 296, 299
Winkfield, Lydie, 149, 240, 269; arrives in Paris, 173–74; birth of Robert, 212; citizenship hinders travel to U.S., 208; courtship with Wink, 177, 194–95; death, 284–85; marriage to Wink, 198–200; racing enthusiast, 173–74
Winkfield, Robert (Wink's

son), 244–47, 252, 253; birth, 212; chooses France over U.S. wife, 280; joins Army, 274–75; marries Jeanine Lefevre, 296; steeplechase jockey, 273–74; weight, 273
Winkfield, Samuel, 203
Winkfield, Victoria, 5–7
Winkfield Casey, Liliane, 248–51; birth, 217; childhood, 226–27; children, 285; graduation, 278; marriage, 278; quoted on her father, 224, 228
Winkfield Parker, Rachael Dancer (Wink's sister), 5–6, 204
Winn, Matt, 68
Witte, Sergei, 87
Wolff, Theodor, 137
women jockeys, 249
World War I, 144–46, 150–54, 158–59
World War II: Kristallnacht (Night of the Broken Glass), 249–50; Paris invasion, 253–58
Worth Race Course, 53
WPA (Work Progress Administration), 265–67
Wyeth (race horse), 66

Yalovicina, Alexandra, 120–21, 134–35, 199; arrives in Paris, 219–20; death, 238; marital status with Wink, 139–40; stays behind in Russia, 155. *See also* Braun, Vera
Yankee (race horse), 81–82
Yusupov, Felix Felixovich, 151, 171–72

Zariba (race horse), 185, 189–90, 210
Zasepa, Antoni, 123–24, 140
Zeppelin, Ferdinand von, 127–29
Zeppelin-Ballon, 127–29
Zoppi, Ryszard, 159, 162